ALSO BY LINDSEY S. FERA

Muskets & Minuets

LINDSEY S. FERA

ISBN (Paperback): 979-8-9867565-0-9
ISBN (Hardcover): 979-8-9867565-1-6

Pompkin Press
Newmarket, New Hampshire

Pompkin Press

For my family

CAST OF CHARACTERS

The Howlett Family

- Mr. Robert and Mrs. Margaret (Peggy) Howlett
- George Bixby Howlett (from Mrs. Howlett's first marriage to Captain Bixby), *b. 1751*
- Jane Catherine Howlett, *b. 1754*
- Annalisa Elizabeth Howlett, *b. 1756*
- William Robert Howlett, *b. 1758*
- Mary Margaret and Henry Charles Howlett (twins), *b. 1762*

The Howlett Household

- Addy, housekeeper from Barbados
- Liza, indentured girl from Ireland
- Dane and Zeke, hired farmhands

The Perkins Family

- Lord John Jackson Perkins II and Lady Elizabeth (Bette)Bixby Perkins
- John Jackson Perkins III (Jack), *b. 1752*
- Oliver James Perkins, *b. 1753*
- Abigail Louisa Perkins, *b. 1755*

- Andrew Richard Perkins, *b. 1759*
- Susan Frances Perkins, *b. 1767*
- Charlotte Elizabeth Perkins, *b. 1774*
- Lord and Lady Brunswick (Aunt Catherine), Lord Perkins's sister
- The late Captain Bixby, Mrs. Howlett's first husband, and brother to Lady Perkins

The Perkins Family Household

- Mercy, indentured housekeeper
- Wheaton, coachman
- Dottie, maid

Friends and Townspeople of Topsfield

- Quinnapin, a Wampanoag Native from Mashpee
- Samuel Wildes, George's oldest friend
- † Captain Gould, captain of Topsfield's militia and owner of the Whispering Willow Tavern
- Martha Perley, courted by William Howlett
- Isaac Perley, Marth's older brother and William's friend
- † Captain Stephen Perkins, second captain of Topsfield's militia and cousin to Lord Perkins
- Mr. Averill and his son Josiah Averill, Patriots
- Hannah French, Lizzie Balch, and Fanny Shepard, gossiping girls of Topsfield
- Elisha Porter, innkeeper at George's Black Water Inn (in Portsmouth)
- † David Perkins, town treasurer and cousin to Lord Perkins

Society of London and Paris

- Lord Essex (Viscount Essex), married Abigail in 1775
- Sarah, chambermaid of the Duchess of Devonshire
- † Georgiana (Gee), the Duchess of Devonshire
- Monsieur Beauregard, French physician
- † Lord and Lady Melbourne
- † Lord and Lady Jersey
- Mr. Fitzherbert, the *ton's* most eligible bachelor
- † Mr. Fox, prominent member of the Whig Party

Continental Army and Patriots

- † General George Washington
- † Henry Knox of Boston, married to Lucy Flucker
- Daniel Bartlett of Menotomy (Cogswell's Regiment)
- † Dr. John Warren, younger brother of the late Dr. Joseph Warren who perished at Bunker Hill
- John and Matthew Whipple of Ipswich (Cogswell's Regiment)
- Dobby, New York camp-follower

British Army, Loyalists, and Turncoats

- Lieutenant Dickens
- Captain Fleming
- Private Lewis
- † Lord General Cornwallis
- † General Howe
- † General Burgoyne

Men of Congress

- † John Hancock, president
- † John Adams, Jack's law partner
- † Thomas Jefferson, wrote the declaration
- † Benjamin Franklin, diplomat to France
- † Silas Deane, sails to France on commission from Congress

† Denotes historical figure

PART ONE
1776-1777

ANNALISA

PORTSMOUTH, THE STATE OF NEW HAMPSHIRE, FEBRUARY 1776

A CLANK OF PEWTER echoed throughout the main room of the Black Water Inn, but the spoken words of Thomas Paine's new circulating pamphlet, *Common Sense*, captivated Annalisa's attention. From the bar, she strained to listen to the gentlemen seated about the largest wooden table, their cheeks pink as roses in the hearth's blazing firelight. They gulped from tankards full of George's flip as they read aloud these new prolific ideals of freedom: that they, the colonists of America, could rule themselves.

Last year's battles showed the Mother Country that the Province of Massachusetts Bay was a reckoning force, but now with General Washington's new army, in tandem with Thomas Paine's eloquently written credos, the birth of a new nation was possible. She saw it now, with far more clarity. *We're at war with England. It may actually happen; we may become independent.*

Buzzing with these thoughts of treason, she returned her gaze to the gentlemen at the table—her husband Jack, and younger brother, William, among them. But she remained poised behind the bar, smiling, though one thought gripped her: *If only George was here.*

"Mrs. Perkins, would you like some madeira?" Elisha Porter's gentle voice enveloped her.

She turned. George's tavern-keep smiled, the candlelight illuminating his velvety, umber complexion.

"No, thank you, Elisha. I'm quite well." She returned his grin. "And please call me Annalisa. I insist."

"I'll try, Mrs. Perkins." He glided behind the mahogany bar and, using a muslin cloth, swabbed a goblet. "You seem melancholy this evening, ma'am. Are you missing Mr. George?"

Annalisa rested her arms upon the bar's ledge. "More than ever."

Elisha produced a note from his black frock coat pocket. "A courier came today. 'Tis addressed to you."

Annalisa took the envelope and flipped it to study the seal. "'Tis from George." She rounded the bar and hastened toward the gentlemen seated about the table. She placed her hands on her husband's shoulders and kissed his temple. "Jack, George has written."

Jack's ocean blue eyes peered at her, and a smile dimpled his cheek. "At last." He stood and embraced her, his lips brushing her forehead. "You've been quite anxious. Come, dear heart, open it."

Quinnapin, a tawny Wampanoag, and Jack and George's closest friend, rose from the table. His rich, sable eyes met Annalisa's gaze. "He must be returned from Ticonderoga."

"I want to see his letter, Annie." William circled the table and met her beside Jack. At seventeen, William finally stood over her tall five-foot-seven frame.

Annalisa's hands shook as she broke the seal and withdrew

the letter. "Give me a moment first, Will. 'Twas addressed to me."

She unfolded the page and read:

> 27th January 1776
> Dorchester Heights
>
> Dearest Little One,
>
> We've finally Returned fromme our Expedition with Knox. The road threw New York was Treacherous, and with the oxen and our cargo in towe, 'twas wors than I'd Imaginned. The snow was thick and deep. I was strong beforre, but now, I Daresay I could easily Kill an ox! We are staid with Washington and his Army at Dorchester Hytes, and will remayne herre until further Notice. Please wryte to Mother and Pa of my safe return. I am not at leisure to wryte as I like. Give my regards to Jack. I want plenty of nieces and nephews upon my return! And tell Elisha I appreciate his unwayvering faith in the Black Water in my absence. And tell Quinn and Wilhelmeena I fully expect to see their hideous faces in the army soon.
>
> Yours &c,
> J.

Annalisa glanced at Jack before handing the page to William. "Here you are, *Wilhelmina*."

Her brother's pale face crinkled at the old nickname, and he snatched the note from her. "Only George can call me thus."

Annalisa chuckled. "He did. In the letter."

"You think he means it?" William looked up from the page. "He truly wishes for Quinn and me to meet him at Dorchester Heights?"

Quinnapin frowned. "I can't join yet. Weetamoo is with child."

Annalisa faced Jack. "Would you wish to join George?"

Jack bit his lip. "I should be glad to, but you know I cannot."

"Why not?" Quinnapin asked.

Jack held Annalisa's gaze with the gentlest candor. "I've responsibilities here—"

"No, sir, you may not use me as an excuse," Annalisa said. "If you wish to join Washington's army, I'm proud for you to go." She bristled at the thought of losing him, but her devotion to the cause overshadowed her doubt. *Jack is meant for more than running George's inn while he's away fighting for what we all believe.*

Quinnapin cupped Jack's shoulder. "I understand your plight, old friend. As a married man, you wish to carry on your lineage. It can only be done one way."

Annalisa's neck and chest burned with her last failed pregnancy, and she left their grouping for the bar. "I'm retiring for the night, Elisha. When Jack is finished with our friends, please you, send him up to me."

"Of course, ma'am. Good night, Annalisa."

She forced a smile, and quit the room with a lantern. From the foyer, she climbed the steep wooden staircase to the second floor. At the end of the hall, she opened the door to the chamber she shared with Jack when they oversaw the inn.

The modest room boasted wide ceiling beams and a four-posted bed. A smoky fire danced within the blue-painted hearth. On chilled winter nights like these, she dreaded undressing to her chemise. Before the fire, Annalisa unpinned her evergreen wool dress from her stays and withdrew her arms from the bodice. It crumpled to the floor. Once untied from her waist, the wool petticoats and pockets tumbled to the floorboards beside the dress. Without the help of a chambermaid, she unlaced her stays, and the whale-boned binding released its harsh grip of her slender torso. It, too, dropped to the floor. She stepped over her pile of clothing and crawled into bed, pulling the woven coverlet up to her chin.

Since their elopement in September, she'd savored the touch of Jack's strong hands undressing her, but the last miscarriage added onus to their nightly romances, leaving her to wonder if he felt slighted by her inhospitable womb. All he'd ever wanted was to join the army, to be part of the cause in which they both believed, but since marrying, Jack refused to join, citing his duty remain with her, as husband and hopeful father. Only recently did her mind turn to the cruel potential for barrenness, but at nineteen, didn't entertain the thought for long.

The hallway floorboards creaked, and the bedchamber door opened and closed.

"Annalisa, please do not be cross with me."

Jack stood by the fire and unwound the cravat from his neck.

"You've just called me *Annalisa*. I think 'tis you who is cross with me."

He sighed and sat on the bed. "I could never be cross with you. I only lament for what I've been unable to give you."

"My body is unable to hold a child. There's no curse upon

your seed, only my womb." Her throat clogged on the last word, and she blinked away her tears.

Jack smoothed her hair, and he leaned over to kiss her. "Dear heart, it will happen when 'tis meant to. I see children in our future—plenty of them."

"You should've married Jane. She's fertile, and ripe with life. No doubt she'll soon birth a boy to your horrid brother." Annalisa rolled onto her side. "She could carry on your family name."

Jack's brows furrowed. "I never could have undergone my engagement to Jane. You know that. How many times must I recount this to you? I love you, and I have never loved Jane." He stood and unbuttoned his waistcoat, flinging it to the floor, then unbuttoned his breeches. "I've promised you time and again I'd sooner die for you than anyone or anything else —this war included."

Annalisa sat upright in bed. "Then why not join the army for me? I know you wish to fight. You've said it enough these several years. Jack, I can't be the reason you withhold yourself from the principles you so strongly believe."

His sinewy body, now uncovered by shirt and breeches, sat by her once more. All sense of frustration from his gaze melted to considerate longing.

"I'm free to choose where I go, yes. And I know this past autumn was spent in Philadelphia with my father—but I was obliged to him. Now that's over, I have no obligation beside my own and the promise I made you the night we eloped. I belong nowhere if 'tis not by your side."

"Jack, I wish to bear you a child. But I also want you to join the army if 'tis what you desire."

"I know you do, dear heart. But I promised I'd give you a child, and I will die trying. I swear it."

Annalisa warmed, despite the chill of the room. "All you say and do is to please me."

Jack edged closer, flooding her with his amber perfume. His lips to her ear, he whispered, "Because I adore you."

Her skin puckered with gooseflesh. "Then let's cease this curtain lecture." She pulled him beneath the coverlet.

⚜

ANNALISA KISSED JACK'S HAND, ONE KNUCKLE AT A TIME. "I pray we have a family in nine months at last."

"In that case..." Jack flipped her onto her back and showered her face with kisses. "We should celebrate your good prayers with another strum. Just to make sure."

Wrapping her arms about him, Annalisa laughed. "You're ready awfully quick, Mr. Perkins."

A knock at the door turned both their heads.

"Who disturbs us at this hour?" Jack threw himself from the bed, pulled on his breeches, and opened the door. William fumbled with a letter, his cheeks rouged with embarrassment. "Will, what's this? Have you no sense we're trying to make a family in here?"

"I'm sorry to disturb, but a note just arrived for you, Jack. The courier was quite hasty." William handed him the letter.

From beneath the coverlet, Annalisa asked, "Who's it from?"

"Lord Brunswick, my uncle." Jack broke the seal and unfolded the page. "Thank you, Will." He closed the door on her brother, who seemed equally eager to flee down the hall.

"Two letters of importance in one night. What are the odds?" Annalisa held her breath, awaiting his response.

Jack sat beside her, and when he finished reading, his unnerved countenance prevailed. "'Tis from Congress. I've been urgently summoned by the Committee of Secret Correspondence."

Her chest tightened with foreboding. "We'll be parted again? To what have you been summoned?"

His gaze lingered upon the page. "To France. Silas Deane will sail upon a different vessel from mine...and upon my arrival in Paris, I'm 'to appear in the character of a merchant'..."

"I'm going with you."

Jack looked up. "Annie, no. 'Tis far safer for you to remain here. We have our family to consider. 'Tis a terrible time to cross the Atlantic. Congress issued a warning for captains of American vessels to take every precaution avoiding British man-of-war ships along the voyage to Europe."

"Will I be without my husband for months, then, or years, while you portray the guise of a merchant to the French courts?" Annalisa gritted her teeth. "I could go with you as your wife—the wife of a merchant. 'Twill seem far less conspicuous for you to appear with me, than present as a congressional agent from the colonies to conduct business..."

"You're not wrong for supposing such a masquerade." On his littlest finger, Jack spun his family's signet ring. "But if we're overcome by a British man-of-war during our crossing, I'll be taken prisoner. I can't risk your life, or our unborn babe's."

She sat upright, disregarding the dreadful cold slipping into her breast. "I'm not some feeble woman, Jack. I can manage crossing the Atlantic, pregnant or no, storm or no, British man-of-war or no."

Jack's face softened and he drew her into his arms. "My darling girl, I have no suitable answers for you. I'm only trying to protect you."

The rhythmic thump of his heart steadied her breathing,

and she buried her face into his chest. She knew she needn't a man's protection—she could keep herself. But on this, she was certain he would acquiesce.

"I'm best protected by your side. Though, with you gone, I could join George at Dorchester Heights as a camp-follower." She omitted enlisting as her secret muse, Benjamin Cavendish, as whom she'd fought at Bunker Hill last June. *Not a camp-follower, but a soldier.* A wave of guilt gripped her. *No, I vowed to put away my breeches for good. When did I come to manipulate those I love?*

She added, "I daresay, crossing the Atlantic is far less dangerous than Washington's camp. Jack, I only wish to be with you."

He remained quiet for some time, then kissed the top of her head. "I'll write my uncle."

2

GEORGE

DORCHESTER HEIGHTS, THE PROVINCE
OF MASSACHUSETTS BAY, FEBRUARY 1776

I N THE TWILIGHT BEFORE sunrise, white wisps
puffed from George's heaving breath. He pitched a spade
into the half-frozen ground of Dorchester Heights, then ran
his arm beneath his dripping nose. The bitter sting of winter
settled into his lungs, and he hacked. This was far more
miserable than the thick humidity last June when he dug
fortifications on Bunker Hill.

He peered at the waters below. The harbor separated
Dorchester from Boston's peninsula, and the British.

Boom!

The discord of cannonade shook him from his charge,
overwhelming the clank of shovels and spades digging
trenches around him.

Boom!

The rupture of cannon-fire, a thinly veiled shroud meant
to conceal their activity from the British yonder, reminded
him of his recent expedition to Fort Ticonderoga; they'd
confiscated the artillery and dragged it the long way back to
Dorchester on sleds affixed with oxen.

Since April, Boston lay besieged by the British. Those who were permitted to leave, and those who'd escaped— either north by Winnisimmet Ferry, or south via Boston Neck —fled the town teeming with Lobsterbacks and Loyalists; a stronghold for the British to isolate the harbor, hindering the trade that kept Boston, and the colony, afloat.

I don't think the province can endure much more of this. George gazed to the west at the Charlestown peninsula. The British had lit the town aflame, leaving it a charred heap on the southern shore. Breed's Hill and Bunker Hill stood covered in snow. From this wintry scene, no one would ever suspect the carnage endured there last June.

He shuddered, recalling that fateful day. Never had he seen such brutality, not even at Concord. And his sister, Annalisa, had witnessed it all dressed as that rogue, Benjamin. How she survived still perplexed him, even offered a shred of awe at her resilience. But her greyed face, beaded in sweat as she nearly expired a month later from a musket wound still haunted him.

"I bet ye Bunker Hill weren't this terrible." Samuel Wildes, his oldest friend, tossed a shovelful of earth behind him.

George tamped away the memories. "I sweat my weight in cider kegs that day. Now, I can barely feel my toes." Another puff of white exited his lips.

Samuel mopped the snot dripping from the tip of his thin, upturned nose. "D'ye really think the Bloodybacks are dimwitted enough t' think nothin' be happenin' out here? That our cannon firin' miles away be enough distraction?"

"I think they've got their heads so far up their arses they'll find any bit of cannonade a distraction. And that squeeze crab, Howe, has his dilberry Lobsterbacks focused on those cannon as we speak."

Samuel snickered. "We'll see come mornin', won't we."

"Private Howlett." An officer approached. "Your strength is needed to help move those two guns into the fortification."

George threw down his spade. "Aye, sir."

"Th' artillery from Ticonderoga?" Samuel asked.

"Aye. Each one," George grumbled. "But these are the final two." He followed the officer down a hill, his heels slipping on ice. "The Devil's cock."

It wasn't enough to have traveled the long way to New York with Henry Knox and confiscate artillery from the British. It wasn't even enough to have dragged all fifty-nine cannon upon sleds fixed to eighty yokes of oxen to Dorchester in the middle of January. No, now he must assist positioning said guns within their fortification on the heights, aimed at Boston. His beloved Boston.

৩৯৩

An officer atop the hill waved. "This way, gentlemen, this way."

A rosy dawn pushed back the darkness as George, along with four other brawny men, thrust the final cannon inside the fort. Despite the bitter cold, perspiration trickled down George's temples. He gritted his teeth and shoved his broad shoulders into the iron. The cannon wheels slid across the slick snow.

The militiaman beside George tripped over his boot. "Easy, Howlett. Yer goin' too fast."

George drove forward with the other three men; the fourth, who'd tripped, sat on the ice rubbing his shoulders. When they'd established the six-pounder within the fortification, George appreciated the ramparts were complete.

"Thank God we finished before the storm," a man beside him wheezed.

The dazzling sun-kissed clouds had faded to show their true grey as snow flurries drifted and danced to Earth. A light dusting already clung to the guns.

"A nor'easter?" George asked.

"Mayhap," the man replied.

Soon, gusts would turn to angry winds, and the flurries to thick, blinding flakes. *A nor'easter to blow the British out to sea.* Sore, George leaned against a cannon and rubbed his throbbing shoulder. He stared at the swollen Atlantic separating them from their oppressor thousands of miles away. Yet, there they were, in the throes of war with Britain, the Mother Country. Perhaps it would only be a matter of weeks before King George realized his madness and withdrew his armies. Enough men had lost their lives, and many more grew ill. They needn't lose more.

George massaged the tender muscle of his left arm. Though ten months had passed since his injury at Lexington and Concord, these excursions exploited his brute strength, and exacerbated the ache. *I wonder if Annalisa still experiences similar tenderness in her shoulder from the round she took at Bunker Hill.* Hopefully, she was safe at his tavern in Portsmouth with Jack. He hadn't heard from either of them since returning to Dorchester Heights.

"Private Howlett, a letter for you, sir."

Startled, he turned. A black man, no older than William, presented him with a sealed note.

"Thank you." George took the envelope and ran his thumb over the oblong blot of red wax. *Jack.* He broke the seal, withdrew the letter, and unfolded the page.

When he finished reading, his gaze lifted to the steel-colored ocean. Annie and Jack were crossing those very waters, bound for France. He sighed, relieved to know the whereabouts of his favorite sister. Annie would also get to see Abigail in London; one familiar face in a vast sea of Tory plums. *The bastards.*

Old bitterness returned at the thought of Abigail, and he stuffed the letter into his coat pocket. He'd been unable to bring himself to write to Abigail, despite the promise he'd made her. It was too hard now that she was wife to that dandy prat, Lord Essex. And if he did write, Lord Essex might uncover the letter. The thought of any harm coming to Abigail sent a wavering tingle up his spine.

George forced her from his mind and faced the ramparts behind him. There was still much to complete within the fortification if they were going to drive the Bloodybacks from Boston; if they were to reclaim their town and end this war. Only then could he return to The Black Water in Portsmouth. Only then could he return home to Topsfield.

3

ANNALISA

THE NORTH ATLANTIC, MARCH 1776

ANNALISA DREW IN A breath of briny sea air, and her nausea eased. "You're sure Abigail and Lord Essex will have received our letter by the time we arrive?"

A cold, salty gust blew Jack's cocked hat from his head.

"Yes." He laughed, grabbing the hat and pulling it to his forehead with a gloved hand. "I sent it the day after Brunswick's letter arrived. If anything, it should reach them a week, perhaps two, before we make port in Calais." He leaned over and kissed her forehead. "Until then, try to rest, dear heart."

The deck of *Liberté*, a three-masted barque of moderate size, was the only place on board Annalisa didn't succumb to sea sickness—or pregnancy. The morbid flux had neglected her since the night Lord Brunswick's letter arrived and had remained absent since they boarded in Portsmouth; Boston's harbor was still under siege. *I pray George is safe at Dorchester Heights.*

"I hope Abigail is in good health. Think you she is pregnant, too?" Annalisa asked.

"She may be," Jack replied. "We'll find out soon enough.

You're sure you don't mind staying with them while I'm in France?"

"Of course not. So long as you return to retrieve me." Annalisa winked.

Jack laughed. "I could hardly abandon you to England." He took up her gloved hand and kissed her exposed fingertips. "I pray our time in Europe is short, and we may return home before the year is out."

Though she pined to see Abigail, she'd never been this far from home. New Hampshire had always been the farthest she'd gone from her beloved town, Topsfield. Now, she drifted in the middle of the Atlantic, nearing Europe each day.

Droplets of rain pattered upon the deck, and Jack peered at the sky. "I don't appreciate the look of these clouds."

She shivered. "There was a brilliant red sky this morning. That is an ill omen of a storm, is it not? A red sky at morning?"

"Aye, but perhaps 'twill only be a bit of rain, nothing worse." Jack stood and offered his arm. "Come. Let's below. I know the air does you good, but this rain will bring on a chill."

☙❧

ANNALISA AWOKE. THE GIANT SEA THUNDERED UPON THE deck of their three-masted barque; a sea that sought to press her flat upon the ocean floor. She clutched her stomach from the roil of nausea made worse by the ship's continuous heaving.

In her bunk, she shivered violently. Near-frozen brine dripped onto her face, mingling with the cold sweat of fear beading at her temples. She reached for Jack beside her and felt space. Frantic, she leapt from her bunk. Her feet splashed into the frigid water swirling about her cabin. Sloshing through the seawater, she staggered into the dark passageway between other cabins at the stern of the barque.

"Jack?" Annalisa wobbled and thudded against the bulkhead. She gripped the beam above as the ship pitched from port to starboard, its timbers giving a low, stressful groan. A lonely lantern swayed from its hook, the flame flickering in darkness. She stumbled and skidded into a barrel sprung from its harness. It rolled with each lurch of the creaking ship and knocked Annalisa to the deck. Her wool dress sodden, she crawled to the roped stair, which led to the upper deck.

"Jack!" She clutched the rope as the vessel gave a stomach-loosening plunge. Her grip on the rope whitened her knuckles, and the dive of the barque propelled her upward. From above, strained voices shouted orders over the roar of the storm.

"Reef the mainsail!"

Trembling against the stair, she dipped a numbed hand into her pocket. Nestled deep within, her fingertips grazed the musket round that had embedded in her shoulder at Bunker Hill; at her neck, the *wampum* feather from her dear friend, Quinnapin. She drew in a sobering breath. Emboldened, she pushed against the heavy door. It did not budge. She heaved again, this time with as much force as she could conjure. It slowly shifted with a groan, and she crawled onto the poop deck.

Annalisa's face stung in the whipping wind. Hail undulated in sheets across the open deck. In the eerie, unnatural glow of early morning, the crew crawled along safety ropes, their shouts muffled by the roar of waves and gales. Jack would never hear her cries over such wrath. Keeping herself low, Annalisa crawled across the slippery wooden planking.

When she reached the rail, she peered over the edge. The

North Atlantic swelled. A wall of water, dreary green at its height, blended into iron-blue. Crests of white spume laced the peaks and lashed at her face. Her wet hair plastered to her forehead, she turned from the rail.

Surely, they would capsize; surely, they would end here, forgotten in a deep, cold grave.

"Annalisa!"

Jack's arm surrounded her waist and pulled her from the edge as a wave crashed down upon them. They rolled as one, flung against a stout wooden bollard.

"This way." Jack hurled them from the poop deck, down to the quarter deck, toward the helm.

The captain shouted, "Abandon course! To point!"

Huddled beneath the mizzen-mast, Jack pulled her close. "Stay with me." He kissed her and pressed his forehead to hers.

A squeal and loud bang sent her shivering in his arms. She buried her face in his neck. Despite the salty wetness of his neckpiece, he still smelled of smoky amber.

"Will we end here?" Her throat clogged as she heaved against him with the tossing of the ship.

Jack brushed his lips across her dripping hair. His silence startled as the world around them clashed and clamored. "This journey. 'Tis my fault." His voice wavered and cracked as if to weep, but she knew he would not, not when he must be strong for her.

Though her mind drifted to her family's farm for only a moment, she shouted over the roar of rain and wind, "If I must, I'm glad to perish in your arms."

Jack's hold tightened.

Fleeting thoughts of George, away with the Continental Army, emerged; her youngest siblings, Mary and Henry, and her pregnant older sister, Jane; poor William left behind at

George's tavern; and Abigail, her best friend and sister-in-law who awaited them on the other side of the angry Atlantic. They had much to live for, but it seemed divine Providence held other plans.

"Lay out the sea anchor! Lay out all chains!"

Another wave—it must've been miles high—swept over them. In the surge that flooded them, Annalisa barely heard Jack's stifled voice as the violent sea pulled him from her. The reefed canvas sails tore from their lashing and spilled from the sky. A tangle of ropes and spars, and the top of the mizzen-mast, crashed around them.

❧ 4 ❧

GEORGE

DORCHESTER HEIGHTS, MARCH 1776

G EORGE SAT BESIDE SAMUEL on a log across from
a crackling fire. He stared at the amber liquor rippling
inside his tin cup. *Vile wibble, this.* Months had passed since
he'd last tasted the warm, bitter frothiness of his flip.

"I hope Elisha is managing the Black Water well without
me. This rum is swill."

Samuel chortled. "It makes no matter, Howlett. This
wibble will have ye wrapped 'n warm flannel quicker'n any
tavern flip."

George lifted his cup. "Then sluice your gob, Wildes."

Their tins clanked, and Samuel's bright tenor sang his
favorite tavern song:

> *"So fill to me the parting glass*
> *And drink a health whate'er befalls.*
> *Then gently rise and softly call,*
> *Good night and joy be to you all!"*

When he finished the song, Samuel reached toward the

three-legged iron spider positioned over the fire. "Now, fer food." From the skillet, he forked a sizzling sausage, bit into it, and chewed.

Despite the rumble in George's victualing office, the greasy smell wrung his insides. Something about the cold March air felt amiss; unfinished, perhaps. And the British remained in Boston. *When will they retreat?*

"Eat somethin', Howlett." Samuel swabbed the juices from his chin with his coat sleeve. "Ye can't work with nothin' in ye vitals but rum."

"I'm not hungry." George gulped the liquor, winced, and set down his cup. He stood over the fire and rubbed his tingling hands over the flames. A burst of warmth pricked his fingers to life. It was a marvel he still had feeling in his tired, calloused farmer's hands. He wondered how Pa got along with the corn husking this past harvest without him, having only William and Henry to help Dane and Zeke. Soon, they'd be plowing and tilling the farm for planting. *And I'll be five-and-twenty come October. Time passes too fleetingly.*

Samuel rose from his seat, picking sausage from his teeth. "Ye know, Howlett, I heard Howe 'n his men be packin'. Word is they might flee Boston."

George turned. "Who says?"

"So says Knox—who apparently heard it from Washington himself."

"I'd sooner become a fart catcher to King George." He turned toward the fire. The heat warmed his cheeks and nose. "Those dilberries have been a plague upon Boston since they arrived in 1769."

Samuel snickered. "Then perhaps ye can follow Anna 'n Perkins across th' ocean an' apply t' be His Majesty's foot servant."

George snorted. "England has to invite me."

"Ye still love Miss Abigail, don't ye."

"You mean *Lady Essex?*" George sneered and returned to the log. He sat and outstretched his long legs. "She's married. What do I care now?"

Samuel sat beside him. "Why don't ye write t' her?"

"Because if her dandy prat husband intercepts it, I'll be no better off than I am now, and she'd risk her reputation—or worse."

Samuel rubbed his chin. "Aye. But ye made a promise, didn't ye?"

George grunted. "So did she."

"Ye can't be cross with her forever. She had no choice in th' matter. Ye know she would've waited fer ye if she could."

"Fie. She could've and she didn't. She was content to let my uncle make decisions for her, and I'll never forgive—"

Samuel smacked his shoulder. "Don't ye say it. I know ye forgive her. Because if somethin' happens t' Abigail, I know ye'll never forgive yerself."

George sat forward and rested his arms on his thighs. It was true. He'd never forgive himself if something terrible befell Abigail. It wasn't her fault she wed Lord Essex; her father, Lord Perkins, had forced her for the advantageous marriage. George burned at his loathing for Society. He'd hardly hid his disdain, even when he met his wealthy aunt and uncle—Lord and Lady Perkins. That dinner at Mr. Hancock's opulent mansion on Beacon Hill had been both impressive and doleful, despite the news of his new-found inheritance. *At least one good thing came of my father's death.*

But even the inheritance wasn't enough for his illustrious uncle to entrust him with Abigail's hand in marriage. Apparently, he, too, needed to be a lord, or member of Parliament.

"I know it wasn't her fault. But the sting of her wedding is still fresh. She hadn't even the courage to tell me." George made a fist then released the tension. "Annie sent the letter detailing Abigail's betrothal. Abigail was a coward, and that, I'll never forget."

"Round it up, ye dimwitted fartleberries." A crass little officer with a misshapen lip loomed. "Back to work, if ye mean to avoid a floggin'."

George stood and towered over the man. He and Samuel turned toward the encampment when, from beyond the rampart wall, a militiaman hurtled forth.

"'Tis true! The British flee Boston!"

The little officer scrutinized the militiaman. "What say ye?"

George pushed past the officer. "Wildes, to the hill. We may make out their ships."

Together, they ran to the edge of Dorchester's tallest mount. George faced north. His Majesty's ships dotted the harbor surrounding Boston's peninsula, much as they had the day he'd fought at Bunker Hill. Except this time, it was the agreeable sight of several ships leaving. Their white sails unfurled, they drifted from Long Wharf, away from Boston.

"Well, I'll be damned." George jumped and turned to Samuel. "Wildes, they're evacuating. The Bloodybacks are evacuating!" He flung his arms about his friend.

"Zounds! We've won th' war, then?" Samuel's light-grey gaze flickered toward Boston Harbor.

"I can't imagine they'd give up so easily, but perhaps I'll be wrong." George clapped Samuel's shoulder. "This is cause to celebrate. Meet me in my tent with the rum. I must write to Quinnapin and William."

They turned to face the fortification, and a different officer approached. "Private Howlett?"

"Aye, sir."

"I've news for you, sir." The officer hesitated, his gaze

darting between George, Samuel, and the letter. "There's no easy way for me to break such information to you, Private Howlett, but I must do so quickly."

George adjusted his leather gloves and cloak against the March chill. "Speak, man."

"There's news of a foundering. It seems your sister and brother-in-law were on board."

"A shipwreck? How far from Europe was the ship? They were sailing to France—"

"The ship's remains were discovered off the coast of Newfoundland by two other passing vessels, one that had departed Quebec City bound for Calais...the other was HMS *Lively*. Washington's been following the whereabouts of the British navy; as you know, they're off the coast of Nova Scotia."

George shook his head, confused. "Jack's ship was bound for France. That cannot be the ship—"

"It was determined the vessel was blown off course by the storm, but the coordinates make little sense," the officer replied. "Perhaps the captain was not bound to his destination. Judging from the barque's departure date, they should've been nearing the Azores; instead, they were only a hundred miles off the coast of Newfoundland." The officer pursed his thin lips. "Washington suspects the captain may have been working with the British...that he may have purposefully rerouted the ship. We're looking into it—"

"Fie! That is preposterous," George roared.

Samuel's hand rested on his shoulder. "'Tis possible, Howlett."

The officer fidgeted with his coat. "No survivors have been reported, save for the captain and a few sailors of the crew."

Blood drained from George's face, leaving his cheeks cool and head dizzy. "No survivors?"

"Surely, they could've been picked up by th' other ship bound fer Calais, aye?" Samuel asked.

The officer's eye twitched. "Perhaps, but not likely."

All air escaped George's lungs as though he'd been punched in the gut. Stunned, he fell silent for several minutes. His body numbed, and the world about him faded into a ghostly pall. He swallowed thickly and blinked away the sting of tears. "They've...drowned?"

"'Tis likely, sir." The officer shifted uneasily, then handed George the note. "My condolences."

George read the dispatch but stopped half-way. His anger bubbled, and he crumpled the page. "They were aboard a barque bound for France, captained by a turncoat."

"That is Washington's theory, Private," the officer replied.

George gritted his teeth. "I want the name of that captain."

5

JACK
HALIFAX, MARCH 1776

JACK'S TEMPLES THROBBED. He opened his eyes. The room appeared blurred and dark. He rubbed his eyes, then curled onto his side. A sharp, shooting pain radiated down his left leg.

"Zounds," he rasped.

"He's waking, sir."

A man garbed in scarlet stood on the other side of a bleary iron palisade.

"Joyce Junior?" Jack's voice cracked. "Is it Pope Night already? Where is your hideous mask, good sir?" He rubbed his eyes again, and the man in red came into focus. Jack startled. This was not Joyce Junior, Boston's notorious commander of the committee of tarring and feathering. His vision cleared, and the iron bars descended from ceiling to floor. Rotting hay piled in clumps over wooden boards, an adzed surface that reeked of excrement. *Not a palisade at all...a gaol cell.*

"Lieutenant Dickens, he's awake, sir." A second man in crimson spoke to a pale, pockmarked, taller man beside him, who removed a set of keys and unlocked the iron door. It opened with a low squeal.

"You've no papers, no dispatches." Lieutenant Dickens stepped into the cell. "No information on you. State your name directly."

"Where...where am I, sir?" Jack cradled his head, suppressing the impulse to retch.

"Your *name*, sir."

Jack massaged his temples. "'Tis Jack."

Lieutenant Dickens pulled a pistol from its holder, gripped the muzzle, and whipped the butt across Jack's right cheek. "Your full name."

Jack gripped his smarting face. "Perkins. Jack...Perkins." He coughed.

The lieutenant smirked and eyed his subordinate. "Mr. Perkins. What was your purpose on board *Liberté*, hmm? Speak, man."

"I...think..." Jack rubbed his cheek. "I was journeying to... visit my sister. Where is my wife?"

"You sound unsure of yourself. Should you enjoy another whipping, boy?"

"No, sir. I...I cannot remember." Jack peered about the prison. *A ship, for certain. But no deep lurch from ocean waves. Perhaps we are anchored at port.* The shorter man stood beyond the deckhead-to-deck rods of the gaol. His arms folded over his chest as he looked on, apparently in study of his lieutenant. Barrels and wooden boxes stacked against the walls, and a roped staircase led to the upper decks. A lone porthole allowed scraps of dying light to pass into the dreary interior. "Please, tell me where I am. Is this not *Liberté*? Have we made port?"

Lieutenant Dickens' leer revealed a row of yellowed teeth,

almost too crowded to fit his mouth. "You're aboard HMS *Lively*, Mr. Perkins."

"HMS *Lively?*" The iron bars and door. The hideous floor. The men in red coats. *Redcoats. Lobsterbacks.* It pummeled back to him: their journey to France, and visit to Abigail in England, Annalisa and their unborn child. They'd been on board a French vessel bound for France. Now, he was on HMS *Lively*.

"Was our ship wrecked?" The memory of a storm felt vaguely familiar, though he remembered little of it. "Or were we overtaken by the British navy?"

"This vessel belongs to His Majesty, King George III."

A British ship, then. Without Annalisa, presumably. Jack's heartbeat quickened at the realization. "Where is my wife, sir?"

"Answer me this, Mr. Perkins: were you, or were you not, sailing to France?"

Jack lifted from the hay to find footing, and an agonizing pain shot down his leg. He toppled to the floor and sucked in the hurt through clenched teeth. He would not relay such information. Jack held the man's black-eyed stare. "I'll ask you once more, sir. Where is my wife?"

"'Tis believed you're a Rebel, headed east on your French barque, for help from King Louis. Am I right, Mr. Perkins?"

"Tell me where my wife is."

His hands clasped behind him, Lieutenant Dickens marched about the prison cell. "'Tis treason to rebel against our king, Mr. Perkins. And it is the likes of such traitors who abscond to our enemies, notably France." He stopped and turned. "I believe you are a Rebel, Mr. Perkins."

"I was headed to England to visit my sister, sir. Now please, tell me where my wife is."

"Our excellent king has done his duty in maintaining a

goodly town of Boston despite this disastrous rebellion. Your abject, Rebel army can hardly keep us at bay, Mr. Perkins. I would have you know this very ship was the first to fire upon your pitiful fortifications at Charlestown last June."

Bunker Hill. Jack compressed his dirty hands until the knuckles whitened. He'd been there that fateful day with William, searching for his Annalisa. "You fired upon provincials at Bunker Hill? This ship...initiated battle that day?"

"Indeed, Mr. Perkins. And from the sound of it, dare I presume your presence at said battle?" He smirked again, apparently pleased by the provocation, and the death of hundreds of men.

"I was not there, sir," Jack lied. His head throbbed with grief. He had been there, the smell of battle overwhelmed him; the sulfuric gun-smoke lingering over the battlefield like storm clouds, the blaze of fires that melted Charlestown to the ground, the coppery scent of blood spilled upon the earth.

And Annalisa, dressed in men's clothing, bleeding. She was blessed to have survived that day. Did she survive this? His stomach wrenched, and a spew of vomitus coated the hay beside him. Jack coughed and heaved until nothing remained within him.

The lieutenant returned to the door and removed his key. "Good day to you, Mr. Perkins. I hope you find the accommodations aboard HMS *Lively* to your satisfaction."

Jack wiped his mouth on his sleeve. "Where is my wife? Tell me where she is, goddammit!"

"That is no way to speak to a commanding officer, Mr. Perkins. Good day to you." Lieutenant Dickens escaped the cell, locking the door behind him. "I hope you enjoy your time on board as we drop anchor at Halifax."

"Halifax?" Jack hurled himself toward the bars, clutching them. "Please, I beg of you, tell me my wife is alive. Tell me she's aboard this ship—that she may return home to our family."

Lieutenant Dickens glided toward the roped stairs. When he reached them, he paused and turned. "The bit about your wife..."

Jack's chest tightened. "Please, I'll do anything so long as you tell me where she is... that she isn't harmed, sir. I—"

"'Tis for another day. Come along, Lewis."

The shorter Redcoat hurried after him.

"No, please." Jack slid his arms through the bars. "Sir, I beg of you—"

"Good day, Mr. Perkins." The lieutenant started up the stairs. As he ascended, he added, "Welcome aboard HMS *Lively*."

"Let me out!" Jack shook the prison rails. His weakened hands slid from the bars. "Please."

Jack slumped into the hay in a coughing fit. When he'd gained composure over his burning breath, he rested his aching head against the ship's wooden wall. He still hadn't inspected what caused the sharp pains in his left leg. With trembling hands, he rolled down the ripped stocking. Dark purple bruising surrounded a reddened bulge at his shin. The bone was unmistakably broken, though had not ruptured the skin.

He grimaced, pulled the stocking over his leg, and slumped into the hay. Despondent, he stared at the deckhead. The world around him swirled into a dizzying mass of gaol cell irons and soiled hay. Beyond the porthole, the sky darkened, and Jack threw an arm over his eyes. *Where is Annalisa?*

6

GEORGE

BOSTON, LATE MARCH 1776

ALONGSIDE SIX OTHER MEN, George trudged through Boston. A skinny rodent squeaked and scurried in front of him, crossing King-street. The town's narrow, winding roads once teemed with merchant sailors, fish mongers, shopkeepers, lawyers, and captains, their chatter and shouts heard at every turn. Now, the barren roads lingered in ghostly stillness.

George clenched his jaw to stave off the sting of tears. It was upon these very streets Annalisa had dressed as a boy, and hurled rocks and ice at the king's soldiers the day of the Boston Massacre. The absence of such turmoil, of life bursting with revolt and fury, echoed even louder in the emptiness. These roads held naught but a vestige of what had taken place upon them.

"We should split our party," Samuel said.

"What if something happens?" Daniel Bartlett, a portly soldier from Menotomy, tugged on his brown coat sleeves. "What if there are still Redcoats lurking?"

Obadiah Reed, a tall, lanky minuteman from Marblehead

—who'd been at the Chelsea Creek skirmish—laughed. "They've gone, Bartlett. We saw them leave."

"Then let us split. I'm going to Long Wharf." George quit the search party before they came to a consensus, and ventured down to Boston's longest pier.

Overhead, the squawk of sea birds accompanied the gentle lap of high tide against the wharf. From the end of the great wooden dock, he turned to face the town. Boston's other wharves studded the eastern coastline. Ships of every build once crowded these piers, but in the wake of the absconded British, only a handful of vessels remained, heaving and straining against their barnacled berths.

A cold gust of salty sea air whipped his cheeks, threatening to lift the cocked hat from his forehead. George nestled it snugly toward his brow and wrapped his cloak about him. Full of empty relief, he wandered up Long Wharf, turned into King-street, then followed up Queen-street, which opened to Treamount. Along the way, empty houses and brick buildings stood dark, and full of shadows. Several older homes had been torn down. While the roads remained free of debris and garbage, the common, on which the British had long occupied—and had once been the green grazing place of cows—was thick with muck, and fortified with muddy ditches and wooden palisades.

Another gust of wind, and George wrinkled his nose against the stench of gunpowder, excrement, and rotting food. Boston had become the derelict and forgotten place he long feared it would. George turned down Milk-street and stopped.

The old north chapel had been burned to the ground.

"No." Anger burning within, George hastened from the site of the ruin, and down Newbury-street. Near the south end stood a sage elm, known in town as the Liberty Tree.

They'd paraded to the tree on Pope Night. When George reached the site, his chest constricted.

A charred stump stood in the tree's place.

"They torched it." He fisted his hand.

"Howlett." Bartlett waved at him. "They've turned Faneuil Hall into a theatre."

George rubbed his thick brows. "The Liberty Tree. They burned it to the ground."

"Fie." Bartlett scowled. "I remember that tree well."

The sight of the Liberty Tree's stump smothered and suffocated the area, and his thoughts turned to the ancient oak at the edge of his family's farm. Its heaving boughs, which rested upon the earth, had been Annalisa's haven. George closed his eyes. *Perhaps her spirit is at peace by the oak.* If only he could venture home for one day to sit in the shade of the tree and be with his sister once more. He struggled to swallow.

"Howlett, Bartlett." Samuel sidled up beside them. "Ye need t' see this."

George opened his eyes and followed Samuel up Newbury-street.

Bartlett scurried behind them. "What is it?"

They arrived outside an unassuming brick workhouse near the waterfront.

"In here." Samuel led them inside the building.

George hacked against the musty stench of mold mingling with seawater. Wooden boxes lined the walls. He approached a crate and lifted the lid, only to find iron surgical instruments, and glass bottles full of powders and liquids.

"Well, I'll be damned." He glanced up at Samuel, and removed one of the vials. George swirled the yellowish fluid. "This might be medicine. We should find the doctor to confirm."

"I'll see if Dr. Scott is present." Bartlett hurried from the warehouse.

When he returned not twenty minutes later, Bartlett had with him Dr. John Warren, the younger brother of the late Dr. Joseph Warren. This man could be no older than George or Samuel, and certainly not Bartlett.

George held his breath, then stepped forward. He, too, had lost a beloved sibling. "Dr. Warren, I'm Private George Howlett. 'Tis an honor to meet you, sir. I was present the day your good brother fell at Bunker Hill. I knew him—he was a fine man. Truly, the best of us."

John Warren's mouth sank. "Thank you, Private Howlett. 'Twas difficult losing him. I studied medicine under him, as you may know. But it pleases me to hear you speak fondly of him." He hesitated, lowering his gaze, as if to ward off tears. With a quick clearing of his throat, he said, "Now, where are these alleged medicines?"

"Over here, Dr. Warren." Bartlett pointed to several boxes.

The doctor stepped over a scattering of other medical supplies, some of which had been stored, and approached the cache of boxes. He peered inside one of the crates, and removed several glass vials, setting them down one-by-one. Taking a bottle in hand, he swirled it, then lifted the cork stopper. Cautiously, with the vial held at a distance, he wafted the scent toward him with his opposite hand. This ritual he repeated for the others.

"At first glance these seem useful medicines." Dr. Warren retrieved three more from within the crate, then stopped. "What is this?"

"Is there something else?" Bartlett asked.

Dr. Warren removed two small bottles—one with a white

powder, the other, yellow. "If I'm not mistaken, these strike me as arsenic."

"Arsenic?" George stiffened. "You're certain?"

The doctor's gaze narrowed at the two containers, his lips pressing into a thin line. "I daresay they are. But I'd like to confirm with Dr. Scott."

⚜

GEORGE AND SAMUEL GATHERED WITH SEVERAL OTHER militiamen and soldiers on Dorchester's tallest hill. Behind them, the great Atlantic swelled in the warming afternoon sun. Henry Knox, the officer with whom he'd stolen British artillery from Ticonderoga, perched on a rock.

"Gentlemen, it has come to our attention by doctors Warren and Scott, the medicines found at the workhouse are unusable by means of arsenic poisoning." Knox spoke with conviction, but George sensed an unease about the encampment. "I may be so bold as to presume it was the intention of the British to poison Boston's citizens upon their return to the town."

A heaviness descended upon Dorchester Heights. *At least we uncovered the workhouse and its toxic medicine before the residents returned. Had we not...*George's skin prickled beneath his coat, and he shuddered.

"This information shall undoubtedly reach the public of Massachusetts in the coming days," Knox continued. "We can only hope such news may propagate feelings of patriotism amongst the people and fuel their anger against the British."

This much was true. And information of this magnitude might embolden more men to join the Continental Army. As for his own contract with the Continentals, George could either return home to Topsfield and his tavern in Portsmouth or sign on for another two years.

Until he'd learned of Annalisa and Jack's demise at the hand of divine Providence, he'd intended to finish his contract and journey home. Life in the military was hardly what he'd supposed it to be. But now, there was little hope of the war ending. The British had fled to Halifax—and most likely planned to attack elsewhere—and Annalisa was dead. There was nothing left for him at home, nothing to do but continue with the army.

George held his firelock, Bixby, and examined its cool steel, its shiny walnut stock. A fleeting memory of teaching Annalisa to load and fire Bixby sped through him. The naturally acquired precision of her shot was quite a feat for a woman. If she'd been born a brother, she could have joined him, and avoided a woman's fate of marrying, of crossing the Atlantic at the behest of her husband's work.

Georges grimaced. He could hardly be angry at Jack for taking her with him. *At least they perished together.* Yet, something about the shipwreck felt odd, and didn't sit well. *But why should it? My sister is dead, sunk to the bottom of that frigid ocean.* The same vast expanse that had claimed Captain Bixby, the natural father he'd never known—the relation that led him to meet his beloved cousin Jack, who now, too, slept in that same cold grave. When he looked up, Samuel had disappeared with the crowd of militiamen, leaving him with Bartlett.

"Private Howlett?"

George scowled. "What is it, man?"

"Will you pack your things?"

"For what?"

"Heard you not the plan?" Bartlett fiddled with the pewter buttons on his coat. "We're leaving for New York."

"Fie, Bartlett, I take orders from Washington, not you," George barked.

Bartlett's round face flushed, and he cleared his throat. "My apologies, but Knox relayed the information. From Washington himself."

George adjusted the firelock at his shoulder. He'd not heard the remainder of Knox's speech after the bit about the poison. "When do we leave?"

"Two days," Bartlett replied. "We march to York Island, to fortify New York City."

"Washington plans to move the entire army there? What of those in Cambridge?"

"Aye, but not at once." Bartlett straightened his coat and stood upright. "We're part of the first brigade to move from Boston. The men in Cambridge will follow."

George sighed, unsure of whether or not he should be pleased to be part of this expedition. Undoubtedly, he'd be tasked with building more fortifications. They would be well-prepared, should the British attack. And if British General Howe was at all the brilliant man he was purported to be, the Lobsterbacks would endeavor to overtake New York City, thereby cutting off New-England from the rest of the colonies.

He bristled at the thought. "This war is far from over. I fear 'tis just begun."

❧ 7 ❧
JACK
HALIFAX, HMS LIVELY, APRIL 1776

"WHY WERE YOU SAILING to France?" Lieutenant Dickens drove the butt of his Brown Bess musket into Jack's stomach.

Gasping, Jack doubled over. "I know...nothing. I've told you...I'm no...spy. I was...to visit my...sister in England."

"Lies. You were aboard a French vessel."

The lieutenant's Brown Bess clipped Jack's chin. He staggered back and leaned against the ship's wooden wall for support, his broken leg throbbing viciously.

"Please...enough." Jack swabbed his hand over his mouth and nose. Bright red blood stained his skin. "I can suffer no more. Please, tell me where my wife is."

"I decide when you've endured enough." Lieutenant Dickens side-stepped, and swiped the musket behind Jack's knees, toppling him to the grimy deck. "Now tell me, once and for all. What was your purpose in sailing to France?"

"No, sir—"

"Mr. Perkins. I will set you free if you divulge the truth." The lieutenant gave a tight-lipped smirk.

Jack shook his head, unwilling to betray Congress and their plans. *Annalisa's life may depend upon it.* "I will not admit something that is untrue."

Lieutenant Dickens raised the Brown Bess to strike Jack again, then paused. He set the musket down and wrapped his long white fingers around the barrel. "You know, Mr. Perkins, we did pick up your wife after the storm. In fact, she answered several questions—including the destination of your ship." The lieutenant quirked a brow. "To Calais."

Jack's breath quickened despite the sharp rib pains. "Where is she? What happened to her?"

"When she'd given us the information, we disposed of her."

A vibrating silence pulsed in Jack's ears. *No, this can't be true.*

Lieutenant Dickens stepped beyond the iron cell, then locked the door with a *clank*. "You must choose, Mr. Perkins. Honor your wife and her confession or continue to dishonor her—even in death—by maintaining collusion with your Rebel lot." He turned from the cell. "Good day, Mr. Perkins."

"No, it can't be. I don't believe you!" Jack gripped the bars and rattled the cell, ignoring the stabbing bark of his broken leg. "Come back here and tell me where my wife is, goddammit!" He crawled from the bars and swung a fist at the wooden plank. "Fie! Fie! Damn you, Lobsterback bastards, damn you!" He threw fistfuls of hay, then slumped against the ship's wall and held his head. "Annie, where are you?" *You cannot be dead.* "I will find you."

THE STAIRS CREAKED OVER THE SHIP'S LOW GROAN OF timbers, and Jack's eyes opened. A lovely young lady with shiny, near-black hair peeked out from her white linen cap. With a lantern in hand, she tiptoed toward the cell.

"Jack?" She hastened forward, set down the lantern, and gasped. "God Almighty. You look a fright."

Jack sat upright and rubbed his eyes. He squinted, and the room and lady came into focus. "Jane?"

His younger brother's wife—Annalisa's older sister—knelt outside the gaol.

"Oh, Jack." Jane's pale blue eyes watered. "I would've come sooner but I couldn't get past the guard. You must know I tried—"

"Pray, know you the truth about Annalisa? Where is she? What have they done to her? Has she...perished?" He choked on the last word, though he willed it to be untrue.

Jane's full bottom lip quivered. "She has."

"No."

"'Tis true, Jack. I'd not lie about this—"

His fist lifted to his mouth, but the wail escaped. "God, why?" With each heave, his ribs shot sharp pains into his abdomen and back, but none compared to the perverse agony within his chest. Each heartbeat swelled with unbearable torment. He gripped his sternum.

"Peace, Jack." Jane glanced behind her. "You mustn't wake the guard. If he hears, 'twill be trouble for us both."

He gasped but could not catch his breath. Life itself sucked from him, as though his lungs filled with the ocean waters that had claimed his beloved. Jack wheezed and coughed to draw in one precious gulp of air but could not. His hands flew to loosen the cravat about his neck, but it was gone. With nothing to constrict his breathing but his galloping heart, he forced in a lungful of air, then expelled it through pursed lips.

"Jack, please." Jane reached for him, but he staggered from the bars.

Jack sucked in several more breaths until he gained composure and rested against the wall. "Pray, is Oliver on board?"

"He is..."

"Then he knows what happened to her. I'm not surprised he hasn't come. A Loyalist to the core. He relishes knowing his Patriot brother, now a widower, remains behind irons. He'd threatened me enough these several years."

Jane pouted. "Never. Ollie's the reason your leg was properly set. He isn't pleased by this, but his hands are tied."

Jack looked down at his broken left leg. Its bandage had been changed. He slammed the wooden deck with his fist. "Fie. If he was able to set my leg, he could free me. And could have saved Annalisa."

Jane leaned close to the iron rails. "You know 'tis not that simple. I would've devised a plan to come sooner...I would've done all I could to save her, but I wasn't here. I was on confinement from giving birth, which was why Ollie left me behind. The baby and I only just arrived in Halifax a fortnight ago."

Jack ground his teeth. "Ollie left you and the infant to travel alone, after your lying in, no less? What sort of husband is he?"

"He is not as you suppose."

"Then did you come by your own volition?"

"He sent for me. And the babe." She paused, and a small grin escaped her lips. "A boy. We named him Thomas John but call him Tommy."

"Congratulations." Jack grimaced, recalling Annalisa and their struggle for a child. "I cannot imagine this ship a fitting place for a newborn."

"'Tis not." A cheerless shadow fell across Jane's wan face; cheeks, he remembered, that once glowed pink like springtime peonies. "I can't care for Tommy on a ship like this. I'm trapped, too, Jack. As you are."

"Then you must insist Oliver let you return home, that 'tis for Tommy's well-being."

"He will not. He demands I be here."

"Would that Annalisa were here." Jack's chest squeezed at the thought of her and the unborn child she'd surely carried. Again, he clutched his shirt, laden with feculence and the scent of pitch, until air returned to his lungs. His breathing steadied, and he studied his surroundings. A guard snored in a chair beside the stairs. "Was...was this the only guard you needed to pass in order to come here tonight?"

Jane nodded.

He cleared his throat. "I've a proposition for you."

She started to shake her head. "Jack, I—"

"If you help me escape, I'll bring you and Tommy home to Topsfield."

Jane looked over her shoulder once more. "I cannot. Of what use could I be to you, Jack? I'm just a woman—"

"No." He gripped the bars. "You're Annalisa's sister. You must be brave. Think like Annie and find a way."

Tears rolled down her cheeks. "I'm not...I cannot."

He reached for her. "I know you can, Jane. Please."

The guard stirred in his chair, and they froze. He grumbled something, then returned to a rattling snore.

Jane dispelled a shuddering breath. "I must go."

"Where is Oliver presently?" Jack asked.

"Quarterdeck, I believe."

Jack seized her hand. "Find me a quill and some paper. I'll write to Elisha Porter. There must be a captain at George's tavern, one with a sloop, or schooner. I'll request they sail up the coast from Portsmouth. Urgently."

"Now?"

"Yes, at once."

Jane backed away from the cell, and tiptoed up the stairs.

THE CLATTER OF HALYARDS FROM ABOVE JERKED HIM AWAKE, as they so often did, and Jack turned onto his side.

"Jack."

A clank, and second rattle, echoed from beyond the bars. Jack lifted his head and sat up. Groggy, he rubbed his face. He was still within the cell; a prisoner, and now a widower. *How much crueler life is when I'm awake.* Jane stood on the other side of the irons with paper, inkwell, quill, and sealing wax in hand.

"Quick, before we're caught. Here." She thrust the writing implements through the bars.

Taking them, Jack set them down and cleared the hay from a patch of wooden deck on which to write. Hastily, he dipped the quill into the inkwell and scribbled his request to Elisha Porter, George's innkeeper at the Black Water Inn.

He looked up at Jane. "The candle, please."

She opened the lantern and handed him the candle from within. Using the flame to melt the sealing wax, little droplets of red clung to the page's fold. When enough had dripped, Jack went to remove the signet ring from his right pinky finger. It was gone.

He met her gaze. "They've taken it. My family's ring." Using his thumb, he pressed the wax until it oozed and hardened. It would have to do. Jack handed her the note. "This must be delivered immediately."

"Then what must I do?"

"Be on the lookout for a reply from Elisha. I've written for him to address his letter to Oliver. Intercept it before it reaches him. I'll require you to borrow money from Oliver to pay the captain. Then you must devise a way to obtain the guard's keys—"

"Jack, this is too much." Her hands trembled. "I can't—"

"You must." He reached through the bars to steady her. "You're my hope of escaping here alive. And I'm your way of returning you and Tommy home."

She nodded. "Quite."

Studying her, Jack fell silent. He recalled the days when first they'd met, the years he'd been so blinded by her beauty that nothing else mattered. And their arranged betrothal. Jack shivered, flooded with guilt. *I should've noticed Annalisa first. How fickle I was, my darling girl.* Now, he held no option but to place his faith in Jane, the fiancée he'd left to elope with Annalisa. *Can I trust her, Annie, my love?*

Jane's full lips parted. "I will return. You have my word." She gathered the writing supplies, retrieved her lantern, and fled up the stairs.

Jack rested against the hay in his cell and wiped a rogue tear from his eye. "Dear heart, how was it you were taken from me? Lord, am I being punished for the way I conducted myself with Jane and Annalisa?" He went to twist the absent signet ring about his little finger, a tic he recognized about himself when Annalisa had pointed it out. *When did they take it?* Not only was his wife gone, but also, the last vestige of his family. Stripped of everything, he had nothing left to lose.

❧ 8 ❧

ANNALISA

PARIS, FRANCE, APRIL 1776

A RUSH OF TEPID air filled her lungs, and Annalisa sat upright in bed. Gasping, she gripped her chemise. As her breathing slowed, she rubbed her hand across her forehead; wisps of hair stuck to her skin. She winced and cradled her throbbing head.

Slowly, her vision cleared.

Bright sunlight drenched a finely wallpapered room in hues of yellow and gold. Above, a canopy of golden damask curtains cascaded over the bed. On either side of the bed stood matching mahogany bedside tables; one boasted a white porcelain vase sprouting with pink flowers, the other, a matching washbasin surrounded by vials of ointments and liquids.

Annalisa lay back and rested her heavy head against the downy pillows.

A white paneled door opened and closed, and a sable-skinned chambermaid entered the room. Her brows lifted. "Miss, you're awake."

"Where am I?" Annalisa's voice croaked as though she hadn't spoken in years.

The chambermaid, with an unfamiliar accent, hastened toward the canopied bed and placed her cool, calloused hand against Annalisa's forehead. "You've broken your fever, Miss." The chambermaid's round face lifted with relief. "I must inform my mistress." She bobbed a curtsey and fled the room.

Not five minutes passed when the door again opened. This time, a lady with a peaches-and-cream complexion, attired in pink silk with skirts fitted over wide hoops, stepped inside with the chambermaid. A ruddy-cheeked gentleman, donning a yellow silk ditto suit, followed.

"*Monsieur* Beauregard, she's awake." The lady clasped her hands and drifted toward Annalisa. The chambermaid remained near the door with the gentleman, who spoke something in French, then quit the room.

"Oh, there, there." The lady sat on the edge of the bed, and a gust of rose and bergamot perfume wafted over Annalisa. "Sarah." The lady regarded the chambermaid, who hurried to retrieve a muslin cloth. Sarah soaked it in some kind of bitter-scented ointment from the bedside table, then draped it across Annalisa's brow.

"You've a terrible head injury, and you bled much. But you're looking well," the lady said. "You mostly slept these several weeks, but when you did wake, 'twas quite the challenge getting to you eat and drink. Nothing but incoherent mumblings, with a few English words peppered in. I daresay, we wondered whether you'd ever fully awaken."

Annalisa closed her eyes to diminish the dizziness. "I...w-where am I, m-marm?"

"You're in Paris, and in very good care," the lady replied. "Sarah's been most diligent in tending to you, under the direction of *Monsieur* Beauregard."

"*M…Monsieur* B-Beauregard?" Annalisa's heartbeat quickened. "Who? W-what happened?" She slowly opened her eyes. The dizziness had subsided.

"So many questions, and rightfully so. And a curious accent." The lady smiled ruefully. "My husband and I were crossing the channel from London. On our arrival to Calais, I took a walk along the pier, near the docked ships…I like to do that when I can. Well, one of them, a French vessel just arrived from Quebec, was unloading a bit of cargo. You were lying, near lifeless, upon a cot on the wharf. The sailors stepped over you and kept moving you from one spot to another…perhaps they knew not what to do with you. I left, but my mind kept returning to you, or perhaps 'twas my conscience. So, I told my man to journey to the dock and if you were still there, to collect you and bring you to our house here in Paris."

A curious accent? Nothing sounded familiar. "F-from where did I c-come?"

The lady shook her head. "I know not, but your ship was from Quebec. You'd no papers on you." She stood. "Let us perhaps introduce ourselves, then, yes? My name is Georgiana Cavendish, Duchess of Devonshire." She gestured to the chambermaid, who curtsied. "And this is Sarah."

The Duchess of Devonshire. "Y-your Grace."

"We've been referring to you as Miss Calais since that is where we discovered you." Georgiana took up Annalisa's hands. "Now, what may I call you?"

Annalisa withdrew her hands from Georgiana's and rested them in her lap. "I kn-know not what you may c-call me, Your Grace."

The duchess tilted her head. "Whatever do you mean?"

Annalisa's chest tightened. "I'm t-terrified, Your Grace. I

kn-know not why I'm here, or w-where I'm from. I kn-know not who I am."

❦

As Annalisa lay in bed that night, she watched the candlelight dance upon the walls from beeswax candles. *Did I come from Quebec? But I don't understand French the way I should if I spoke it in Quebec. Why was I aboard that French vessel? Why am I here?* Such existential questions were examined by most humans, including herself, at any moment in time, but they held a far different meaning to her, now. Each attempt to uncover her memories appeared as black voids; no faces, names, or places. Not even her own. Just the vacancy of a life once lived, now unknown.

Her head throbbed with a dull ache, and her eyes welled for the memories lost, and forgotten. *Should I mourn? For what do I mourn? Perhaps I left a grievous past, one riddled with despair and sorrow. Perhaps I succumbed to indentured servitude to an unkind master or mistress. Mayhap, I should be grateful to be employed now, in the presence of nobility, with their immense kindness offering me convalescence. But what if I left a good life...a husband, children...loving parents?*

Sarah entered the room with a silver tray. "Good evening, Miss. Mr. Beauregard thinks you should eat something."

Annalisa sat up, and Sarah propped the pillows behind her. "Th-thank you."

The chambermaid lifted a silver cover to reveal a steaming bowl of broth. "'Tis not much, but Mr. Beauregard insists you eat slowly."

"Who is M-mo...Mr. Beauregard?" Annalisa took the spoon, but hesitated before dipping it into the bowl.

"He's the doctor, Miss."

Annalisa dipped the spoon into the liquid, rich with thyme, rosemary, and sage, and she sipped. Her insides warmed. "This is w-wonderful."

Sarah cocked her head. "You like it?"

"Very much. It tastes like s-something I've eaten before." Annalisa set down her spoon and sulked. "Th-though I cannot remember where, or when. Or who m-made it."

"'Twill return to you in time, Miss." Sarah lifted a mug of tea and handed it to her.

Annalisa gripped the hot, steaming cup, and her cool hands burst to life from the warmth. She drank. The tea tasted bitter, but also herby, with a hint of sweetness.

"I've had this b-before."

Sarah's brows lifted, and she blurted, "You have?" Rapidly, she added, "Forgive me, Miss. 'Tis not my place to ask."

Annalisa bit her lip. "At least I th-think I have. B-but I can't r-recall how."

Sarah's jaw hardened as she retrieved the mug and set it upon the tray. "'Tis not likely you've had this tea before, Miss. Perhaps something similar."

"Yes, you're pro...probably right." Annalisa's eyes welled with tears. "Does anyone m-miss me? Have I family? A husband, or ch-children?"

Sarah's downcast gaze avoided hers. "'Tis not my place, Miss—"

"Please, Sarah. Whatever should I do?" Her cheeks flooded. "Whatever sh-should *they* do?"

The chambermaid's face softened, and she smoothed Annalisa's hair. "All will be as 'tis meant to, Miss. We'll take care of you." Her soft voice hummed a simple melody, and the warmth of her hand upon Annalisa's brow eased the pain.

Annalisa's eyelids drooped, and as she drifted to sleep, she reached for Sarah's other hand. "Thank you."

JACK

HALIFAX, LATE APRIL 1776

THE SHIP'S TIMBERS GAVE a low grumble. Lulled by the familiar sound, Jack rested in the hay and plucked strands from his tattered wool breeches. He recalled the day he discovered Annalisa in the woods beyond the oak tree. She'd been firing George's fowler in the clearing, and he'd been lost along the way to her house. As he'd picked burrs from his fine coat and stockings, she'd cleverly remarked about his readiness for country life.

Jack's heart squeezed and the pressure returned, rendering him incapable of drawing a satisfying breath. Recognizing the stricture in his chest, Jack closed his eyes and inhaled through his nose. He imagined expelling a long tendril of tobacco smoke as he exhaled. This he did until the dread subsided. Nothing would return Annalisa to him, and wallowing in misery would only worsen his predicament. *I must focus on escaping this place. Annalisa would want me to keep fighting.*

The sound of wood screeched across the deck, and Jack opened his eyes. Oliver stood beyond the cell. The guard on duty had gone.

Jack balled his fists at the sight of his capricious brother. "Why have you come?"

"To dress your leg."

Jack fell silent as Oliver removed keys from his pocket, opened the cell door, and stepped inside.

"I was hardly expecting you to be awake," Oliver said. "Each time I've come to change your bandages, you've been fast asleep." He knelt and unraveled the old linen, stained with blood and dirt, from Jack's leg—the same leg that had been injured at Concord a year ago. With a wet muslin cloth, Oliver washed away the crusted residue. Jack started at the sight. Beneath the old injury just below his knee—which had healed well—was a large purple welt that had begun its fade to yellow.

"This looks better. The swelling reduced tremendously." Oliver wrapped the strips of clean linen about Jack's shin.

"Why tend to me, but keep me imprisoned? Ollie, you know the torment I've endured these several weeks. Surely, you know the agony." Jack winced. "Where is Annalisa? Tell me what happened to her."

"She's gone, Jack."

"No. Tell me where she is."

"She's gone. There's nothing I can do. Annalisa is gone, and you're imprisoned. My hands are tied—"

"Fie!" Jack slammed the wooden deck. "I'm your brother, yet you collude with the Redcoats as though you're one of them—"

"I am one of them," Oliver snapped. "You forget I've joined His Majesty's regulars of my own accord. I don't believe in this rebellion, Jack. You've known this about me for years. Why does it surprise you now?"

"Then release me. I'm of no use to you here, or at home in

Topsfield. Send me back and I'll be no nuisance to you, or the king's army."

"I can't do that." Oliver finished tying the linen around Jack's leg. "We've orders to follow."

"Damn your orders," Jack growled. "I'm your brother, your flesh and blood, yet you're content to have me imprisoned like some beast. Have you no integrity, no sense of duty as a brother? A father and husband?"

Oliver scowled. "You dare accuse me unfairly. Jane and Tommy are safe here. I'm honorable and shall support our king as he's maintained our colony—as I keep my family."

"A king who's rendered us inept," Jack said. "The man is a despot. And your selfish disdain for our family is no better."

"Disdain?" Oliver twirled a gold ring about his littlest finger. "I'm the one of our family who wishes to uphold the name."

"My ring." Jack's heart skipped. "'Twas you who stole it."

"*My* ring, as I intend to inherit Father's estate when we've won this war." Oliver huffed. "You may have seduced our uncle, Lord Brunswick, with your work in Congress, and convinced him to keep you his heir apparent, but I don't believe Uncle will keep his promises once he discovers you've been imprisoned and tried for treachery. Then I shall inherit both estates."

Jack started. "'Twas Brunswick who wished for me to remain his heir apparent. I did no such convincing. And 'twas by Uncle's own admission he thought my work in Congress well done."

Oliver crossed his arms. "You mean to defend your Congress. 'Twas not I who led my wife to death out of a misplaced sense of duty to those traitors in Congress."

"That storm was of divine Providence," Jack cried. "How

dare you accuse me of my wife's death. You still have a wife—and a child. You're a fool to lead them on this path."

Rapid footsteps pattered down the stairs, and Lieutenant Dickens kicked the cell. "Silence, whelp. Or shall I recount your wife's death to you?"

"That won't be necessary, sir." Oliver stood and stared down at Jack. "I've finished here." He stepped beyond the gaol, and Lieutenant Dickens locked the door. Before fleeing up the stairs, Oliver's backward glance sent Jack's skin pricking.

The officer jingled a set of keys. "I heard much of your wife's death."

"No." Jack shook his head. "I won't hear more."

A screech of iron followed silence, and Dickens stood inside the cell with a jester-like leer upon his pointed face. "Before they tossed her overboard, I heard she moaned like a whore as the crew ravished her."

"Enough!" Jack stood slowly, but his leg gave out. The butt of the lieutenant's musket clipped Jack's face, and he collapsed, rubbing his cheek. "You dare slander my wife."

"Slander?" The officer chuckled darkly. "'Tis but the truth." He leaned over Jack, his dry, bitter breath suffocating him. "I was there."

A fit of anger bubbled up and Jack swung at the officer's face.

Lieutenant Dickens clutched his nose as blood dribbled through his fingers. "You maggot. I'll have you thrown to the sharks."

"Do it." Jack ground his teeth. "End my misery."

A light clatter of steps echoed from the stairs, and the flowery scent of lavender overtook the stench of decay. "Sir—Lieutenant Dickens. Oh, you poor dear," Jane crooned.

Lieutenant Dickens turned. "You needn't be down here,

ma'am. Please you, return to your quarters."

"My husband wishes a word with you, sir."

The lieutenant's gaze tapered, but his face softened. "As you wish, Mrs. Perkins. But I shall warn you, the prisoner's agitation is that of a beast." He withdrew from the cell and locked the door. Before ascending the stairs, Jane offered him a linen handkerchief for his bleeding nose.

When Lieutenant Dickens disappeared above the deck-head, Jane approached the gaol. "Has he hurt you?"

"It matters not," Jack snapped. "Pray, is Oliver truly meeting with him?"

"No. 'Twas a lie."

"Then how can we expect our intercourse to go unnoticed here?"

She grimaced as though she weren't sure of herself, or her plan.

"Hurry. Before he returns," Jack whispered.

"Your letter reached Elisha. The captain—a Mr. Richard Duncan—found me directly at port. Elisha had instructed him thus. He's here, Jack. In Halifax."

"Elisha?"

"No, the captain."

Slowly, Jack stood, and hobbled toward her. He reached through the bars, and she handed him the letter. He cracked the seal.

"Richard Duncan." Jack scanned the script, then held Jane's stare. "We leave tonight."

"Tonight?" Her eyes rounded. "How am I to get the keys and break you free so quickly?"

"Do what you must. Just get the keys."

"I'll try—"

"No. Do it. For Annalisa. Do it for Tommy."

Jane's lips pressed together, undoubtedly to ease their

quiver. "I'll do what I can."

"You must. Captain Duncan wrote he'll have a rowboat ready after midnight. This is our only hope." He thrust the letter beyond the bars. "Take it. Memorize his words, then burn it."

৩১৫৩

BLACKNESS BLANKETED THE PORTHOLE. *MIDNIGHT. SURELY, 'tis midnight.* Jack wobbled about his cell. If only he had a crutch to lean on to ease walking. The guard had fallen asleep hours ago. Now, he required Jane. But after her clumsy visit that afternoon he doubted she would come at all. Jack chewed his lip. After the lies she'd conjured about her pregnancy, and how cruelly she'd treated Annalisa, there was little reason for him to trust her. Though, she had been truthful when forced. *If only she was more careful when she lied to Lieutenant Dickens.*

Hopefully, Tommy's well-being proved enough motivation. The plan benefited them both, unless she truly didn't wish to leave. *Perhaps her visitations were at the behest of Ollie to expose me as a traitor.* A coldness slipped into his chest. He hadn't fully considered Jane might betray him. *Betray me to the British. Perhaps Annalisa isn't dead at all.* His stomach roiled, and he balled his hands as he hobbled about the cell.

No. Jane will do this. She will help. She must.

The guard's snore rumbled beyond the gaol. If only he could escape without Jane; fashion a way to pick the lock. Jack patted down his person, though he knew nothing remained within his pockets. The sting of his lost signet ring still burned. *I would've been better drowning in the North Atlantic.*

The stairs creaked, and the dim glow of lantern light followed. Jane emerged with a bundle wrapped in blankets.

Jack met her at the bars. "Pray, you've got the keys? If not, the guard's been asleep at least two hours. They should be on his person."

She approached the cell with a strange, serene calm upon her face. "This is your nephew, Tommy." The newborn rested in the crook of her arm, near the curve of her breast.

Forgetting why she was before him, he smiled. Tommy's pink little cheeks and long dark lashes marked him as Jane's son. Still too new to the world to show both his parents' traits, Jack wondered if the child would one day inherit Oliver's blond hair, or coffee eyes.

"He's lovely." Jack stuck his hand beyond the bars to stroke the baby's forehead. As he glanced up from Tommy's gentle repose, he noticed a bite mark upon Jane's bosom.

She met his gaze, and her pale eyes turned cold. "He's why I'm here. I said you could trust me."

A roil of nausea rocked him, then guilt took its place. Though he suspected the awful truth, he asked, "What did you suffer?"

Jane lowered her stare and removed the keys from her pockets. "I made sure the rum flowed freely tonight."

"Are you hurt?"

"No more than I'll be if we're discovered. Please, hurry."

Jane handed him the keys, and he fumbled to find the correct one for the cell door. After trying three, the fourth clicked. He turned it and opened the door.

Jane looked at the guard, who shuffled in his chair. "Quickly. He stirs."

Jack fled the cell with the lantern and led the way up the stairs.

"I see you've seduced my wife into freeing you."

Above him, at the top of the stairs, Oliver blocked their way to the upper gun deck. "I had a feeling something was amiss."

"Ollie, please," Jane whispered. "I wish to return home with Tommy. A ship is no place for a newborn. I'm fearful he'll die—"

"He's safe here, and so are you." Oliver grabbed Jane's arm and pulled her up to his side. "As for you, *Brother*. Or, should I say, *Traitor*, back to the gaol with you. I can't have my superiors finding us here. Go on. Go to."

Jack advanced up the steps until he was eye-level with Oliver. His brother's blond hair was tied in a neat queue, and he boasted the scarlet uniform of a British regular.

"You'll do as I say, else I'll sound the alarm," Oliver jeered. "No one enjoys a prisoner escape quite like the captain, I assure you."

"I'll take my chances." Jack swung his fist into Oliver's chin. He grasped his face, and Jack heaved his elbow into Oliver's stomach. He doubled over with a groan and crumpled to the ground.

"Hurry." Jack stole his brother's pistol, and together with Jane, he limped onto the upper gun deck.

"Captain Duncan is on the starboard side," Jane said, breathless.

Jack shuffled to the right side of the ship and peered out one of the open cannon portholes. In moonlight, a rowboat bobbed in the waters below. Though his leg screamed with fury, Jack hastened tying a rope around the cannon, then tossed it through the aperture.

"Give me Tommy. I'll have you descend first."

Jane hesitated, kissed the baby's cheek, and handed him to Jack. "Be gentle with him."

"I will. Now go."

In her layers of petticoats, she squeezed through the port-hole and shimmied down the rope. Jack stuck his head out the opening and watched her descend to the rowboat.

"You there. Stop where you are."

Jack turned. A sailor pointed his pistol at him. He gripped Oliver's weapon and aimed it at the sailor. "I've a child. If you shoot, you'll kill an innocent babe."

The sailor cocked his pistol. "Another move and I'll—"

Crack-bang!

Jack fired, and Tommy wailed.

The sailor staggered, clutching his arm. "Wretch!"

Jack buttoned the screeching baby into his tattered coat, then gripped the rope with one hand. Carefully, he wedged out the porthole, a task far trickier than he'd supposed, shimmying down a rope with a mending leg and a baby tucked against his chest. But he breathed through his leg pain, loosening his grip on the rope in increments, and lowered to the waiting vessel.

"You've almost made it." Jane's voice surrounded him, and he felt a pair of hands upon him. He dropped into the rowboat, and Jane tugged the screaming Tommy from his coat.

"Quickly, sir, quickly." The captain tossed an oar at Jack. "My name's Captain Duncan. I'll have us in Portsmouth by midday tomorrow."

Jack gripped the oar and plunged it into the water. "Thank you, sir." Relieved, and ignoring the throb in his leg, he sucked in a breath of the first clean air he'd smelled in weeks. As they started to row, a head appeared at portholes.

"This is hardly over, Jack," Oliver called out. "We'll meet again. Next time, on the battlefield."

The threat sounded anything but sincere, merely a rallying cry of a bitter younger brother. Yet, the warning had been made. Be it in earnest or no, when next they met it would be a duel.

❧ 10 ❧

ANNALISA

PARIS, MAY 1776

"YOU LOOK WELL TODAY." As Georgiana traversed the room, her dangling jeweled earrings caught the sunlight.

Annalisa sat up in bed and beamed. "I feel w-well today, Your Grace."

The duchess returned her smile. "'Tis our last evening in Paris before we leave for London." Her musical voice was one of the few Annalisa had come to know and enjoy this past month, though all voices sounded unfamiliar these days.

Georgiana settled by the window and gazed outside. "Look at this gloriously clear day." She turned from the damask curtained window. "Paris in springtime is the loveliest."

Annalisa slid from the bed and slipped on the green silk dressing gown Georgiana had lent her. With assistance from Sarah, she'd begun pacing the bed chamber, but to walk outside would be lovely, indeed. "I've n-never been to Paris. I find m-myself lucky to b-be here." Annalisa scowled at her stutter. "M-my apologies, Your Gr-grace."

Georgiana held up her hand. "That troublesome stutter will improve with time. Mr. Beauregard has assured me. 'Twas from the nasty blow to your head."

Annalisa joined the duchess in sunshine, and her arms and chest warmed beneath the rays spilling through glass panes. *How inviting after countless weeks in darkness.*

"You remembered you've never been to Paris," Georgiana said. "I told you your memory would begin to return."

Annalisa touched her head where the large bruise had been. If not for abducting her memory and causing her stutter, she was grateful the injury no longer plagued her with terrible headaches and dizzy spells. "I hope I haven't b-been too much of a b-burden, Your Grace. You and Sarah have..." she slowed her speech, "been...so kind...to me."

"Nonsense." Georgiana reached for Annalisa's hand. "I think 'twas part of God's plan, Calais."

Annalisa twisted her lips to hide her frown. Calais was not her name—she knew that much—only the place they'd found her. "I must be s-someone, from s-someplace, Your Grace. How can it...be...I cannot at least recall m-my Christian name?"

Georgiana removed a couple of trinkets from her pocket. "You're well enough to see these. Perhaps they'll spark a memory or two." She handed Annalisa a small lead musket round, a purple and white feather carved from some kind of stone, and a sapphire ring, the gold band etched with leaves. "These were found on you."

Annalisa gasped. "Is this a w-wedding band?"

"Perhaps. Perhaps 'tis a family ring," the duchess replied.

Annalisa studied the duchess's youthful face. Georgiana was certainly no older than she, though Annalisa could only presume her own age, and Georgiana married the duke in 1774. *'Tis entirely possible I now hold my own wedding ring.* Her chest tightened with an even greater conviction to recall the man who may have given it to her. She closed her eyes and ran her fingers over the etched leaves of the band. Annalisa's eyes pricked, and she opened them.

"I can't remember."

Georgiana's face softened. "I suspect this ball was lodged here." She pressed the soft space beside Annalisa's right shoulder. "You've a scar to match. Whatever you've suffered, perhaps 'tis best you not remember it."

A scar? Annalisa went to the looking glass, slid the neckline of her shift from her right shoulder, and examined the healed wound. "I've n-no recollection of how that came to be, Y-your Grace." She pressed the heels of her hands to her eyes. "How can I have n-no memory of m-my life?"

"Hush." Georgiana smoothed her hair. "All will be well." She tied the necklace about Annalisa's neck, and the carved feather rested at her throat. "This was fastened about you. Mayhap it will bring you luck."

Annalisa touched the stone, smooth on one side and carved on the other, hoping to stimulate a memory.

"I daresay, it looks to be made by a Native of the Americas," Georgiana said.

Annalisa's thumb ran over its surface several times. Maybe it was not stone. It almost felt like a shell of some sort. "P-perhaps I'm from the colonies. You said the ship I was upon m-made b-berth in Quebec."

"You're not fluent enough in French for that to be true, though your accent is sufficiently different. Mayhap you're from one of our colonies in America." Georgiana's face brightened. "Why don't you practice reading poetry with Sarah in the gardens today? Surely, 'twill help your stutter."

"Y-you think so, Your Grace?"

"Yes. I'll send Sarah in to dress and ready you. Then 'tis off to the garden with you." Georgiana drifted to the door, and paused with her hand on the latch, "Ah! I've the perfect book for you," she said as she left the room, closing the door behind her.

Annalisa returned to the looking glass. The purple and white feather dangled at her throat. *What kind of stone is this? And how did it come to me?* She slid her shift from her shoulder to examine the healed wound. *More importantly, how did I come to bear such a wound?*

"Miss?"

Annalisa recognized Sarah's voice on the other side of the door. "Yes, come in."

Sarah entered with a steaming bowl of water and fresh linen towels. "I was told I'm to accompany you in the garden today, Miss."

Annalisa grinned. "Y-yes. 'Tis been months since I've felt the sun upon m-my face, and I'm quite in raptures b-by it."

❦

PINK BLOSSOMING CHESTNUT TREES LINED THE GRAVEL PATH Annalisa and Sarah walked. Beyond the pathway sprouted puffy pink and white peonies, burgundy tulips, white irises, and little blue forget-me-nots. Fresh lilac and delicate rose perfumed the warm garden breeze.

"'Tis a m-magical place." Annalisa drank in each flower as she passed by. "I c-can imagine Shakespeare's play *A Midsummer N-night's Dream,* in a garden such as this." Annalisa paused in their walk. "'Tis my f-favorite of his p-plays."

"Something else you remember, Miss." Sarah's lips upturned.

Annalisa's heart fluttered with delight. "I daresay you're right." She continued to walk, clutching Sarah's arm. Chattering bird song filled the silence between them. *Perhaps this is exactly what I need today—a pleasure-walk through life's garden.*

"You're taking much stronger strides, Miss."

"Today f-feels better than yesterday."

Georgiana stepped from the house with a white parasol perched over her head, and joined them. "I've found you this book of poetry. I think you'll take a liking to it." She handed Annalisa a leather book with worn edges—a beloved volume of the duchess's, no doubt.

Annalisa opened the cover and read, "*Poems and Fancies with the Animal Parliament.*" She gasped. "Margaret Cavendish." Closing her eyes, she held the book to her chest. *"Mixed rose and lily, why are you so proud, since fair is not in all minds best allowed?"*

"Ah, *A Dialogue Betwixt Wit and Beauty*! You know Mad Madge," the duchess cried. "And your stutter melted away."

Annalisa opened her eyes. "I do. I know M-mad Madge very well, indeed."

The duchess, Annalisa, and Sarah sat in the shade of a blooming chestnut tree, and Annalisa recited Mad Madge's prose with ease. For the first time in weeks, her body coursed with the sensation of what she perceived to be pleasure; the joy for a splendid day bestowed upon her by divine Providence; elation for the physick of Margaret Cavendish's poetry upon her stutter; and delight to be in the presence of such agreeable company.

Georgiana beamed with giddiness, something Annalisa had not yet witnessed in the duchess. "Calais, I daresay, you'd be a prize among us this evening. Pray tell, would you indulge me and join us after dinner tonight in the drawing room?"

Annalisa hesitated, unsure of whether she could answer the duchess's request without stuttering.

Georgiana added, "I would ask you to dine with us, but as

our guests have not had the pleasure of making your better acquaintance. And while we still know nothing of your origins, they would object to your presence at dinner. But after, formality is of less consequence. No one could protest to your being among us."

Annalisa shook her head. "Your Grace, I cannot. M-my stutter. I'd make a fool of m-myself—"

"Nonsense. 'Tis only a small dinner party. I know you'll fare splendidly. Then we'll be off to England for June. In London, we can officially introduce you to Society, then there shall be no objections to your dining with us."

Annalisa bit her cheek. "And shall you introduce me as Miss Calais?"

"No." Georgiana smirked. "Let's call you Miss Cavendish, since you've such a penchant for our dear poet. Mad Madge is one of my husband's distant relations, a cousin I believe. The Duke and Duchess of Newcastle." She rose, and added with eager zeal, "Come, let's ready you for tonight, Miss Cavendish."

⚜

ANNALISA STOOD BEFORE HER LOOKING GLASS. THE SCAR under her right eye, another curiosity to bewilder her, burned beneath a layer of porcelain-colored paint. Below brows lined in burnt clover, her forest green eyes, though looking quite hollow, sparkled in candlelight. *A face I do not entirely recognize. Miss Cavendish. A name that sounds familiar...*

Her honey-brown hair, pomaded and powdered and curled into a high roll, sat atop her head. A single lock wound its way over her shoulder. She fisted her hands, resisting the urge to scratch her scalp. Rather, she adjusted the white and purple feather at her throat, then smoothed the gold silk skirts of her *robe à la française* gown—a gift from Georgiana—of which the *panniers* stuck out wider on either side of her hips than was comfortable.

"You look lovely, Miss Cavendish," Sarah said.

Miss Cavendish. Is this something I would have worn?

Annalisa turned from the mirror. "I wish I knew if I always dressed like this in m-my former life." She gave a tight-lipped smile. "Wearing this much silk feels...uncomfortable."

"Then perhaps you've been blessed to a new life with better society," Sarah replied.

"That may be true, but I think I'd r-rather remain here with you. I find your c-company quite comforting."

"Miss Cavendish—"

"I wish I could tell you to call me by my Christian n-name, Sarah. *Miss Cavendish* feels too...unlike me. Who-whoever I am." Annalisa hesitated. "What name w-would you give me?"

Sarah frowned. "'Tis not my place, Miss."

"Please, think of a name for me, Sarah. I beg it of you."

A rapping sounded from the door. "Miss Cavendish, are you quite ready? Dinner is almost adjourned. The guests will soon be headed into the drawing room."

Annalisa cleared her throat and found her voice of this new young lady, Miss Cavendish. "Yes, Mr. Smith." She went to the door and opened it. Before stepping into the hall with the servant, she whispered to Sarah, "Think on a name. Please."

She followed Mr. Smith down the staircase, through a white paneled hallway lined with golden sconces and beeswax candles, and into the drawing room. A grand rectangular room, papered in florals, the drawing room boasted mahogany tables of varying heights and sizes, and at least ten white upholstered chairs rimmed in gold. A marble fireplace jutted from one of the long walls, and a pink velvet sofa with matching settee positioned before the fireplace. At the far end of the room, the sky turned to indigo beyond the panes of a tall window curtained in pink velvet. Beside the window, a gleaming pianoforte. Annalisa's heart skipped. She drifted toward the instrument as though a rope had been knotted between the pianoforte and her, pulling her to it. A yearning, a need, pulsed through her.

She slid onto the bench and poised her fingers upon the keys. The gleam of her sapphire ring upon her fourth finger caught the flicker of candlelight, and she started to play. The melody escaping her fingertips sounded familiar, as though she'd played it countless times. Perhaps she was accomplished in her previous life; perhaps she was of higher society. Resolve and joy surged through her in tandem as she played. *I can sit among Georgiana's company and feel at ease.*

"*Mon dieu.* She plays the pianoforte." A gentleman wearing a white powdered wig advanced toward her. "*Mademoiselle* Cavendish." He bowed slightly, and grinned. "You remember me, *Mademoiselle?*"

Annalisa stood, and curtsied. "I do, sir. *Bonsoir, Monsieur Beauregard.*"

"*Bonsoir, ma chérie.* How wonderful to see you like this, *Mademoiselle.* Come, the duchess wishes to introduce you."

Georgiana's blue and black silk gown decked in ribbon and lace was unlike anything Annalisa had ever seen—or at least, could recall. The duchess wore her light brown hair powdered and curled in an enormous high roll, which threatened to graze the top of the doorframe. She eyed Annalisa at the far end of the room and approached with quickened step.

"You look lovely, Miss Cavendish." Georgina took up Annalisa's hand. "Come with me." She added in a whisper, "Your playing is most accomplished. What a splendid surprise!"

At the discovery of her facility, Annalisa beamed.

Georgiana introduced her to several guests, ending with a gentleman who appeared to be in his late twenties. "Miss Cavendish, may I present Mr. Fitzherbert."

He bowed. "Pleased to make your acquaintance, Miss Cavendish."

With a straight nose almost too long for his face, and a chin dimple that reminded Annalisa of another man—though could not remember—he was handsome.

"A pleasure, sir." Annalisa curtsied.

Mr. Fitzherbert leaned in, flooding her with amber perfume. "The pleasure is all mine, Miss Cavendish."

She shivered at his intoxicating scent. "Y-you're too kind, sir."

When he had gone, Georgiana whispered, "Fitzy has a vast fortune, no less than twenty thousand pounds a year. His grandfather was in the shipping business, and his cousin is a member of the House of Lords. I daresay, 'tis only a matter of time before Fitzy claims a seat in Parliament. He's our circle's most eligible bachelor."

The man is handsome and wealthy. If Georgiana is enthusiastic about him, perhaps I should also be.

When everyone was seated about the drawing room, deep in conversation, Annalisa found her way back to the pianoforte. Far more comfortable upon the bench than in the company of strangers, she sat. Her fingers upon the keys, she waited for them to recall a song. A first note, followed by a second, then a third, and the song flowed from her without the assistance of music, but from the memory of her heart. As she played, she tuned her ears to whichever conversation resounded loudest.

"I daresay, Lord North's oppressive Coercive Acts have caused quite the predicament in America." The sentiment came from a man sporting blue hair powder, introduced to her as Mr. Fox. "Since the evacuation of Boston, I heard Washington's moved his illustrious American army to New York. Thankfully, it seems the Americans are willing to put up a fight."

"Hear, hear."

Annalisa continued to play until Mr. Beauregard joined her.

"Miss Cavendish, such talk must bore you, *non?*"

"I'm surprised to admit I find such political speech r-rather amusing, *Monsieur.*"

He chuckled. "In what way, 'amusing'?"

Annalisa grinned. "Forgive me. Perhaps amusing is incorrect. Interesting, fascinating. I do wish to l-learn more, *Monsieur.*" She glanced at her hands springing about the keys, then lowered her voice. "I daresay, there's much to garner from well-bred gentlemen speaking about s-such topics of importance."

"Such as?" Mr. Beauregard sipped his port. "The rebellion in America?"

"Yes. I'd forgotten there's a rebellion."

"I fear 'tis no longer a rebellion, *Mademoiselle.* 'Tis war. You must know, France is upon the very same precipice as England's colonies."

Annalisa shuddered. "I knew not, f-forgive me."

She finished the jovial melody of the sonata's *allegro* with a final staccato cadence, and a purposeful double ending of the tonic chord. In the absence of song, clapping filled the room. Annalisa bowed modestly, though wished to jump from the bench with glee. Reeling in her triumph, she met Mr. Beauregard's pleasant smile.

"Your stutter has improved much," he said.

"Thank you, *Monsieur*. The duchess lent me her poetry book. 'Twas one I'm familiar with."

"*Mon dieu!*" Beauregard laughed. "Another breakthrough. This is a blessing, *ma chérie. Très bien.*"

"I see you're in good company with Mr. Beauregard, Miss Cavendish." Mr. Fitzherbert joined them and set his glass of port upon the pianoforte.

Annalisa's face heated. "Good company, indeed, sir. We're talking of America. Pray, any news from that distant shore?" *Mayhap he can offer information that will remind me of where I'm from.*

Mr. Fitzherbert exhaled through pursed his lips. "Let me see. Since the evacuation of Boston?"

"Pray, when was Boston evacuated?" Annalisa asked.

"March, I believe," Beauregard replied.

"I think our military remains off the coast of Halifax," Fitzherbert added, "But word has it, Lord General Cornwallis may be headed to New York. As is Washington, per report from our robust Mr. Fox."

Annalisa's chest squeezed, and she remembered Boston's harbor had been under siege. *The British evacuated in March?* "It has been that long," she gasped.

✤ 11 ✤

JACK

PORTSMOUTH, THE STATE OF NEW HAMPSHIRE, MAY 1776

A HEAVINESS DESCENDED UPON Jack, and his breath shortened. Startled, he huddled beneath the coverlet. His throbbing leg hardly noticeable against the agony of breathing, he strained to inhale a lungful, but pressure, followed by a dull ache, coursed through his chest. Sweat beaded at his temples and dripped down the side of his face.

"Oh, God," he gasped. "Save me, please."

A knock sounded from the door.

"Jack?"

"I...can't...I can't...breathe," he rasped.

The door flew open and Jane rushed to the bed. "My God, what's happened?" She ran a hand over his forehead. "You need a doctor—"

Jack clutched his chest. "I can't..."

Jane hurried from the room, and returned with Elisha, George's innkeeper. In his hand, Eisha held a glass vial filled with rust-colored fluid.

"Mr. Perkins, drink this if you can."

Elisha removed the cork stopper and lifted the bottle to Jack's lips. He drank the bitter fluid, and Jane sat beside him, her hand rubbing his back.

"Shh, everything will be all right," she cooed. "All will be well."

The minutes passed with her delicate hand upon him, and the fluid warmed his insides. His breathing slowed. One breath, then two, and his chest tightness eased. Jack inhaled a deep, rendering breath, then sighed.

"My God, Elisha, you've saved me." Jack peered at Jane. "Thank you, both of you."

Elisha handed Jack the bottle. "'Tis laudanum. Drink a small amount when you're in a fit as you were, but use it sparingly, else you might come to depend upon it."

When they left his room, Jack rested against the pillows. Two days had passed since their escape from HMS *Lively*; two days into his recovery from torture. He closed his eyes and fought the onslaught of memories from his imprisonment: the beatings, the lies, the anguish of his wife's death.

He threw an arm over his face. *I wish to feel nothing... remember nothing.* The laudanum offered drowsiness, and a gentle, encompassing warmth. Jack turned over and pulled the cork from the bottle and sipped. The unpleasant fluid burned its way into his stomach, but eventually heated his body with comforting relaxation. This time, the agreeable sensation spread from his torso to his manhood. His beloved Annalisa returned to his thoughts, and his arousal grew. Jack reached down and unbuttoned his breeches.

❦

EACH NIGHT THAT FOLLOWED, THE FEAR OF A CONSTRICTED breathing fit led Jack to the bottle of laudanum. And each night, he drifted to sleep with not a thought of HMS *Lively* to torment him, only the hollow satisfaction of self-pleasure encouraged by the warm fulfillment of physick.

Eager to induce his nightly ritual, Jack unbuttoned his breeches and reached for the bottle. It was empty. His heart palpated, and he jumped from bed. Leg throbbing, he buttoned his breeches, threw on his waistcoat and coat, and grabbed his crutch.

Jack hobbled down the stairs. The inn was mostly dark this time of night, with only one lantern burning at the bottom of the stairs. He took the light behind the bar and scoured Elisha's box of ointments and physick. *No laudanum.* Frantic, Jack left the bar and fled the tavern for the streets of Portsmouth. *Surely, there must be some sailor or merchant awake to direct me to an apothecary.*

With his crutch, he limped down to the wharf, where he sighted two sailors drinking outside some bawdy establishment.

"Good evening, sirs. Might you be able to tell me where I may find an apothecary?" Jack asked.

"An apothecary? At this hour?" One of the sailors laughed. "Doubtful anyone will be awake to receive you. What is it you seek?"

"Laudanum," Jack replied.

The second sailor asked, "Have ye tried opium?"

Jack shook his head, desperate. "No. Is there a place I may go?"

"Behind you." The first sailor pointed, "Down those steps, you'll come to a blue door. Knock once, and the rogue will let you in."

Jack hesitated, unsure of whether this man could be trusted. But his need to forget led him from the sailors, and down the stairs. The dingy blue door before him, he knocked once.

A burly man of George's height opened it. "Aye?"

Jack stammered, "I was sent here...for opium."

The man stepped aside and gestured for Jack to enter the cellar. The room smelled of sweet smoke and glowed with candlelight. Three other men sprawled over settees of varying lengths. A buxom lass with brunette hair took him by the hand and led him to an unoccupied settee.

"You look new to this, sir," the lady said. "I've not seen you before."

Trembling, Jack shook his head. "This is my first time. Really, I require a bottle of laudanum. It helps my breathing."

The girl smirked. "This will help your breathing far quicker than laudanum." She left him for a moment, then returned with a long pipe. "Make yourself comfortable," she said, helping him recline. Using a long, thin needle, she held a dark ball of opium paste over a candle flame until it swelled and bubbled. Speedily, she placed the pea-sized ball into the pipe and allowed candle flames to lick the opium. She lifted the pipe to his lips. "Inhale."

Jack pulled from the pipe, and a burst of warmth enveloped his entire self. "My...God." He slumped against the sofa and closed his eyes.

"The relief is quite immediate. Is it not?"

"Mmhmm," he mumbled, unable to lift his eyelids.

His body in complete capitulation, the world, too, surrendered its heaviness, lightening the burden upon his chest and conscience. Strange joy filled him with hopeful absolution, and his faith restored. Jack outstretched his arms, and a warm body, smelling of smoke and jasmine, joined him. Soft lips met his, their bodies moving in rhythm to another place and time, and the gentle mouth drifted to his pego, where it consumed his arousal. Jack's arm slid over his face, his inhalations steady and deep, until he burst with relief.

When he came to, Jack sat upright. The girl had gone, and the three other men slept. *How long have I been asleep?* He removed his pocket watch.

"Zounds." *Five o'clock.* He'd promised Jane they would leave for Topsfield in the morning. His head aching, Jack hoisted himself from the settee and grabbed his crutch. But first, he must to the apothecary.

❦

THE ROAD SOUTH TO TOPSFIELD FROM PORTSMOUTH WAS long enough on horseback, but inside a juddering carriage with a screeching infant, it proved insufferable. As Tommy howled, Jack pursed his lips to hide his chagrin. His head still throbbing from the opium, he glanced at Jane, who coddled and rocked the child. Noticing the purple circles beneath her eyes, he wondered if he, too, looked as offensive as he felt.

"May I?" Jack reached for the three-month-old.

Jane hesitated but surrendered the screaming baby.

"There, there, little man," Jack crooned, settling the babe into his arm.

Tommy seemed much smaller in the crook of his arm than in Jane's. He studied the boy's round face, red with distress, and his heart quaked. In his soft baritone, Jack sang:

> *"The last time I came o'er the moor, I left my love behind me.*
> *Ye powers, what pain do I endure, when soft ideas mind me!*
> *Soon as the ruddy morn display'd, the beaming day ensuing,*

*I met betimes my lovely maid, in fit retreats
  for wooing..."*

Tommy's breathing eased and his eyelids drooped.

"Your voice is physick to his ears, and mine." Jane rested her head against the seat and closed her eyes.

Jack stared at his nephew. If only this child were his, a gift of his and Annalisa's perfect union that he could forever cherish in her now infinite absence.

The verdant, rolling farms and swaying trees of Topsfield tightened his breath. Beside him, Jane slept, and in his arms, so did Tommy. Jack shuffled sideways in his seat and inched his hand toward the new bottle of laudanum he'd purchased from the apothecary that morning. Careful not to wake the baby or Jane, he reached into his coat with his free hand and retrieved the vial. Using the hand that cradled the child to hold the bottle, he removed the stopper, raised the bottle to his lips, and swallowed a small amount of fluid.

In minutes, his lungs filled with life-giving air, his body relaxed, and Jack gazed favorably upon bucolic Topsfield; the revered farming town in which he'd fallen in love with Annalisa.

The carriage pulled into the drive of his father's estate. The three-story yellow clapboard house, perched atop a small hill, piped smoke from one of the four chimneys into the temperate May air.

"We've arrived," Jack said.

Jane opened her eyes. "I can take him now." She lifted Tommy and cradled the child to her bosom, which still bore the yellowed ghost of a bruise. She caught his stare and adjusted her neck handkerchief over her breast. "No one need know what befell us aboard HMS *Lively*."

"I only suspect what befell you aboard HMS *Lively*," Jack replied.

"And you never shall know."

"Was it Lieutenant Dickens?"

When Jane did not answer, Jack ground his teeth. *The villain.*

Wheaton, his father's coachman, helped Jane and Tommy from the carriage, followed by Jack, and led them to the front door. Mercy, their indentured servant, answered.

Her face paled as she gasped, "Mr...Perkins. Mrs. Oliver, do come inside. Lady Perkins is in the drawing room with the girls and Andrew." Mercy stepped aside and, after taking their travel cloaks, ushered them into the elegant, turquoise-papered drawing room.

The room smelled pleasantly of Mother's orange blossom perfume mingled with remnants of woodsmoke. The fire would have been lit in the chill of the morning, but now glowed with embers. His family sat about the room, the windows ajar.

Mother looked up from her needlepoint, and gasped. "Can it be?"

"Jack! Janey!" His nine-year-old sister, Susan, bounded toward them, her golden curls bouncing. Susan wrapped her arms about them, and two-year-old Charlotte sat at Mother's feet.

"Brother." Andrew, sixteen and standing taller than Jack remembered, stepped forward and embraced him as Susan stepped away.

Mother's coffee-colored eyes—the same Oliver, Abigail, and Susan had inherited—misted. Droplets streamed down her cheeks as she rose from the chair and hastened toward Jack. She held him, heaving against his shoulder.

"My darling boy. My son. My first-born son," she sobbed.

"God has returned you to me. I prayed every day. Every day." When she'd composed herself, Mother turned to Jane and kissed her cheek, then peered at Tommy bundled in blankets. "How pleasant to see my grandson again. I was quite worried when you left for Halifax."

"Tommy's been healthy and strong, but a ship is no place for a child," Jane replied.

Susan and Andrew crowded around Jane and the baby.

"May I hold him?" Susan asked.

"Let your brother and Jane settle in—there's much to discuss." Mother returned to her chair and picked up her needlepoint.

Jack lifted his youngest sister, Charlotte, kissed her crown of light brown hair, and set her on his lap as he sat beside Andrew on the sofa.

"You look well, Brother," Jack said.

"I cannot believe you're here." Andrew gave a crooked smile that echoed his own. "You're alive."

Mother shook her head. "I'm near speechless. Have you written your father? He's in Philadelphia at Congress, you know."

Jack glowered. "I've not. I've only just recovered from my ailments."

"Where've you been these several months? We heard your ship capsized...that you and Annalisa," Mother choked on her words, "had expired."

He rubbed his sweating palms over his breeches. "Annalisa has. There's much I don't understand, or remember, but I was rescued by a British naval ship off the coast of Halifax. They took me prisoner when they learned I'd been aboard a French barque bound for Europe. Jane and Ollie were on board." He eyed Jane, and she nodded.

"'Twas terrible what they did to Jack, but Oliver was quick

to tend to him, and had him released." Jane repositioned Tommy at her breast. "And Jack offered to take us home."

He bristled at her version of Oliver's betrayal. *She means to protect him.*

"Thank the Lord." Mother dabbed her tears. "We're still grief-stricken. Mr. and Mrs. Howlett did not leave their farm until the middle of last month. They've been in mourning ever since."

Charlotte squirmed in Jack's lap, and he set the toddler on the floor. "Has George written? Does he know of the shipwreck, or of Annalisa?"

Andrew shook his head. "I know not. No one has heard from him."

Unnerved, Jack asked, "What of Abigail and Lord Essex? Have they written?"

"They remain in London, grieving your loss." Mother's lip quivered. "Abbie expressed a wish to come home, but she was too close to giving birth. 'Tis now May. I daresay she should be delivered of her baby by now."

"I'll visit the Howletts on the morrow." Jack glanced at Jane, then stood. "If you'd like to accompany me, your family would be glad to receive you. If you'll excuse me, I must retire."

Alone in his bedchamber, he threw open his trunks and sifted through old clothing and trinkets. "It must be here," he muttered, frantic. "I know 'tis here."

Buried at the bottom of the second trunk lay a white bauta mask with gold edging he'd bought while touring Venice with Oliver in 1772. He lifted the mask and took it to the looking glass. Placing it over his face, only his blue eyes stared back. *Perfetto.*

Fatigued, Jack tossed the mask into his haversack, then crawled into his canopied bed. He'd shared this space with

Annalisa on their wedding night. This grand estate would've one day been theirs. Now, it was to be only his. *A widower.* A dull ache crept through him.

He gazed across the room, out the window at the bright blue sky. Spring was his favorite season. It had also been Annalisa's. *We should be in Paris now, soon to visit Abbie and Lord Essex in London.* Jack tugged at his lip, unable to recall the shipwreck, let alone Annalisa's face that frightful night. At the foreground, his torture aboard HMS *Lively* pummeled forth, and his breathing labored. At the age of four-and-twenty, he was a widower. *A tortured widower who escaped imprisonment and must travel with a mask for fear of capture.*

Jack reached for the bottle of laudanum, pulled out the cork, and sipped the contents. He closed his eyes as heat gently flowed through him, and his breathing eased. He set the bottle on his bedside table.

⊙⊛⊙

THE FOLLOWING MORNING, JACK SAT IN HIS FAMILY'S carriage, which conveyed him two miles down the narrow lane to the Howlett farm. His leg, though healing, prevented him from riding his mare, Morgaine. From the road, the recognizable green, fertile landscape, separated by rows of rock walls, sprawled before him; the Howlett farmhouse, a large brown saltbox with center chimney, stood nearest the road. As much as he cherished this view, the anticipation of seeing Annalisa was what he'd once coveted most.

Wheaton opened the carriage door, and Jack shuffled out with his crutch in hand, refusing assistance. He ambled up the path to the front door on his own and knocked.

A friendly, umber face answered. Her hand over her mouth, she uttered, "Mr. Perkins."

Jack entered the old farmhouse. It smelled exactly as he'd remembered it, smoky with hints of clove. Disregarding propriety, he embraced the housekeeper. "Addy."

"Oh, Mr. Perkins." Addy held him, then stepped back. Her warm eyes examined him, and she shook her head. Greying hair peeked from the edge of her linen cap. "I can't believe you're here."

"'Tis been a nightmare."

She blinked several times. "I been keeping up with your house with Mr. Quinnapin. You let me know if you wish to return. I know it might be hard without Miss Annie."

Jack sucked in a breath. "I'd sooner live alone at the house we shared than anywhere else."

Addy nodded. "Let me see you into the drawing room." She took his cocked hat, then helped him down the hall.

How strange, how foreign this drawing room feels without Annie at the spinet playing Mozart.

"Jack!" Mrs. Howlett, seated in a blue upholstered chair by the window, stood. She set down her needlepoint canvas and spanned the room to embrace him. "You're alive."

Allowing her tears to soak into his velvet coat, he enfolded his mother-in-law for several moments before pulling away.

"You look well, ma'am," he said.

Mrs. Howlett sniffled. "As well as a mother can be when she's lost a child to the sea. How strange and cruel the ocean should claim George's father, and now Annie." She straightened her skirts. "Please, sit. Mr. Howlett's gone to Ipswich, but William, Henry, and Mary are here. They'll be in, presently."

"You'll be glad to know I've returned with Jane and little Tommy," Jack said. "She told me to inform you she will visit on the morrow."

Mrs. Howlett's shoulders relaxed as she settled into her chair by the window. "My dearest Janey. I'd been so worried about her on that ship with a newborn."

William rushed into the room with the twins, Mary and Henry. "Jack!"

Jack embraced his brother-in-law, and the thirteen-year-old twins. "I grieve to be here without Annalisa."

"I think Annie lives," Mary blurted. She smoothed her skirts, a trait she likely learned from Jane. But unlike her eldest sister, Mary's hazel eyes held an inquisitive glint, akin to Annalisa's.

Jack regarded the girl curiously. Mary was now the same age Annalisa was when first they'd met. He repressed a shudder. *How quickly time passes.*

"'Tis not likely she survived, Mary," Henry murmured. "I'm sorry to say."

Mary shook her head. "She came to me in a dream last night. Today's the twentieth of May, her birthday."

"Mary Howlett," Mrs. Howlett wailed. "Enough. We're in mourning."

Jack's heart thudded. *My darling girl. You were Mary's age when we met, and today you would've been twenty. How could I have forgotten?* He took up his sister-in-law's hands and pulled her onto the sofa beside him. "Do tell, Miss Mary. What did she say in this dream?"

Mary smiled, and for a brief moment he saw Annalisa, two months shy of her fourteenth birthday, at his Boston home that cold March of 1770.

"Annie was dressed in silk with plenty of fine ribbons and lace. She looked quite content." Mary's gaze bore into Jack with the sweetest candor. "I daresay you were beside her, Mr. Perkins. She looked on you as dotingly as any wife would."

Jack smiled wistfully. "A wonderful dream. Would that she would visit mine."

"Yes, Mary." Mrs. Howlett swept a handkerchief beneath her icy blue eyes. "Now, Jack, tell us what befell you since the shipwreck. We all thought you dead."

He sucked in a lungful of air, and recounted all he understood of his rescue, imprisonment, and escape from HMS *Lively*.

William's mouth gaped. "My God."

"Thank goodness you made it home with my darling Janey and my sweet little grandson." Mrs. Howlett fanned herself. "Who shall care for my Jane with your brother away in the British army?"

Jack swallowed hard. "I can, ma'am. So much as I'm able. As will my mother and Andrew."

Mrs. Howlett's shoulders relaxed. "Thanks be to the Lord. Mr. Howlett and I are proud Oliver joined the British. He's always been loyal to our king, unlike my headstrong George." She shook her head. "Who knows where he may be?"

"George was in the militia. He's a man grown," William snapped. "He's able to do as he likes, marm."

"Nonsense!" Mrs. Howlett glared at William with an iciness that could have frozen the province. "George does nothing to quell my nerves."

"Peace, Mother. George does what's right by him," Henry said.

Mrs. Howlett scowled. "But could he write me but one letter from that traitor's camp? I think not!"

"I've heard mail is hardly reliable these days, ma'am," Jack replied.

William folded his arms. "I've not received any letters, either."

"'Tis well enough. I know not where he came to rebel so

ardently. Mr. Howlett, as you know, is Loyalist, and George's natural father was a naval officer before captaining his own merchant ship." Mrs. Howlett harrumphed. "Until George returns to this farm a Loyalist, he's no son of mine."

George's natural father was a British naval officer? Jack squirmed in his seat, wondering how much George knew of Captain Bixby.

"I should like for this war to end quickly," Mary said.

"'Tis not likely." Henry adjusted a clock upon the fireplace mantel. He turned to address the room. "Not with Howe's men in Canada. They're forming a plan of attack, no doubt."

William scoffed. "And where'd you come by such information?"

"When last I was at George's inn," Henry replied coolly. "Next time you're there, it might behoove you to listen to others."

Jack marveled at young Henry. The boy was young, yet spoke with more thoughtfulness and insight than both his older brothers.

When Jack took his leave, Mrs. Howlett saw him to the door and handed him a flowered red and indigo neck handkerchief wrapped about a small book. "I found it in the girls' room. 'Twas Annalisa's. I know all else was lost at sea, but I think this was rather important to her."

"Of course, Mrs. Howlett. Thank you, ma'am." Jack kissed her cheek and limped upon his crutch down the path toward his carriage. He paused, gazing at the farm. In the distance, at the edge of the property, the ancient oak beckoned. With Annalisa's belongings tucked beneath his other arm, he hobbled beyond the path and into the fields until he reached the sage tree.

He sat upon the limb he'd shared with Annalisa the night of the Strawberry Festival. High in the branches, a chickadee tweeted its unassuming melody. Sunlight dripped through the vast canopy, spilling lacy patterns onto Jack's lap. He unwrapped the book from the fabric, and a gust of Annalisa's lilac perfume overcame him. The small book looked familiar. It had to be the one she'd often carried with her.

He opened it; Margaret Cavendish's poetry. In the margins, he read Annalisa's penciled script: *notes on poetry; notes on writing prose.* He smiled at the scrawling about him: *Notes about Jack Perkins: this poem reminds me of Jack. I should like to read this to Jack.* His interest piqued as he read, *notes on Benjamin Cavendish.* Jack flipped the pages and found instructions on how to load and discharge a firelock; lessons from George, no doubt. *But who is Benjamin Cavendish?*

Rather than return to his father's estate, Jack asked Wheaton to drive him to the house he and Annalisa had shared. It belonged to his father's cousin, the town treasurer, David Perkins. After Jack had saved Stephen Perkins—his father's other cousin, and captain of the militia—during the battle at Concord last April, David offered to let the house to him and Annalisa.

The modest dark brown saltbox with large central chimney stood on a small plot of land near the gristmill. Beside the house, adjacent to the rear door, was Annalisa's quaint kitchen garden she'd cultivated in late September. Already, clusters of herbs sprouted, herbs she would've dried and used in cooking, and Addy's physick. His gut wrenched at the sight, and he entered the house as swiftly as his leg allowed.

Minimally furnished, it still smelled of woodsmoke. In the kitchen, mounted above the large brick hearth, rested Annalisa's musket—a gift he'd given her back in December. He removed the weapon from its hold and ran his fingers over the walnut stock. *Her keen eye was deserving of such a piece.* Jack forced a sigh from his tight chest and replaced the musket upon its nails.

From the lone wooden cupboard, he retrieved a bottle of brandy and filled a dram glass with the amber liquid. Slowly, he made his way up the narrow stairs to the largest bedchamber. A feeling of emptiness loomed as he opened the door. Their canopied bed stood at the far end of the room beside the window, and across from the fireplace. The bed was made, as though they'd return to it that night. Aside from a woven rug, and a chamberstick on the lone bedside table, the room was bare. They'd been married only a short while, the house itself as blank a canvas as their marriage.

Jack set the dram upon the bedside table, next to the chamberstick, then pulled off his coat and laid it over the end of the bed. He removed Annalisa's neck handkerchief and poetry book from his coat pocket and held the bit of fabric to his nose. *Is this the same neck handkerchief she'd pulled from her dress that night in the carriage house when we were first intimate?* He tried to recall details of her, but his memories returned fuzzy and grey. *If only I could dream of her as vividly as Mary.*

He plucked the bottle of laudanum from his waistcoat pocket and placed it on the bedside table beside the brandy. Jack untied his cravat and tossed it, along with his waistcoat, to the floor. Taking up Annalisa's poetry book, he lay against the pillows and flipped through its pages. Surely, he'd missed something within the margins, some other dictation revealing more of her inner thoughts on this Benjamin Cavendish fellow. He discovered three other details she'd written on Cavendish: *he is well-liked and outspoken, a fervent Patriot, he gleans much from his surroundings.* Jack scanned the other pages until he reached the final at the back of the book. There, upon a page without printed text, he read Annalisa's script:

Benjamin Cavendish knows me Better than Anyone in this Worlde.

He is my Muse, my sence for living, my Sun in daytime and my Moon at night.

He shall be Me, as I shall be him. One day, we shall live as One.

His heart skipped a dreadful beat. *Was she in love with this man?* The thought chilled him, though his palms sweated. Jack shook his head from the grievous assumption. Of course, she loved no other. She loved him with every breath she breathed. And he believed it. Yet, she'd never mentioned this man, this unknown Mr. Cavendish of whom she'd written accolades and notes upon her poetry book's margins. How little he supposed she could have loved another before him, or the secrets of her heart.

A bubbling of acid burned his throat. *When will these tiresome symptoms cease? Will I be plagued by such illness the remainder of my days?* His neck hot with indignation, he chucked the poetry book across the room. "No more Benjamin Cavendish, dear Annie." He reached for the bedside table and retrieved the dram of brandy and bottle of laudanum.

ANNALISA

DEVONSHIRE HOUSE, LONDON,
JUNE 1776

U NLIKE THE COLORFUL, FLOWERY paradise of
Paris, the gardens at Devonshire House in London
offered green hawthorn hedge and billowing willow trees.
Under direction from Georgiana, the servants kept ajar the
windows, allowing sweet fragrances of honeysuckle and elder-
flower to eliminate all traces of stale air within the house.

Annalisa circled the pebbled garden paths with the
duchess. Overhead, delicate bird song reminded her of
familiar woodland sounds upon a steep, forested path. She
focused on the birds' melody, hoping to remember, but could
only vaguely recall the place. *I think perhaps there's also a large
tree?*

"The ball is tonight, Miss Cavendish."

Pulled from her thoughts, Annalisa lifted an eyebrow.
"Your Grace?" The dinner party in Paris, for which she was
semi-present, had been daunting enough. *I sound like my
brother.* Annalisa gasped. "Heavens. I remember something."

"What is it?"

"I've a brother...though I can't recall his name. But I'm

certain of it. I have a brother, Your Gr-grace." She gripped her skirts, heart pounding. "Nay. I've three brothers."

"How marvelous!" The duchess's orange blossom perfume overwhelmed the delicate honeysuckle as she squeezed Annalisa's hand. "I daresay, their names will follow in no time at all." They returned to their walk. "But I've a small delicacy to discuss with you—one I can't ignore now we've returned to London."

Annalisa studied the duchess's profile: her straight nose, her dark brown eyes beneath thick lashes. "Your Grace."

"You've been with us for months, Calais. I daresay you must be feeling quite yourself, save for your memory, of course." Georgiana linked her arm with Annalisa's. "We've only introduced you to our small circle in Paris, but I think 'tis time we gave you a debut...of sorts." She hesitated. "People are talking."

"T-talking, Your Grace?"

"Yes. Society is talking. I think tonight's ball would be an ideal opportunity to alleviate any...misgivings people may have. 'Tis a masquerade."

"I don't think I've been to a m-masquerade, Your Grace."

"Well, can you dance a minuet? Or an allemande?"

Annalisa hesitated, unsure of herself. But considering her competency at the pianoforte, she replied, "I daresay I can."

"Marvelous." Georgiana clapped her hands with girlish glee. "I'll have you practice the rest of this morning with Mr. Renwick. He tutored my sister and me since we were little girls. He'll have your dancing polished and shining by afternoon. Then, we ready for the ball." She squeezed Annalisa's hands in a way that made her believe they were the closest of friends. The gesture filled Annalisa with a dark loneliness, and a yearning for her best friend—an unknown person of her past, if she could be so lucky.

*

GUESTS ATTIRED IN SILK AND LACE, WIGS AND HATS, AND OF course, elaborate masks, paraded into the Devonshire House assembly room. Girlish lavender and gentlemanly musk perfumes gusted in, certain to mask the body odor threatening to emerge later that evening.

Georgiana stood beside Annalisa inside the large rectangular dancing hall. Windows stretched from floor to ceiling, where gold filigree surrounded paintings of heavenly cherubs, and from which elaborate crystal chandeliers dangled. Hundreds of candles within chandeliers and wall sconces illuminated the room in opulent luminescence.

The duchess, with a gift for recognizing each guest even behind their mask, made several introductions to Annalisa, including Lord and Lady Melbourne, and Lord and Lady Jersey—neither of whom had been in Paris.

"Your Grace, how wonderful to see you." Lady Jersey removed her gold mask to reveal a pointed face reminiscent of a rat's, caked in white face paint. Her beady eyes examined Annalisa from shoe to high-roll. "Miss Cavendish. A pleasure."

Annalisa adjusted her blue columbina mask covering only the upper half of her face, and curtsied. "My lady."

When Ladies Melbourne and Jersey had slipped into the chatter-filled assembly room, Georgiana whispered to Annalisa, "Lady Jersey makes a cuckold of her husband with any man who will have her. Now that you know her person, observe her tonight—she'll dance with anyone but he."

A gentleman sporting a black and white domino mask approached. His warm amber scent mingled with the crisp evening air wafting in from the outdoors. Annalisa shivered with delight.

"Your Grace, and my dear Miss Cavendish." The gentleman bowed. "How marvelous a ball you've conjured, Your Grace."

"Anything to celebrate the season." Georgiana regarded Annalisa. "Now she's had her debut with Society, we've a splendid season of events in which Miss Cavendish can partake."

The gentleman bowed. "It would be my honor for you to dance the first with me, Miss Cavendish."

Annalisa curtsied. "I would be delighted, sir."

Two party guests advanced toward them; a lord and lady, no doubt. They boasted matching lavender silk garments, and white and purple masks rimmed in silver, the gentleman's having a large, beak-like nose. The lady wore a black beauty patch beneath her right eye. Her curled, blonde hair complimented her husband's sand-colored wig.

"Your Grace." The gentleman bowed and his lady curtsied.

Georgiana greeted them, then turned to Annalisa. "My Lord and Lady Essex, may I present Miss Cavendish."

Lord Essex bowed and his lady curtsied. "Miss Cavendish, delighted."

"Likewise, my lord, my lady," Annalisa replied.

"If only we could see your face, Miss Cavendish." Lady Essex tittered. "'Tis but my first masquerade, and I've still many more in Society to know. Imagine when we meet again after tonight. I shall not know you at all!"

They all laughed.

"I'm new to London as well, my lady," Annalisa replied. "Perhaps we may be introduced to Society together."

Lord Essex appraised her. "You're quite tall, Miss Cavendish. I daresay I'd know you after tonight for your height alone."

Lord and Lady Essex took their leave and slipped into the ballroom.

"Lord Essex is Mr. Fitzherbert's cousin," Georgiana whispered. "I daresay, you've taken quite well to Lady Essex. Fitzy is bound to notice."

From the far end of the room, strings sounded Handel's sedate *minuet in G minor*. The duchess winked at Annalisa. "'Tis time for the first. Your gentleman is waiting."

Annalisa hurried to the set of dancers and stood across from her partner in the black and white domino mask. His shapely lips upturned into a charming smile, and she couldn't help but return a shy grin.

A minuet. I know this dance. I practiced it well today. To a count of six, Annalisa stepped in time to the music. The duchess and her dance partner—presumably anyone but the duke—promenaded down the center of the room first, while the non-dancing guests gawked from the perimeter.

Annalisa and her gentleman promenaded last. Each step of the dance matched his as she made her way back to the set. When they'd completed the final promenade, and the music ended, they acknowledged one another with a formal bow and curtsey, and Annalisa left the set. Eager for some wine to quell her nerves, she took up a glass from a servant's tray and sipped the claret.

"Miss Cavendish."

She turned. Her dance partner had followed her from the set.

"You dance a beautiful minuet," he said.

"Thank you, sir. I'm unsure why, but your praise feels unwarranted."

He grinned. "Miss Cavendish, if I may—"

"Sir, I must confess, it bothers me everyone here knows my name, yet I know not who they are."

"Such is the mystery of a masquerade," he replied with a wink.

"But I was introduced to Ladies Melbourne and Jersey, and Lord and Lady Essex..."

"They are the duchess's closest friends," he said. The gentleman adjusted his white waistcoat beneath his black frock coat, and leaned in close, inundating her with amber. "I daresay you know me, Miss Cavendish."

Annalisa pursed her lips. "Mr. Fitzherbert?"

"Indeed. Miss, I wish to have you upon my arm for the entirety of this night."

"Behind a mask, anyone has rank and a title, Fitzy," Lady Jersey hissed as she passed by with Lady Melbourne.

Annalisa's cheeks burned behind her mask.

Lady Essex approached. "For shame. This lady is lovely—something which you know nothing about."

"Who is this person?" Lady Jersey sneered. "Are you Essex's new wife?"

"'Tis a masquerade. 'Tis not for you to know," Lady Essex snapped.

Lady Jersey disappeared into the crowd with Lady Melbourne. Mr. Fitzherbert laughed—a musical sound that filled Annalisa with tingling warmth. He bowed to Lady Essex. "Well done, my lady."

"Thank you, Lady Essex." Annalisa's scalp itched from the pomade and powder. She resisted the urge to scratch. "I daresay I have very few friends here."

"Nonsense. You have a friend in me." Lady Essex hesitated. "I have few friends, too. You see, I've just been delivered of a daughter, and haven't had many opportunities to make acquaintances. I'm from the American colonies."

"America?" Annalisa rasped. "Whatever's brought you here?"

"My husband. We met in Boston at a ball. He became besotted by me for whatever reason. We married and ventured to London. But he's promised we'll return to the province next year." Lady Essex paused. "Your accent is much like my own. Are you not from America as well?"

Annalisa bit her lip. "I'm not sure, my lady."

"Miss Cavendish's origins are questionable," Mr. Fitzherbert said. "But we're intrigued by her grace and good manners."

Lady Essex nodded. "Of course. I, too, am no stranger to questionable origins with good manners. Society certainly has a way of discounting one of their own, even if we are of documented good breeding."

"Who is your father, my lady?" Annalisa asked.

"Lord Perkins. My father was magistrate in Boston until the massacre in 1770. Since then, we relocated to a small farming town north of the city. But I am his blood, as much as Society likes to discredit him."

"Lord Perkins." Annalisa considered the name. "I daresay that name is familiar."

Lady Essex's eyes narrowed behind her mask. "Is it?"

Lord Essex appeared behind Mr. Fitzherbert and offered his arm to his wife. "Home, I think, my dear."

Behind a fabricated smile, his wife hid her disappointment well. "Of course, my lord." She turned to Annalisa. "Until we meet again, Miss Cavendish."

Annalisa watched the couple leave the bloated assembly hall, and she wished to chase after Lady Essex. Something about her voice and eyes comforted her in this strange, foreign place.

❧ 13 ❧
JACK
TOPSFIELD, JUNE 1776

JACK'S FINGERS GLIDED OVER the strings of his violin, and the somber melody of Mozart's *adagio* from the second piano sonata filled the room. A soft evening sunset trickled through the window of the drawing room and onto the spinet, his wife's beloved instrument. Not even the sound of his proficient violin compared to her accomplished playing. He set the violin aside.

Tommy's piercing screech penetrated the room. Jack stood from the bench, retrieved his cane, and limped into the hallway and up the stairs. His nephew's wail led him into Jane's bedchamber. The curtains were drawn. He hobbled to the window to open them. Evening sunlight flooded the room, illuminating his nephew in the basinet.

"There, there. Hush." He lifted Tommy and rocked him, singing the child's favorite song:

> *"The last time I came o'er the moor, I left my*
> *love behind me.*

*Ye powers, what pain do I endure, when soft
ideas mind me!"*

"He rarely ceases to cry when I sing to him."

Jack turned. Jane stood in the doorway and stepped into the bedchamber. He returned his focus on Tommy.

"He must be fond of his uncle's voice. He knows you well," Jane said, reaching for the child. She cradled him to her breast. Her blue eyes softened a moment before turning to ice. "You're more father to him than his own."

Jack faced the window. A robin flitted from a maple tree in the yard. "I know too well Oliver's selfishness. He hurts me, as he does you and Tommy. But do not call me *father* to this child. I beg it of you."

"How many nights have you sung him to sleep, Jack? How many nights have you helped change his swaddlings?" Jane gently touched his arm. "You're more father to this child, whether you like it or not. I've only one letter from Oliver since we absconded from *Lively*. One." She looked away and blinked several times.

Jack's throat clogged. "He's the son I wish Annalisa might have borne me." He swept a delicate thumb over Tommy's cheek. "Know you a Benjamin Cavendish?"

Jane eyed him curiously. "Why?"

He shook his head. "Something I read in one of Annalisa's books—"

"Yes. I know the name."

Jack hesitated, unsure of whether or not he wished to know the answer, but asked, "Who? Who is the man? Was she in love with him?"

"I know not the man, only the name." Jane's gaze lowered, but when she lifted her stare, she held his with resolve. "She never spoke of him, but I daresay, she sneaked off many mornings. Annie kept secrets."

Jack heaved a shaky breath. "So it seems."

"Forgive me." Jane grazed his shoulder. "'Twas not my intention to speak poorly of our dear Annalisa."

"No, forgive *me*. 'Twas I who asked." Jack limped across the room, cane in hand, without looking back.

"Jack, wait."

He hesitated in the doorway. "I'm meeting William and Quinn at the Whispering Willow. I'll be returning to my house later tonight. You'll see me tomorrow. Give Tommy a good-night kiss for me."

"Since we returned, you've spent every night at the Willow, Jack." Jane chased after him. "I'm worried for you— the laudanum...the brandy. Please, stay here. I know your mother would wish it so—"

"You know I can't." Jack walked down the stairs and out the front door. He spent as little time as he could at the house he'd shared with Annalisa, but neither was he comfortable at his father's estate. It mattered little where he slept, except for the lingering lilac perfume upon Annalisa's pillow, which haunted him in their bed each night.

His leg now healed enough to ride, Jack mounted his mare. Morgaine's hooves clopped upon the hardened soil of the narrow lane to the Whispering Willow tavern. At this hour, when the sun's golden rays cast slanting shadows across the road, he could hardly stand the encroaching loneliness of night. At least he had his friends and the tavern to help him forget.

He tied Morgaine to a wood fence surrounding the perimeter of the old, clapboard establishment, hobbled to the front door, and stepped inside. Beside the unlit hearth, the jovial jig, *The Gobby-O*, emanated from Mr. Averill's fiddle.

Aromas of fermented hops mingled with smoky, banked embers from this morning's fire.

"Perkins." Quinnapin, his old friend, waved from the rear of the room.

"Quinn." Jack embraced him and sat beside William on the bench.

"You're looking well." William's blue eyes sparkled with drink as he offered Jack a pint of ale.

Jack took the tankard. "I suppose I look better than I feel."

"I think we all do," Quinnapin replied.

"Hear, hear." William raised his mug.

Captain Gould of the militia, an older man with greying hair and stubbled chin, slid beside Jack on the bench. "Ye ole whip jackets. I've missed the jerrycummumble George caused me. Pray, has he written?"

"I've written him. I'm still awaiting his reply." Jack eyed his brother-in-law. "Has he received any of your letters, Will?"

William shrugged. "I'm not sure. I've written a dozen letters and only received one from him about a month ago."

"Last I heard, Washington's army be at York Island," Gould grunted. "Also heard Howe 'n his men be sailing fer New York." He stood from the bench and straightened his leather apron.

Jack pursed his lips. "All the more we should aid Washington." He looked to his friends. "Any plans on joining the Continentals, gentlemen?"

"Aye, Weetamoo and I are headed west to visit my Mohican friend," Quinnapin replied. "From there, we'll be headed to New York to join George."

"I'm leaving for Ticonderoga," William said.

Quinnapin's brows lifted. "Your father is Loyalist. Will he let you join the Continentals?"

"George signed on. And I'm my own man. I'll be eighteen come September." William crossed his arms and sat back. "I'll join the Continentals if I please."

Jack fiddled with the bottle of laudanum in his coat pocket. "If I don't hear from George by month's end, I'm riding to New York to enlist. I can't remain here and wallow in my misery any longer. Life in Topsfield without Annalisa is unbearable."

"I'd offer to bring you with me to Ticonderoga, but the ride is long." William gripped Jack's shoulder. "Can you march, or even ride such distances with your leg?"

Captain Gould returned to their table with a large steaming pitcher of flip and three pewter tankards. He poured the liquid into each mug. "Enjoy, abrams."

"I can. And I will." Jack took a swig of the flip and finished it in two gulps. The bitter, earthy concoction of rum, ale, and molasses settled in his stomach with a satisfying warmth.

Quinnapin leaned over the table, his long, black hair trailing over his shoulder. "Running away won't heal your heart any faster, Friend. And neither will flip, nor ale, mask the pain of loss."

Jack wiped the froth from his upper lip. "I know. But I've been adrift. I need a purpose. I know she's gone. Believe me, I know it. But I've lost myself along with her. I've wished to enlist since Bunker Hill. Now's my chance. I just need George to tell me where to meet him—"

"You needn't George to tell you." Quinnapin shook his head. "He's most likely at York Island. Just go. I promise, Weetamoo and I will join when we can. You have my word, Friend."

"Thank you." Jack peered at William. "When do you leave?"

"Next week."

Quinnapin slammed the table. "You've not told me this! *Ku-noo-seeh*. Talk to me, Will."

"I've told no one, lest it get back to my father. He cannot convince me otherwise. I'm leaving with Josiah Averill and Martha Perley's brother, Isaac." William's pale face blushed. "When this war's ended, I wish to make Martha my wife."

"Well done, Will," Jack said, smiling. "Miss Perley is a lovely girl, and I've always enjoyed my time in the minutemen with Isaac."

They finished the pitcher of flip and ordered a second, then a third. By the end of the third, the sun had long since set beyond the windowpanes, and the room, lit by flickering yellow candlelight, spun like the wheel of a ship.

Jack stood. "Abrams, I'm disguised. I must leave you, else I'll wake in the morning on the common for all of town to ridicule."

Quinnapin laughed. "Will you not attend the Strawberry Festival tonight, then?"

"Nay. But I'll see you on the morrow." Jack stumbled out the front door with his cane and mounted his horse.

He arrived home with a shred of moonlight to guide him. How empty, how sad and hollow his spirit as he stabled the animal. Quinnapin was right. No amount of laudanum or liquor could mask, or cure, the emptiness inside—or betrayal. *What did Annalisa keep from me? Who is Benjamin Cavendish?* In his altered state each night, Benjamin Cavendish permeated his thoughts, eating away all reason.

Jack hobbled through the front door of his empty house, and in the darkness, tripped. "Damn."

He fumbled for a paper spill to light the candles. When he found one, he held it to the banked embers of the kitchen hearth, lit a candle, then two, then three. He sat at the wooden kitchen table and poured himself a dram of brandy. *Come tomorrow, I'll drink no more. Come tomorrow, I'll leave for New York and do what I've yearned to do. Quinn is right. I needn't wait for George to write.*

Jack rested his head upon the table and closed his eyes.

Knock, knock, knock.

Startled by the rapping, he stood and limped into the foyer. Perhaps it was Quinnapin or William to ensure he made it home. He opened the door.

"Will you let me in?"

Jack stepped aside, and Jane floated into the foyer.

"Why are you here?" Not waiting for her to join him, he meandered back to the kitchen. "Did you come from the Strawberry Festival?"

"Yes." She followed and planted herself before the table with hand upon her waist. "Are you disguised again?"

"Where's Tommy?" Jack finished the brandy, then sat at the table.

"At home." Jane reached for the bottle of liquor and set it on the fireplace mantel, beneath Annalisa's musket. "I told your mother I would come and retrieve you after the festival was ended. 'Tis not safe for you to be here alone, by yourself."

"Safe?" Jack sneered. "I'm a man of four-and-twenty. Why should I not be safe, alone in my own home?" His head drooped, and he held his face in his hands. "I'm leaving. Come morning."

"To go where?"

"New York. I'm joining the Continentals."

"You can't leave, you can barely talk, let alone ride a horse." Her hands made their way to his shoulders. "You must return to George's inn, as you promised Elisha. Jack, you're a strong, capable man who's done more for Tommy and me these several weeks than Ollie has in the past several months. We need you. You have a purpose here."

He looked up at her. "I'm not your husband, Jane. Nor am I Tommy's father. I have no responsibility to either of you—or anyone else, for that matter."

She slapped him. "How dare you. Those are neither the words of a gentleman, nor the words of a beloved uncle and brother-in-law. Your mother would be ashamed. As would Annalisa."

Jack held his smarting cheek and swallowed the stale dryness of liquor in his throat. "Each day I wake and wonder why God hasn't taken me. Why he didn't take me instead of Annalisa. I question His plan, and I damn Him. I curse Him." He stood. "I look at Tommy, and I loathe Oliver—for all he abandoned. I pray he never returns from the British army."

"These are harsh words you can't mean. You must quit grieving, Jack. Annalisa would want you to—"

"Do I even know who Annalisa was?" He faced Jane. "I'm plagued by her journal and all she kept from me. What secrets did she hold, and why? I kept nothing from her. I gave her my heart—my whole heart, Jane. But why did she withhold hers? Could she not trust me?"

Jane pouted. "No woman can fully give her heart, Jack. Annalisa was no different. She had many confidences, things she told not even me."

"How can you be so certain?"

"Because I, too, read her book. The man, Cavendish? I never met him, but I daresay, he was always at the foreground of her thoughts." Jane bit her lip. "As you were often at the foreground of mine."

"None of that." Jack turned from her. "You always had eyes for Oliver. Don't deny it."

"I always thought well of him." She moved toward the

mantel and adjusted a pewter plate. "He's well-bred and cultured—like you. There was something in his air when he walked into a room...he commanded it. And he doted on me as a lady deserves." She paused. "Perhaps I was too quick to judge. Would that Oliver loved me like you loved Annie."

"Love." He held her gaze. "I still love Annalisa."

"Quite." Jane fiddled with her wedding band. "And even with her secrets, you still love her. I should be lucky to hear such declarations from Ollie. I daresay, oft I wonder what my life would be had we wed...you and I." Her lips upturned in a lamented smile. "If Tommy was yours."

"Tommy is not mine." *A horrid lie she'd told, one that almost cost me Annalisa.*

"I know." Her mouth parted as though she meant to say more, but rather, her gaze drifted over him with longing. Jane stepped closer, near enough to smell the brandy upon his breath, and indulged him with a coy smile of invitation. "I daresay, loneliness can be a good thing to share with someone, Jack."

He recoiled when, with a delicate finger, she trailed along his neckpiece and down the front of his waistcoat, leaving a wake of lilac perfume. *Annalisa's perfume.* Jack closed his eyes. The scent dizzied him and tugged at his heartstrings. *Why does she wear Annie's perfume?*

"You did fancy me once, did you not?" Jane whispered behind him.

He felt her hands upon him as they glided into his waistcoat, and over his chest. His eyes opened and he turned. "Aye, but no...more." His eyelids drooped, heavy from the grog.

"Perhaps you require this." Jane handed him the bottle of laudanum. "Here."

Jack opened his eyes and sipped from the vial. Eyes closed

once more, he leaned back in the chair as pleasantness overcame him.

Soft, velvety kisses upon his neck and cheek inched closer
to his earlobe, and for the first time since leaving Portsmouth,
his manhood, goaded by the intoxicating laudanum mixed
with the scent of lilac perfume, overtook him. Induced by
loneliness, he pulled Jane close and fused his lips to hers. She
returned his kisses with as much eagerness and unbuttoned
his waistcoat and the front of his breeches. In a storm of
desperation disguised as passion, Jack sprawled her over the
kitchen table and pressed himself on top of her. He pulled the
neck handkerchief from her bodice and tossed it to the floor.
His mouth covered the ample curve of her milky bosom as
she hiked her skirts above the knee. Jack guided his arousal
into her, and she locked her legs about his hips. Basking in a
pleasure that perhaps even she required, he thrusted into her
for several moments atop the kitchen table before pulling
away and leading her up the stairs, into his bedchamber.

Jane removed her dress and unlaced her stays, tossing
them to the floor. His head spinning with lust and liquor, Jack
shook free of his waistcoat, pulled his shirt over his head, and
stumbled to where she lay beneath the coverlet. With one
hand, Jane led him into her and indulged with him until he
burst, releasing the first wave of pleasure he'd felt in months.
The room spun and, his body spent, all faded to black.

✤ 14 ✤

ANNALISA

DEVONSHIRE HOUSE, LONDON, JUNE 1776

"MISS CAVENDISH." SARAH ENTERED the breakfast parlor with an envelope. "A letter was delivered for you, Miss."

Georgiana tilted her head and set down her glass of wine. "Who sends it?" She glanced at Annalisa and winked. "Mr. Fitzherbert, perhaps?"

"Lord and Lady Essex, Your Grace." Sarah bobbed a curtsey.

Annalisa lowered her spoon from the soft-boiled egg in the eggcup and took the letter. She ran her fingers over the ivory-colored paper, and the ornate crimson wax seal with the Essex family crest. "May I open it, Your Grace?" Georgiana nodded, and Annalisa broke the seal and unfolded the page. "Lady Essex asks that I dine with them, Your Grace. Tonight."

The duchess pouted. "But we've Mr. Sheridan's play, *The Duenna*, tonight. I thought they were planning to attend."

Annalisa shook her head. "Lady Essex writes: *my husband and I are dining at home this evening and wish for the pleasure of your company so as to know you better within our circle.*" She looked up. "I can decline the offer, Your Gr—"

"Nonsense." Georgiana drew her wine glass to her lips, sipped, then set down the glass. "I think 'tis a marvelous idea for you to attend—on your own. It means you're one of us, now. You needn't me there to make introductions."

"I'm forever in your debt, Your Grace," Annalisa replied.

"Never." Georgiana finished her glass of wine, then added with a mischievous grin, "You need only tell me if Mr. Fitzherbert is there. I suspect he may be attached to you."

Annalisa smirked. "Of course, Your Grace."

"Please," the duchess held up her hand, "call me Gee."

"Of course, Your Gr...Gee." Annalisa glanced at Sarah, who stood silently by the door awaiting dismissal. "I've one favor to ask...Gee."

"Anything."

"I'd like Sarah to accompany me this evening. As my chaperone."

⚜

ESSEX HOUSE STOOD IN AN AREA WEST OF LONDON, KNOWN as Twickenham—according to Georgiana—and perched on the banks of the River Thames. The large Palladian villa rose three stories high and faced the glistening water.

Their carriage, drawn by two matched pairs, approached the drive, and Annalisa sat back in her seat, awaiting the carriage to stop. Sarah sat across from her, jaw set and arms folded.

"Thank you for accompanying me, Sarah."

"'Tis as you wish, Miss."

Annalisa leaned forward. "Sarah, is it so hard to believe I truly enjoy your company?"

Sarah stared hard at her. "Is it so hard to believe I want anything but to be here? To be anywhere but England?" She balled her hands. "That I should like to see my mother again instead of being forced into servitude under the pretense that 'tis protection? Your enjoyment of my company is the last thing I consider, Miss Cavendish."

Sarah's bitter words stung in a way Annalisa had never expected them to. Flush with the embarrassment for her perception of their relationship, and her blindness to Sarah's position in life, Annalisa replied, "You're quite right, Sarah. And I'm sorry."

"Sorry won't bring me home or help me find my mother and grandmother."

"No. It won't. Where is home?"

"Barbados."

"I hear 'tis beautiful there."

"I hardly remember it," Sarah replied.

Annalisa bit her lip. "I wish I could remember where I'm from, too...though I know we've vastly different experiences."

"My apologies, Miss. I spoke out of turn."

"No, please don't apologize." Annalisa caught Sarah's gaze. "You spoke truth, and I commend you for it. I wish for nothing but to speak truth, so let me state mine. Slavery is an odious state of affairs, and nothing may support it, Sarah. Nothing."

"I'm not a slave. My mistress pays me quite well."

"And I thank God you make a livable wage, because many others you resemble do not." Annalisa hesitated, looking at her own bronzed forearms. "I know not my own truth, but you know yours. There is no reason to ever apologize for that." Slowly, she reached for Sarah's hand, but Sarah crossed her arms. Annalisa leaned back in her seat. "I hope one day things are done right by you, Sarah."

"I needn't your help, Miss Cavendish. I'm perfectly capable of securing my own fate."

The carriage door opened, and Annalisa let the coachman assist her from within, though she wished to continue her intercourse with Sarah, who followed behind.

Lofty, Roman-style columns flanked the entryway into the breakfast parlor, and across from it, the assembly hall. Gold filigree adorned the edges of each doorway and ceiling panel. A servant led Annalisa and Sarah down a wide corridor to the ladies' parlor.

Annalisa's breath caught. River-facing windows spilled sunlight upon light green, damask-covered walls. White upholstered chairs and a sofa faced a marble fireplace opposite the windows. Porcelain vases perched upon cherry-wood tables overflowed with purple columbine. Sarah studied the room with a judgmental eye—surely, she would inform the duchess how Lady Essex's rooms were decorated.

"Do sit, Miss Cavendish, Miss Sarah." The housekeeper, a pale, older woman, gestured to the sofa by the fireplace. "Lady Essex was detained by her daughter's nursemaid shortly before you arrived but will be along presently." She dipped a curtsey and left the room.

"The view of the river is lovely." Annalisa meandered toward the windows but shifted her attention to the Roman columns framing a polished spinet. Inspired by the Italian architecture, she sat at the bench and played Scarlatti.

Sarah joined, her lips upturning slightly. "It seems like music gives you much joy, Miss Cavendish."

Annalisa beamed. "It does."

"May I present Mr. Fitzherbert," the housekeeper said, the handsome dinner guest in tow.

Annalisa stood, and the music yielded to a chiming clock

upon the mantel. "Sir, 'tis a pleasure. I knew not you'd be here."

Mr. Fitzherbert hastened toward her, grinning. "Miss Cavendish, please do not cease playing on my account."

"First, may I present Miss Sarah." Annalisa gestured to Sarah, who curtsied. If she was nervous, she hid it well; her smooth face told nothing, save for polite composure. *Something she must be painfully used to.*

Mr. Fitzherbert bent at the waist. "Miss Sarah, a pleasure."

Lady Essex hurried into the room. She tucked a loose pin into her golden hair and smoothed her periwinkle skirts. Lord Essex advanced behind her, looking less harried. Annalisa studied their faces, now unveiled since the masquerade.

Lord Essex's grin deepened a prominent chin divot. "Fitzy." He glanced at Sarah, who stood beside Mr. Fitzherbert.

"My lord, may I introduce Miss Sarah," Annalisa said. "My chaperone."

Lady Essex, whose pleasant face had lifted in their jovial greeting, deflated, and her freckled cheeks paled. Her husband stuttered an obtuse welcome.

"My lord, my lady, whatever's the matter?" Mr. Fitzherbert asked. "Are you dazzled by our dear Miss Cavend—"

"Annalisa?" Lady Essex's eyes welled. "Is it really you?"

Annalisa's heart skipped. "I beg your pardon, marm?"

"'Tis me." Lady Essex approached the spinet where Annalisa stood frozen. "'Tis me, Abigail."

Beyond the windows, the sky had darkened with storm clouds, and a roll of thunder shook the house. Rain spattered upon the windowpanes as Lady Essex's cheeks pinked, then glistened with her own overflow of tears.

"My lord, please, tell her." Lady Essex cupped a hand over her mouth to stifle the cry.

Lord Essex stepped closer. "We thought you dead."

Mr. Fitzherbert offered a handkerchief to Lady Essex. He asked, "Know you Miss Cavendish?"

Drying her tears, Lady Essex nodded. "Quite intimately. She's my brother's wife." Lady Essex wailed, and her husband held her. "*Was* my brother's wife. My brother is dead."

Annalisa lifted a tremulous hand to her breast. "Are you certain?"

Sarah sidled up beside Annalisa and grasped her free hand. "My Lady Essex, as the duchess's personal chambermaid, I've been under direct instruction to care for Miss Cavendish, and I must inform you, Miss Cavendish has suffered from profound memory loss. I daresay there is much to discuss, should she wish to discuss it."

"Yes." Annalisa met Sarah's concerned stare and squeezed her hand. "I do wish to discuss it."

🪷

DESPITE THE QUANDARY OF THEIR AWKWARD introduction, and much to Annalisa's dismay, the formal dinner proceeded as planned. Beneath the dinner table, Annalisa picked at her thumbnail. The ceremonial chatter over the clink of silver and porcelain served as a welcome distraction from Lady Essex's, or rather, Abigail's, scrutinizing gaze. At first, her study caused much anxiety, but the more Annalisa met her stare, the more familiar it felt.

With her fork, Annalisa slid the greasy roast mutton across her plate, then sipped on sweet madeira. Across the table, Mr. Fitzherbert smiled. It was a comfort he looked upon her so favorably, though he knew as little about her as she herself.

After dinner, the ladies withdrew to the parlor, and

Annalisa dawdled by the spinet. She ran her fingers over its glossy finish, then sat upon the bench and started to play.

"This is Mozart. It gives me joy knowing you still play." Lady Essex meandered toward Annalisa and Sarah. "And to hear you playing this piece."

Sarah looked to Annalisa. "It seems Miss Cavendish never forgot music, my lady."

"'Tis Mozart's second piano sonata. Of that much I'm certain." The muscle memory of Annalisa's fingers performed each note, cadence, and trill, but the music came from her heart. *I must've played this piece a hundred times in my former life.*

Lady Essex settled beside her on the bench. "This piece is more to you than just Mozart's second piano sonata."

"Tell me how I know it, my lady."

"As you wish, dearest friend."

Dearest friend. Annalisa warmed at the sentiment, that someone considered her a dear friend. *If only I could reciprocate such fond feelings toward Lady Essex.* She glanced at the blonde woman beside her, robed in periwinkle silk and smelling of rose and bergamot perfume. From the redness encircling Lady Essex's eyes, she'd sobbed rather heavily on her husband's shoulder before dinner.

"Keep playing. Perhaps 'twill jog your memory."

Annalisa continued the sonata, moving to the second movement, the *adagio*. At the first melancholy sounds, her hand quivered upon the keys.

"Oh, Annie," Lady Essex murmured. "You know not the trembling of my heart. I can only imagine yours."

"I wish I could remember." Annalisa inhaled a shaky breath. "I fear I've not a single memory before the shipwreck, nor even my rescue. Only what I've been told."

"And what were you told?"

"I was found by the duchess on a wharf in Calais."

"And you don't recall how you came to be upon a pier in Calais?" Lady Essex asked gently.

Annalisa shook her head, the sad melody of the sonata's *adagio* overcoming her.

Lady Essex frowned. "You were to meet us. You and Jack. Tell me you remember him."

Annalisa forced away the prickle of tears. "No, I'm afraid not."

"Oh, 'tis worse than I feared." Lady Essex blew an anxious sigh and looked to Sarah. "Had she nothing on her person that detailed her life?"

"Only the necklace, her ring, and a small lead round, my lady," Sarah replied.

Lady Essex's eyes misted once more. "The lead ball. That was a horrific day."

"What of the ball?" Annalisa asked.

"You fought at Bunker Hill and trapped a ball in your shoulder."

"I did no such thing."

"Yes, you did." Lady Essex gestured to the sapphire ring upon Annalisa's left fourth finger. "And Jack was your husband. This ring belonged to my mother's mother, my grandmother Bixby—the grandmother I share with your half-brother, George."

Mozart's *adagio* settled over Annalisa with heaviness. "Jack is truly dead?"

A solitary teardrop rolled down Lady Essex's freckled cheek, and her mouth parted to speak, but she did not. She patted away the tear and in a low voice, said, "We heard news of a shipwreck, and neither of you were accounted for among the living."

"But...how?" Annalisa fought the mourning for a husband she did not remember, but now grieved. "Where are our families?"

"The Province of Massachusetts Bay."

Annalisa reached for Sarah. The music ceased and silence overtook the room. "Georgiana was right, I'm from the colonies." She looked to Lady Essex. "How long were we married? Pray, what did Jack look like?"

Lady Essex smiled sadly. "He was very handsome, too handsome—the most agreeable man in town. He had blue eyes the color of the Atlantic, soft chestnut brown hair, and dimples when he smiled. And he was taller than you—a feat for some gentlemen."

Annalisa warmed. "With such an appealing husband, have I any children?"

Lady Essex shook her head. "No—"

"Miss Cavendish bled much shortly after we found her, my lady," Sarah chimed.

Annalisa started and regarded Sarah. "You never told me..."

"We could not confirm if it was a failed pregnancy, Miss. Mr. Beauregard said if it was, you were not far along."

"I'm a childless widow." Annalisa's face fell, and she returned her gaze to Lady Essex. "My wedding?"

Lady Essex's hand slid down Annalisa's arm. "My poor friend, you've been through much. I think we should continue this another day—"

"My wedding, Lady Essex. Tell me about my wedding, please."

Lady Essex inhaled sharply "You eloped. In September." She waited for Annalisa's reaction. When she said nothing, Lady Essex continued, "Sadly, when I arrived here, I learned the Marriage Act of 1753 does not recognize elopements as legitimate."

"I must be terribly humiliated back at home." Annalisa

crumpled the fabric of her green petticoat. "Perhaps my family will forgive me, if they've been at all grieving me."

"Of course, they've been grieving you," Lady Essex replied.

Annalisa slid her first finger along the spinet's ivory keys. "Lady Essex, if this is all true, you must write home at once."

Lady Essex squeezed Annalisa's hand. "Of course."

"I should think I'd like to return if I can."

"Quite." Lady Essex reached for the necklace at Annalisa's throat. "I see you wear Quinnapin's *wampum*."

"Is that who gave this to me?"

"Yes. He's Wampanoag. He carved that feather from a quahog shell. He's a dear friend of yours and Jack's." Lady Essex hesitated, and a shadow of disquiet settled over her. "And George."

"My brother," Annalisa replied.

"Yes," Lady Essex whispered. "He's one of three."

"And the others?"

"William, who must be seventeen now. And Henry, Mary's twin. I daresay the twins should be thirteen or so."

Annalisa clutched her bosom. "I've a sister as well?"

"You've two. Jane, your elder sister, who married my brother, Oliver." She stared at Annalisa suggestively, perhaps expecting a reaction. When it did not come, she added, "And Mary."

Comforted for the first time since April, Annalisa said, "I can at least rest happily tonight knowing my own name."

"I'd never lie to you, Annie. I love you as my dearest friend and sister." Lady Essex returned her smile, albeit sadly. "You are Annalisa Perkins, née Howlett—if we choose to recognize your marriage." She sucked in a shaky breath. "I think we shall. We're at war with England. And we owe it to Jack."

15

JACK

TOPSFIELD, JUNE 1776

JACK AWOKE TO LIGHT kisses fluttering along his neck. Eyes still closed, he grinned and wrapped his arms around the warm body beside him. He kissed the top of her head. "Let's try again for a child."

A light soprano giggled.

His sleep fog lifted and Jack's stomach dropped. "Jane?" He slid away and leapt from the bed, covering himself. He sifted through an array of clothing scattered about the wooden floor and tugged on his breeches. "What is this? Have we strummed?"

She scowled. "You don't remember?"

"Should I? Have I?" He pulled at his hair, his temples throbbing after a long night of liquor and laudanum. "My God, what have I done? What have *we* done!"

"You're a widower, Jack. 'Tis no crime. I came here to comfort you." She reached for his hand. "Dare I say we're two lonely people looking for love?"

Jack snatched back his hand. "I've committed adultery, madam. Your husband, my brother, is not dead. And for what 'tis worth, I'm still grieving Annalisa." He paced the room, repressing the urge to retch. "Did I inject you with my seed? What if you get with child?"

"I cannot. I'm still nursing Tommy. The nursemaid says I can't get in the family way until I stop."

"You're certain?"

"Yes."

He sat on the edge of the bed and sighed. "There's at least some solace in that." His hands cradled his head. "As if my heart weren't heavy enough."

Jane rested her chin on his shoulder, and an aroma of lilac overwhelmed him. *She never wears lilac.*

Jack stood. "Why do you wear Annie's perfume? Mean you to torment me? Or tempt me?"

She glowered. "I meant neither torment, nor temptation." Jane wound the coverlet about her naked form and rose from the bed. "I know I can never replace Annalisa. But if we're alone and despairing, I can't see the harm in sharing one another's company."

He pulled his linen shirt over his head. "I will not. My brother—the scoundrel he is—still lives and deserves not to be cuckolded." Jane's bottom lip quivered as though she would cry. Softened, Jack lifted her hand. "I can't give you what you seek. My heart belongs to Annalisa—in life and in death." He choked on the last word, and when he composed himself, he dropped her hand. "I'm leaving for New York. I'm joining the Continentals. I must." He plucked his waistcoat from the floor. Fighting the wave of crippling nausea, he added, "I'm shamed for what I did. You deserve far better than this."

Jack quit the room and hurried down the stairs—as quickly as he could without his cane—and into the kitchen, where he grabbed the bottle of brandy upon the fireplace mantel below Annalisa's musket, and the vial of laudanum upon the kitchen table. He rushed outside. There, upon the stone front-door step, he emptied the brandy. When only the glass remained, he withdrew the cork stopper on the vial of laudanum. The rust-colored fluid poured into the puddle of golden brandy that dripped and dribbled across the stone. No more liquor, and no more laudanum to numb his senses, or his sensibility. If God had indeed heard his prayers through his curses, this final travesty brought on by his melancholia could be tempered with humility and reconciliation.

❧

JACK AND JANE HAD BEEN SEATED WITH HIS MOTHER IN THE parlor not ten minutes when the clop of horse's hooves, and the crunch of carriage wheels upon gravel, shook them from their charge. Jack lifted from his chair and looked out the window.

"Father. He's returned from Philadelphia."

"Thank Heaven." Mother, who'd been silently working her needlepoint, sighed. "I'd written him weeks ago of your return."

Jack commenced into the foyer, and Mercy opened the door.

"Jack. My dear boy." Father, in his black travel cloak and cocked hat, stepped inside and embraced him. When he pulled away, Father blinked several times, and removed his spectacles to wipe tears from his eyes. "My God, you're thin. But I thank God you're alive. You must tell me what happened. Congress has been in an uproar since the shipwreck. That foul captain of *Liberté*—"

"The foul captain?" Jack stepped back from his father. "Whatever do you speak of?"

Father removed his hat and cloak and thrust them into the housekeeper's outstretched arms. "A dram of brandy, Mercy." He appraised Jack for a moment, then led him into the parlor, where he greeted Mother and Jane.

When Father was sat in his favorite chair by the fireplace, Jack asked, "Sir, what of the captain of *Liberté?*"

Father lit his pipe and drew in a long sip. "Yes, the captain." He expelled the sweet pipe tobacco into a tendril. "The captain spied for the British. He never meant to sail to France. He knew—"

"Annalisa and I were on board, destined for France as per Congress," Jack completed his sentence. "I now understand how it was we wrecked off the coast of Halifax, and I imprisoned upon HMS *Lively*. But, pray, Oliver was aboard, and confirmed Annalisa's death...did she truly pass?" A dim flicker of empty hope that his wife still lived—somewhere—led him to regard Jane, who sat silently on the sofa between Susan and Charlotte.

Jane met his stare. "Yes, Jack. We've been over this."

"There was a storm." Father took the brandy given him by Mercy and sipped the amber fluid. "'Twas of divine Providence. No British spy could conjure such a storm. You're lucky—or unlucky, if you should see it as such—to have been rescued by HMS *Lively*."

"'Twas a nightmare on that ship," Jack barked. "Of course, 'twas unlucky. I'm now a widower with a tormented mind because of that imprisonment."

"Peace, Jack." Father crossed his leg then pulled again from his pipe. A long strand of smoke circled his head. "I understand you're recovering, but Congress would like you to return. The Committee of Secret Correspondence requires you. Mr. Deane has established contacts in Paris. We must persist upon France—"

"I will not."

"Think on it. You're of the Committee of Secret Correspondence. You can hardly abandon your duties—"

"I'd already abandoned them when I was shipwrecked and presumed dead," Jack snapped. "And I've escaped imprisonment. The British will be looking for me. Don't deny it, sir. 'Tis all the more reason I must escape town and join the Continentals."

"But you said Ollie was on board HMS *Lively*." Father glanced at Jane. "He could not release you?"

"Oliver's allegiance lies with his army," Jack replied. "He did mend my leg but claimed he could not release me."

The vein on Father's forehead bulged. "That is troublesome to hear." His gaze settled on Jane. "And you, my dear, were on board as well. With my grandson?"

"Yes, my lord." Jane smoothed her skirts. "I suggested it an unsuitable place for the child, but Oliver insisted it safe for us. 'Twas I who assisted with Jack's escape. He brought Tommy and me home." She hesitated. "I love my husband, sir. But a ship is no place for a babe."

Father lifted his hand. "You've strong motherly instincts, my dear. I commend you for that." He turned toward Jack. "My heart all but stopped the day I learned of the wreck. You are my first-born." Father adjusted his spectacles, perhaps to ward off more tears. "I'm devastated for your loss, Jack. And while 'tis proper you should be in mourning, I think you must join me in Congress."

Jack shook his head. "No. I'm riding to New York. I'll be signing with the Continentals."

"Washington's on Long Island," Father replied. "He's having a tremendously difficult time signing on soldiers."

"All the more I must join."

Father studied him from over the rim of his spectacles.

His white wig held less luster, and his forehead carried more creases than Jack remembered. "In Congress, we're drafting a declaration of independence from Britain. The colonies can, and should, establish trade with Europe, as well as proclaim independence."

Jack's heart thudded remembering Thomas Paine's pamphlet, *Common Sense*, which articulated just that.

"Your uncle, Lord Brunswick, wishes for your return, as does Adams," Father added. "You must be part of it."

John Adams. Jack would never forget his apprenticeship with Adams during the Boston Massacre trials. Now, they were law partners—one of the few trades acceptable to a gentleman. It felt like years, not months, had passed since he'd last stepped inside the office he set up in town. Now, the colonies were at war with the Mother Country, and he, an escaped prisoner. *How can I presume to cultivate client relationships at a time when so much plagues me and my reputation?*

His hands trembling, Jack tugged at his lower lip. "Pray, Brunswick still wishes me his heir apparent?"

"Of course." Father chuckled. "You've signed the paperwork. Twice. 'Tis done."

Inheriting both his father's and uncle's estates and titles would afford him the means to attend Congress, no matter his law practice, but he could also afford to join the Continentals.

His foot tapping anxiously, he lifted from his seat and excused himself from the room. *None of this matters until I quit the laudanum. I need to be a better man.*

Jack left his family's estate and rode to the outskirts of town where Topsfield's land abutted Ipswich. There, he called on Quinnapin and Weetamoo, who hadn't yet left for New York.

"Jack, *wuneekeesuq*," Quinnapin greeted in his native Wampanoag.

When Jack didn't enter their home, Quinnapin stepped outside, his face falling with concern.

"I need help." Jack's voice broke, "I must quit laudanum. I've come to depend upon it, and I know not how to be without it."

Quinnapin's hand rested on Jack's shoulder. "Of course. I can help you through the worst, old friend. But you must know you're going to be sick for several days. Quite sick."

Jack lowered his gaze and nodded. *How has this become my life? How did I let myself fall this far?*

"Come, let's inside. You can stay with us." Quinnapin guided Jack into his house and closed the door.

✤ 16 ✤

GEORGE

YORK ISLAND, NEW YORK, JULY 9, 1776

GEORGE HURRIED DOWN THE street and slipped. He threw out his arms for balance, escaping a fall. Peering down at his shoe, he grimaced at the stench of excrement.

"Fie."

George made his way to the nearest shop and perched his shit-covered shoe against the iron scraper outside its door. *This had better be horse dung...*

"Good day to you, sir." A prostitute missing two teeth managed to whistle at him from a narrow alleyway across the street. "Are you lookin' to have your Thomas milked? Perhaps a proper bagpiping?"

"Not today, marm."

In his youth, a lover was a lover, or, rather, a strumming was a strumming. But not with these lasses. Not even to forget Abigail, lost to Lord Essex. He'd spent enough time at Mount Whoredom and Damnation Alley while living in Boston to know the morts of New York City were no better than Boston's pox-filled doxies; and he meant to keep himself from the syphilis. His shoe moderately clean, George hurried away. He'd need far more than a pint of ale—or six—for such strumming.

Northwest of the town, along the Hudson River, George met with the rest of his militia. They'd secured Fort Washington, while across the river in New Jersey, a separate brigade of provincials safeguarded Fort Lee.

Bartlett and Samuel sat near a small fire, singing Samuel's favorite tune, *The Parting Glass*:

> *But since it fell into my lot*
> *That I should rise and you should not...*

Samuel looked up. "Mount any lasses today?"

A few plump sausages sizzled in the spider; the casing of one burst open. A squirt of grease landed in the flames, causing them to dance with the added fat. George's stomach roiled.

"I'd rather shite through my teeth."

Samuel and Bartlett snickered.

Bartlett handed George a canteen. "Rum."

"Sluice your gob." George drank.

Samuel outstretched his arm. "Howlett, give me ye bayonet. I need something t' cut me sausage."

George chuckled and handed his friend the bayonet. Samuel sliced into the sausage and more juices spurted into the sizzling fire.

"At least 'tis good fer somethin'." Samuel handed George his weapon, then popped a lump of sausage into his mouth.

George appraised his bayonet as he cleaned away the grease. "The Bloodybacks are at Staten Island. Won't be long before we need these."

Samuel chewed voraciously, then swallowed. With the

back of his sleeve, he dried his chin. "We be sittin' here since April. I doubt Howe 'n his Lobsters be any closer t' a plan now than when they left Boston."

Bartlett, with one foot bare before the flames, peered up from darning a hole in his stocking. "I heard General Washington will be gracing us with his presence today. Seems he's eager to see how we've advanced Fort Washington."

"I think we've done well. When it comes to recruitment, I've been telling rogues about the Bloodybacks' plan to poison Boston. Most are eager to sign on." George took another swig of the canteen. Already, the cheap rum lightened his head. "Those Lobsters can sail down this river as they like. They won't make it very far."

"Howe will attack. We best ready ourselves," Bartlett replied, then returned to his stitching.

A stout captain with a ruddy, pockmarked face advanced toward their campfire. "Private Howlett, the commander of artillery wishes a word with you."

George rose from his chair and followed the captain into a tent.

There, on an old wooden stool, sat Henry Knox. He peered up at George and motioned for him to approach. "You may leave us, Captain." When the officer left the tent, Knox said, "Good to see you, Private. How are you faring these months in New York?"

"Well, sir. Not since our venture to Ticonderoga did I think I'd return within the year," George replied. He glanced about the tent. Layers of maps and dispatches littered Knox's desk; before him, a ledger.

Knox's thick lips curled. "Quite." He returned to his ledger, signed it, and set it aside. "I've summoned you for three reasons. As you know, the British have arrived at Staten Island."

"Aye, sir."

"The first reason I've asked to see you is under orders from General Washington. At my compliments on how well you conducted yourself on our expedition to Ticonderoga, and our fortification of Dorchester Heights, and now, Fort Washington, I inquired about a promotion." Knox paused, waiting for George's reaction. When he gave none, Knox continued, "And he agreed."

George grinned. "Well, I'll be damned. A promotion, sir?"

"Aye. To sergeant."

"I'm humbled. And most undeserving."

"Nonsense. The men follow you. I see it. I daresay, General Washington sees it." Knox gestured to the ledger. "Sign here, if you please."

George took up the quill and scrawled his name upon the page. "Thank you, sir. I'm most obliged."

"Don't thank me, Sergeant. Keep up the discipline and recruitment, and you'll probably be a major someday." Knox sprinkled sand over the ink to dry it, then set the ledger aside. "'Tis always good to see us Boston men sticking together. I remember you from when Lord Perkins lived in town. You're his nephew, yes?"

"Aye. I spent a few months studying under Mr. Hancock, then the bloody massacre happened and my family summoned me home. 'Twas a shame. I think I left my heart in Boston, sir."

"I left my heart in Boston, too. My poor wife, Lucy, hasn't seen me in months."

"Lucy Flucker." George guffawed. "I kissed her on Pope Night. 'Twas all in good fun, I assure you."

"Ah yes, infamous Pope Night. I daresay, I was brave enough to attend one or two of those raucous evenings." He chuckled, then leaned forward. "Pray, did you ever meet the man who called himself Joyce Junior, the chairman of the committee of tarring and feathering?"

"I met him that night," George replied. "My cousin Jack and I were chased by Sons of Liberty to Long Wharf, where we encountered the mighty chairman himself. His mask was as hideous as they say. He ordered the tarring and feathering of that loyalist plum from Nantucket, Mr. Chatham. We escaped only by admitting our allegiances lay with the Sons of Liberty."

"Never saw the man but read much about him in the *Gazette*. You and Jack were lucky to have escaped." Knox paused. "Would that your cousin could join us, now."

George stiffened. "My cousin is dead, sir. Died at sea in a shipwreck."

Knox gave a lamented headshake. "I heard. You have my condolences." He hesitated, then continued, "This brings me to my second point. Some information has come to light regarding that wreck."

"I understand the ship was captained by a turncoat..."

"Aye. The captain was a spy for the British."

"Mean you to say they were deliberately placed in harm's way of the storm?"

Knox shook his head. "No man can predict a storm by divine Providence. But the ship never made it farther than the coast of Halifax."

George curled his fists. "I'll maim every Bloodyback I can, sir. You have my word. Pray, has the captain a name? Was he captured? I've been trying to locate the rogue since we left Boston."

Knox looked about his tent as though to ensure they were alone. "Captain Fleming. But you heard nothing from me, Sergeant." He stared hard at George, then glanced at a brief upon his desk. "The third and final. General Washington received a proclamation...a declaration of independence from Congress. Several officers have been instructed to read it aloud to the men. I'd like you to read it to ours."

His vigor renewed, George slapped Knox's desk with enthusiasm. "Aye, sir. I'll read it."

Knox handed George the roll of papers, neatly tied with twine. "I'll follow shortly, Sergeant."

When George returned to his friends, Samuel was cutting another sausage with his bayonet.

He looked up. "What's happened?"

George snatched the bayonet, swabbed it clean with a handkerchief, then handed it back to Samuel. "No more cutting food with bayonets. We're going to require them, presently. Knox promoted me to sergeant. Jack and Annalisa's ship was captained by a British spy, and—"

Bartlett gasped. "Not a turncoat?"

George shrugged. "Spy...turncoat—"

"Yer joking, Howlett," Samuel said. "Quite th' load of news."

George made a fist, wishing he could assault the villain captain. "His name is Captain Fleming. Apparently, their ship never made it beyond the coast of Halifax. The Lobsterback bastard will pay. Now I have his name, I'll find him and make him suffer."

"Easy, Sergeant," Bartlett replied.

Samuel glanced at the rolled paper in George's unclenched hand. "What 'ave ye there? A dispatch?"

George winked, then hollered, "Fall in, abrams. Orders from Washington!"

"Orders from Washington? Yer promoted not ten minutes 'n ye 'ave a proclamation t' read?" Samuel snickered.

Henry Knox emerged from his tent. "Fall in, gentlemen!"

The militiamen about the camp stopped their tasks and, grumbling, formed lines before George and Henry Knox.

"Sergeant Howlett has an announcement to read from Congress and General Washington," Knox yelled over the murmurs. "Attention!"

George slid the twine from the paper and unrolled the page. He read: *The unanimous Declaration of the thirteen united States of America. When in the Course of human events, it becomes necessary for one people to dissolve the political bands which have connected them with another, and to assume among the powers of the earth, the separate and equal station to which the Laws of Nature and of Nature's God entitle them, a decent respect to the opinions of mankind requires that they should declare the causes which impel them to the separation."*

George paused and studied the sea of eyes fixed on him. Not one man uttered, coughed, or blinked. He swallowed, then continued to read to the end, a lengthy proclamation detailing Congress's intention to separate from the Mother Country. His hands quaked as he reached the end, and the energy of the soldiers before him buzzed.

Hats flew into the sultry summer air.

"Huzzah!"

"Hear, hear!"

In a mad frenzy, the men dispersed about the encampment, perhaps to celebrate, perhaps to cause a jerrycummumble.

"Rogues, they've done it. They've declared independence." George bellowed a joyous laughter he'd not felt since the days before Lexington and Concord—when his sister and cousin were alive, and all that concerned him was the tavern, and the drinking of flip.

"Aye, 'tis cause fer celebration," Samuel cried.

Not an hour after he'd read the declaration, George and

his friends passed around several canteens of cheap rum as they sat about the rustling campfire.

"Are ye wrapped in warm flannel yet, Howlett?" Samuel's Irish accent slurred.

George guffawed and loosened his cravat. "'Tis either this fire, or I'm utterly disguised, rogues. This rum is vile."

"When we're independent from Britain, I daresay we conjure better ways to make rum," Bartlett said, his eyelids drooping. "No more slave trade."

George and Samuel lifted their tin cups. "Hear, hear. To ending the slave trade."

A group of six or seven soldiers toted a metal statue of King George III. Drunkenly, they tossed it to the ground, landing beside the fire with a heavy thud.

"Th' reptile." Samuel spit on the statue.

One of the soldiers who helped lug the replica said, "How else can we desecrate him, rogues?"

Another unbuttoned the flap of his breeches and made water over the king's head.

George jumped from his seat, ready to piss on the king's forehead, but stopped. "Let's melt him and make musket rounds that'll find their way into the hearts of his Lobsterback bastards."

✿ 17 ✿

JACK

PHILADELPHIA, AUGUST 2, 1776

M R. JEFFERSON READ ALOUD their Declaration of Independence to the flushed audience before him. Many of these men, Jack included, had been absent at the first signing last month, in July. He peered about the airless meetinghouse at the gentlemen fanning themselves. They wafted about air, thick with body odor. Seated beside his father and John Adams, who sat still, perhaps impervious to the heat, Jack stuffed two fingers between his neck and cravat to loosen the tie.

His leg aching, Jack shifted in his seat, and stretched it forward. A trickle of sweat dripped down his back. He eyed Father to his left, who nodded complacently at Jefferson's proclamation. To his right, John Adams rapped his cane with an occasional, "Hear, hear."

Each word that left Jefferson's awkward tongue would perhaps be interpreted by the prime minister, Lord North. *Will the king even read the document? Will it even reach England's shores? Surely, the original would almost be there by now.* Jack leaned forward, resting his forearms upon his thighs. Annalisa

would have absorbed each word from Jefferson's lips; she had
been as much a Patriot as he and George.

If any of Jack's letters reached George, his cousin would
be shocked to hear of his survival, only to be promptly disappointed to learn Jack had journeyed instead, to Philadelphia.
He'd given considerable thought to joining the Continentals,
but the lameness of his leg ultimately decided for him. There
was no way he could withstand marching countless miles
upon a limb so weak and feeble.

Jack slid to the edge of his seat, relieved by Congress's
declaration. It construed a long-standing sentiment he'd felt
since the Boston Massacre in 1770. Jack gripped the arms of
his Windsor chair and recalled the cold, blustery night in 1773
when he'd jettisoned crates of tea into Boston Harbor. Each
of those nights had culminated in the first battles of 1775—
Lexington and Concord, and Bunker Hill. *Finally, Congress
acknowledges the hardships we've suffered for years in Boston at the
hands of the British.* In some ways, the sedition he'd committed
was validated within the declaration of independence.
Though that treachery felt a lifetime ago, he would commit
new treason today by signing the proclamation.

*"We, therefore, the Representatives of the united States of Amer-
ica, in General Congress...solemnly publish and declare, That these
United Colonies are, and of Right ought to be Free and Independent
States..."*

Jefferson's voice returned Jack to the meetinghouse. A
rather quiet and gauche speaker, Mr. Jefferson had neverthe-
less formulated the most poetic and well-versed document
he'd ever heard. The declaration had been made public nearly
a month prior on July the fourth, but now the others who'd
been absent from Congress at the original signing meant to
add their signatures to the finalized copy on parchment.

"And for the support of this Declaration, with a firm reliance on

the protection of divine Providence, we mutually pledge to each other our Lives, our Fortunes and our sacred Honor."

The Congress erupted into a symphony of applause, rapped canes, "Huzzahs!" and "Hear, hears!"

Jack clapped and glanced at Father; he knocked his cane upon the floor for a job well done, as did John Adams. *How infrequently my law partner smiles.* The heat and emotion overwhelming him, Jack stood and excused himself, and found his way outside the meetinghouse.

At once, the Philadelphia breeze cooled his face. As he wandered from the brick building, Jack imagined last summer. June, at the Strawberry Festival, when he'd asked to court Annalisa; only weeks later, Bunker Hill had threatened to part them forever. He shuddered at the memory. They'd endured much leading to this moment in Congress; hundreds having lost their lives, including Annalisa, in the name of declaring independence from Britain. *She may rest now, knowing her death was not in vain. We will become an independent nation, my love. And you did your part.*

His throat thick with melancholy, Jack leaned against an old cherry tree. It had been months since he allowed himself to feel sorrow, to remember the pain endured aboard HMS *Lively*. The laudanum had numbed everything, but was no longer a part of his life, thanks to Quinnapin, and five grueling days of sickness and agony. Now, he must relearn to feel.

The cherry tree's welcoming shade reminded him of the Howletts' ancient oak. Perhaps Mary and Henry occupied that space this very moment, laughing and climbing the tree's thick, wide branches. Hopefully they did, for now with a proclamation of independence, war was certain to persist, and perhaps rage on for years to come. *These will not be easy times.*

Mr. Greeves, Hancock's assistant, approached with steadfast step. "Mr. Perkins—you're required, sir."

Jack followed the assistant and reentered the stuffy meetinghouse.

"There he is, and looking a bit flushed, I must say," John Adams said with a nod of approval. "The color in your cheeks does improve your complexion. We were quite astounded when first we saw you, looking so thin and pale." Adams regarded Jefferson. "I've known this lad since he graduated Harvard and became my law apprentice. Indeed, he learned well; we're now partners."

"And I'm grateful to you, sir," Jack replied. "My imprisonment upon HMS *Lively* did me quite the disservice, but I'm recovering well. My leg grows stronger each day."

"So I've heard, Mr. Perkins," Jefferson remarked. "We're right heartily glad for your return to Congress. Pray, what do you think of the declaration?"

Jack beamed. "'Tis a marvel, sir. Better written than any good man here could've done—and each gentleman present is more than capable of conjuring such profound sentiments, but to put it to writing is quite the task. 'Tis been an honor to be part of such a moment, sir."

"And your moment will come, too, Mr. Perkins. We still hope to court France. They would prove a most powerful ally," Adams added.

Father rested a hand on Jack's shoulder. "I couldn't have said it better, Mr. Jefferson. I'm most pleased by your fine, diligent work. Have we each signed the parchment yet?"

John Adams eyed the meetinghouse door. "We're awaiting Dr. Franklin. He went to the necessary."

As Adams finished speaking, the meetinghouse door opened, and in stepped Dr. Franklin. A glint of sunlight reflected off his large patch of receding hairline, which yielded to long, greying hair. Franklin peered at the room from over the edge of round spectacles. "Shall we sign again, gentlemen?"

The men clamored about the room, surrounding Mr. Hancock at his desk. Jack joined his father and John Adams. He'd met Mr. Hancock several times when living in Boston. It had been at Hancock's grand manor that George was bequeathed a sum of money from an old life insurance policy held by George's natural father, Captain Bixby; Bixby had been contracted by Hancock's late uncle. *A night I'll never forget; and I'm certain, neither will George.* The annual sum had allowed his cousin to purchase the Black Water Inn in Portsmouth.

Mr. Hancock dipped a white quill into the inkwell and scraped off the excess black ink. He scratched a flamboyant signature, quite largely, onto the parchment. "Is it substantial enough to match the one sent to King George?"

The gentlemen laughed, and each took their turn signing the page. When it came to Jack, he hesitated, and met the eyes of those in the room.

"Gentlemen, I wish to speak on things I've contemplated since the creation of this document."

"Go on, Perkins," Franklin said, though a few others, Congressmen from the southern colonies, groaned.

"'Tis a privilege to sign such a document, but 'twas equally an honor to fight. I was there at Concord, and likewise present at Bunker Hill. I stand before you today, gentlemen, not as a vessel of Congress, quick to sign my name, but as a militiaman who fought the British on each of those fateful days. The people of Massachusetts have been fighting since 1770." Jack's throat clogged, but he composed himself. "'Tis been six long years for the people of Massachusetts, and I pray the rest of these alleged *united states* partake in the fight that has solely been ours. New-England has long been the head of Dr. Franklin's famed serpent, and I'm overjoyed to see the other colonies join with us as the body."

Jack dipped the quill in ink and signed his name. "This is for each man who remains on the front lines of battle, each man who has fought, and each man whose injury or death has been the cost of this document. This is for Bunker Hill." Though he spoke the word *man*, he envisioned Annalisa, the woman who fought and survived Bunker Hill, the woman who'd traveled with him in the name of Congress and had lost her life. For Annalisa, he signed.

The gentlemen clapped.

"Hear, hear, Perkins."

"Huzzah!"

Adams rapped his cane. "For Bunker Hill."

Mr. Hancock nodded. "For Bunker Hill, Mr. Perkins."

When the last signature was upon the parchment, Jack addressed Congress once more. "Now, we must all hang together, gentlemen."

Dr. Franklin chuckled, landing a hand upon Jack's shoulder. "Indeed, young Mr. Perkins, we must all hang together, for if we do not, we'll all hang separately."

ANNALISA

DEVONSHIRE HOUSE, LONDON,
AUGUST 1776

ANNALISA SCREAMED INTO THE NIGHT. She bolted upright in bed and clutched her bosom. Her chemise was drenched in perspiration.

Sarah hurried into the room with a chamberstick in hand. She placed the candle upon the bedside table, and clutched Annalisa's trembling body. "Hush, Miss. All will be well."

In the darkness, Annalisa eased against the chambermaid, her scent of herbs comforting. "'Twas a nightmare." Annalisa shook herself free of it. "I dreamt of my husband...he clutched me close as the world around us shattered. I can hardly understand why...'tis all too disconcerting."

"Just a dream, Miss. Morning will be here, and in the evening, you'll attend Lady Melbourne's ball." Sarah brushed away Annalisa's hair. "All will be well."

"I wish you could join, Sarah."

"You know how I feel about that." Sarah released Annalisa from her arms. "But I daresay, you'll fare just fine without me." She offered a small smile. "You're close to remembering. I can feel it."

"You think so?"

Sarah nodded. "Mmhmm. I think meeting your old friend Lady Essex—Abigail—has helped. Just the other day, you mentioned something about a large oak tree at the edge of your family's property."

"I did. I recall a...v-venerable tree. I feel I used to climb its branches." Annalisa chuckled. "Perhaps I was not so well bred as the duchess suspects."

Sarah grinned. "See? Memories have come, at last." She stood from the bed. "Now try to get some rest, Miss."

Annalisa reached for her. "One day, I hope you find your mother and grandmother."

Sarah nodded. "Me too, Miss."

⚜

THAT EVENING, ANNALISA STOOD BESIDE GEORGIANA, THE duke, and Mr. Fitzherbert at Melbourne House's grand assembly room. Like every other great hall boasting gold filigree and wainscoting, at least four gleaming chandeliers lit the room in luminous glow, and an array of perfumes saturated the air. *How strange that these balls have come to feel commonplace and tiresome, when I was so fearful of them.*

"Your Grace." Lord and Lady Melbourne greeted their most esteemed guests, and then Lady Melbourne fixed her gaze on Annalisa and Mr. Fitzherbert. "Miss Cavendish, Mr. Fitzherbert."

"My lord, my lady." They each bowed and curtsied.

"Come, Fitzherbert. Your sister only just arrived." Lord Melbourne gestured toward a grouping of young ladies.

"Maria's here?" Mr. Fitzherbert's face glowed. "I knew not she was invited." He turned to Annalisa, and the duke and duchess. "If you'll excuse me, Your Grace." He disappeared with Lord Melbourne into the crowded room.

Lady Jersey curtsied, and eyed the duke, who swiftly excused himself. She turned her beady gaze to Annalisa. "I believe Lord and Lady Essex have arrived. I've been informed of your newly...intimate...friendship with Lady Essex, Miss Cavendish. How splendid to be so accepted among us."

The duchess regarded Annalisa. "Miss Cavendish has indeed become a dear friend of mine, Lady Jersey. 'Tis no surprise to me Lady Essex has taken to her as well."

Lady Jersey's shrill laugh bordered on witch-like cackle but sounded trained enough to maintain decorum. "How fortunate. The Americans should stick together, should they not, Lady Melbourne?"

"Americans?" Lady Melbourne asked, seemingly aloof.

"Quite. Lady Essex is from the colonies. Knew you not? And 'tis been uncovered Miss Cavendish is as well. I daresay, if the Americans desire independence, they should take it...if they can. Last I heard, their army is nothing but a pitiful amalgamation of farmers," Lady Jersey snickered.

Annalisa's heart skipped. *Independence?*

"Lady Jersey, hush," Georgiana scolded.

From across the room, Annalisa saw Lord and Lady Essex. "Do excuse me, Your Grace." She left the ladies forthwith and approached Lady Essex, who beamed as Annalisa neared.

Promptly, Lady Essex removed a piece of paper from her reticule. "I'm so glad to see you. I've news from America, but come this way. I don't wish for our English brethren to overhear. Particularly that mule, Lady Jersey."

Annalisa's heart pounded as she followed Lady Essex through a doorway, and down the corridor.

Lady Essex peered behind her. "Lady Melbourne has this room for her own particular use. 'Tis best we utilize it now, before some unsuspecting lady and gentleman borrow it later."

She creaked open the paneled door and slipped inside the darkened room. A pale twilight trickled through the window at the far end of the room, and Lady Essex hastened toward it. There, in the day's remaining light, she unfolded the page and read aloud, *"For cutting off our trade with all parts of the world. For imposing Taxes on us without our consent...for taking away our charters..."*

A memory returned to Annalisa. *I dressed as a boy and threw oysters and ice at the Redcoats in Boston.*

"...He has plundered our seas, ravaged our Coasts, burnt our towns, and destroyed the lives of our people..."

Annalisa listened to a litany of reasons why the colonies should separate from the Mother Country, and she saw her brother, George, at his tavern surrounded by friends, and herself, garbed in men's clothing hidden within a keg vestibule. *I used to listen to the rhetoric from that small room.* Another remembrance of her firing George's fowling piece, followed by another, playing the spinet while her sister, Jane, danced a minuet.

Recollections returned, slowly at first, then gradually, they overtook. Peoples' faces—beloved faces, including Lady Essex's—poured into her mind.

The morning George left to join the Continental Army. William at George's knee, reading his aunt's letter. Mary and Henry beneath the ancient oak. Mamma scolding me for firing George's firelock the day I burned my face. Papa in his chair with tobacco smoke swirling from his pipe. Jane with her pregnant belly. Jane marrying Oliver. Abigail shucking corn with me at the corn husking. Quinnapin offering me the wampum feather. Jane ogling Jack at Lord Suffolk's ball. Jack, seated beside me on a branch of the oak. Jack at George's

tavern the day we married. Jack dancing with me at the Strawberry
Festival. Abigail, my best friend...

Annalisa gasped. "Abbie." She clutched her oldest friend,
and Abigail's familiar rose perfume engulfed her. "Oh, Abigail,
'tis you."

Abigail held her. "I knew you would remember, dearest
friend."

"What torment have I caused you these several months?"
Annalisa wept.

"I was at peace when I knew you lived." Abigail released
her, peered down at the declaration, and chuckled. "To think,
these are the words which brought you back to us."

"Of course, they are." Annalisa smiled through her tears.
"Have you written home?"

"Several times. But I've not received any reply." She
squeezed Annalisa's hand. "Oh, Annie, if only Jack were
living. I'm so very sorry."

Annalisa's throat tightened. "Then 'tis true. I c-can't imagine
m-my life without him. I know you told me he died in the sh-
shipwreck, but that was before now...before I remembered
him." Annalisa wiped the tears as they fell, but they endlessly
flowed. Unable to catch her breath, she said, "I n-need air."

"Follow me." Abigail led her from the darkening room and
through another door, which led to an outdoor terrace.
There, Annalisa drank in the warm August evening, full of
jasmine.

"Why, Lord, have you t-taken him from me?" Annalisa
threw her hands to her face. "I want to go home, Abbie. I
need to see m-my family. They must know I'm alive."

"I've written them, Annie. I have yet to receive a reply."
Abigail dabbed her handkerchief across Annalisa's cheek. "My
heart grieves with you, dear friend. You're a widow at twenty,

and 'tis fitting for you to be in mourning. But remember, you have plenty of years ahead to marry again one day, and birth children."

"I don't wish to remarry," Annalisa sniffled. "I feel haven't properly grieved him until this v-very moment."

"I know." Abigail kissed her forehead. "You haven't. And tonight, after we've had our festivities, and everyone has gone to bed, you may weep and grieve to your heart's content. You owe it to yourself, and Jack."

To quell the stutter, Annalisa recited Mad Madge's poem, *A Dialogue Betwixt Wit and Beauty*. When she finished the poem, she exhaled, calm. "Should I tell Georgiana my memory's returned? She and the duke have been so kind to me..."

Abigail shook her head. "Not tonight. Perhaps in the morning you might wish to speak of it. Surely, they'll be glad to hear it. But for now, chin up—"

"Shoulders back, and smile." Annalisa's lip quivered as she reached for Abigail's hand and squeezed it. "I'm so glad you're with me."

❧

LATE-MORNING SUNLIGHT STREAMED THROUGH THE OPEN windows of the ladies' parlor as Annalisa and Georgiana awaited Abigail's arrival. Sarah loitered by the door.

"What is it, Miss Cavendish?" Georgiana asked. "You're alight with glowing resignation. Is it Mr. Fitzherbert? I saw you danced three last night."

"No, 'tis not Mr. Fitzherbert. 'Tis better than that, Your Grace." Annalisa eyed Sarah. "I wish for you both to be present when Lady Essex arrives."

The housekeeper entered the room and announced Abigail, and not a moment too soon. "Your Grace, how kind of you to receive me today." Abigail nodded to Annalisa. "Miss Cavendish."

"Lady Essex, you might recall Miss Sarah. She was my chaperone the day I visited your house." Annalisa gestured to Sarah, who curtsied.

"Please sit, Lady Essex." Georgiana offered a pink damask chair adjacent to the sofa upon which she and Annalisa sat. "I know nothing of what Miss Cavendish has to say but am eagerly awaiting her good news."

"Georgiana, you've been so kind to me these months as I recovered. I've known not who I am, or from where I came—I've been living a m-masquerade of my whole life." Annalisa paused, composing herself. "But last night, Lady Essex read to me news from America...a proclamation for independence. The colonies wish to separate from England, and 'twas from those written words I remembered."

Georgiana gasped. "You know yourself?"

"Oh, Miss Cavendish, that is good news," Sarah said, smiling.

"You may call me Annalisa, or Mrs. Perkins, if you like. My husband was aboard the same vessel but did not survive." She trembled speaking the words aloud, "I'm a widow, and shall be in mourning."

"Oh, Miss Cav—Mrs. Perkins." Georgiana reached for her.

"Lady Essex is my late husband's sister." Annalisa looked to Abigail. "I call her Abbie. And her other brother, Oliver, married my older sister, Jane. You see, our families are intimately entwined."

"There's more," Abigail added. "My daughter is your niece."

"Yes, who I've yet to meet," Annalisa said with a chuckle.

"But my family remains in the Province of Massachusetts Bay. I wish to return home, Gee."

Georgiana nodded. "I understand. I should never think to keep you for myself, though I'll miss you tremendously."

"There's more, Your Grace," Abigail said. "I would like Annalisa to stay with us at Essex House until we depart. I've written to our families several times since we discovered her, though I've yet to hear from anyone. Your Grace, has the mail been slower for you as well, since the war's begun?"

Georgiana cocked her head as she considered the plight. "I've not noticed a change, but I've not sent any letters across the Atlantic. I did hear General Howe landed in New York. He plans to attack Washington's troops. At least that is what Mr. Fox informed me. He's been following the hostilities closely." Georgiana reached for Annalisa's hand. "You do have friends in Parliament, Calais. The Whigs strongly support America's quest for independence."

"My brother, George, is in the Continental Army, Gee." Annalisa looked to Abigail. Her dearest friend had loved George long before Lord Perkins consented to her marriage to Lord Essex. "I'm certain he's in New York." She suppressed a shiver as memories of Bunker Hill clouded her with sulfuric gun-smoke and chest-rattling cannon-fire.

Would that I were with him.

🐲 19 🐲

GEORGE

BROOKLYN HEIGHTS, NEW YORK,

AT THEIR BROOKLYN HEIGHTS fortification, George lingered near the guns, slick with rainwater. The artillery had managed to fire on the British well into the previous night, despite the continuous rain. In deepening twilight, he studied shadowy figures of Redcoats acres away in their muddy trenches.

"'Twas no small task keeping the gunpowder dry in this weather, rogues. I know not how we'll endure this," George lamented. "With the East River to our backs, we're trapped here."

Samuel, who buffed the muzzle of his musket with a dirty linen cloth, peered at him with red-rimmed, bleary eyes. "Aye, we know it. I been without sleep since we lost th' battle fer Long Island."

"'Tis only a matter of time." Bartlett joined George by the cannon. "We must surrender, Sergeant."

"I can't give that order. You know that," George replied. *When did our cause dwindle to this wretched state? What brought us here, ready to kneel to that squeeze crab, King George? Is everything for naught?* He turned his back on the British and appraised the barracks. The East River flowed, and across it lay York Island. *Perhaps there's a chance yet for us to escape this position.*

Colonel John Glover, a bulky man with a strong jaw, of the Massachusetts regiment from Marblehead, advanced. "Sergeant Howlett, prepare the others. 'Tis been decided amongst the generals we're retreating to York Island."

"York Island, sir?" Bartlett asked. "But how?"

"Silence." The colonel eyed George. "Any questions, Sergeant Howlett?"

George's spirit vibrated, driving away his weariness. "The plan, sir?"

"My regiment is mostly fishermen and sailors. 'Tis been decided we'll begin evacuating across the river after nightfall. Mifflin and his men from Pennsylvania will make up the rear and hold the line while we retreat. They'll be last to leave."

"Cross the river?" Bartlett's eyes widened. "Howe and his men will see us escape."

Samuel smacked Bartlett upside the head. "Shut it, ye dimwitted fartleberry. 'Tis an order."

Several yards away from their position, the dark waters lapped lazily at the shore. Peering across the river devoid of ships, George said, "'Tis a wonder there's been so little wind. The British haven't filled the river, sir. Think you we've time?"

"General Washington made a similar remark." The colonel studied George a moment, then straightened his coat. "We must make haste. Gather the sick and wounded and get them to the Brooklyn Ferry so they're at the ready to evacuate first."

"Aye, sir."

The colonel turned and disappeared into the dimly lit barracks. Twilight already had given way to stars in an indigo sky. George returned his attention to his two friends. "Let's get a band of rogues together to get these invalids to the ferry."

Samuel clapped George's back and followed, with a reluctant Bartlett, through the encampment.

"You, Private." George pointed to a soldier, no older than his younger brother, William. "Get to the sick tent and help them to the ferry."

The private, with round doe-eyes, asked, "How many are wounded who need assistance, Sergeant?"

"I'm not sure," George replied. "Just get to the sick tent with some abled-bodied men and get the wounded to the ferry."

"Aye, sir." The private hurried away.

George led his friends to one of the larger tents housing the injured. He wrinkled his nose against the sour putrescence of festering wounds.

"'Tis agony...my leg, my leg," a militiaman cried.

Though the guttural scream prickled George's skin, he knelt beside the man who'd just lost his leg to the bone saw, the stump wrapped in bloodied linen. "Come now, Private. We've got to get you to the ferry."

"I can't," the man said through clenched teeth. "I can't walk."

"We'll carry ye, mate." Samuel positioned himself at the foot of the cot.

George looked behind him for Bartlett. His portly friend supported a man who hobbled with a crutch. They left the tent.

"Here, bite this." George handed the amputee a piece of leather. "We're evacuating to York Island. This is our only chance, aye?"

The man nodded and shoved the leather between his

teeth. With Samuel, George lifted the cot, and they trans-
ported the man to the ferry dock.

By eleven o'clock, every sick and wounded soldier started
to cross the East River with Colonel Glover and his regiment.
Satisfied, George hustled through the fortification to rally the
remaining militias loading wagons. *Everyone and everything
must cross the river tonight.*

"Speak not a word, rogues, and muffle your wagon wheels,
lest you wish to be hanged by Bloodybacks," George said.

"We be cuttin' close, Howlett." Samuel's lanky form sidled
up beside him and looked about the fort. "We've far too many
men 'n wagons left t' ferry across before dawn. We'll never
make it."

Bartlett joined, fidgeting with his coat. "We've not even
seen half the troops cross."

His friends' faces were caked in sweat and grime, their
hands soiled with mud and the dried blood of the injured.
This was a new kind of weariness, George decided, weariness
beset with futility and desperation, unlike anything he'd experienced at Concord or Bunker Hill.

"'Twill be close, rogues. But we'll make it." George gripped
his friends' shoulders. "We must believe it."

Six times, the ferry boat traversed the river, and a pink
dawn loomed, with still more men to evacuate. George
hurried through camp, seeking delayed soldiers, when he
stopped. General Washington, tall and regal, lingered within
the barracks, with hands clasped behind his back. He
appraised the muddy surroundings, now mostly barren of
tents, wagons, and horses.

George hesitated before approaching his superior. "Sir, 'tis
nearing six of the clock. Have we many left to vacate the
fort?"

The general's stern gaze met George's, then returned to

their surroundings. "There seems to be a fog rolling in, Sergeant. An act of divine Providence, indeed, if it masks us from our adversaries yonder."

George appreciated the fog. "Quite, sir." He waited a moment beside the commander in the hushed stillness of early morning, their environs besieged in mist. A moment of ethereal wonder, George knew he'd not forget it in his lifetime.

"Better make haste, Sergeant. The ferry shall wait for no one." Washington left his side, headed toward the East River, then turned once more. "'Tis an order, Sergeant."

❧

FOUR DAYS PASSED SINCE THEIR MIDNIGHT EVACUATION from Brooklyn Heights, fatefully concealed in rain and fog. The battle on Long Island, a colossal loss for the campaign, was also behind them. George gazed at the sparkling brackish waters of the Hudson and East Rivers as they flowed into one at the southern tip of York Island. Here, they stationed at Fort George.

His shoulders rounded, he cleaned his musket with gunpowder-stained linen. Beside him, Samuel stared at the bay, his long face expressionless. *Will Samuel stay the course, or will he desert and return home, like many already have?*

Samuel must've felt his stare. He eyed George, and a small smirk formed on his thin, cracked lips. "Think it not, Howlett. I'm with ye 'till th' end."

"You read my mind, rogue."

"I can tell when yer thinkin' like a doxie," Samuel snickered, then ran a hand through his sandy blond hair. "I been fightin' with ye since the beginnin'. I won't desert ye now, ye ole gollumpus."

George pulled Samuel into an embrace. "I'd have it no other way, you cock robin."

Washington's aide-de-camp sped toward them. "The general requests you, Sergeant Howlett."

George left Samuel and chased after the officer through rows of wedge tents, to Washington's quarters. He stepped inside the large tent behind the aide-de-camp.

"Sir, I've Sergeant Howlett for you." The aide-de-camp removed himself as hastily as he'd introduced George.

General Washington was a tall man, but George towered over him by three or four inches, something he hadn't noticed that foggy morning at dawn.

The general motioned for George to sit. "Sergeant, I've seen the valor with which you fight in battle, and this evacuation proved no different. 'Twas perilous and tiresome, but you maintained a steady vigor that inspired others." He paused. "Your persistence and fervor are notable."

George remained still as stone. "I'm a veteran of Bunker Hill, sir. Nothing I've seen has shaken me quite like that day. But I've been with your army since you occupied Cambridge." He swallowed thickly. "My sister and brother-by-law died in a shipwreck...I've little left for me at home, sir. I daresay, I may be with you till the end."

Washington nodded, his mouth pressed into a thin, flat line. He plucked his quill and scrawled upon a piece of paper. "This campaign has been no easy task, Sergeant. I'm certain you've noticed the number of deserters. No doubt, their defeated hearts are heavy for a cause which knows no favorable outcome to a new army. We're undisciplined and lack motivation."

"Sir, I beg your pardon, but we might yet prove victorious. We may lose many battles, but with your leadership, there will be far more victories, sir."

Washington's brows lifted. "You speak with assuredness, Sergeant."

"I've believed in this cause since the night of the massacre in Boston, sir—I was there. I also fought last April at Concord...and had the grave misfortune of seeing the good Dr. Warren perish at Bunker Hill."

Washington sat motionless. "Then it may come as a surprise to you 'tis been decided we must also abandon New York City."

"Abandon the city, sir? We've only just arrived—"

"Indeed." Washington pointed to a pin embedded within his map. "Howe and his troops now sit on Montresor's Island with plans to attack. While we cannot burn the city to the ground, we're not at leisure to hold it. 'Tis been the consensus among my officers, and I've been outnumbered. Four thousand men will remain here with General Putnam. The remainder of the army shall march north to Harlem."

A beat passed between them before George said, "Aye, sir."

"Sergeant, the captain of Cogswell's regiment has absconded. I wish to promote you to captain. 'Tis within the militias we see least loyalty. It shall be your task to command the field, as well as inspire a sense of vitality and devotion so others may not desert." General Washington signed the ledger. "Should you accept, Cogswell's regiment will remain here under Putnam's command. Are there any objections to the terms I offer?"

"None, sir."

"I ask you to sign here, Captain Howlett."

George scribbled his name onto the page. Unfortunate, he must remain in New York City with Old Put and his vapid commands, but at least he'd have the title of captain over Cogswell's regiment.

"You have carte blanche with your recruitment...Boston's poisoned medicines worked nicely," Washington added with a wink. "Good day to you, Captain."

"Thank you, sir." George stood and bowed, then stepped from the tent. He'd not made it six feet from Washington's quarters when a courier found him.

"Sergeant Howlett, a letter for you, sir."

"'Tis Captain Howlett now," he barked, and snatched the letter. As he walked back to where he'd left Samuel, he broke the unfamiliar seal and read the familiar script. He stopped midstride. "Well, I'll be damned." George ran toward the campfire around which Samuel and Bartlett sat. Both tended to an iron pot swinging over open flame.

"Howlett, what is it, man?" Samuel asked. "Did Washington tell ye t' move on t' Harlem?"

George laughed, a sense of elation coursing through him. "I was promoted to captain of our militia, but this letter far outweighs anything Washington could've told me."

"Well, what be it, *Captain?*" Samuel snickered. "A letter from that doxie, Dobby, ye been strummin' these two days?"

"A letter, indeed." Grinning, George handed Samuel the note. "'Tis from Jack. My cousin is alive."

"The one who drowned in the shipwreck?" Bartlett asked.

"I can't understand how—he's written quite the tale—but he's alive, and in Philadelphia at Congress with my uncle."

"Perkins lives!" Samuel finished reading, then met George's gaze. "Will ye write t' Abigail, then?"

"Surely she knows her brother is alive," George said, retrieving the letter. He folded and stuffed it into his waist-coat pocket.

"I wouldn't be too certain," Bartlett replied.

"Ye should write t' her," Samuel said.

It would give him reason, that was certain—and he'd

promised he would write. *But is it too late after all this time? She will be incensed by my negligence. She'll think I stopped caring for her.* But it was no matter. Jack lived, and whether Abigail already knew it or not, he would write to tell her; this reason was better than any. He would write of his promotion, and that he meant to remain in New York City with Old Put. With his advancement, and Jack being alive, George's hope for the cause was restored.

"I can recruit Perkins." George removed his canteen of rum. "Sluice your gob, rogues. To Jack."

Bartlett and Samuel raised their tin cups.

"To Jack." They saluted.

20

JACK

TOPSFIELD, SEPTEMBER 1776

A FTER TWO DAYS ON horseback, Jack's leg quivered. He rested a moment within the stable and removed the letter from his mother. He re-read her frantic script:

12 August 1776
Topsfield

Dearest husband and Jack,
My Heart braykes to wryte these words.
I've receeved a Letter from General Burgoyne,
and he has informed us that Oliver has Perished
in Battle. He was Our son, John. Jack, he was
you Brother. The Girls are devastated, and
Andrew is being Strong for each of us. Please,
if you may, make Hayste home. We need you
Here.

Yours &c,
Bette

Jack stuffed his mother's letter into his waistcoat pocket. Father was at least a three days' drive away, having taken the carriage home. *My leg would've preferred the carriage ride.* As he limped to the front door of his family's home, he removed his bauta mask and placed it into his haversack. The late summer trees, ready to burst with autumn color, swayed in the September wind. Above, dark storm clouds swirled, a buttress to the grave news he carried.

Susan ran outside. "Jack," she cried. "Jack's home!"

He scooped his sister into an embrace and kissed her cheek. "How's my favorite girl? You've grown since last I saw you. Are you well?"

"I am."

He set her down. "How does Mother? Jane and Tommy?"

Susan grimaced. "Janey's in bed. Mamma and Mercy have been by her side most of the time, but Mamma is sad. I've been helping Dottie with Charlotte."

Jack knelt before her. "Are you sad, too, Susie? Wish you to talk about it?"

Her blonde curls bobbed as she shook her head, though she sulked.

She's an image of Abigail. Jack kissed her freckled cheek, then hurried inside the house, Susan trailing behind him. The scent of his mother's rose and bergamot perfume filled the air.

"Mother," he called.

Andrew entered the foyer. "Brother, you've returned."

Jack clutched him. "This is all too much. I can hardly believe it."

"Nor I." Andrew led him into the parlor, where he handed Jack the clay pipe he'd been smoking.

Jack sipped on the end until a wisp of tobacco smoke lifted from the piece. After he exhaled, he asked, "Are you well?"

"As well as can be, given the circumstances. It feels like we've only just received word from Burgoyne's army about Ollie, but I think 'tis been closer to three weeks. Mother wrote you and Father as rapidly as she could."

Jack hung his head. "Father regrets he couldn't ride. His carriage should have him home by Thursday. How did this happen? Was there any indication of how Ollie came to...fall in battle?"

"No. Only that there had been a battle at *Trois-Rivières*, and Ollie took a ball to his chest."

Jack pinched his nose to stave off the tears. *Oliver is dead. My brother.* "I had much unresolved with him."

Andrew's hand found Jack's shoulder. "I know."

Had I known when I escaped HMS Lively *I'd never again meet Ollie...*Jack shook his head, unable to complete the thought. "How fares Jane?" His poor sister-in-law, who'd helped him escape imprisonment, who aided him during the dark days of laudanum, now, too, faced widowhood.

"She's not well. She's in mourning."

In light of Oliver's untimely death, the anticipation of seeing Jane flooded him with guilt; he could hardly confide in Andrew of their charade back in June. Nauseated, Jack made his way up the stairs and down the hall.

Mother closed Jane's door as he approached. "Jack, darling." She threw herself at him and kissed his cheek. "Thank God you've come."

"How are you?"

"Not well." Her voice wavered, "I've lost a son. I thought I lost one in springtime, but you've come back to me. Now, I've lost another. 'Tis a lot for my heart to handle."

"Maybe Ollie is alive, yet."

"I pray. I pray the dispatch is wrong, but how could they mistake him? 'Twas signed and sealed by General Burgoyne himself." Mother dried her tears. "Ollie wasn't perfect, I know that, but he was my son."

Before now, Jack hadn't noticed the creases etched into the corners of her eyes, her thinning lips, or the worry lines carved into her forehead. *Mother has aged much this past year.*

She gestured to the chamber door. "Be delicate with Janey, but I know she'll be glad to see you."

Jack held his breath and opened the door. Jane sat in the canopied bed, propped by two pillows. Her white chemise and bedding blended with her ivory face; her long dark hair flowed in shiny ribbons over her bosom.

She turned toward him. "Jack."

He went to her and clasped her chilled, slight hands. "I'm so very sorry."

"Thank you. I know you and Ollie were at odds, but he was your brother. I'm grieved you lost him, too."

"There's much I wished to reconcile with him." Jack averted his stare to their hands. "Are you in good health, at least?"

"I'm tired, and I suffer the heartache of loss. Tommy is well, at least." A tear rolled down her cheek, and she rubbed it away before he could.

"The boy will be a reminder of the love you and my brother shared."

"It does me good to see you at last." Jane's eyes closed, and a river flowed down her face. Jack's heart swelled for her. Such grief he understood all too well.

"Oh, I deserve this pain," Jane sobbed.

He sat beside her. "Whyever would you believe that? You've not been so terrible a person as to deserve widowhood with a small child."

She sniveled. "I was unfaithful to my husband."

His throat tightened with culpability, but he summoned strength for her, as she had for him during his first days of mourning. "Aye, something we're both guilty of. But we can't alter the past. 'Twas a mistake we'll never make again. We can atone for our sins, Jane. I swear it."

Jane reached for a handkerchief and dried her eyes. "Oh, I'm a fool."

"Tell me." The instant the words left his mouth, he regretted it.

"I'm with child."

His face and body iced, and an acidic burning erupted in his throat. "I beg your pardon?"

She threw her arm over her face and sobbed. "Please don't loathe me, Jack. I meant not for it to happen."

"How long have you known?"

"Since I missed my monthlies."

He rubbed his temples. "We were intimate in June. You must be...at least three months along. You said you couldn't get with child so long as you nursed Tommy."

"I guess 'twas an old wives' tale. I never got in the family way with Lieutenant—"

Then it is true, she lay with that fiend Lieutenant Dickens to help free me. Jack clutched her hand tighter.

Jane studied their grasp for a moment. "When Annie and I were little girls, I tried to make her like me. I tried teaching her French, and how to dance a minuet. But all she wished to do was fire George's fowler. And I grew to resent it. The older we became, the more I saw her as a rival than a sister—particularly after we were acquainted with you and your family. I didn't want her out in Society...not because I thought she'd humiliate me, but because I knew her wit would outshine my beauty; that somehow, she'd capture your heart." Jane started to sob again. "And she did. So much that you married her instead of me."

He quaked, hearing her words. He'd never spoken with Jane of their broken engagement, that perhaps she truly did fancy him more than Oliver. "Jane, I never meant to break your heart, but I can't change the past, nor how my heart chose to love. Have you a desire to confess your sins and mine to the reverend?"

"No." Jane wiped her leaking face on a handkerchief. "When I'm no longer in mourning, your mother wishes for us to marry."

He started. "She knows about this child?"

"Yes, but not that 'tis yours. Jack, I had to tell her I was in the family way. I was beginning to show and could only lace my stays so tight."

"She believes the child belongs to Ollie?"

"Yes, I told her we lay together before escaping HMS *Lively*." She appraised him, pouting. "You look troubled."

Jack grimaced. "Of course, I'm troubled. My brother's dead, and I just learned I impregnated his wife by means of adultery...as though the infidelity weren't burdensome enough."

"I've never known such despair until now," she replied. "But 'tis strange how fate should align itself as 'twas meant to. We shall be married as was arranged."

Jack's neck heated with a burst of anger. "My brother is not even laid to rest, and you talk of marrying me." He stood. "Madam, good night."

"Your mother suggested it, not I."

He rubbed his temples. "I feel as though I'm reliving the

charades of last autumn, but this time the babe actually is mine." Jack wandered to the window and peered outside. A great gust rustled the leaves on the trees, scattering a few from their branches. The clouds would burst any moment; a late summer storm.

"'Tis the correct thing to do, Jack. We're both widowed. And my children will be fatherless. In this arrangement, we may both atone for our sins..."

"How unlucky for us to have survived such short marriages." He continued staring at the darkness overtaking the grounds of his father's estate. Beyond the property, the narrow lane to Annalisa's house faded beneath black storm clouds. *I was supposed to end my days an old man with Annalisa beside me. Not Jane.*

Overwhelmed by the disastrous turn of events, in tandem with the guilt of impregnating his late brother's wife, he muttered, "Our misdeeds led us to this path, and now we must live with the consequences. I only pray that Oliver and Annie rest peacefully...and they forgive us."

Jane sat upright. "Think on it, Jack, please. You're my best chance for a husband. What other gentleman of good breeding will take me as I am, widowed with one child, and another on the way? This babe within me is yours—"

He turned from the window. "But no one knows 'tis mine. You told my mother 'tis Ollie's."

"Yes, to save us both from the shame of adultery."

Jack returned to the bed and sat on the edge. "We've created an impossible predicament, Jane, you and I. I could've been a loving uncle to Tommy, and supported you as my widowed sister-in-law, but now, you carry my child...but you're telling me no one can know 'tis my child, yet you wish to marry me." Head shaking, he rose from the bed. "I'm ill thinking on it, because you're right; no man of good breeding will take you as you are. And you're carrying my child, Jane. *My child*. What other option have we?"

Jane's face lifted. "Then you're agreeable to the nuptials?"

"'Tis the last thing I wish for myself. I'll never stop loving Annalisa, but have I another choice?"

"I swear it, Jack. When we're married, we'll tell our families about the child...that you're the true father."

"Why not hold ourselves accountable, now? The deed is done. Let's face the ridicule and be done with it."

Jane shook her head. "No...we can't. Not yet. Society expects me to grieve Ollie, which I do...then we may marry. After the birth, when Society has perhaps lost time of when Ollie perished, we may reveal the nature of this child's fathering."

Jack's hair rose at her devotion to Society. "Damn Society. I care little for what they think—"

"A man may father as many bastards as he likes. But not a lady. Ladies have reputations to uphold, and I'm asking this of you. Please, Jack. I lay with Lieutenant Dickens for you, to help us abscond from HMS *Lively*. Now, I'm asking you to do this for me."

His chest bloated with conviction. It was true, she'd upheld her position in their plan, though he never intended for her to lie with anyone, save for Oliver, her rightful husband. Nonetheless, she was the keystone to their escape, and she'd comforted him well during his first days of convalescence. Despite his screeching scruples, perhaps he was bound to accommodate her and abide her wishes, for now.

21

ANNALISA

ESSEX HOUSE, LONDON, OCTOBER 1776

ANNALISA AND ABIGAIL SPRAWLED on a blanket in the gardens of Essex House. The summery scents of honeysuckle had vanished, leaving only cool, dry wisps of sweet autumn leaves. Louisa, Abigail's daughter, clung to Annalisa's bosom. Her heart ached for the lovely girl at her breast, and for the children she'd hoped to conceive with Jack. Sarah mentioned she'd bled much shortly after they'd found her. *I thought I was with child when we set sail. Had it been another miscarriage?*

Louisa reached for the necklace at Annalisa's throat.

"No, no. Naughty girl." Annalisa chuckled, and unwound Louisa's fingers from the *wampum* feather.

"She loves to pull my hair these days," Abigail said. "The viscount is especially amused when she grabs his wig."

Annalisa and Abigail giggled at the image of Lord Essex losing his wig to his tiny daughter's hands. Louisa was not yet six months but was growing into herself. She stared up at Annalisa with brilliant green eyes. *Just like George.*

"Abigail, have you heard from anyone from my family? I've written as well and have heard nothing."

Her friend's gaze lowered. "I've not."

Annalisa quirked a brow. "Not even George?"

Abigail fiddled with the deck of cards, splaying them over the blanket upon which they sat. "Well, I did write him—when we discovered you."

"And?"

"And when Louisa was born."

Annalisa glanced about the garden for loitering servants. Satisfied they were alone, she whispered, "Louisa is not the viscount's, is she?"

Abigail wavered. "No. She's not."

Annalisa's heart skipped. "Oh, Abbie. How did this happen?"

"I don't know." Abigail's face and neck flushed, and her face contorted as though she would cry.

"Shh." Annalisa reached for her. "Peace, dear friend. All will be well. Pray, what happened?"

Abigail released a long breath as she ran her hands over her yellow bodice. "George and I were...together...several times before he left for Boston last August. Before I was married. And I did nothing to protect myself." She adjusted her shoulders back and jutted her chin. "I loved him, you know."

Saddened by her friend's arranged marriage, and the child born of a different father than she ought, Annalisa asked, "Think you Lord Essex suspects?"

Abigail adjusted her straw hat against the October breeze. "Charles holds her less. Often, he remarks, *'how came this child by such green eyes and black hair?'.*" She lifted Louisa from Annalisa's arms. "'Tis obvious, Annie. Neither of us boasts such features."

"Then you don't deny it?"

"I do. I tell him my father's hair, before it greyed, was chestnut brown, like Jack's."

Annalisa recalled Jack's long, smooth locks, tied with black ribbon at his nape. *How handsome he is. Was.* She blinked against the onslaught of tears threatening to burst, and focused on George, who, as far as she knew, still lived. Her brother's long, inky hair was unlike any of her other siblings'. In this, he was most unlike them—a trait he'd inherited from his natural father, Captain Bixby.

Abigail continued, "I tell Charles my mother's mother, my grandmother Bixby—Louisa's namesake—had green eyes. I'd only met her but once when I was a child, but I remember her eyes." She studied Annalisa. "Eyes quite like yours. Pray, how came you by such a color when you and George share only your mother? I remember your mamma's as icy blue, like Jane's and William's."

"She does. But my father's mother was Agawam. Papa said her eyes were forest green, that I resemble her most."

"Then we've both green-eyed grandmothers." Abigail smiled, then looked toward her great stone mansion. "Charles can't refute what I say, and for that, I'm thankful." She paused. "But I've reason to suspect he's not the man he says he is."

A gust of chilly air lifted the hat from Annalisa's head. She bristled as she grabbed it, though was unsure if it was the breeze, or her friend's ominous conjecture, puckering her skin.

"Whatever do you mean?"

Abigail removed two letters from her pocket. "I've been meaning to show you these for weeks but could never find the time to steal them from Charles's desk." She unfolded the pages and handed them to Annalisa, who scrutinized the broken seal.

"The Prime Minister?"

"Yes. Lord North."

"Why is Lord Essex in correspondence with Lord North?" Annalisa asked. "The Prime Minister is not a Whig."

"It says here," Abigail reached for the second letter and read, *"My old friend, I will do whatever you ask of me, so long as I have your support in Parliament."* She scoffed. "Is it not clear enough? North is vying for Charles's support in Parliament."

Annalisa bit her lip. "In my time at Devonshire House, I learned from the duke's Whig Party dinners, Lord North is wildly unpopular these days. Perhaps he's merely trying to gain votes by whatever means possible."

"La!" Abigail groaned. "But why write to Charles? Think you 'tis possible North's written similar letters to other Whigs? Think you the Duke of Devonshire holds a similar note?"

"I know not. The duke is rather taciturn. But I should think Lord North, a man in danger of losing his popularity, and hence, his position of power, would do anything necessary to secure himself." Annalisa reached for Abigail's hand. "Be not too quick to render your husband a traitor to his party."

Looking quite uncomfortable, Abigail diverted her gaze. "Perhaps you're right. But I've a sour feeling about it."

Annalisa glanced at the house. "Is Lord Essex hunting all day today?"

"Yes."

They both stared at the mansion.

"Care to peruse his study with me?" Abigail asked.

Inside, they dallied on the first floor until the nursemaid ascended the stairs with Louisa, then slipped down the hall.

Abigail led them through a wide, white painted corridor affixed with bronzed sconces, until she reached Lord Essex's study. She lifted the latch and closed the door behind them. With floor to ceiling windows and white bookcases, natural light bathed the space in unusual brightness, far unlike the dark mahogany study Annalisa had imagined it to be.

"I'll search his desk if you look through that ledger," Abigail said.

Annalisa took the large leather book from his desk to an oak Windsor chair and sat, setting the tome on her lap. She flipped through the pages, all of which had written numbers upon them. "These are his accounts." Her brows knit. "Wish you to know the expenditure of his estate and finances?"

"No. Charles assures me I may buy whatever I like—"

"He's in debt." Annalisa looked up to meet her friend's anxious stare.

Abigail, seated at the desk, faced her. "I beg your pardon?"

Annalisa rose from the chair and took the ledger to the desk. "Look, his account can barely afford this house. Pray, who is his bookkeeper, his estate manager?"

"La!" Abigail cupped her mouth. "Whatever could he be spending his money on? He's assured me countless times... how could I have been so foolish?"

"Don't be too harsh on yourself." Annalisa returned to her chair. "How could you have known? He probably wishes not to worry you." She read another page and scratched her head. "But he may have to let this house. I can't see how you can continue living beyond your means."

"Let the house?" Abigail looked as though she would weep. Frantically, she reached for another letter from the pile upon the desk. "This estate has been in his family for hundreds of years...Mr. Darby has been the estate manager since Charles's father was alive. I can't imagine he'd lead

Charles astray." She unfolded another letter, and her gaze darted across the page. Her face grew wan.

"Abbie, what is it?"

The page wavered in Abigail's hands. "A letter from George."

Annalisa rose from her seat. "What does it say?"

"He wrote of his position within the Continental Army." With a wistful upturn of her lips, added, "He's a captain now... they're in New York." Her hand flew to her mouth. "Zounds!"

"You frighten me. What is it?"

Abigail's eyes rounded with disbelief, and she whispered, "Jack's alive."

❧ 22 ❧

ANNALISA

ESSEX HOUSE, LONDON, OCTOBER 1776

ANNALISA GRIPPED THE DESK as the room spun. She pulled the letter from Abigail's trembling hands and read. It was George's handwriting. Annalisa read and re-read her brother's script as she paced before the desk.

"My God. How? When was this letter received? George dated it for August. Why would Lord Essex withhold such information from you?" Annalisa looked up from the note. "From me? We must write home at once."

"I know nothing. But, Annie, this is our chance...the perfect opportunity for us to let the house and return to Massachusetts. Charles can't refuse. I won't let him." Abigail reached for Annalisa. "We'll reunite you with your husband."

A trembling joy replaced the leaden darkness of loss, and Annalisa's breathing slowed. She ran her thumb over the sapphire ring on her finger. "Jack lives. I can hardly believe it."

"I'll speak to Charles tonight," Abigail said.

"How? We're to Vauxhall this evening."

"It matters not. Charles will listen. He'll book us passage on a ship to take us home—"

"No." Annalisa circled the desk and gripped Abigail's shoulders. "He'll know we've been in his study. We must be tactful. Perhaps we could confide in Georgiana. Mayhap the duke could suggest traveling to America, or letting the house..." Annalisa threw up her hands. "Oh, Abbie, I know not how to approach the subject, either."

"I think you have the duchess's ear. She'd listen to you and help," Abigail replied. "Her husband is one of the most powerful men in England. If Charles listened to any man, it would be the Duke of Devonshire."

"Aye, but you know not the relationship the duke has with Georgiana. I've seen it—his indifference toward her is alarming. I'm convinced he must be the only man in England not besotted by his wife."

"Then we'll find a way to divulge this information to Georgiana. She could influence Mr. Fox, or some other Whig in Parliament who could persuade Charles." Abigail anxiously gathered the letters. "We must do *something*!"

"And we shall. But we must be rational and practical. Any sudden outburst or display of emotion will set off the viscount." Annalisa stared hard at her friend until Abigail met her gaze. "Yes?"

Her friend nodded. "I will control myself. You have my word."

"As much as I wish to be in Jack's arms this instant, the rush to return mustn't be made in haste. Jack's alive." Annalisa beamed, and she embraced Abigail. "Oh, he's alive! 'Tis all I need to know until we formulate a design. For all we know, Lord Essex received this letter and has a plan for us to sail back by the New Year. We mustn't discredit him yet." Annalisa pulled from Abigail and startled at her friend's grave stare. "What is it? Do you not agree?"

Abigail bit her lip. "The letter was addressed to me, Annie."

⚜

DRESSED TO THE NINES WITH ABIGAIL AND LORD ESSEX, Annalisa strolled through the lush Vauxhall Gardens. Little crimson berries dotted the green hawthorn hedge lining the pathways, and yellow and orange trees swayed in the chilled evening air. Sweet aromas of autumn flowers and fallen leaves left Annalisa yearning for her family's farm, now, perhaps, within reach.

A melodious reprieve of horns and strings distracted her from the unsatisfied sensibility of missing home.

"The orchestra." Annalisa turned to Abigail with girlish enthusiasm. "'Tis Haydn's newest symphony, number sixty-one in D major."

Abigail regarded her husband. "My lord, may we go to it?"

"Yes, of course," Lord Essex said with a chuckle. "But first we must meet the rest of our party."

They glided through the gardens to a main portico where they joined the Duke and Duchess of Devonshire, Lord and Lady Melbourne, and Lord and Lady Jersey. In the distance, the orchestra already concluded the first movement, the *vivace*.

"Your Grace, how good to see you." Annalisa curtsied for Georgiana and the duke.

The duchess linked arms with Annalisa and turned from their party. "You're looking well, Calais."

Fond of the nickname she'd initially disliked, Annalisa smiled, as it now reminded her of the devoted care she'd received at Devonshire House.

"Is Sarah well?" Annalisa asked.

The duchess nodded. "She is."

The ladies left the gentlemen behind and walked along the lantern-lit pathways.

"'Tis a good night for a *dark walk*," Lady Jersey said. Her unblinking eyes glimmered in the evening twilight.

"Ah. And who shall be the lucky gentleman?" Lady Melbourne asked.

"I've my eye set on the Earl of Carlisle," Lady Jersey muttered. "When last we met, he was as clay between my hands."

"Not a difficult feat for Lord Carlisle," Georgiana replied with a giggle.

The ladies laughed, and Annalisa fell behind with Abigail.

"Lady Jersey speaks like a mule in heat," Abigail whispered. "Think you the duchess cares for her?"

"Nay. Georgiana says she can hardly stand Lady Jersey," Annalisa replied.

"Tell me, Lady Essex..." Lady Melbourne paused in her walking so they could catch up. "It seems your husband holds quite an interest in Lady Caroline. Who is it you desire to bed?"

Abigail suddenly fell silent.

"Don't be a fool, Lady Essex." Lady Jersey swept an insect from her gown. "Come now. There are hundreds of well-bred, handsome gentlemen present this evening, most of whom can boast a title, each of them with an eye for the dark walk, and none of whom wish to spend it with their wives. Surely, you see *someone* agreeable."

"I suppose I would choose Mr. Fitzherbert," Annalisa blurted, diverting attention from her friend. "He's always been kind to me, and he's hardly unpleasant to look at."

Lady Melbourne replied, "But you're not married, Miss Cavendish—"

"Ah! And there he is," Lady Jersey trilled.

Annalisa flushed, hoping Mr. Fitzherbert hadn't heard what she'd said.

"Why don't you join him, Miss Cavendish." Lady Jersey pushed Annalisa from the well-lit path toward the notoriously unlit pathways, known as the *dark walk*.

"Good evening, ladies." Mr. Fitzherbert wore an evergreen velvet suit in ditto, with a black beaver-felt cocked hat upon his head. He strode toward them with cane in hand. "Miss Cavendish, a pleasure."

"I believe Miss Cavendish would fancy a turn about the dark walk, sir," Lady Jersey said.

Annalisa shook her head. "No, I'd like to hear the orchestra—"

"Then let's to the orchestra." Mr. Fitzherbert held out his arm. He led her from the ladies, and Annalisa turned for Abigail.

"What of Lady Essex? She wished to hear Haydn's symphony as well..."

"They'll follow when they're ready, Miss Cavendish," he replied.

Hesitant, Annalisa let him lead her down a darkened foot-path, arm-in-arm, in undisturbed silence. The music growing fainter behind them, her heart raced, and she dipped her hand into her pocket for the Bunker Hill round. The weight of the little ball reminded her of the strength she'd mustered that day. *I saved Nathaniel.*

They came to a bifurcation, and Mr. Fitzherbert guided them down a narrow stretch, into a small inlet between hedges.

"Where've you taken me, Mr. Fitzherbert? I hear not the orchestra—"

"Miss Cavendish."

A whiff of his amber perfume dizzied her, and the darkness, which obscured his smooth face, full lips, and bright
eyes she knew by daylight, nearly fooled her into believing
Jack was before her. *And his voice is as melodious as Jack's...*

"I know your Christian name, but I came to know you as
Miss Cavendish. Forgive me as I continue to refer to you as
such."

"'Tis quite all right, sir."

"I must admit, I've been rather drawn to your provincial
nature these several months. You're a tantalizing creature
with most refreshing American manners."

She tilted her head, the spell about her, broken. "American
manners?"

"Indeed." His hand slid down her left arm and lifted her
hand. "Your skin is still quite bronzed from summertime.
We've oft contemplated your origins, Miss Cavendish. Pray
tell, are you not fully English?"

Annalisa's skin prickled. "Sir, that is none of your business." These were not the kind words of the gentleman she'd
known since springtime. *Jack would never have commented on
such things...*

His thumb ebbed across her cheek and over the silvery
scar beneath her right eye. "Then will you indulge my
curiosity and divulge where you acquired this?"

She averted her gaze from his. Though she had no reason
to withhold the truth from him, he hadn't earned the right to
learn it either. *But 'tis a part of who I am.* Annalisa cleared her
throat.

"My brother, George, taught me to use a firelock in the
clearing behind my family's farm. One day, I loaded it with
too much gunpowder, and the discharge burned my face."

"Zounds! A farm. Then you're a country lass. This
astounds me. You play the part of a lady quite well." He

laughed. "You even danced a minuet! I daresay, you've fooled us all."

"I beg your pardon? I've tried to fool no one—"

"'Tis no matter." He fused his lips to hers, pulling her close with hungry kisses.

Annalisa found herself in the Perkins's parlor of their Boston home, and it was Oliver's mouth accosting her. Her heart galloped, and she pushed him away.

"How dare you." She slapped him.

Mr. Fitzherbert's eyes rounded with shock as he held his cheek. Before he could speak, Annalisa rushed from the hedgerow, and onto the path. She ran until she met the lantern-lit pathways, and Haydn's orchestrations resounded into the night. Annalisa clawed at her bodice, gasping. *This is Vauxhall, in London.* Boston was thousands of miles away, as was Oliver Perkins, and the assault six years ago. *How odd it should resurface now in such a foreign, unknown place.* Annalisa caught her breath and hurried toward the music, hoping to find Abigail.

"Annie." Her friend hastened from the crowd and embraced her. "Are you all right? What's happened? Where's Mr. Fitzherbert?"

"I'm fine." Annalisa shivered. Never again would she allow any man to treat her as Oliver had, or Mr. Fitzherbert. "We must plan to leave London. I'll ask Gee to help us, in the event Lord Essex fails us." She wound her arm about Abigail's, and advanced toward the crowd listening to the orchestra. The duchess, standing between Ladies Melbourne and Jersey, acknowledged Annalisa with a gleaming eye.

Annalisa straightened her shoulders, and she towered above the three titled ladies. "A word, Your Grace."

"Calais, how was the dark walk?" Georgiana asked with a wink.

"Not what I'd expected, Your Grace. I thought we meant to come here for the music."

The duchess's face fell, and she left her friends. Annalisa and Abigail walked with Georgiana to the outskirts of the audience.

"What is it?" Georgiana asked.

"Abigail and I must return to America. Could you help us?"

The duchess nodded. "Of course. But won't the viscount plan such a journey?"

"My lord is in debt, Your Grace," Abigail replied. "I doubt he could afford passage on any ship."

"I knew not. If there's any way I can help, I've the cheques you may require."

"You're too generous, Your Grace." The way Abigail smoothed her skirts reminded Annalisa of Jane. "The passage will be more than enough. Once we let the house, we'll be able to repay you. At the very least, I may obtain the funds from my father's estate—"

"Nonsense, Lady Essex. Consider it my parting gift to you both." The duchess smiled sadly at Annalisa. "Finding and caring for Calais these months offered me something I didn't know I required."

Annalisa squeezed the duchess's hand. "Thank you, Gee."

❦

WHEN THEY RETURNED TO ESSEX HOUSE, ANNALISA settled in the drawing room at the spinet. Mozart's music flew from her fingertips with joy. With Georgiana's help, they could return to America, and she would see Jack again. *How long has it been since last I held him? Does he believe me dead as well?* She shivered at the thought, despite the roaring fire.

"You've kept us in London long enough, my lord. I think 'tis time for us to return to America. You promised me no longer than a year in England." Abigail's voice carried through the walls.

Annalisa stopped playing.

"Let's into the study to discuss this," Lord Essex replied. "I don't wish for the servants to hear the anger in your tone. You forget yourself."

"I forget myself, sir? What of the secrets you've withheld from me? Have you forgotten those?"

"I've kept no secrets from you," he snapped.

"What of your debt? Is that why you've not bought us passage to America?"

"I'll not be interrogated in my own home."

"Sir, is it true?" Abigail asked.

"You forget your place, young miss—and my business is my own."

"But is it true, my lord? As your wife, you owe me a simple answer."

"As my wife, you're obligated to fulfill your duties to me, in case you've forgotten. A son, and an heir. Why don't you tell *me* the truth—is Louisa mine?"

Annalisa stood from the bench and approached the door. *He's done it, he's asked about Louisa.* She held her breath, awaiting Abigail's answer.

"Of course, she's yours," Abigail cried.

"Lies!" The viscount roared.

"You must book us on the next ship to America, or I will do so myself," Abigail replied.

"Madam, I do not take nicely to demands."

"Is that so, sir? I'll have you know the Duchess of Devonshire will buy us passage. Surely you wouldn't wish to disappoint the duke."

Oh, Abbie, no. Annalisa bit her thumbnail.

"If you so much as accept a shilling from the Duchess of Devonshire, I swear you will never see Louisa again."

Crash. Another door slammed, shaking the one through which Annalisa listened. She waited in the stillness for several minutes before entering the parlor.

Abigail sat on the sofa before the fire, her face in her hands, heaving with each sob. Annalisa rested beside her on the couch and curled her arms about her.

"Shh."

"Heard you the whole thing?" Abigail sniffled.

"The viscount will not take Louisa from you. He cannot."

"But he can. And he will." Abigail mopped her tears. "How can we leave?"

Annalisa pulled Abigail close, so she rested upon her shoulder. "We'll fabricate a plan. I promise. But we mustn't be rash. To act with temerity will be our demise, yes?"

Abigail nodded.

"Tomorrow, you must make amends with Lord Essex. Apologize for the outburst and accusations, and reassure him of your devotion."

"Annie, how? I've offended him so—"

"He's your husband. You must." Annalisa lowered her voice. "And in the meantime, you and I shall scheme of a way home. The duchess is willing to help."

"But what if my lord suspects?" Abigail asked.

Annalisa stroked her friend's hair. "Remember my old friend from Bunker Hill, Benjamin Cavendish?"

Abigail sniffled. "I think so?"

"'Tis time we resurrect him."

❧ 23 ❧

GEORGE

YORK ISLAND, NOVEMBER 1776

"HOLD STILL." GEORGE GRIPPED Dobby's bare buttocks as he concluded a letter to Jack. The curve of her lower back and rear end proved a difficult writing surface, yet a demonstrated abundance on which to clutch when strumming. Yes, the women of New York—and particularly, Dobby—were eager to please; a small consolation for the travesty of battles lost. But as his pen scratched across the page, his thoughts turned to Abigail, lost to Lord Essex and London. He'd not heard from her since she left Boston, though he'd written her at least thrice. Now, he had Dobby to distract him, a brunette from York Island with a buxom apple dumpling shop, who'd attached herself to the fort as a camp-follower.

Dobby squirmed. "You keep poking me with your quill."

"Then hold *still*," he chuckled.

"Aye, Captain."

George signed the letter and tossed it aside to dry. "You're daft to remain in this city."

"I can't leave you," Dobby said with a pout. "How can I

leave you now? The British keep trying to take Fort Washington. Wherever should I go?"

George rolled off his cot, displacing her, and pulled on his
breeches. "Major General Greene is in command of Forts Lee
and Washington—Old Put was sent to Philadelphia—I fear
things will only grow worse."

"But you said Washington was victorious at Harlem." She
pulled a wool blanket over her rounded, voluptuous breasts.
"Surely, you'll be able to keep Fort Washington."

"Not likely." He buttoned his waistcoat. "Kip's Bay was a
disaster. Know you how many militias fled?" *And were injured?*
Samuel lay in a sick tent, wounded from a ball to his arm—
shattered upon impact.

Dobby shook her head.

"Too many." George slid on his coat, retrieved the letter
he'd written to Jack, and folded and sealed it.

"Where are you going?"

"To see Samuel, and hand my letter to the courier." He
gave a playful, exaggerated bow. "By your leave, my lady."

George stepped from the tent and into the grey
November morning. The stronghold—comprised of wooden
palisades and dirt trenches—perched on the tallest mount of
York Island. They'd been able to ward off the Hessians and
British since October, but recent news of Washington's defeat
at White Plains lingered on his mind. *I must recruit. I need
Jack.*

George located the courier and handed him the letter,
then ventured inside the sick tent. He suppressed a gag
against the waft of feculence greeting him at the opening. To
diminish the stench of decaying wounds, George covered his
mouth and nose with his handkerchief.

Samuel lay on a cot in the corner, his arm—the forearm

having been amputated—tucked against his chest by a sling. A light sheen of perspiration covered his dusky forehead.

"Howlett, that be ye?"

"Aye." George knelt beside the cot and offered a cheeky grin. "'Tis Captain Howlett to you, Private." When Samuel didn't laugh, George grimaced. "How fares your arm, old friend?"

Samuel coughed and pulled the wool blanket over him. Though he shivered violently, Samuel's skin burned beneath George's hand. "Th' doc keeps sayin' th' wound be festerin'. Damn th' Bloodybacks. Damn th' militia."

"Rogue, you fought hard at Kip's Bay. Blame not yourself."

For a moment, Samuel's shaking ceased, and he closed his eyes. "What'll ye do with me gone? Will ye write t' Perkins?"

"None of that. You sound like a cock robin." George forced a laugh. "But I did write to Jack. I pray the mail is delivered to him."

"Good. Ye need Perkins." Samuel coughed again, and flecks of blood trickled from his lips. "I'll not make it t' see Christmas."

"Speak not of it." George removed his handkerchief and wiped Samuel's mouth. "We'll get you well enough to flee this place. Hessians and British keep firing on us, but Greene seems to think we can hold them off. He's a fool, like Old Put...and that squeeze crab, Colonel Magaw."

"Aye, Howlett, maybe ye should be in command," Samuel snickered, then elapsed into a fit of coughing. "If this wound won't kill me, 'twill be ye." His light grey eyes, once full of gleaming mischief, now held George's stare with deathly hollowness. "Yer goin' t' command the lot o' them. And the men'll follow ye...ye hulking...gollumpus." Samuel's eyelids drooped, and his mouth relaxed. His breathing slowed, and for a moment, George believed he slept. He clasped

Samuel's icy remaining hand, until his friend's chest no longer rose.

"Wildes?" George's hand slid across Samuel's forehead, but his friend's eyes neither opened, nor lips parted to inhale. "Wildes, come now, you old doxie." He searched for Samuel's pulse. An absent throb. "No, no." George crumpled over Samuel's body. Between silent sobs, he sang, *"But since it fell into my lot that I should rise and you should not, I'll gently rise and softly call, good night and joy be to you..."*

"Captain Howlett, you're required, sir."

George lifted his face from Samuel's body. A soldier, no older than sixteen, stood before him. "What is it, Private?"

"Colonel Magaw reports the British are attacking, sir."

George rubbed his face and jumped up. "Explain yourself, Private."

The private stuttered, "The...the eastern defenses have been overwhelmed by Cornwallis, sir."

"Fie." *Bloodyback bastards!* Before leaving, George kissed Samuel's forehead. "See that Private Wildes is buried at once." He strode from the tent.

A militiaman shouted, "The Hessians are charging!"

George dashed to his tent. Inside, Dobby was already dressed, and packing a brown, leather haversack.

"You must leave. Now."

She glanced up. "I heard. The Hessians are attacking."

"The eastern defense is overwhelmed. Go. Now."

"Where?"

"To Fort Lee, across the river in New Jersey." He studied her a moment. "Either that, or return yourself to the lower part of the island and consider yourself a Loyalist."

Her round face expressionless, Dobby nodded, and fled the tent. Swiftly, George checked his cartridge box and firelock, and left the confines of his tent.

THE DISCHARGE OF MUSKETS AND FOWLERS RESOUNDED A deafening *boom!* Through the clouds of gun-smoke, the British and Hessians advanced.

"Load your firelock," George ordered.

Any well-trained militiaman or soldier could fire three volleys a minute; that was what he'd taught Annalisa when they fired Bixby in the clearing beyond their house. Now, he must set an example with his men.

"Make ready. Fire!"

His militia assaulted again. Still, the Bloodybacks pressed on.

George glanced about the fort for his superior, Colonel Magaw. Only he could give the command to surrender.

"Load and prime, rogues," George ordered. "Make ready. Fire!"

His chest rattled with another eruption of musket-fire.

"Colonel Magaw," George called. "We can't hold them off any longer, sir!"

The colonel appeared through the thick gun-smoke, his chubby face sagging with defeat. "Retreat, men, retreat," the colonel shouted.

George turned to Bartlett, who stood by. "Bartlett, gather as many of our militia as you can. Colonel Magaw is surrendering. Any of us remaining will fall prisoner."

Bartlett rubbed his grime-covered face. "Where will we go, Captain?"

"Across the river to Fort Lee. But I daresay, it won't be for long. Go. Now!"

Bartlett and eight others of their militia dashed toward the river, but Bartlett turned back for George. "Captain Howlett, you're coming with us, no?"

"Aye, I'll be along presently. I need to gather the others of our militia. I'll not abandon them. Now, make haste. 'Tis an order."

His friend delayed a moment, gripping his coat. "Aye, sir." Bartlett fled after the others, down to the river.

George turned his back on the river and hastened through the barracks. "Cogswell's regiment," he hollered. "Cogswell's regiment!"

John and Matthew Whipple, a father and son duo from Ipswich, sped toward him. "Captain Howlett?" the father asked.

"Whipple, I've ordered our militia to cross the river to Fort Lee. Make haste, man. And bring any of ours you see along the way."

John Whipple's harried stare darted across the encampment about to fall to British and Hessians. "Aye, sir."

George ventured deeper into the camp, seeking the rest of his militia. Gun-smoke ebbed through the air, and another round of musket-fire rumbled the barracks.

"Cogswell's regiment," he bellowed over shouts and clamor.

"Halt! Bleib wo du bist."

George started. Three Hessians breeched the redoubt, weapons engaged and aimed at him.

His hand gripped his fowling piece. "Come at me, you dilberries."

"Stay where you are, Provincial." A British officer, presumably a sergeant, joined the Hessians. "This way."

"'Tis Captain Howlett, you Bloodyback bastard." George charged the sergeant. Two Hessians held him back, and the third joined the British officer, laughing.

"My apologies, *Captain* Howlett," the sergeant chuckled. "Militia, I presume? You wear no epaulets, *Captain*."

"Aye, reptile. I'm captain of Cogswell's regiment, per General Washington himself. You'll treat me with the dignity and privilege deserving of a field officer. Is that understood, *Sergeant?*"

The sergeant shifted uncomfortably and glanced behind him. Higher ranking British officers, a colonel and a major, crested the mount, and entered Fort Washington. He nodded. "Yes, Captain, of course. Such are the rules of war, sir."

Though he clenched his jaw, George sighed, somewhat relieved. A prisoner of war, he was destined to one of their prison ships now docked in the harbor, but as a captured officer, he might be offered parole.

❦ 24 ❦

JACK

TOPSFIELD, EARLY DECEMBER 1776

JACK'S FINGERS THRUMMED UPON his wooden escritoire. He stared at the soft snow falling beyond the glass window-panes. Oliver was dead. Jane was with child. Each week, her belly swelled larger than the last, his babe nestled within. The culpability of bedding his brother's wife had been burdensome enough. Now, Oliver having met his end in battle, the accountability proved inescapable. *I've much I wish to say to him, much to atone for.*

Yet, for the first time since losing Annalisa, the innocent life growing within Jane left him hopeful. Despite the war and the year's hardships, come March, he would be a father; there was a chance for a new beginning.

Jack's gaze returned to the letter upon his desk. The bauta mask propped beside it cast an oblong shadow across the page, but George's summons remained legible: *join us, we need men.* Partially obscured by the mask, the words taunted, rekindling his unease for travel. *I must overcome this. I must meet my cousin in New York.* Quinnapin and Weetamoo had already left for New York. Perhaps they were already with George.

He folded the note and stuffed it into his letterbox, along with every letter he'd received from Annalisa. The anniversary of their wedding day had come and gone, as though she'd never been married to him at all. These several weeks since learning of Oliver's death hardly afforded him time to lament the day. *I should fight for you, my darling girl, as you would've had me fight.*

Rising from the chair, Jack made his way to the window. The imperfect glass, embedded with tiny bubbles and wavering patterns, proffered a distorted view of the outside world. His reservations for joining Washington's army proved just as altered. A pang of remorse surfaced as Tommy's screech seeped into his bedchamber from beyond the door. Jack hastened from the room, down the hall, and into the nursery. Tommy's little red face glistened with tears. Wrapping his arms about the boy, Jack lifted him from the cradle.

"There, there, little man." His nephew wailed as though he knew of Jack's plan to leave. "I won't be gone long, I promise." But it wasn't just Tommy he'd abandon; it was his family, and Jane, pregnant with his child.

"Fatherhood suits you."

Jack turned at the voice. His own father stood in the doorway.

"I meant not to startle you." Father stepped into the room. Walking toward them, he peered down at Tommy. "I had many ambitions and dreams as a young man, but I don't think I ever quite knew my purpose on this Earth until you made me a father." He removed his spectacles. "And losing a son...losing a child is something no parent ever wishes to endure. Yet it happens—fevers...illness. As parents, we suppose these things may claim an infant, or young child. But your mother and I were lucky. Healthy births and infancies, each of you. Now, to have one of my grown sons taken is...

well..." His voice trailed to a whisper, "Nothing lessens the pain. It makes me ask God *'why'?*"

Jack chewed his lip. "I ask God why he took Annalisa every day."

Father's hand rested on Jack's shoulder. "'Tis but divine Providence." He looked down at Tommy's face. "Perhaps she met her end because Oliver was meant to leave his children fatherless."

When Jack said nothing, Father added, "You know 'tis the right thing to do. Jane will require a husband. Her children need a father."

"And I could lend my support as their loving uncle," Jack replied, his conscience gutting him. *I wish to be the unborn child's father. I wish for our families to know it.*

"Quite. Jane could remarry, some gentleman of good breeding. Our family and hers could support her until she does, but you stepping into that place eliminates the unknown, and keeps her children safe. We know the sort of gentleman you are, Jack. There's no guarantee Jane may marry a man as kind or honorable as you—a man willing to rear two boys who are not his own."

"'Tis true. I've contemplated the matter much, and I suppose I've no reason to refuse the task now my own wife is gone." The onus for what Jane endured with Lieutenant Dickens in order to free him from prison weighed heavily on him. Wedding her was one way he could atone for his sins, and hers, though it was the last thing he wished to do.

Father's lips formed a tight smile, and he nodded with approval. "There's a good lad."

Jack studied the dark curl of Tommy's lashes, his round, rosy cheeks; he resembled Jane more with each passing day. *Will anyone question her second child as Oliver's?* His jaw tightened with conviction. "I'll marry Jane. 'Tis the honorable thing to do. But I'm leaving for New York."

Father's face reddened. "You wouldn't dare—"

"At four-and-twenty, I'm a widower without children of my own, about to wed my deceased brother's wife and become father to his children. Sir, I can, and shall, do as I please."

"'Tis hardly the appropriate time—"

"Sir, there will never be an appropriate time. Now is the correct time."

۞

New York

AN EARLY WINTER DRIZZLE SATURATED JACK'S WOOL CLOAK, and his skin puckered against the frigid wetness. Droplets dripped onto his bauta mask from his cocked hat. He'd ridden long days, stopping only thrice along the highway through Connecticut to feed and water his horse, before crossing into New York.

The low winter sun dwindled as he neared York Island. The surrounding land, grey with barren trees, teemed with British and German Hessians. *Has the fort fallen?* Old fears seized him, and his grip on the reins tightened. *How am I to cross without being discovered?* On the eastern side of the river, across from the northern end of the island, Jack arrived at a checkpoint at King's Bridge. A Redcoat held out his hand.

"Your papers, sir. And remove your mask."

"My name is Mr. Bixby, sir, and I cannot remove the mask...I've pox upon my face. I have no papers, sir. I'm just a man traveling to New Jersey and must first cross to York Island."

"What is your purpose in New Jersey?" The Redcoat's

pointed jaw jutted as he peered at Jack from beneath his black cocked hat rimmed in white.

"I'm visiting an old friend who is taken ill with dropsy. His wife wrote me—"

"No one crosses the river to York Island without papers."

Jack went to spin the signet ring that had been absent from his finger for months, which now lay in some grave upon his brother's rotting finger. *Cursed Redcoats.*

"I understand, sir. Orders from Howe, yes? I assure you, I'm no spy. I'm no rebel; just a man who wishes to see his friend before God takes him. Can you please let me cross, sir?"

The private glanced at his peer beside him, another Redcoat with somber face to match the algid December day.

"No."

His anger rising, Jack clenched the reins. "Good day to you, sirs." He turned his horse and trotted back up the road, away from the bridge. *New York has clearly fallen. Is George even within the town?* He could continue riding north, and cross into New Jersey by way of the Hudson at Peekskill, but he needed to uncover where Washington's army had gone. Surely, they escaped York Island to New Jersey, but he needed to be certain.

As daylight waned, Jack rode to the nearest establishment —The Running Fox Inn. There, he paid for a room, and to stable and feed his horse for the night. Inside the murky tavern, Jack sat by a window through which the sky beyond faded from navy to black. If only Quinnapin and George were seated beside him. *If only I wasn't alone amongst these Loyalists.*

A potboy served the tankard and mince pie he'd ordered. The bauta mask, positioned away from his mouth and chin by design, allowed him to sip the brown ale. Refreshed by the smoothly fermented hops, Jack bit into the pie. Savory juices dripped down his hand. Promptly, he dabbed away the mess on his chin.

"They make a good pie, don't they, sir?"

Jack glanced toward the voice. A man no older than he, with russet hair tied into a queue, and skin still freckled from summertime, stood from his table. He boasted a green velvet coat and riding boots.

"Aye, sir. I've not had one this good since Portsmouth."

"New Hampshire?"

"Aye. My cousin's inn makes the best mince pies." With no one to make an introduction, Jack gestured to the seat across from him. "Care you to join me, sir?"

"Thank you." The man gave a gentlemanly bow before sitting. "Captain Fleming, at your service, sir."

Jack replied, "Pleased to make your acquaintance. I'm John Bixby."

"What brings you to New York from New Hampshire, Mr. Bixby?" Captain Fleming motioned for the potboy to bring him a tankard of ale. "And why the mask?"

"It covers my pox, sir."

Captain Fleming's nose wrinkled.

"My friend's taken ill with dropsy," Jack continued. "I'm trying to cross the river to York Island. I've had a hard time of it though—there's a checkpoint at the bridge, and I've no papers."

Captain Fleming pursed his lips. "Sounds about right. Washington's army fled through New Jersey. We've secured the area from rebel forces."

Jack sat forward in his chair. "That is good to hear, sir. Pray, when did we overtake the city?"

"End of November, I believe. We've captured over two thousand rebel prisoners, so I heard. They plan on paroling the officers, though."

Jack bristled at the news but gave a satisfied nod. *George might be among those officers. I need to get to the island.*

Captain Fleming raised the tankard left for him by the potboy and clicked his tongue. "'Tis a shame, the state of our colonies." He sipped his drink, belched, then rested the tankard upon the table. "Have you a wife? Children?"

"I've three children at home, and a lovely wife, my Anna— the great-niece of the late governor, Benning Wentworth." He smirked, satisfied to be hidden behind the bauta mask. *Quite the masquerade I've conjured for my loyalist life.*

"A lucky man you are, Mr. Bixby." Captain Fleming smirked. "I've a small sloop. I'd be glad to sail you to York Island. Wouldn't sit well with me if your friend met God before you got to say good-bye to him."

Jack's spirits lifted for a moment. "I would be in your debt, sir—"

"I insist. We brothers must have allies in all corners of the colonies." Captain Fleming scratched his patchy side-whiskers. "If I take you to York Island, I only ask that if we meet again, we meet as Loyalist brethren."

Jack nodded and held out his hand. "Aye, sir."

They shook.

Captain Fleming finished his ale, then stood. "I'll meet you here at dawn, Mr. Bixby."

⚜

AT DAWN, JACK FOLLOWED CAPTAIN FLEMING DOWN TO the water, where his single-masted sloop diligently rocked against the pier. When they were on board, Jack tied his horse to the mast, and assisted Fleming with releasing the sails.

"You've a bit of a limp, Bixby." Captain Fleming's brows

creased with concern. "Were you injured on your long ride? I've something I can bandage your leg with—"

"That won't be necessary, sir, thank you. But yes, 'twas injured along the King's Highway in Connecticut."

The ship swayed into the sparkling Hudson. Though the sun had climbed higher into the sky, the wintry air remained quite chilled. On either side of the river, trees, stripped of their late autumn crowns, clung to sparse brown leaves. Snow would soon blanket that wilderness, and quiet the earth. *How fast time passes. 'Twas only a year ago Annalisa and I witnessed Abigail wed Lord Essex, and Jane marry Oliver.*

Once they were well into the middle of the river, Captain Fleming asked, "Pray tell, Bixby, what is your friend's name?"

"James. James Cochin," Jack replied. *How readily I'm able to lie. Am I despicable?*

At the wheel, Captain Fleming's reddish hair appeared dull against the cloudy skies. As the sloop rounded the northern tip of York Island, Jack watched the New Jersey shore for Fort Lee, overtaken by British troops. He shuddered at the thought of thousands of Continental soldiers, now prisoners within the very encampments they meant to hold. Men like his cousin. *I must find George.*

"Bixby, how'd you meet your wife? You mentioned she's the great-niece of..."

"The late governor...Benning Wentworth." Jack paused, checking his story. "New Hampshire's governor."

"Who is governor in New Hampshire now?"

"'Tis...another Wentworth." His mind drew a blank, and his palms moistened. "John Wentworth. My apologies, sir, I'm not as sharp as usual. I've not been the same since the pox. Truly, I'm blessed my wife and daughters have abided the slowness of my mind."

Captain Fleming left the wheel to adjust the sails. He peered at Jack, squinting against the grey clouds. "No sons?"

"One son. And three daughters."

"Forgive me," Captain Fleming cocked his head, "I thought you said you had three children."

Jack's face heated behind the mask. "I do. Three daughters by my Anna. My son was born to me out of wedlock—before I met and married my wife."

Captain Fleming gave a cheeky grin. "Aye, we've all one of those, don't we." He slapped Jack's back and continued to adjust the sails.

"And what of you, Fleming?"

The captain heaved a jovial belly-laugh. "Not married. I did leave a girl back in Rhode Island, before I commissioned a voyage to Europe."

Jack's sensibility heightened, followed by a relative unease. "What voyage was that?"

"February, I was to sail to France—or so I thought. She was a lovely barque, the *Liberté*. This sloop's nothing compared to her."

Unable to breathe, Jack's fist tightened around a rope. "You were captain of that ship?"

"Aye. My father commandeered her from a Frenchman in Quebec during the last war." Captain Fleming scowled. "'Twas a horrible winter storm that wrecked her and nearly all on board. In truth, we never meant to make it to France. The British bought me out. For hefty coin, I couldn't refuse. I was instructed to sail to Halifax instead. The fatal mistake, I'm afraid. Not worth the pounds in the end."

Fort Washington, perched on the island's tallest mount, drew closer. At the wheel, Captain Fleming stood with his back to Jack. *I should kill him, murder the man who bargained life for money, and captained the ship that took Annalisa's life.* His skin burned despite the chilly December wind, and before he could reconsider, lunged for one of the ropes. He flung it over Fleming, yanking him to the deck. The captain swung, his fist clipping Jack's chin. The bauta mask flew from his face, and Jack wrestled the rope around the captain's body, positioning it over his neck. Fleming's cheeks transformed from crimson to a light shade of purple.

"Release...me," Captain Fleming choked. "Please."

In a brief moment of clarity, Jack dragged the captain to the helm and tied him to the mast, beside his horse. Contented Fleming was thoroughly secured, he loosened the rope about the captain's neck, and made his way to the wheel.

Fleming coughed. "Why, you've not the pox. Your face is as pretty as a dame's."

"Aye, so my wife told me. We're headed to Fort Washington, where you're going to help me free my cousin."

"I knew you were a rebel lout," Captain Fleming sneered.

"A rebel lout who commandeered your sloop, reptile. You'll either help me find my cousin, or I'll toss you overboard by the rope about your neck."

❧ 25 ❧

JACK

YORK ISLAND, NEW YORK, DECEMBER
1776

THEY DROPPED ANCHOR AFTER sunset in a small undisclosed cove just north of Fort Washington. With Captain Fleming bound in rope, they descended the sloop and waded in the frigid water to shore.

"Fie! This is freezing," Fleming gasped.

"Shut your potato trap," Jack hissed, though he shivered.

They continued onto the river-bank, and trudged south through dried brush, toward the fort. A narrow road snaked beyond the bushes, and Jack followed the lane, his wet clothes stiffening in the cold air. His bauta mask upon the sloop, Jack's breath puffed into white clouds. Anxiety piqued his nerves. *Am I daft? What am I to do once we arrive at the fort? I pray Lieutenant Dickens remains upon his wretched vessel.*

"You there. State your name."

A Redcoat blocked the path.

Jack's heart pounded. *What would George do?* He summoned his strength and, with Captain Fleming in tow, barreled toward the private, knocking him to the hardened earth. Jack swung at the soldier's chin, rendering him unconscious. With the rope binding Captain Fleming tied to Jack's wrist, he quickly undressed the private, and shed his frozen clothes for the uniform.

"Red is rather becoming on you, Bixby," Fleming snickered.

Jack hauled the Redcoat from the road. "Another word from you—"

"You should've left me aboard the sloop."

"And risk you breaking free, only to abandon me on this godforsaken island? I think not." Jack yanked the rope, secured the tie through Fleming's mouth, and dragged him toward the barracks.

A sergeant neared. "Private, have you orders to take this prisoner?"

"Yes, sir. He's a captain with the Continental Army," Jack replied. "Sir, please show me the way to the imprisoned officers—I've not been informed where they're kept."

"Officers are within the barracks, Private. All others have been transferred to the prison ships in the harbor."

To Jack's surprise, the sergeant said little else, and led them inside the fortification. Jack followed a long corridor lit by lanterns until the sergeant stopped outside a locked wooden door.

"In here." The sergeant removed a set of keys and unlocked the latch.

Stepping inside the dingy cell, Jack held his breath. A solitary lantern swung from its hold, illuminating unknown faces caked in filth. When he could hold his breath no longer, the fetid stench, reminiscent of his cell aboard HMS *Lively,* assaulted him and he coughed. A chill ebbed up his spine. *Focus, Jack. And breathe.*

"Well, I'll be damned."

Jack turned at the familiar bass, his spirits vibrating.

George sat in a corner, his face and hands soiled with dirt, his clothes encrusted in mud. Jack grimaced at the miserable sight of his fearless cousin, reduced to a scrap of prison trash.

"I...I've information," Jack announced, avoiding his cousin's anxious stare. "'Tis been decided by...General Howe... officers shall be granted parole."

The officers within the gaol stood, their murmurs growing in intensity. The Redcoat beyond the door popped inside the cell.

"What's this, Private? I was not informed—"

"'Tis orders from General Howe, squeeze crab," George bellowed. He jumped from the squalid ground and hastened toward the door, the other officers crowding behind him.

Jack hauled Captain Fleming toward the front. "Gentlemen, if you please, come this way." He led them from the cell and, with George, seized the sergeant, tossing him inside gaol and locking the door.

"Hurry, gentlemen," Jack said. "And quietly." He commanded the group of officers down the corridor, and outside.

"'Tis a prisoner escape," a Redcoat shouted.

"No, 'tis the officers," Jack cried. "Orders from the general, they're to be paroled."

Behind him, George gave a rakish laugh. "Perkins, you're daft."

Jack ushered them from the barracks, still clinging to the rope tied about Captain Fleming. Their group disappeared down the road, where they fled into the surrounding brush until they reached the cove. Icy, brackish waters lapped the rocky shoreline.

In this brief stillness, Jack addressed his beloved cousin. "I had to think like you, Cousin."

George chuckled as he waded toward the sloop. "Aye, daft like me. Pray, what ship is this?"

"My prisoner's," Jack replied, nodding to Captain Fleming, whose mouth was still gagged by rope. "I'll explain when we arrive at Washington's camp."

Shivering and soaked, they boarded the small vessel. On board, George helped Jack tie Captain Fleming to the mast, then turned his attention to the wheel. One of the other officers had already overtaken it, while others made ready the sails. George looked to Jack, and gripped his arm, still encased in the enemy's crimson wool.

"Perkins, I'm impressed. And I'm so very glad to see you, Brother-cousin."

"Me, too." The exhaustion overtaking him, Jack pulled George into an embrace. "My God, I've never been so glad to see you, Brother."

❦

New Jersey

Settled into his wedge tent, Jack wrapped a wool blanket about him and rested upon his cot. Never had he imagined conjuring one escape from gaol; now he'd fled two. Perhaps it was Annalisa who guided him each time. *My darling girl, my angel.* He closed his eyes, ready to succumb to a sleep of dreams. It had been a long two days reaching Washington's camp from York Island, and longer since he'd slept a full night.

"Perkins, are you awake?" George's voice boomed beyond the tent.

Jack groaned. "Aye, what is it?"

His cousin stepped inside. Bathed and clean, George

stood before him dressed in a blue wool coat with white facings and waistcoat; his right shoulder boasted a gold epaulet, and upon his black cocked hat, a yellow cockade— insignias of his rank as captain that had been absent from his clothing during the rescue.

"Look at you," Jack said. "You look well. I daresay, it suits you to be captain."

"Are you well?" George sat on the edge of the cot. "I know we've to discuss what befell us in our time apart."

Jack stifled a yawn. "I'm as well as can be, given the circumstances." The brief silence magnified Annalisa's absence, and his thoughts returned to Jane and his unborn child. A roil of nausea rocked him. "Not a day passes when I don't think of Annalisa."

George hung his head. "Aye, my dear sister."

"I know she loved you better than anyone."

"Save for yourself." George winked.

"She loved us equally well." Jack focused on the dancing orange flame within the solitary lantern. Its glow cast dark shadows that stretched across his tent walls. "I hate to say you've no idea of the grief, because you lost her, too."

George grunted. "Too much death. When I learned about you and Annie, we were still at Dorchester Heights, but when we arrived at New York, I hadn't time to grieve. Truthfully, it never improves. The stench of each battle consumes you, and you've no time to pluck at your heartstrings."

Jack grimaced, hesitant to share what befell him while in mourning. *This is my cousin, he is hard-pressed to judge.* "I'm quite ashamed, actually...after my imprisonment aboard HMS *Lively*, I became rather dependent on laudanum. I spent the better part of springtime deep-rooted in the indulgence and clouded in stupor. It numbed every bit of me...I had no reason to grieve because I couldn't feel. Annie would be humiliated to call me *husband* if she knew." Jack pinched the bridge of his nose. "I'm well rid of it, now. Quinnapin helped me quit the stuff. I only pray Annalisa's soul forgives me."

George lifted his head and met Jack's stare. His cousin's green eyes, reminiscent of Annalisa's, appeared dark in the candlelight. "I'm grieved to hear you suffered so."

"I've only more sorrowful news, I'm afraid. I'm not sure you heard, but Ollie's...dead." Jack quailed with guilt beneath the blanket; he hadn't said the word aloud to anyone, save his family. "My mother received word from Burgoyne in late summer."

George's jaw stiffened. "My condolences. But I'm remiss to admit...I find more sadness in Samuel's death."

"Samuel's died as well?" Jack's face tingled. "When? How'd it happen?"

George cleared his throat as though it would rid himself of sadness. "He took a ball to his arm at Kip's Bay. They amputated, but the wound festered. It eventually claimed him." He ran his palms over his breeches, then stood. In the lanternlight, his face glowed a deep orange. "'Tis our lives now, Perkins. Hard to believe only eighteen months ago we were merry-making at the Strawberry Festival."

Jack allowed himself the memory of Annalisa sitting beneath the venerable oak, and his fingertips brushed his mouth. The kiss they'd shared still tingled his lips.

In the way he seemed to ward off emotion for Samuel, George cleared his throat again and turned from Jack to face the tent wall. "Would that I had let Annie join the army with me. Mayhap she never would have met her end upon that ship with you."

Jack started at his cousin's words. His lips parted, about to ask George what he meant, but George turned to face him.

"Pray, who is the cock robin you hauled with you?"

"He's with the other British prisoners, aye?" Jack asked.

"Aye."

"Good. You'll be interested to know the man. His name is Captain Fleming—"

"A turncoat who captained *Liberté*, the ship that took Annie's life," George said with a growl. "I've waited months to claw his eyes out. When Knox revealed his name to me, I vowed to find him, but never could."

"I met him at a tavern in New York. I was unable to cross the bridge to York Island. He, a proclaimed Loyalist, offered to sail me across the river...once he believed I, too, was Loyalist. When he told me he'd captained *Liberté*, something inside me grew sinister, as though a demon, or the Devil himself overtook me. George, I loathe the evil I've experienced. Upon HMS *Lively*, I conjured thoughts as no man should." Jack shivered and gestured to the bauta mask peeking from his haversack. "I wear that now when I travel on horseback. I can't be too careful...Lieutenant Dickens knows my face. He'll find me—"

"Peace, cousin." George knelt beside the cot. "You're far from HMS *Lively*. We'll harness that experience when we meet the Bloodybacks and Hessians in the field, aye?"

"Aye." Jack quelled his breathing, and asked, "How came you to lose New York City?"

"Damn him, that twiddle poop General Greene," George muttered. "Would that he retires a fart-catcher. I warned Washington of my concerns, and the Hessians overtook the fortification anyhow. Over two thousand of our men were taken captive, many more were wounded or killed, *and* we lost countless reserves of ammunition and artillery. This war has been an utter disaster. I fear Washington believes it, too. I'm lucky—we're all lucky—you released us. The Bloodybacks dallied with paroling us officers, but thousands of our men remain aboard those prison ships."

A wintry gust rattled the tent flap, and Jack curled the blanket over himself tighter. "I know all too well the torment aboard a British prison ship."

George lifted his canteen. "Aye, but you're a prisoner no more, and neither am I. here's to outwitting the Bloodybacks and the Hessians. Let's rid ourselves of this wibble." He guffawed. "This stuff will make you shite through your teeth."

❧ 26 ❧

ANNALISA

ESSEX HOUSE, LONDON, DECEMBER 1776

ANNALISA ADMIRED THE WHITE, wooden bookcases carved into the walls of her bedchamber, each surrounded by decorative beryl blue wallpaper. Perhaps she would miss this house, but not as much as she yearned for home. None could ever rival her family's unassuming farmhouse in Topsfield, or the modest saltbox she'd shared with Jack after they eloped. Even the luxurious Devonshire House, where she'd spent two months in convalescence, barely competed with Topsfield, three thousand miles away.

She closed her eyes and envisaged Jack's gaze. His eyes always reminded her of the first time she glimpsed the ocean, the way it sparkled in sunlight her initial visit to Boston. *And Jack's alive. I may lose myself again in his eyes.* Titillating thoughts of her husband's caresses drew her to the canopied bed. She rested upon the silk coverlet and lifted her skirts. Heat radiated from the fireplace, warming the space between her legs. Annalisa closed her eyes and imagined Jack's hand as it glided up her thigh. She found the indulgent space his fingers and tongue pampered when they were intimate and bit her lip.

How long has it been since I've known pleasure? It matters not...Jack's alive, I may enjoy life again. She could dare to hope to one day bear his children.

"Annalisa, are you ready?" Abigail's voice sounded from the other side of the door.

"Y—yes." Heart pounding, Annalisa threw down her skirts and leapt from the bed. She washed her hands in the basin, applied a bit more lilac perfume, then opened the door. "Yes, I'm quite ready."

Abigail smirked. "What were you doing in there?"

"'Tis none of your business." Annalisa fled the room, her friend behind her. "We can't keep the duchess waiting."

LONDON'S STREETS REEKED OF FECULENCE, BUT ANNALISA was quite used to foul odors from her family's farm. Without so much as a grimace, she and Sarah followed behind Georgiana and Abigail, who chattered endlessly a few paces ahead.

"I wish to be honest with you, Sarah, but I must insist upon your confidence." Annalisa peered at the duchess's chambermaid walking beside her, and waited for a reply.

"Miss Cavendish, I swear I'll not speak a word."

Annalisa stared ahead. "Lady Essex and I are planning to buy passage on a ship to America."

Sarah joined her stare. "Will you take me with you?"

"If you can afford passage, and wish to join us of your own accord, you're more than welcome."

Sarah's voice was low, "I've enough saved from my time working for the duchess. How much closer is America to Barbados?"

Annalisa pursed her lips. "I'm unsure. Wish you to find your mother?"

"I'm uncertain my mother's in Barbados, Miss Cavendish."

Sarah stopped walking and faced Annalisa. "I don't know where she is."

Annalisa reached for her hand, and Sarah let her hold it. "If trying to find her is something you wish to do, let me know if, or how, I can help."

Sarah held Annalisa's stare. "I want to go with you. I want to go to America."

"Ladies, come along," the duchess called from up ahead.

An unassuming brick building in Oxford-street housed the seamstress's shop, who, according to Georgiana, was the best in all of London. Annalisa stepped inside, behind the duchess, Abigail, and Sarah.

"Your Grace, how wonderful to see you." The seamstress, Mrs. Sandown, bowed. "For what may I take measurements today, Your Grace?"

Georgiana looked to Annalisa with a strange eagerness that rounded the duchess's wide eyes.

Annalisa stepped forward. "A man's suit. For myself."

"And one for me as well," Abigail said, as she moved toward a display of colored silks.

"I beg your pardon, Miss?" Mrs. Sandown asked.

"'Tis for a masquerade," the duchess replied with a playful grin. "We shall be dressing as gentlemen for Twelfth Night."

The ladies all laughed.

"Ah, of course," Mrs. Sandown cried. "What fun!"

Annalisa stepped toward the fabric. "I'll require this for the stockings, and this one for the neckpiece. I'd like this white linsey woolsey for the waist coat and facings, and this indigo wool for the coat. And this leather for the knee breeches. The linen here for the shirt will do nicely."

The duchess sighed. "Such modest choices, Miss Cavendish. Why not choose silk and add some embroidery?"

"Oh, no. I wish to dress modestly, Your Grace," Annalisa said.

Georgiana beamed. "'Tis nice to hear you speak so assuredly of yourself, Calais."

"Indeed, it is," Abigail replied.

Sarah pointed to one of the hats. "Miss Cavendish?"

"Ah, I nearly forgot the most important piece. Mrs. Sandown, black beaver-felt for the cocked hat, if you please."

"Of course, Miss." The woman held up a long piece of measuring tape. "May I begin?"

❧ 27 ❧

GEORGE

PENNSYLVANIA, DECEMBER 1776

AFTER BEING PURSUED BY Cornwallis through New Jersey since their escape from New York, George received orders from General Washington. Cogswell's militia was to follow the army back into Trenton, New Jersey. They'd only been in Pennsylvania a handful of days, and with the arrival of some provisions—notably, blankets—spirits had somewhat lifted.

George made his way to General Washington's quarters. Snow blanketed the ground and the wild wind whipped, icing his toes within his shoes. Despondent from battles lost, and interminable retreats, he wondered how they could be victorious in the coming year. At the close of November, they lost nearly two thousand men when contracts expired; they would lose at least another thousand by December's end.

As 1777 loomed, he couldn't help but question if their effort was for naught. *Will Congress accept defeat?* According to his superiors, and Jack, who'd received word from Lord Perkins, Congress's plights upon France had materialized little more than furtive financial efforts, and scant materials.

"Sir?" George tipped his hat to the general as he entered Washington's quarters.

"Captain Howlett, have a seat." Washington gestured to a wooden chair before a large, oak escritoire. Upon the desk sat neat stacks of paper, books, a ledger, and an inkwell.

George sat, resting his hat in his lap.

"Captain, what know you of the state of affairs across the river?" Washington asked.

"Not much, sir."

"The Hessians patrol the other side, and Howe returned to New York with his men, and Cornwallis has accepted leave to return to London."

"Then we appear to be stagnant, sir," George replied.

"Precisely." The general kept his voice low. "And how does it feel to be chased thus, as we have been, by the enemy, Captain Howlett? How does it make you feel each day we remain here, in constant observation of the Hessians?"

George thought for a moment before answering. "Sir, it sends the men into fits of frustration. Therein remains an obscurity, a layer of utter darkness clouding the cause. Notwithstanding the past months of pursuit, the men are dejected that we remain, enduring such conditions when they could be home, warmed by the fire with their families." He paused, eyeing his superior. "Sir, I shall never desert the cause, but I fear many will continue to flee."

Washington paced the tent, hands clasped behind him. "Captain Howlett, I know of the men you speak, and I too, feel a foreboding that imprisons my very soul; that a victory against the British is but a whisper in these bitter gusts of ice and snow. I fear if we wait too long, we'll have neither the men to fight, nor the spirit. Retention has been horrific. But gazing across the river each day at the Hessians, I've discovered in myself a renewed vigor. A fervor, if you will, for our cause. I've exhausted my deliberation over our next advancements, and 'tis come to my attention that come springtime, an attack on Philadelphia is inevitable. We must hasten ourselves now and dampen whatever onslaught may come."

"We're to cross the Delaware again, sir?" George asked.

Washington nodded. "Indeed. This time, in a clandestine incursion upon the Germans. I fear such an act is required in order to revive morale."

George had never seen a man so vulnerable and distraught. Though General Washington stood tall, he seemed to carry the weight of the entire globe upon his shoulders. Despite this, he spoke with the conviction of a man who only ever held a notion of victory.

Inspired, George nodded. "Of course, sir."

When he returned to his tent, Jack and Bartlett sat within. *If only Samuel was here, too. And Quinn. But at least Quinn still lives.*

"I've news from the general," George said. He surmised from Jack's haggard stare that his cousin's spirit needed lifting. "Howe's decided to march his Lobsters back to New York to take up winter's quarters. And Cornwallis, the dilberry, received leave to return to England. All we're left with are bloody Hessians. As you've probably noticed."

"Aye, their camp is at Trenton," Jack replied, his voice hoarse. "Things are looking bleak."

"No doubt our dedicated Commander in Chief shares our sentiments," Bartlett said. "Though, I attest he experiences these burdens far greater than we."

George kicked his boots into the frozen earth to rouse his toes. His breath turned to smoky vapor as he cleared his throat. "I want for us to be victorious."

"Then we shall." Jack handled the tin lantern and opened

the tent flap to peek outside. "Perhaps our luck has finally won out."

Snow and freezing winds blew about the camp.

George sat on his cot and buttoned his spatterdashes. "We're going to cross the Delaware, abrams...and surprise the Hessians Christmas Day."

Jack grinned, and pulled the cork free from their bottle of rum. "Then let's finish this wibble."

"Give me some of that." George reached for the bottle.

A BRUMAL CHRISTMAS NIGHT, SLEET, SNOW, AND FREEZING rain battered George like icy razors. At home, he'd call this kind of tempest a *nor'easter,* and he'd have a warm hearth by which to sit. Instead, before him, the Delaware River swelled and spun with massive chunks of ice. That night they would make their surprise attack on Trenton. That night, they would cross.

George drew a diagram in the wet snow for Jack and Bartlett. "Seven hundred men are to follow Ewing at the Trenton Ferry. There, they'll seize the bridge and approach Trenton from the south. Next, Cadwalader will lead another group across the river, further south as a diversion, striking von Donop's regiment. This is meant to occupy the Hessians long enough to prevent reinforcements, thus allowing us to cross and march on Trenton with Washington. If all goes accordingly, we may even push forward to Princeton and New Brunswick."

Jack raised a dubious brow. "And if the strategy doesn't work? The weather is less than desirable for marching distances, much less crossing the Delaware's rushing rapids."

George dug his foot into the map he'd drawn in the snow.

Blowing warm air into his hands, he rubbed them together. "Then at least we hold the spirit of our revolt to carry us onward, rogues. We cripple any incursion that may come upon Philadelphia. 'Tis imperative—she's our capital city, and an encroachment on her is inevitable. This ambush should slow the Bloodybacks and may even win us Trenton."

"I daresay we've come to a point where we sorely require victory," Bartlett said. "This assault must end triumphantly."

George swiped the ice from the tip of his nose. "We'll do the best we can." Glancing about their encampment, he doubted the weather would allow for Washington's rigid timetable. The general intended to have all men across the river by midnight to march south to Trenton by five in the morning.

"Cogswell's regiment, fall in," George ordered.

His men lined themselves along the bank of the turbulent river. As the wind howled and moaned, it whipped frosty bits of his hair into his face. Shaking, George shifted in his shoes, his spatterdashes barely warming his legs. The sleet and freezing rain welted his skin as he and his men stepped onto the crowded ferry. George stood behind Jack and Bartlett and handed them each a package of rations.

The flatboat pulled from the shore, guided by several men along its cable. Cutting into thick layers of ice, and against bitter rapids, the barge rocked and swayed. George lurched but caught himself with a bend of his knees. The other side of the river lay at a mere three hundred yards, but in the black night, with only a small lantern and a torch as their guide, it appeared miles away.

"Steady on, pull harder," George hollered to the men on the cable.

"The current's too strong, Captain," Matthew Whipple called over the roaring winds.

Matthew, sixteen, helped his father, John, at the oars, steering the barge along the cable. George pushed to the front and slipped alongside the great wheel of their cannon. He shoved Matthew aside, and, grabbing the long oar in his frozen hands, heaved with all his strength. On the opposite side, Jack overtook the other oar from John Whipple.

"Easy, Perkins," George shouted.

Exposed to the elements on open waters, freezing rain and snow caked George's clothes, soaking him. But the bitter chill never seeped into his body as he hoisted and maneuvered the oar against the rushing currents.

"Careful, Perkins, we're nearly there," George roared.

The flatboat docked, and George led his militia up the slippery bank. Several men hauled the cannon barefoot, their toes blue and purple against crystalline white snow. Others marched with ruptured shoes. Beside him, Jack and Bartlett kept the pace, their heads bowed against the wind. *This army is broken in more than just spirit. Please, Annie, let us be victorious against the Hessians.*

"Soldiers, keep by your officers," Washington bellowed. "For God's sake, keep by your officers!"

The long walk pulsed warm blood to George's frozen feet, awakening his toes. By the time they marched on Trenton, the winter sun had already risen, illuminating a quiet town still in repose.

"It seems the Hessians sleep much after celebrating Christmas last night," Jack said.

George's chuckle faded behind the crack of gunfire.

Snap-crack!

Boom!

Hessians, half-dressed, emerged from houses, confused and unaware of the attack.

Over the clamor, George cried, "Cogswell's regiment, prime and load. Make ready...fire!"

Click.

"My powder's spent," Jack hollered.

The gunpowder, incapable of catching fire in sleet, George ordered, "Cogswell's regiment, engage your bayonets."

His militia followed Washington's men, and advanced their attack.

Jack shouted, "Cousin, look out!"

George aimed his weapon at a Hessian, but a sharp pain sliced his left shoulder.

"Zounds!" George swung the butt of his musket into the German's stomach, knocking him to the ice-covered ground. With a quick jab, he stabbed the Hessian's chest, and steaming blood spilled from the gash.

Jack hastened to his side and peered at the slash through George's coat. "'Tis not too deep, but you'll need it treated."

"Your arm," Bartlett huffed, darting toward them.

"My wound at Concord felt worse than this," George replied. "Engage your weapons, rogues."

George attacked with his regiment, and Hessians fell, naïve lambs slaughtered by the starving provincial wolves. After nearly an hour of skirmish, George supposed about one-hundred Germans were wounded, and over twenty lay dead; they captured nearly a thousand as prisoners.

Jack sidled beside George, his face and neck crusted with dried blood. "I daresay, this was the victory we needed."

George grinned, though his body shuddered with weariness, and his shoulder burned. He ordered his regiment, cold and exhausted, to follow Washington back across the Delaware to their encampment. *On to winter's quarters.* He peered up at the sky. *Thank you, Annie.*

ANNALISA

DEVONSHIRE HOUSE, LONDON,
JANUARY 5, 1777

TWELFTH NIGHT, AT LAST. Annalisa touched the silvery scar beneath her right eye as she stood before the looking glass in her suit for the duchess's masquerade. *How long ago it was I incurred this injury. Now, 'tis but a faded memory.* She ran her hands over the fine wool coat and leather breeches clinging to her body. Georgiana had thought it quite the jest for ladies to costume as men, and men as ladies. How little the duchess knew of Annalisa's exploits in breeches as a member of the Danvers militia. Though she'd fooled them readily, she never owned breeches of her own, always donning the clothes her brothers had outgrown. Now, each garment properly hugged her exact form.

How long has it been since last I wore Benjamin's clothes? Her breath caught. *June of 1775. Bunker Hill.* She reached into her pocket for the lead round and shivered with the return of her memory; the pungent, sulfuric gun-smoke, Charlestown burning, the bodies bloodying the hills. *I will never forget.*

The year had just turned to 1777. How quickly time passed when she wasn't herself. She'd lost nearly a year of her life, time that would never be returned to her. Yet, here she remained, on the other side of the Atlantic, patiently awaiting Lord Essex to bring them home.

Her attention returned to her reflection. The leather breeches, white waistcoat, and navy wool coat with white facings appeared more informal than what other guests were certain to wear. But she cared little. This suit would prove more useful than a mere costume at a masquerade; it would be her penultimate guise as Benjamin Cavendish upon their return to the colonies. In such a well-fitted suit, she could join Washington's army with little question. Providence had bestowed upon her height and a slender frame, which easily concealed her womanly features. Her greatest challenge, she knew, would be the morbid flux that came upon her each month.

This masquerade ball, she held little worry; the morbid flux had come and gone two weeks prior, leaving her agile and slim. There would be no bulky period apron tucked between her legs to worry her of bleeding into her breeches while dancing.

Satisfied, Annalisa plaited her honey-brown hair into a queue, tied on her white domino mask, and donned her new black beaver-felt cocked hat. She was no longer Annalisa Howlett Perkins, nor was she Miss Cavendish. Tonight, she was Benjamin. The only thing missing was her beloved musket Jack and Quinnapin had forged for her. She recalled the weapon perched over the hearth in the home she shared with Jack. *I pray 'tis there upon my return.*

Giddy, she grinned into the mirror. "Hello, old friend."

Vivaldi's *Concerto for Flute and Strings in F major, Op. 10, No. 1* reverberated intricate trills and cadences into the majestic assembly hall of Devonshire House. Lords and ladies, dressed as the opposite sex, gathered about with glasses of claret. Georgiana, in a teal silk suit in ditto adorned with scrawling gold embroidery, welcomed her guests with an eagerness Annalisa only witnessed in the duke's absence. Luckily for Georgiana, the duke was visiting Paris. In his nonattendance, the duchess already wielded two glasses of wine, and opined for a lofty game of faro when dancing ended.

"I think I recognize this fellow." Georgiana greeted Annalisa with a gracious, masculine bow.

"Your Grace." Annalisa returned the gesture.

Abigail, with legs encased in evergreen silk breeches and ivory silk stockings, scampered toward them. Annalisa admired her friend's physique, something she'd never noticed until that moment. Though shorter than Annalisa by several inches, and with wider hips, Abigail's shapely legs were long and trim. In fact, each woman boasted pleasing thighs and calves, always hidden beneath petticoats and dresses. *How freeing, how satisfying to show such fine bits of human form without fear of disgrace or humility. Ah yes, the paradox of a Twelfth Night ball.* A masquerade on any evening could afford to bend the rules of Society, but particularly Twelfth Night dissolved nearly all of Society's ridiculous decrees.

Behind Abigail, Lord Essex materialized in an evergreen silk ladies' gown. He laughed behind his coordinating green mask.

"Good evening, Your Grace." He curtsied.

Georgiana bowed, and replied with a chuckle, "My lady."

Lord Essex retrieved three glasses of claret and brought

them to his wife, Georgiana, and Annalisa. "I daresay, this is the first masquerade I've donned a dress."

"You and every other gentleman this evening, my lord," Abigail replied. "I must say, breeches are rather agreeable articles of clothing." She winked at Annalisa, as though to say she understood her excursions as Benjamin Cavendish.

Late into the night, a line of dancers formed at the end of the assembly hall, nearest the orchestra. Handel's *Water Music* played, and Annalisa relocated to Lord Suffolk's ball in Cambridge, before Bunker Hill. That night she'd had her debut with higher society and stumbled during the minuet. *How mortifying. Though not nearly as humiliating as when Oliver tripped me.* Her chest heated at the memory of her sister's cruel husband. *Would that he's absent upon our return to the colonies.*

Lord Essex led Abigail to the set of dancers, and Annalisa retreated to the perimeter of the hall to drink her glass of claret.

"Will you dance tonight, Calais?" Georgiana asked.

"Not if I can help it," Annalisa replied. "My muse, Benjamin Cavendish, has renounced the minuet."

Georgiana laughed. "Then drink up, Mr. Cavendish. I expect you in our game of faro later this evening." She bowed and took her leave, disappearing into the crowd.

"Miss Cavendish."

Annalisa turned.

A woman with satiny umber skin, dressed in yellow silk breeches with matching coat, stood beside her. A yellow columbina mask covered the upper half of her face.

"Sarah?"

Sarah grinned slowly. "Happy Twelfth Night, Miss Cavendish."

"Oh, I'm so glad you're here." She embraced Sarah, and

when she pulled away, added, "I quite like this color on you. It adds a cheeriness to this dismal winter season."

"The duchess's house staff are always permitted to attend her Twelfth Night masquerade." Sarah ran a hand over her coat sleeve. "I was fortunate Her Grace was kind enough to commission this suit for me this year. From what I recall, the color reminds me of the sunlight in Barbados." She peered about the hall and leaned in close. "I said I wished to join you and Lady Essex on your trip to America. That still remains so. Have you bought passage yet?"

Annalisa shook her head. "No."

"I've asked Her Grace, and she's agreed to release me from my duties."

"She has?" Annalisa gripped Sarah's hand. "That is wonderful news. I promise I'll write to you as soon as Abigail and I buy passage."

Laughter and chatter filled the space between them, and Annalisa caught Mr. Fox's voice in a lull. "Apparently, Howe's men have pursued Washington's army through New Jersey. Last I heard, Cornwallis was summoned home to London."

Annalisa pulled Sarah with her toward Mr. Fox, who spoke with two other gentlemen, all three donning silk *robe à la française* gowns. "Sir, I couldn't help but overhear your intercourse. Pray tell, what news of the army?"

"We've overtaken New York City," Mr. Fox said. "Washington's army escaped New York City in autumn and spent the better part of December running from Howe and Cornwallis through New Jersey."

"My brother fights with Washington." Annalisa swallowed through her tightened throat. "Mr. Fox, you couldn't possibly know how many have died, or were taken prisoner in New York, could you?"

Mr. Fox shook his head. "I know nothing of the sort."

Sarah tugged her from the group of gentlemen. "Your brother is fighting?"

"Yes. I've not seen him since August of 1775." Annalisa hid her wavering frown by sipping her glass of wine. "I'm certain he believes me dead, like everyone else at home."

"Then you'll surprise them all when you see them again." Her strong chin jutted. "I'd be honored to witness such a reunion."

"What's this?" Abigail joined. "You've heard from George?"

Annalisa started, surprised by Abigail's outspokenness about George when Lord Essex lingered nearby. "No. Washington's army has been pursued by Cornwallis and Howe since the British overtook New York City—"

"But…George was in New York, was he not?" Abigail's hand flew to her chest. "He must've escaped with the army, yes?"

"I know nothing else, Abbie—"

"Someone must know something." Abigail turned about, as though to scan the room for people who knew George personally. Annalisa reached for her friend to stop the outlandish display, but it was too late. Lord Essex approached with brows knit.

"Whatever's the matter, my lady? You appear vexed."

Abigail replied, "'Tis Annie's brother, George—he's with Washington's army and they've been overrun from New York City—"

"Not here, my dear." Lord Essex's face colored, and he lowered his voice. "We're at a masquerade. 'Tis Twelfth Night. This is hardly a topic of conversation for tonight."

"My lord, there's a war raging across the ocean," Abigail cried. "And people we love are fighting—"

"People *you* love? Or people Mrs. Perkins loves? Last I

knew, 'twas Mrs. Perkins's relation who fought, not yours," Lord Essex said.

"George is my kin," Abigail said. "I, too, love him—"

"I know who George is." The viscount's face grew redder than a boiled beet. "I had the opportunity to make his acquaintance at Suffolk's ball. Pardon us. I think we've had quite enough wine and dancing for one evening."

Annalisa and Sarah followed Lord Essex, who hauled Abigail by the arm, from the assembly hall.

When they reached the main portico, he stopped. "I will not be made a fool...a cuckold...before the people of our circle."

"A cuckold, Lord Essex?" Annalisa stepped forward and stood between them.

Lord Essex's brown eyes rounded with rage. "Aye, cuckolded. By *your* brother, Mrs. Perkins." He reached for Abigail and pulled her down the stairs and outside.

Annalisa followed, Sarah trailing behind, and into the blustery January night. "My lord, why do you indict her thus? Abigail has been faithful to you, sir."

Lord Essex called for his carriage, then faced Annalisa; his hand rested at the waist of his dress's bodice. Annalisa hid her smirk at the sight—an established lord dressed in women's clothing, reproaching her like Jane or Mamma.

"Perhaps you've not taken proper study of my daughter, Mrs. Perkins," he barked.

Abigail shrieked, "I've told you time and again, my lord, Louisa is your daughter—"

"Then you won't mind not seeing her again, will you, Wife?"

Abigail gasped. "Whatever do you mean? She's still my daughter!"

"Still. Your. Daughter." He lowered his voice, "When you

journey to America, you'll do so without the child. And me. If she is mine, you won't mind leaving her with her father until you return to London."

"Never," Abigail whispered. "How could you even propose such a plot—"

"Lord Essex, this is preposterous," Annalisa said, though she had anticipated this reaction. He never held any intention of returning them to America. "You're journeying with us, are you not, my lord?"

He eyed Sarah carefully before speaking again. "I'll not be spoken to like some delinquent child. I'm Viscount Essex—"

"My lord, your carriage," the valet said.

The four-in-hand pulled up, and the valet opened the door. Lord Essex stepped up, tripping on the skirts of his gown. "God dammit!" He ripped the mask from his face, threw it to the ground, and hurled himself inside.

Abigail lingered, reluctant to enter. Eventually, she pursued her husband. Annalisa took Sarah's hand and followed after her.

◈

"I TOLD YOU, IF YOU SO MUCH AS ACCEPT A SHILLING FROM the Duchess of Devonshire, you'll never see Louisa again. Am I clear?" Lord Essex paced the parlor. He'd long since changed from the masquerade gown, and Abigail sat by the fire, biting her fingertips.

"I've asked you a question, Lady Essex." He turned to her. "Do you understand?"

"She heard you, my lord." Annalisa rubbed her friend's shoulders. "She will abide by whatever you decree, my lord. But we must return to America. 'Twas never your intent to return us, was it, my lord?"

His jaw stiffened. "You'll return without Louisa. Until my wife admits her adultery, I'll not allow her to play *mother*. Not to someone else's child."

"But she's my child," Abigail sobbed into her hands.

Annalisa wrapped her arms about her. "Shh, there, there."

"Why do you care, my lord?" Abigail lifted her face to Lord Essex. "She's not the son you require. Leave her to me. Please, don't take her from me."

His face grew wan. "Then you admit it? She belongs to another?"

"No, my lord—" Annalisa started.

"Yes." Abigail nodded. "'Tis true, my lord."

"Abbie, no!" Annalisa cried.

Lord Essex stared hard at his wife. "Speak his name."

Abigail shuddered in Annalisa's arms. "George Howlett."

The viscount walked toward the door. "I shall return to America and I will challenge him."

Annalisa cowered. "No, please, my lord. I—"

"Get out of my house. Now!" He slammed his fist against the wall, and the clock rattled.

Annalisa whispered to Abigail, "I'll take Louisa to Georgiana. Meet me at Devonshire House when he's gone to bed. Pack only what you can carry." She fled toward the parlor door and left the room. When the door had closed behind her, Sarah met her in the foyer.

"Pray, what's happened?"

"We're taking Louisa to Devonshire House. Gee will have us. From there, we'll book passage to America."

Annalisa rushed up the stairs and down the corridor to the nursery. There, tucked into white, lacy blankets, Louisa slept. Annalisa scoured the room for all manner of Louisa's things, packed them in a satchel, then lifted her eight-month-old niece from the bassinet. With the child tucked to her breast within her men's coat, Annalisa scurried from the nursery.

"Quick," she said to Sarah, who loitered in the foyer. "To the stable. We ride."

⚜

THE DUCHESS WAS AMIDST A LATE GAME OF FARO WHEN SHE received them.

"This way, this way." Georgiana hustled them inside and up the stairs to the room Annalisa had inhabited. "Pray, have you all you might require? Or shall I send someone to Essex House to retrieve your things?"

Annalisa sat on the bed with Louisa in her lap. She felt for the *wampum* necklace, her Bunker Hill round, and the wedding ring upon her finger. "Everything I could need is on my person."

Georgiana looked to Sarah. "And shall I expect Lady Essex as well?"

"Yes, Your Grace," Sarah replied.

Georgiana made her way to the bed, where she sat beside Annalisa. She held out her hand to Louisa, who grabbed the duchess's finger. "What a sweet child. Would that I had one of my own."

"Likewise, Your Grace," Annalisa replied.

The duchess pouted. "After all this time, you still address me so?"

"I apologize, Gee. Surely you know how I'm in your debt for all you've done for me—"

"No, you're a dear friend, Calais. Whatever I can do to help, I trust you know I shall."

Annalisa met Sarah's dark stare, and she sucked in a deep inhale. "Abigail, Sarah, and I must return to America. We thought perhaps Lord Essex might buy us passage despite his poor finances. He had no intention of ever returning us, Gee. Can you buy us passage on the next ship bound for New-England?"

Georgiana gazed toward her feet and rested her mouth upon her fist. For a long time, she did not move or speak. Annalisa wondered if the duchess wished to join them, abandon her unhappy marriage, and travel three thousand miles across the Atlantic to a land she'd never been. *To begin life anew, like the rest of us.*

"Of course." The duchess's gaze lifted. "I'm glad to do it. I said I would that night at Vauxhall." Georgiana, the most beloved, and loneliest lady Annalisa had ever met, rose from the bed and glided toward the door. "By this time tomorrow, I swear you shall each have passage home."

PART TWO
1777-1778

❧ 29 ❧

ANNALISA

THE NORTH ATLANTIC, MID-FEBRUARY
1777

ANNALISA CLENCHED THE WOODEN rail, her knuckles white. The last time she'd been on a ship it wrecked in a winter storm, and this passage across the Atlantic left her trembling. Before her, the grey ocean ebbed and flowed, rocking the creaking ship from port to starboard. Above her, the white, red, and blue Dutch flag flapped against a frigid gust. She shivered and turned from the rail. Today marked the better part of six weeks at sea, and each day, a struggle. The journey felt longer than she remembered, though she had little to compare it to. She barely recalled her previous crossing, but Abigail insisted this trip west was indeed longer, as their vessel sailed against easterly flowing ocean currents.

"I was hoping the air would warm the nearer we came to America." Sarah drew a blanket about her shoulders. "The weather in England was dismal compared to what I left in Barbados. Is not the weather in Boston better?"

Annalisa shook her head. "No. The springs, summers, and

autumns are fair, but winters are cold when snow and ice blow in. We call them nor'easters."

Sarah shrugged. "At least I'm free to leave it."

Annalisa grinned. "Indeed, you are."

"But I think I should like to remain with you, Miss Cavendish, until I'm able to book passage on a ship to Barbados."

"Of course. You may come and go as you please, but you always have a place to stay with me." Annalisa shivered again and pulled her cloak tighter about herself. "I'm going to check on Abigail and Louisa. Will you join?"

Sarah shook her head. "No. I never tire of this view. This free world." The past six weeks, Sarah had spent long hours each day on deck, and long after dusk. "It may be cold, but 'tis wild and boundless. I've never seen such sunrises and sunsets, storm clouds, or vast sameness. The stars in the nighttime sky...'tis but a dream."

Annalisa had been similarly bewildered by the endless ocean and sky; and nights so star-filled, if not for an occasional ripple, the reflection all but tricked her into believing their ship floated within a starry void of blackness. Yes, she understood Sarah's awe, but below deck, Louisa and Abigail looked pale and retched often.

Annalisa returned to her cabin. Abigail lay with Louisa in a small wooden bunk, stroking her inky black hair.

"My poor Louisa is ghostly. We've been aboard this ship over a month. I fear she may not make it to America." Abigail wiped her tears. "I fear *I* may not make it."

Annalisa, garbed in her men's clothing, knelt by the bunk. The sour, putrid air dizzied her. "Hush, dear friend. You needn't worry. Louisa will live. You will live."

Abigail rested her head on the straw pillow and scratched her scalp, the fleas and lice abundant. "I pray you're right. Think you Lord Essex is crossing this very moment?"

"No. I don't."

"What if he is?"

"We'll be several weeks ahead of him," Annalisa replied. "And we may hide away at George's tavern in Portsmouth. Essex knows not of that place."

Abigail closed her eyes. "I pray you're right. Will you sing for us?"

"Of course." Annalisa cleared her throat. *"Farewell and adieu, to you English ladies..."*

"Those aren't the words, Annie," Abigail chuckled.

> *"We'll rant and we'll roar like true American*
> *sailors,*
> *we'll rant and we'll roar across the salt seas.*
> *Until we strike soundings in the channel of*
> *old Boston,*
> *from Winnisimmet to Topsfield, 'tis twenty-*
> *five leagues."*

Abigail giggled. "I like your lyrics better."

That night by lantern light, Annalisa scrawled a letter to Jack. Whether his eyes meant to read them or not, she'd written one every day they'd been at sea. *How soon I may see him, and my family.* She folded the note and added it to the stack of others. She'd been absent from the colony for a year. How much had changed, if anything at all? *Is Jack well after our shipwreck? Has he healed properly?* Her mother and father, too, may have aged or ailed in her time away. The thought tightened her breast.

Despite the potential for her aging parents' afflictions, it was for George she mostly worried. Away with Washington's army, perhaps he was still in New York; maybe he was in New Jersey. She had no way of knowing his whereabouts or well-being. *Is he even alive? Is he taken prisoner amongst the British who now occupy York Island?* She pushed the thought from her mind and yearned for the pages of her Margaret Cavendish poetry book. If only she'd taken it with her to Europe—though it would now have been lost to the ocean depths. But why hadn't she? *I suppose I'd little use for it. After I wed Jack, my hopes of joining the army diminished.*

As she nestled in her bunk wearing only her shift, her breeches and coat hung upon a nail, Annalisa knew she would don them often once they arrived in Boston. Masquerading as a man was fruitful, not only for joining the army, but also for protecting Sarah, Abigail, and Louisa on board the ship. The crew still believed her their male chaperone, and no one so much as dared look at them. *I'm fortunate to be tall. I play the part well.* Annalisa smiled into her straw pillow. She'd learned much from her dear brother, George.

❧

"I don't think I can live another day at sea," Abigail sniveled.

Annalisa repressed her own urge to retch. "We're one day closer to America, and one day further from England. We must be nearing the shore."

Louisa wailed, filling the small cabin with impenetrable noise.

"How can you be sure?" Abigail cried. "You've said the same silliness the last two weeks, and I can't hear it anymore!"

Annalisa massaged her pounding head. "Let's go on deck. Mayhap the fresh air will do you good."

"I can't." Abigail sobbed with her eight-month-old daughter. "I'll jump overboard with Louisa—"

"My ladies."

Sarah's voice startled Annalisa; she'd been on deck since dawn.

Annalisa asked, "What is it, Sarah?"

Sarah's face glowed with excitement. "We've sighted land."

"Praise God," Abigail sighed, sinking into her bunk.

Annalisa hastened from their quarters and onto the main deck with Sarah. After weeks surrounded by a heaving, slate abyss fading into eternal grey, Boston Harbor's verdant islands dotted the horizon.

"We've made it." The salty air, though hardly different from the past six weeks, refreshed, and the sun, which had been hidden by clouds, dazzled the glittering waters—waters so azure Annalisa saw Jack's gaze.

Sarah joined her at the rail. "That is your land, Calais?"

Relieved, Annalisa beamed. "Yes."

Abigail met them at the rail with Louisa, who no longer cried. "'Tis beautiful."

"It is." Annalisa stroked Louisa's back. "I was beginning to worry for this little one."

Abigail kissed Louisa's cheek. "She's strong. She's got Bixby blood in her, a captain's granddaughter. I daresay she may be meant for sailing more than I."

"Definitely more than you," Annalisa chuckled. "But you forget, her father's a captain now as well."

"He is." As abruptly as Abigail's freckled face brightened, it fell. "I pray he's alive so he may meet my greatest joy."

Her friend's words prickled the skin beneath her wool coat, but Annalisa fixed her gaze upon the horizon. Boston's harbor islands rose by inches, and as they neared the peninsula in the final few hours, Annalisa appreciated the absence of the British flag.

30

ANNALISA

TOPSFIELD, LATE FEBRUARY 1777

T HE COACH WHEELS OF their rented carriage
crunched and skidded over the icy road into Topsfield.
At the sight of familiar snow-covered fields, Annalisa reached
for Abigail. Her friend slept since they left Boston, and
Louisa's little mouth hung agape at Abigail's chest, deep in
slumber.

Notwithstanding the weeks they spent crossing the
Atlantic, they'd traveled over a day since docking at South
Battery in Boston. But all wariness vanished as the Perkins's
home, a large yellow clapboard house with four chimneys—
two at each end—perched diligently upon a small hill, came
into view.

"Abbie, we're here." She shook her friend. "We've arrived."

Abigail's eyelids fluttered open, and she yawned. "I feel
like I've slept for days." She peered at her daughter, still
asleep at her breast with a string of drool moistening her neck
handkerchief. "I can't wait for Louisa to meet my family, and
yours."

"This is your house, Lady Essex?" Sarah asked.

Abigail gazed wistfully at the snow-covered gardens that, come spring, would be lush with flowers. "Yes. I know 'tis hardly the kind of estate my husband or the Duchess of Devonshire inhabit in London, but 'tis home."

Sarah smiled. "I think 'tis lovely, my lady."

Perched upon the front steps, they awaited Mercy to open the door. Annalisa's heart fluttered like the tiny wings of hummingbirds that suckled from flowers in her kitchen garden. She slid her sweating palms over her leather breeches, and the front door opened.

"Lady Essex..." Mercy's ivory face, which had brightened as she greeted Abigail, paled as she sighted Annalisa. "Mrs. Perkins." Her round, astonished eyes rolled into her head, and she collapsed.

⚜

In the Perkins's parlor, Lady Perkins trembled in Annalisa's arms.

"I'm speechless. Utterly without words. I'm overjoyed." Lady Perkins pulled away and stepped back to look at Annalisa. "Upon my word, and dressed as a man. But you look well. Heaven knows we've prayed...and mourned. Jack prayed—"

"Daughter-in-law." Lord Perkins tugged her into his embrace as he left Abigail and Louisa, and Lady Perkins went to her daughter and granddaughter. "You've no idea the joy I feel upon seeing you here in the flesh. These have been tortuous months."

"I'm relieved to be home, my lord," Annalisa replied. "Pray, where's Jack? I must see him."

Lord Perkins stiffened. "He's away, I'm afraid...joined the Continentals."

Her heart sank.

"Abbie!" Andrew, the youngest of the Perkins boys, handsome with grey eyes and chestnut hair, now nearing seventeen, burst into the parlor with Susan and Charlotte. He held Abigail, then hugged Annalisa. "Annalisa! My God, look at you." He stepped back. "You look well, even in breeches."

She laughed. "'Twas a masquerade to keep us safe aboard our ship—"

"Yes, where is Lord Essex?" Lord Perkins asked. "Will he be along presently?"

Abigail, lingering by the fireplace, bit her lip. "No, sir..."

"Then he remains at his Boston home?" Lady Perkins asked.

"No..." Abigail shook her head. "He's in London—"

"Young miss," Lord Perkins boomed. "You mean to tell me you spanned the Atlantic without your husband? Pray tell, whyever would you do something so foolish?"

Annalisa eyed Andrew, who had taken a seat on the blue damask settee by the window. She joined him.

"I was protected well by Annalisa in men's clothing," Abigail replied.

"And with your babe-daughter, no less!" Lord Perkins adjusted his spectacles. "Have you truly gone mad?"

"Peace, John." His wife rested a hand upon his chest. "Abigail will explain why she left her husband in London."

Abigail placed Louisa into her mother's arms. "Louisa's the reason. Charles threatened I would never see her again if I returned home."

"Essex is a reasonable man. Why would he speak such folly?" Lord Perkins asked.

Abigail sucked in a breath. "Because Louisa is not his."

Beside Annalisa, Andrew hid his face in his hands and muttered, "Unbelievable, our family."

Lord and Lady Perkins fell silent, and Annalisa studied

Sarah, who stood near the parlor door observing the scene. *Poor girl, what did she happen upon?*

"'Tis not true," Lady Perkins whispered. "You didn't—"

"I did," Abigail replied. "Before ever I wed him, I lay with George. Louisa is his."

Lord Perkins sat in his chair by the fireplace and drew up his pipe from the side table. He pulled from it for several minutes, and sweet tobacco smoke swirled about his head. Lady Perkins peered at the babe in her arms.

"She is uncannily like my brother. And George is an image of his father." She handed the girl back to Abigail and joined her husband by the crackling fire.

"I...I know you're disappointed, but Lord Essex was not the kind man you believed him to be. He...he spoke cruelly to me and...and one day he poured his soup over my head when I told him the morbid flux was upon me." She sobbed, "I wished to give him a son, but I could not."

Annalisa rose from the settee. "Friend, you never told me this."

"I was ashamed." Abigail's lip quivered, but she held her shoulders back and stood tall. "He was unkind, and to be married to such a brute—title, rank, or no—is nothing I wish for myself, or my daughter." She adjusted Louisa at her hip. "I will divorce him and marry George. And there's nothing either of you shall do to stop me."

Lady Perkins's hand lifted to her bosom. "Abigail, what will Society think?"

Lord Perkins set down his pipe, and held up his hand. "Peace, Bette. I'd not send Abigail back to such a man if what she speaks is true." He rose from his chair, crossed the room, and embraced her tightly.

Annalisa ached at the way Lord Perkins cared for his daughter—such love, such devotion—but she could tell he was tired, weary from the grief of the past year. Two years prior, when he'd forced Abigail into marrying Lord Essex, Annalisa had been certain Lord Perkins valued the match over his daughter's happiness. Now, he seemed quite altered in how he viewed matrimony, and Society.

"Pray, where's my sister?" Annalisa asked, suddenly aware of Jane's absence, and Oliver's.

Lady Perkins met her anxious stare. "She's upstairs, lying in."

"Is she well, my lady?" Annalisa asked.

"She's with child, and about to give birth any day now," Lady Perkins replied. "Though Ollie will not be joining us."

Abigail's head turned. "Whyever not? Has he joined the British, then? They'll not allow him leave?"

Lord Perkins led Abigail to the chairs before the fireplace and drew up her hand. "Oliver's deceased, my dear. We received word from Burgoyne late August—we wrote you..."

"Charles was withholding my mail." Abigail sniffled as her father's news about Oliver settled over her. "Then 'tis true? Ollie's...dead?"

Lord Perkins nodded. "He is, my dear."

Abigail clutched her father's shoulder and sobbed. "Then Jane is a widow, and with child?"

Lord Perkins regarded Annalisa as he held Abigail. "Jane was with Oliver aboard HMS *Lively,* the ship that rescued Jack after that storm wrecked *Liberté.*"

"Except Jack was taken prisoner," Andrew added spitefully.

Annalisa gasped. "Prisoner? Mean you to tell me they held Jack captive after they rescued him, even after learning his brother was on board?" Her neck burned with deep rage for Oliver. "Could Oliver say nothing to dissuade them? My lord, what is it you wish for me to know about Jack? He's joined the Continentals? When did he leave?"

"Come, Miss." Andrew looked to Sarah, still shriveled near the door. "Please, sit beside us." His crooked smile dimpled one of his cheeks, reminding Annalisa of Jack. Sarah hesitated, then with a sureness of step, joined them upon the settee by the window.

"Pray, what is your name?" Andrew asked.

"How rude of me." Annalisa warmed, though she suspected something was amiss. *Why do they evade my questions about Jack?* She gestured to Sarah. "May I present Miss Sarah..."

"Devonshire," Sarah completed the introduction. "I met Lady Essex and Miss Cav...Mrs. Perkins at London."

Lord Perkins nodded. "Pleased to make your acquaintance, Miss Devonshire. You're most welcome here."

"I apologize for not insisting you be introduced sooner," Lady Perkins added. "This has been a most...interesting reunion with my daughter and daughter-in-law. As you can see, there's been much to speak of."

"Yes, much," Annalisa agreed. "About Jack—"

"How did you come to meet my daughter and daughter-in-law, Miss Devonshire?" Lord Perkins asked.

Sarah relayed to the Perkins family of Annalisa's rescue, and of her time caring for Annalisa during her ailment and convalescence from the head injury.

"My countless thanks to you, Miss," Lord Perkins replied. "She's clearly benefited from your devoted care."

Annalisa stood. "I suppose I should like to see my sister, if I may."

Lord and Lady Perkins rose from their chairs by the fire, and Andrew lifted beside her.

"Annie," Andrew began, taking her hand. "There's something you must learn."

"Annalisa, dear, we all thought you dead—" Lady Perkins almost wheezed with exasperation. "We had no idea you survived."

Abigail's face distorted. "Mamma, whatever's the matter?"

Lady Perkins looked to her husband, who approached Annalisa. He cupped her shoulder in the gentlest of ways and gazed upon her with a depth of sadness Annalisa had never quite appreciated from him.

"Before you hear it from Jane, you must hear it from me, as it was my idea in the first."

Annalisa fisted her tingling hands. "My lord?"

Lord Perkins cleared his throat. "You must know this decision was made in everyone's best interest...your sister is soon to be mother to two children, neither of whom will ever know their father. Jack, too, was a widower—"

"No." Annalisa shook her head. "No."

"Jack and Jane were wed, my dear. Just last week."

"Fie! How could you?" Abigail shrieked, and Louisa awoke with a sudden wail.

The blood drained from Annalisa's cheeks, and her face grew cold and numb. "N-no." Her eyes welled. "How c-could you?" A heaviness returned to her chest she'd not experienced since she believed Jack dead. The weight of the past year engulfed her in a disorienting blackness—the shipwreck, her memory loss, the restoration of her speech, her escape from London—and her knees gave out.

31

ANNALISA

TOPSFIELD, FEBRUARY 1777

ANNALISA OPENED HER EYES to a blurry Abigail seated beside her. She sat upright, but Abigail shook her head.

"Easy, sweet friend."

Annalisa rubbed her eyes. "What room is this?"

"My bedchamber, at my parents' estate in Topsfield. You recall we've come home, yes?"

Annalisa nodded. A fire rustled and snapped in the white-painted fireplace. "How long have I been asleep?"

"Only a half-hour or so. You learned information most odious. I would've fainted as well."

News of Jack and Jane's marriage pummeled her into soberness, and Annalisa tossed her arm over her face. "How can this be? After all I've endured? After all Jack's endured? How could he agree to something so vile?"

Abigail stroked the coverlet over Annalisa's leg. "I know not. 'Tis the worst of luck. But I do understand it. Everyone believed you dead, Annie. Everyone, including Jack. Imagine his horror when he discovers you're alive and well."

Annalisa's breathing slowed as she considered this. *Jack doesn't know I'm alive. How horrible for him when he uncovers the truth. But what if he's fallen in love with Jane?* She sat up once more. "We must write him at once. He must know I'm home —that you're here with Louisa."

"My papa's writing to him as we speak."

"Does Jane know?"

Abigail shook her head. "My mamma was going to her. Though she's worried such news might induce labor."

Annalisa scowled. "Then let her give birth if she will. She has the life I wished for; Jack as her husband, and two children...something I couldn't give him."

"But they're not his children, Annie. They're Ollie's."

"What if he loves her?" Annalisa choked.

"La! Jack's merely risen to the duty charged him by my papa. He does right by Jane in her time of need, and nothing else. What other man of good breeding might consider her? Jack's honorable, you know that."

Annalisa considered this as well. Jack was honorable to play father to his deceased scoundrel-of-a-brother's children. *How lamentable for him.* Yet, she could hardly bring herself to see Jane.

"Will you go to her?" Abigail asked.

"I will, but I can't stay here. I must return to my family. I need my mamma and papa." Annalisa's cheeks moistened. "I need Mary, and William, and Henry." Her sob heaved her chest. "I need George."

Abigail held her, allowing the tears to soak through her dress sleeve. "I understand it. I do." She smoothed Annalisa's hair from her face. "There, there, sweet friend. Let it out."

When she'd sniveled every bit of fluid from herself, Annalisa pulled from Abigail and dried her face. "I must look a fright."

"You look as anyone would who learned their love has wed their sister. I assure you, Jane will be as melancholy to speak with you."

"Will you take me to her?"

Abigail nodded. "But let's get you washed and out of these clothes. I've a dress that might fit you."

Annalisa noticed Abigail had freshened herself and changed from her travel clothes.

When Annalisa doffed her menswear, donned Abigail's stays and petticoats, and pinned on her dress—which was too short—she loosened her hair from its queue. Her long, honey-brown locks flowed down her back.

There came a knock at the door, and Sarah entered holding a steaming mug. "Calais, I found the kitchen and had the cook brew this tea. 'Twill calm you."

Annalisa left the bed and took the cup from Sarah. "Thank you." It smelled sweetly of chamomile and lavender. She sipped, and her spirits quieted. "This is exactly the remedy for my soul, Sarah. Your physick is like magick."

Abigail, Sarah, and Annalisa gathered in the hall beyond Jane's bedchamber door. Her nephew's cry echoed from within—Jane's first-born son, whom she learned they called Tommy.

"We'll wait in the hall for you," Abigail said.

Annalisa squeezed their hands and knocked. Jane's soprano sounded tired as she instructed her to enter. Jane lay in a canopied bed, her round belly large beneath the coverlet. Dark chocolate, shiny hair drifted over her bosom in a tidy plait. Jane's porcelain skin that once bloomed like summer-time peonies appeared pale and translucent; her icy blue eyes rimmed in circles of red and purple.

Tommy, a boy of nearly one, crawled about the bedstead, boasting a head of flaxen hair, like his late father's. A pang of guilt and wretchedness overwhelmed Annalisa. Her poor, innocent nephew would never know the man who'd gifted him life.

"Janey," Annalisa croaked.

Her sister met her gaze. "Oh, Annie, we all thought you dead."

"Would that I had," she whispered.

Jane shook her head. "No, please, don't speak thus." Her gaze focused on the child staring at Annalisa. "Tommy, this is your Auntie Annie. Go on, Annalisa. Meet your nephew."

Annalisa hesitated before reaching for the child. "Hello, Tommy." She lifted him into her arms. How strange he felt compared to Louisa, whom she'd grown to know and love so well. "Have you met your cousin Louisa?"

Tommy reached up and grabbed Annalisa's *wampum* necklace. "No, no, naughty boy." She chuckled. "Louisa did the same. You're quite similar."

Jane smirked. "'Tis so good to see you—you've no idea how distraught we've been. When we learned of the ship-wreck...Mamma and Papa have not been the same since."

Annalisa sat on the bed with Tommy in her lap. "I've no words to describe the torment of this past year." She paused. "And to return, only to learn about...you and Jack," her voice cracked. "Well, I suppose there's been nothing worse that's been done to me."

"You must know 'twas because we both believed ourselves widowed." Jane bit her lip. "You heard about Oliver, yes?"

Annalisa nodded. "My condolences."

"I know you cared little for him, but I wept for weeks. Given the condition Ollie left me in," Jane ran her hand over her round stomach, "Lord and Lady Perkins felt it fitting Jack marry me. Jack was honorable enough to agree. I can't say he's happy about it, but I believe we both found comfort in one another these past several months. He's been quite tormented, too."

A wave of jealousy crashed over Annalisa at her sister's words, that Jane was with him when she was not. "How long has he been gone? When did he join the Continentals?"

"He rode to New York in December to be with George. They're now in New Jersey at winter's quarters."

"And he obtained leave to wed you?"

"Yes." Jane hesitated. "Last Sunday."

"Timing is everything, is it not?" Annalisa picked a loose thread from Abigail's green quilted petticoat. "Well, according to Abigail, Lord Perkins is writing to Jack. I suspect he'll return again, soon."

Jane fell silent.

"And when he does, I expect you to dissolve your marriage forthwith."

"A divorce?" Jane's icy glare met hers. "We've only just been wed."

"Jack and I are still married."

"You were believed dead."

"I'm not any longer."

"I'll not petition for divorce, Annalisa." Jane smoothed the coverlet over her belly. "On what grounds have I to petition?"

Annalisa fisted her petticoats. "The man you've wed is already married."

"But you were presumed dead…"

"It matters not." Annalisa replaced Tommy upon the bed. He crawled toward his mother. "When Jack returns, he'll petition if you will not."

"Under what pretense?" Jane asked. Though her voice was curt, she appeared fatigued. "A magistrate will not grant divorce unless there's reasonable cause."

Annalisa gritted her teeth. "Adultery, if I must."

Jane's full lips quivered, and Annalisa thought her sister would cry. Rather, Jane replied, "I think we've said enough. Shall we resume this intercourse on the morrow?"

"No. I'm returning home to Mamma and Papa. I'll stay there until Jack returns, then we'll resume our life in our house," Annalisa said.

The color rose in Jane's cheeks. "Know you anything of what Jack endured aboard HMS *Lively*? Of the agony after his imprisonment? I helped him escape, you know—"

"How could I? I was recovering from my own traumas, if you cared to know."

"I was there, Annalisa." Jane's gaze fixed ahead, at nothing in particular. "I saw Jack's broken leg, and the abuses he suffered at the hands of Lieutenant Dickens. I comforted him when we returned to Portsmouth, when he was poorly, and consuming laudanum."

Annalisa prickled at the image of Jane soothing Jack when it should've been her. "Oliver could've persuaded his officers to have him released. How can you sit here and tell me you did anything to rectify Jack's imprisonment? Your husband was a member of the British army." Tommy wailed, and Annalisa's throat clogged. "Forgive me. I mean not to terrify the child—"

"Get out." Jane grabbed her son and cradled him. "I've nothing more to say to you."

Annalisa turned to leave. When she reached the door, she added, "If you care to know, I was rescued and cared for by the Duchess of Devonshire, when I lost my memory and remembered nothing. The duchess cared for me. She bade me call her Georgiana. I have friends in high places, Jane, and I'm not afraid to utilize them."

Two miles down the narrow lane from the Perkins estate sprawled her family's homestead. The twenty acres of lush farmland, divided by rock walls, was now blanketed in snow, and would be verdant and fertile in a few months' time. The familiar sight of the place, where her heart truly remained, tightened Annalisa's chest. With conviction, she, Sarah, and Abigail with Louisa upon her lap, exited the Perkins's carriage—the same carriage in which she and Jack had first been intimate back in 1775. Annalisa could almost smell his amber perfume and feel the touch of his hands upon her for the first time. *Too many recollections, thankfully, most of them pleasant.*

She stepped outside and shook herself of the memory. Her shoes squeaked against the snow-shoveled path as she led her friends to the front door. Annalisa knocked, and almost immediately, the brick-red wooden door opened.

"Miss Annalisa." Liza, their indentured Irish girl, paled, and stepped back. "Is it really ye? Yer not a specter?"

"No, Liza." Annalisa shook her head. "'Tis me. I've Abigail with me, and our friend from London, Miss Devonshire. May we enter?"

Liza flushed, and she stepped aside. "O' course. Yer mam 'n da be in the drawin' room with Henry 'n Mary."

Annalisa followed Liza down the hall, her house smelling familiarly of cinnamon and clove mingled with woodsmoke, as it always did this time of year.

"Mr. 'n Mrs. Howlett—ye have guests—"

"My goodness, Liza, you must announce guests...before they enter—" Mamma's mouth fell, and her face grew wan. Her needlepoint canvas dropped to the floor.

"What is it, Peggy?" Papa turned his head, and his black eyes widened. "My God—our prayers have been answered." He jumped from the chair and hastened toward Annalisa, enfolding her in his arms. She sniffed the pipe tobacco on his linen shirt, overcome with the familiarity and comforts of home. "I've prayed and prayed, dear Annie."

"My Annalisa." Mamma lifted from her chair and tugged her from Papa's embrace. "God be praised." Annalisa's shoulder cooled from Mamma's tears soaking through her clothes.

"Annalisa!"

She stepped from Mamma and appraised Mary and Henry as they bounded into the room. *How the twins have grown in one year. They will be fifteen this August!*

Mary's eyes watered. "Mamma, I knew she lived. Did I not tell Jack I thought Annie lived?"

Henry kissed her cheek—her sweet, handsome youngest brother with smooth, light brown hair and hazel eyes to match Mary's. *His skin is still quite bronzed from summertime, more than I remember it.* Her youngest siblings shared hers and their Native grandmother's alleged tawny complexion, though Mary proved fairer, for spending more time indoors.

"Pray, where's William?" Annalisa asked.

"He's at Fort Ticonderoga," Henry replied. "He left in June."

Even William, who was afraid to defy Papa, has joined. Now two of her brothers belonged to Washington's army.

Mamma and Papa greeted Abigail, and Annalisa introduced Sarah. When they each were seated about the modest drawing room, Mamma's light-blue gaze focused upon the child in Abigail's lap.

"There's much we wish to know, and I'm certain you've much to tell us. But first, who is this little one?" Mamma asked.

Abigail beamed. "This is Louisa, named for my mamma's mamma." She hesitated. "The grandmother George and I shared...Grandmother Louisa Bixby. This girl is your grand-daughter, Mrs. Howlett."

"La!" Mamma gasped. "*My* granddaughter? How do you mean—?"

"Is it not clear, Mother?" Henry laughed. "Look at this child—she is George."

Mamma's hand rested on her bosom. "Is it true?"

Abigail nodded. "Yes."

"But what of Lord Essex?" Papa asked.

Abigail's freckled face pinked. "Before I wed Charles, George and I were...together. Before he left for the Continentals."

Mamma and Papa fell silent.

"Mr. and Mrs. Howlett, 'twas not without love, I swear it. I would've married him had he asked...had my papa not consented for me to marry Lord Essex." Abigail hesitated. "I still love George."

"Has your husband not come with you?" Mamma asked coldly.

"No, he's not come with us." Abigail relayed to them the horror that had been her life in England—a dreadfulness Annalisa never knew, nor witnessed, but only suspected.

Mamma's fingers clutched the edges of her neck handkerchief. "What cruelty. I'm glad you escaped, my dear, but what will Society think?"

"Damn Society, Peggy." Papa's face hardened, and he directed his discomfited stare toward Annalisa. "What of you, dearest?"

"I endured much this past year, sir." She elaborated how she'd been cared for by the duchess, how she'd been introduced to Society once her speech improved—this pleased Mamma very much—and the return of her memory when she'd reunited with Abigail. "We only just arrived to the Perkins's yesterday."

Papa's face fell.

"Then you've seen Janey," Mamma said.

Annalisa reached into her pocket and fingered her Bunker Hill musket round. "Yes. I know about her and Jack."

Mamma added, "We all thought you dead, dear."

"It matters not. Lord Perkins has written to Jack. I expect him to return in the coming weeks, and he can petition to divorce Jane."

Mamma's brows lifted. "You would do that to your sister? She's with child...and widowed."

"And Jack is my husband," Annalisa said. "My rightful husband."

Papa's thin lips pursed. "Annalisa, you eloped—"

"We were married by Reverend Wildes by the Book of Common Prayer. George was witness—'twas a legal marriage, I assure you." Annalisa watched her siblings. Mary and Henry lowered their gazes to the wooden floor. "Know you something I don't?"

"English law does not recognize elopements, Annalisa," Papa replied. "We may be at war with England, but this is a Loyalist home...and in this house, we observe English law."

"I know...but 'twas a legal marriage—"

"Enough." Papa held up his hand, and he scratched his thin face, bronzed and wrinkled from years in the fields. His hooded eyes sagged as he held her harried stare.

"The Marriage Act of 1753 does not recognize elopements, Annalisa," Mamma said.

"But you let us live together," Annalisa replied. "You let us live in our house down the lane. Papa, we'd been trying for children...how can you now nullify our marriage and all we experienced as a couple? Mamma, how can you ignore all of it and proclaim Jane his lawful wife?" She heaved, unable to catch her breath. "What other m-man will have me, n-now I've been deflowered, and without ch-children? What sort of future have I, if not with J-Jack? Please, Mamma, Papa. Please."

Mamma frowned. "There's little we can do, Annalisa. Society—"

"I suppose I'll return to my house by the gristmill." Annalisa stood and turned to her friends, seated silently on the sofa. "Come. I've plenty of room to host you."

"Annie, wait—" Mary chased after her. "Take me with you."

"Mary Howlett, be seated," Mamma hissed.

"I only wish to spend the night at Annie's," Mary replied. "I want to hear her stories of London and the Duchess of Devonshire."

"Tomorrow, Mary. I'll retrieve you. You too, Henry." Annalisa fled the drawing room with Sarah, and Abigail and Louisa.

❦

THE BLACK SILHOUETTE OF HER MODEST SALTBOX WAS etched against a late winter dusk. In just a month's time, the sun would set noticeably later and rise earlier, a precursor to spring and the rebirth of everything. The irony was not lost on Annalisa as she stepped up to her house—a home she'd not entered in over a year—an awakening of sorts.

Addy answered. "Miss...Annie, it is you?" She clutched Annalisa. "Oh, Heavens, child, it is you."

Annalisa inhaled Addy's familiar scent of herbs and woodsmoke. "I've missed you so." She stepped into the foyer with the old housekeeper and gestured to Sarah—Abigail had returned home for Louisa's fussiness—and introduced her newest friend. The two women acknowledged one another.

"Pleased to make your acquaintance, Miss Addy." Sarah curtsied as any other London lady would. Though she'd been the duchess's chambermaid, it was evident Sarah's etiquette eclipsed others' within her station.

"The pleasure's mine, Miss Sarah," Addy replied. "You've accompanied my Miss Annie well, it seems."

"I accompany her of my free will, Miss Addy," Sarah replied.

Addy nodded. "And I'm employed by the Howletts of my own free will. Come in. The fire's roaring. I just knew something would happen this day. Something in the wind felt different." She led them into the kitchen and stood by the large, brick hearth.

Annalisa reached for her musket above the mantel, and ran her fingers over the smooth wood exterior. "I'm sure you heard Jack's no longer my husband."

"I did, Miss Annie, when last I was at your parents' house. Miss Janey is with child, and widowed. We all thought Jack were widowed as well." Addy swiped her thumb across the scar beneath Annalisa's right eye. "And here you are. In the flesh."

"Pray, is Quinnapin about?" Annalisa asked, eager to see him. "I would love to see him, too."

Addy's frown deepened. "Mr. Quinnapin lost his wife, Weetamoo. You remember her, yes?"

Annalisa clutched her bosom. "Oh, poor Quinn. Whatever happened to Weetamoo? She was exquisite, and so kind..."

"Lost her to the Iroquois, he said," Addy replied. "On their way through New York from visiting Mr. Quinn's Mohican friend."

"Were they traveling to meet George?"

Addy nodded. "But he's returned. If you wish, I can retrieve him."

"No." Annalisa shook her head. "I couldn't possibly disturb him with my troubles—"

The front door opened and closed.

"Trouble who?" Quinnapin, tall and tawny with unbound long, black hair, strode into the kitchen. He was handsome, as Annalisa remembered, with square jaw, and sable eyes.

"Quinn." She hurried to him, and he embraced her. He lifted her into the air and spun her around.

"Look at you." He stepped back and studied her. "You're radiant, in a returned-from-the-dead kind of way."

Annalisa laughed. "'Tis true, I suppose. Everyone thought me so, yet here I am." She gestured to Sarah and introduced her friend. "And this is Quinnapin, my old friend. He's Wampanoag."

Quinnapin kissed Sarah's hand. "The pleasure is mine, Miss Sarah."

"What is Wampanoag?" Sarah asked.

"My nation of people, *Wôpanâak*. It means *people of the first light*," he replied. "We're from the lands south of Shawmut, or Boston, as Miss Anna calls it. I'm from Mashpee but journeyed to Shawmut, where I came to meet this lass through her brother and husband—" He caught himself. "Forgive me. May I call Jack your husband?"

"He was when I left this place, was he not?" Annalisa said. "I love him."

Quinnapin nodded. "When you meet again, you may say to him: *kuwamônush*, I love you."

Tears gathered behind her eyes. *"Kuwamônush."*

Quinnapin smiled. His hand drifted to her neck and lifted the small, carved feather. "I see you kept the *wampum*."

Sarah exclaimed, "Ah, so this is Quinnapin who made you that necklace."

"Yes, I did." He eyed Sarah. "Are you from the same place as Miss Addy?"

"I'm from Barbados," Addy replied.

"Me, too," Sarah said, her face pleasantly alight with joy.

"Where?" Addy asked.

Sarah lowered her gaze. "I know not. I was ripped from my mother before I could learn of the place."

"Sarah wishes to return to Barbados," Annalisa replied.

Addy sighed. "Barbados is a long way from here, and full of all kinds of dangers if you don't know where you're headed." Addy, probably noticing the deflated look upon Sarah's face, reached for the girl's hand. "It don't matter, child. I'll tell you all about our island, yes? Mayhap one day we'll return, you and I."

Sarah nodded, her mouth sweetly lifting. "I'd love that, Miss Addy."

"Very well. Now, let me make us some coffee." She glanced at Annalisa. "We're still a house that don't serve tea, yes, Miss Annie?"

Annalisa nodded. "Aye. There's no tea in this household."

32

JACK

MORRISTOWN, NEW JERSEY, MARCH 1777

H AVING BEEN NEWLY INOCULATED against smallpox, Jack's body ached and his head burned with fever. He threw down his quill from the page, unable to write to Jane, and rubbed his neck and face. She would soon be delivered of their child, and he was at Morristown. *Annie is dead, I know, but Jane can never replace her...*He shuddered. Their marriage had been sparse, only family in attendance while Reverend Emerson wed them in his family's parlor. The memory haunted him nearly as much as his time aboard HMS *Lively. I never wished to marry her, dear heart. I never wished to...* Jack's throat clogged, and he pinched his eyes. *I loathe that I betrayed you, my darling...that I allowed my unmitigated scorn for Benjamin Cavendish to cloud my judgment.*

"Perkins, a letter for you."

Weary, Jack peered up at George, who tossed a folded page at him.

20th February 1777
Topsfield

Dearest Jack,

There is no way to Express the unmitigated and unbelievable Thing I am about to write. And it comes at a time most inopportune with your marriage to Jayne. Your late wife, Analissa, has but graced Us with her presense this day with your Sister Abbie and a daughter she bore to George Howlet—a Girl she named Loveesa, after your mother's mother...

"Zounds!" Jack's heart galloped and he stopped reading. Looking up, his cheeks tingled. "My God! Have you read this?"

George shook his head. "I've not. 'Twas addressed to you. You look pale. Is it the letter or the inoculation?"

Jack handed him the note. "Read it."

George scanned the page and his eyes rounded. "Well, I'll be damned! Annie's alive!"

A renewed sense of vigor overcame his fatigue, and Jack jumped from his cot to embrace George. "And you're a father. My wife's returned to me by the grace of God, and I'm uncle to your daughter."

"Louisa." George rubbed his chin, re-reading the letter. "Not the name I'd have chosen, but I suppose 'tis fair Abigail name her."

"'Tis for our grandmother—my mother's mother," Jack replied. "The grandmother we share."

George guffawed. "Then 'tis a fitting name, indeed."

As quickly as Jack soared higher than the sky and clouds toward the reaches of Heaven, the Devil reeled him back to the earth and far below, into the fiery pits of his dark caverns.

"I've just wedded Jane..."

George jutted his square jaw. "Poorly timed nuptials. But you and Annie were married first. Can you not annul this marriage?"

Jack went to spin his absent signet ring. "I know not, but I must return to Topsfield at once. Will you grant me leave?"

"Will I? I'll obtain leave for myself as well." George bellowed a boisterous laugh. "Louisa. Think you she will take my name? Louisa Howlett?"

Jack grinned. "I should think so—"

"But Abigail remains married to that plum Lord Essex. Pray, think you he accompanies her?"

Jack reread the letter. "My father's mentioned nothing of Essex. I daresay, he's not with her, but I can't be certain."

"It matters not," George replied. "I'll challenge the plum."

Trembling from fever and thrill, Jack packed his haversack. "Let us ride at dawn."

33

ANNALISA

TOPSFIELD, MARCH 1777

B ANG, BANG, BANG.
Addy answered the door, and a cold gust of March air swept inside the house. "Miss Abigail."

"I need Annalisa, most urgently."

At the familiar voice, Annalisa, seated by the kitchen hearth stitching a hole in one of her stockings, set down her things and hurried into the foyer. Abigail stood with Addy, her mouth creased with concern.

"What is it, Abbie?" Annalisa asked.

Abigail fiddled with her gloves. "'Tis Jane. She's requested your presence."

"No." Annalisa shook her head. "I've not spoken to her since we returned to town—"

"Please, Annie. She's in labor."

ANNALISA LINGERED IN THE DOORWAY TO JANE'S bedchamber. Beyond, her sister lay in the canopied bed breathing heavily, a sheen of sweat coating her face, neck, and bosom. Mamma paced near the foot of the bed as Dr. Brown, and his midwife, Mrs. Curtis, examined Jane.

"I want...my sister," Jane huffed. Seemingly delirious, she turned to Lady Perkins, who stood beside her. "Please...I want...my sister."

"Yes, of course, dear." Lady Perkins nodded for Annalisa to enter, and she stepped into the room.

"Mrs. Perkins requires rest." Dr. Brown finished his exam and handed his instruments to Mrs. Curtis. "The child is tucked within her. We've still some time before he begins to descend."

"Give her this to quell the anxiety." Mrs. Curtis handed Mamma a small bag of dried herbs, then whizzed past Annalisa, and hastened from the room with Dr. Brown.

Lady Perkins summoned Mercy, who popped her head into the room. "Please you, fix this tea for our dear Janey."

Mercy took the small bag from Mamma and left the room.

"Where is Oliver?" Jane cried. "Where is Jack? He shall miss the birth."

Her anguished screams made Annalisa's skin crawl. *Such are words I should've said.*

Mamma stroked Jane's head. "My love, your child comes. Be not saddened by Jack's or Oliver's absence, for tonight you shall bear Ollie a most beloved son. But look, Annie's come to see you."

Annalisa inched forward until she could clearly see the haggard fatigue upon Jane's face. "I'm here." She kissed Jane's brow, though she trembled at the sight. *How horrid she looks. Is this what the childbed looks like?*

"Leave us," Jane cried.

"But darling," Mamma crooned, remaining by the bed.

"I must speak with Annie. Alone."

Annalisa avoided Mamma's harsh stare as she stepped from the room with Lady Perkins and Abigail. When they'd gone, and closed the door behind them, Annalisa settled upon the bed.

"What is it, Jane?"

"If I die...I must confess..."

"Hush, you mustn't tempt fate." Annalisa dabbed her sister's forehead with a damp linen cloth.

"Please, Annie...I must confess."

"Jane, I'm not a reverend." Apprehensive, Annalisa rose from the bed and hastened to the door. She stuck her neck into the hallway. "Mamma, she wishes to confess her sins. Shall we call the reverend?"

Mamma and Lady Perkins, their faces warped with concern, rushed inside the chamber.

"Janey, you've no sins to confess." Mamma perched upon the bed and smoothed Jane's hair. "I can't imagine it."

The hours passed, turning Jane's porcelain cheeks from pink to crimson, and her tormented cries to tortured screams. Abigail entered to the room and stood by Annalisa, who dawdled as far from the birthing bed as possible.

"'Tis a fright, is it not?" Abigail said quietly.

Annalisa shuddered. "To think, we willingly seek to place ourselves in that childbed."

"Abbie, darling, fetch Andrew," Lady Perkins said. "Ask him to call upon Dr. Brown."

"Yes, Mamma." Abigail fled the room.

"You must endure, my Janey." Mamma stroked the wet hair from Jane's face.

Jane shook her head. Her eyes squeezed shut, she emitted a primal groan. "Where is my husband?"

Annalisa reached for the *wampum* feather at her throat. *Jack is not this babe's father. Call out for Oliver. He did this to you.*

"His...son..." Jane's voice diminished to nothing, caught in a short a moment of intense squeeze. Then, her eyes wide with terror, she gazed hard at Annalisa. "This...child." Her guttural cry filled the room, rendering her incapable of speech.

Dr. Brown and Mrs. Curtis meandered into the bedchamber behind Abigail. With him, Dr. Brown hauled a large buckskin bag of medical tools. Mrs. Curtis made her way to Jane and examined her.

"I believe 'tis time, Dr. Brown."

"There, there, Mrs. Perkins. Everything will be all right." Dr. Brown opened his bag. "If I may..." He glanced at Mamma and Lady Perkins, and they stepped aside. Dr. Brown then turned Jane to her side and commenced with an invasive exam. "I feel the child's head. Mrs. Perkins, if you could please curl up your knees."

Jane tucked up her knees as she lay on her side, away from Dr. Brown, who never once looked at Jane, only felt.

"Now, you must push," he said.

Annalisa tamped away her fear of the childbirth, and rushed to the other side of the bed, and knelt. "Janey, you must push as fiercely as you can."

"Oh God, I can't," she shrieked.

"You must," Abigail said. "'Tis is the only way. Come, you've done this before."

Annalisa stroked her sister's head, and Jane, squeezing her eyes shut, inhaled and held her breath.

"Yes, keep it up." Dr. Brown removed a strange instrument from his bag, but he seemed not to require it as the baby's head emerged.

After the head, a small body, with strange skin coated with fluids, followed. A piercing cry flew from the mouth of the infant, and Dr. Brown held up the child. A boy. When the cord was cut, Dr. Brown handed him to the midwife, who cleaned and wrapped him in a muslin towel.

"Oh darling, he's wonderful." Mamma beamed at her third grandchild. "He's the handsomest."

"'Tis a...boy?" Jane's voice cracked as she spoke, her whole self now fluid as water. A tired grin lifted her mouth, then promptly faded. Jane sobbed as the doctor placed the newborn into her arms. The boy cried, and Annalisa's eyes stung with tears. Was it envy, or merely the miracle of birth?

"You must now be delivered of the afterbirth," Dr. Brown said.

Annalisa looked to Mamma, Lady Perkins, and Abigail, who all seemed to know what this meant, though none of them met her anxious stare. Mrs. Curtis retrieved the newborn from Jane, and Annalisa stepped forward.

"I'll take him."

She reached for the bundle and cradled him. How tiny, his little fingers and toes, the nails even smaller. How came a complete person—with ten fingers and toes, two lovely eyes, one button nose, and two perfectly shaped lips—from the inside of another? The awe, not envy, tightened her throat. When she looked up, Dr. Brown carried a bowl filled with bloody meat, the long birthing cord still attached.

"What is that?" Annalisa cried. "Is Jane all right? Have her insides come out as well?"

Abigail laughed. "'Tis the afterbirth, Annie. It comes out after the baby's born." Her hand slid down Annalisa's arm. "Worry not, you'll one day come to know these things."

"This is my first time...seeing. I knew not that happened. Pray, what is it?"

"I'm not even sure...but I believe 'tis where the baby lives inside us," Abigail replied.

Lady Perkins joined them by the door. She peered at her

grandson and beamed. "When you were born, Abbie, we had no doctor present, only the midwife and other women to support me." She eyed Dr. Brown. "Was a doctor present at Louisa's birth?"

Abigail nodded. "Yes, and a midwife, and my chambermaid, along with several others."

"'Tis a newness to their practice, I suppose. Why not add midwifery to their list of skills?" Lady Perkins regarded Annalisa. "Is this the first newborn you've held, my dear?"

"It is, my lady." Annalisa's gaze fixed on the boy. He was too perfect, a tiny angel from Heaven, asleep in her arms. "Would that I could have one of my own." She broke her stare from the child and thrust the babe into Lady Perkins's arms. "I must take air. I beg leave."

Annalisa quit the chamber and closed the door behind her. In the silent hallway, she drew in a staggered breath. *How may I one day endure such torment? Surely, it can't be as terrible as battle...*From the first floor, the front door opened and closed, and a man's soft baritone floated up the stairs.

"Pray, is she well?"

Annalisa perked at the voice and ran down the stairs, stopping on the bottom step, her fingers gripping the banister, her heart threatening to beat through her breast.

Jack stood in the doorway, erect, as though he were at attention from a commanding officer. He was as handsome as she'd remembered, though a bit gaunt. Perhaps it was a leanness that came from marching hundreds of miles, or the manual labor required within the Continentals. Her heart galloped into her throat as she caught his harried stare.

"Annalisa." He staggered a moment, perhaps unsure of whether to whisk her from the step or bow to her as friends.

"Jack."

He advanced toward her, and she threw her arms about his neck.

"Annie." Jack crumpled to the floor with her.

She pulled from him, and they each cupped the other's face. Her fingers slid over the wetness upon his cheeks.

"'Tis you. 'Tis truly you." Jack glanced up at his father, who stood by, and pulled Annalisa to her feet. "Sir, may we have a moment?"

Lord Perkins removed his spectacles and pinched the space between his eyes. "Of course. Come into the drawing room. No one shall disturb you there."

✣ 34 ✤

ANNALISA

TOPSFIELD, MARCH 1777

ANNALISA STOOD BY THE fire, allowing the heat to dry her damp face. She ran a hand over her green dress, one that always complimented her eyes. *How strange I should care how Jack sees me.*

As he closed the drawing room door and approached, she trembled.

"Jack," she choked. *How can he be my brother-in-law?* Only a cruel God would bestow such a travesty upon her.

Jack's thumb slid across the scar beneath her right eye, then lifted her hand and kissed it. "I cannot believe 'tis you." Stepping back, he studied her, then shook his head, his cheeks dimpling with a laugh. "You're incandescent—as though nothing ruinous ever passed between us. I'm not sure how, but I'd forgotten how tall you are."

She fiddled with her hands, suddenly nervous before him. "I know not what to s-say. It feels like the f-first time we m-met."

"No need to be anxious, dear heart." Jack's face softened, and he drew her into his arms. "'Tis only me."

Lulled by his amber perfume, she melted into him. Her head against his neck, she shivered, recalling his gentle whispers that once tickled her ear. *How long since our last night together? What I wouldn't do to relive it.*

She pulled from him. "I suppose I know not how to be with you."

His head tilted. "How do you mean?"

"Now that," she swallowed, "that you've m-married Jane."

Jack's face hardened.

"Of course, I know. 'Twas one of the affairs I learned when first I returned." She drew away from him. "I understand it, as much as I can—everyone thought me dead..." Her voice broke, and she brought the heels of her hands to her eyes. "Would that I had d-died in that shipwreck than endure all this."

"No, Annalisa." Jack pulled her to him once more. "No, please. Right now, listen to me..." He lifted her chin with his thumb and forefinger. "In this moment, speak to me as your husband, for that is who I am. Yes? Before any of this befell us, when last I saw you, you were my wife." He drew her toward the sofa facing the fire and sat. "I want to know everything since the shipwreck. But if 'tis too painful to recount, I'll share all I endured."

She shook her head. "I remember little, if anything, of the wreck itself, only what I was told by my rescuer."

"I thank God you were rescued." He kissed her hand, one knuckle at a time.

A small smile lifted her lips. "The Duchess of Devonshire. She found me upon a pier in Calais."

Jack's brow quirked. "The Duchess of Devonshire?"

"She called me Calais when I could not remember my name." Though she grinned at the memory, a look of horror spread across his face.

"You could not recall your name?"

"I remembered nothing of my life. Not even myself."

"This is grave to hear." He glanced above her, then to the floor. "My heart breaks...that you suffered such terror."

"'Twas distressing, I assure you, but my living conditions atoned for any physical or emotional suffering I bore. I was nursed to health at Devonshire House. I knew the duchess, and we became friends. She bade me call her Gee...for Georgiana." Annalisa bit her lip. "My greatest grievance was upon recovering my memory—when I learned you had died."

"Oh, Annie." Jack's lips found hers. They were soft, but he kissed her reverently and passionately, as she'd dreamt this past year. "We both believed the other perished."

"How could we have not?" She held his hand and ran her fingers over the calluses. "I received no word from our families—"

"But Abigail?"

"When I reunited with Abbie, we learned her husband is not the man we believed him to be. He withheld Abigail's mail. 'Twas how we discovered you lived...we uncovered a letter that had been addressed to her. 'Twas after that, we plotted to quit London."

"Then you were as much prisoner as I." Jack scowled. "You may have heard I was held aboard HMS *Lively*."

She prickled. "Jane told me, but not all of what befell you."

He bit his full bottom lip. "'Twas agony, mourning you each moment I was awake, grieving you in my dreams when I slept...between abuses." He touched his leg. "My leg had broken badly. I daresay 'tis healed, but still aches when I ride or march too far."

"The same leg you injured at Concord."

"Aye, it is." He paused. "You heard about Ollie?"

"Yes."

"I know you cared little for him. I too, held many griev-ances with him aboard HMS *Lively*. But he's no longer upon this earth. I must learn to speak of him with peace in my heart and love him as a brother should..." Gloom twisted his face. "It distresses me greatly to have you beside me, as I've wed Jane. I lost my faith, Annie. I curse God for all he's taken from us. He's a cruel, unjust God."

"No. Speak not so, love. He brought us together again. I'm here. And so are you. We survived against all odds."

A small, crooked smile dimpled his cheek. "I love you." He pulled her onto his lap and showered her face and neck with kisses. "I've never stopped loving you, Annalisa. Never."

He spoke her name with such desirous desperation, she shivered, sparking her womanhood. She pulled him down on top of her.

The yearning in his eyes faded to angst, and he sat upright. "I can't."

"Whatever do you mean?"

"Jane's just given birth...I..." He held his face in his hands. "Annie, I'm married to Jane. Fie! If I could alter the course of divine Providence, I would. I abhor the arrangement, Annie. To my very core, I loathe everything about it, but I—"

"You what?"

"I can't commit adultery, not when she's just given birth."

Her mouth bent. "But...I'm your wife. Yes, we eloped, but 'twas still legal...you said so yourself."

"Aye, 'twas legal." Jack drew up her hands. "Annie, we all believed you dead."

The way he was overcome by the last word, she knew he fought back tears.

"But I'm here, now. Does this mean nothing to anyone?"

"Of course. You mean everything. But I can't ignore all

that's passed while you were gone. Believe me, I wished for none of this. 'Twas forced upon me by my father, and in your absence, I agreed it was the honorable thing to do. I never thought...I never—" Jack pressed his hands to his face. When he'd composed himself, his red-rimmed gaze held hers. "I never thought you'd return to me."

He fell silent for a moment, then recited, "'*I love the man that can smile in trouble, that can gather strength from distress, and grow brave by reflection. 'Tis the business of little minds to shrink; but he whose heart is firm, and whose conscience approves his conduct, will pursue his principles unto death.*' Thomas Paine wrote those words in his latest essay, *The Crisis*. I found they rang true to me, dear heart."

From his candid stare, she knew he spoke truth. And the tormented integrity which anguished him seeped forth until she, too, tripped inside his moralities, incapable of affording the fantasy. He was not hers to love. She could no more force him to be beholden to her than she could've within that cold grave everyone believed her to be. Gazing down at the ring he'd given her, she tugged it from her finger; one of the relics she'd so cherished in trying to return her memories to her, no longer belonged to her.

"I'll not obstruct your principles." Annalisa handed him the ring. "You must go to Jane. We've said our piece."

Jack hesitated a moment, his gaze fixed on the ring. Without saying more, he stood and turned from her, but he delayed again, perhaps unwilling to leave her after all they'd endured. He faced her.

"Meet me at our house. There, we can at least have some semblance of privacy to talk. I can't promise you I'll remain with you the night, but—"

Annalisa rose from the sofa and placed a finger to his lips. "I'll meet you." Despite his impassioned speech from Thomas

Paine, a glint of determination bubbled up. "I promise I won't tempt you into our bed."

Jack lifted her hand and grazed his lips across the knuckles. "By your leave, Miss." He quit the room, not looking back.

❧ 35 ❧
JACK
TOPSFIELD, MARCH 1777

JACK CLIMBED THE STAIRCASE with a heaviness he'd not known since he learned Annalisa had died. Closing the door on her now was the penultimate sacrifice of his sins committed, and the last thing he wished to do. Rather, he yearned to take her to his bedchamber and hold her; to strum her again and again until the sun rose, never to release her from his embrace. He would make up for time lost this past year, when his desperate days had been spent longing for her, mourning her in a haze of laudanum-induced numbness. Now, rather than remain in the arms of his beloved, he must reap the consequences of his behaviors made in haste, during the darkest night of his lamentations.

He knocked on Jane's chamber door, then entered. His mother and Mrs. Howlett spoke in hushed tones while Abigail rocked a small bundle at her breast.

"Jack." Abigail handed the baby to Mother and hurried to embrace him. "Oh, Brother. You look well, though a bit thin. Pray, is Morristown terrible?"

"We'll leave you two alone." Mother settled the newborn

into Jane's lap, and advanced toward the door with Mrs. Howlett. "Abigail, come along."

"In a moment," Abigail hissed.

When Mrs. Howlett and Mother left the room, Jack spoke carefully about their horrendous winter in New Jersey —men ridden with smallpox, the number of deserters, but that he and George had been inoculated, and maintained health.

"Where's George? He's not joined you?" Abigail's eyes misted.

"He couldn't obtain leave," Jack replied. "He sends you his love. Pray, how is Louisa?"

Though Abigail's face fell, she smiled. "She's well at ten months. You'll meet her in the morning." She looked to Jane, who rested with her eyes closed, but kept the child close to her breast. "You have another nephew. She's not yet decided on a name, but 'tis her second son. He should be named for Mr. Howlett." Abigail shook her head. "'Tis no matter...I think she wished to discuss it with you—her *husband*."

Jack flinched at the way she said the word with hardened spite.

Abigail gripped his arm. "Pray, how did this happen? How came you to marry her?"

"I thought Annalisa died. I never would have wed Jane if I'd known Annie lived," he whispered. "When we learned Ollie had been killed, leaving Jane widowed with one child and one on the way, how could I not replace him? What other gentleman of good breeding would have her in such a state? 'Tis my duty as heir to this estate, Abbie."

"Now what will you do?"

"I know not. Can I divorce Jane when she's just given birth? When we've just been wed? I know not a single magistrate who would condone such a petition."

Abigail shrugged. "You're the lawyer, I suppose you would know. Perhaps you've reason to divorce her on the grounds you're already married. You never know what the magistrates will say."

"Father was magistrate. I know what the magistrates will say," Jack snapped.

"'Tis worth at least trying, Jack. If it means you can be with Annalisa."

"Jack?" Jane's head turned in their direction. "Is it you?"

Jack left Abigail and sat beside her upon the bed. "How do you feel? You look quite fatigued."

Her full lips parted. "As do you. The ride from Morristown was long?"

"Quite. I was inoculated not long ago. But I heard—"

"Annalisa lives. And so you came to see her." Jane sat up and peered at the bundled baby in her arms. "Would you like to hold him?"

Jack swallowed. "Aye." His hands shook as she placed the newborn into them. How small he felt compared to Tommy, his brother's son, now nearly one. But this boy was his. *Will he inherit my eyes? My smile?* The child slept peacefully in the crook of his arm. Yes, his face was perfect and symmetrical in the most beautiful of ways—evidence of his foolish and despairing union with Jane. *How was such a divine creature borne of such despondency?*

He turned. Abigail had left the room, leaving them quite alone.

"You wished to name him with me?"

"Yes," she replied.

Perhaps she's willing to now reveal the boy's fathering. "He should take my father's name, since he's my first-born son—"

"But he was born of scandal," Jane replied. "Society will know I lay with you before Ollie died, my reputation will be ruined. He's my second son, and must be named for my father, Robert William."

Jack bristled. "You said if I agreed to marry you, we could tell our families I fathered this child after he was born. He's now born. It must be done."

"No...we can't, Jack. I can't betray Ollie's memory—"

"But this boy is my son, my first-born." He reached into his arsenal of reason, and added, "He can inherit my titles if I acknowledge him."

This gave Jane pause, and he held his breath awaiting her reply. Titles and rank always pleased her, perhaps as much as marrying advantageously. But she shook her head. "No. No one can know what we've done, Jack. We must call him Robert, for my father. That way no one can question his birth."

His face heated. "Reputation be damned. The truth must be told, for if not, this information will veer its nasty head one day, with or without our consent."

"Annalisa can't know," Jane blurted. "I nearly told her during my labors...I believed myself near death. But I know now what a foolish endeavor that would've been."

Jack started. "Annalisa must know. If she discovers this when the child is grown to look like me, or the information is mistakenly spilled by one of us, she will loathe us for eternity."

Jane diverted her stare. "I care little for whether or no she loathes me. This is my child, and my secret to bear. As it is yours. Do you really wish for the people of town to call me 'harpy' or you, 'lecher'?"

"I'd rather Society call me 'lecher' than ignore the birthright that is deserving of my son, or have Annalisa believe me deceitful." With one hand—the other still cradling the baby—he loosened his cravat, the air stifling him. "She was my wife, Jane. And I still very much love her. We must do right by her and our families…and our son."

"You'll always love her, won't you?" Jane said bitterly. "You'll leave me for Annalisa now that she's alive. I'll be a widow with two children to raise on my own." She hesitated. "You saw her, didn't you…before you came to me. Before you met your son."

"The son you won't allow me to recognize." He stiffened at her resolve, and his loathing returned. Jack gritted his teeth. "And yes, I did see her. I thought I'd lost her forever. But when we met, I did nothing to compromise your integrity, or mine. We spoke of things that passed between us, and I upheld my marriage vows to you. But none of that changes how I feel for this boy, and what Annalisa must know. 'Twill hurt her, yes, but will devastate her more if this secret is kept."

Jane reached for the boy, and Jack handed him back to her. "If you tell Annie, I swear upon Oliver's soul, I'll have her poisoned—"

"This is absurd," Jack cried. "I don't take well to threats, madam. If you so much as look at Annalisa in an unfavorable light, I swear upon Oliver's soul, I will pursue a divorce petition, and everyone will know the truth about our son."

"Then I shall poison myself and our child," she hissed. "I swear it upon *my* soul, *and* Oliver's."

Jack's stomach churned at the hideous, cruel threat, and stepped away from the bed. *What madness has descended upon her? This is not the same Jane Howlett I've known all these years…* She'd always been preoccupied with Society and upholding her reputation, but this was beyond reason.

A simper escaped her lips as she peered down at the newborn, and she stroked his tiny head. "Jack, don't you see? There's no way for this to end well for any of us."

JACK

TOPSFIELD, MARCH 1777

JACK STEPPED INSIDE THE house he'd shared with Annalisa when she was his wife. It was quaint but comfortable, and sparsely furnished with borrowed items from his father's cousin who owned the property. Annalisa sat at the kitchen table, her back to the fire blazing within the brick hearth. Her head, uncovered by her linen cap, hovered over her hands as though she studied something within them. His heart panged; it was as though they'd never left this life, as though she'd always been there, and he, always beside her.

As he moved toward the table, he noticed her musket above the mantel—a gift he'd given her with Quinnapin. Jack tugged a chair adjacent to where she sat and pulled it beside her. Sliding into the seat, Annalisa peered up at him, and he saw she studied a musket round. He smoothed the soft curls from her angular face and recalled Jane's words. *Can I believe her threats?*

"I'm glad you came," Annalisa said. "I was worried you wouldn't."

Jack kissed her forehead, and Annalisa nestled her face into his neck, adding, "I know not how to be with you when I've longed for you this past year..."

"Then speak to me as your husband, lover, and friend. You're my dearest, most cherished friend, indeed." Jack inhaled the powder and pomade clinging to her hair, laced with the faint sweetness of lilac. "When I was Adams's apprentice, I observed him and his wife with great interest; he used to tell me she was his greatest friend and confidante. I envied their friendship...I wished for such a marriage myself."

"Would that I could be your Mrs. Adams."

"You were far better than Mrs. Adams. You were my Mrs. Perkins."

Annalisa entwined their fingers and kissed his hand. "There's not another man like you in this world. I daresay I'd rather spend my life alone than marry again."

"Speak not so." *This is too hard. How can I look upon her as my sister-by-law when she was once my wife?*

"'Tis but the truth, and I'm not ashamed to admit it. I met plenty of eligible gentlemen in Europe, and not one compared to you." Annalisa fell silent for some time. "I wish you were with me in London."

"Do tell me of London."

"The *ton* is riddled with gossip. Georgiana, the Duchess of Devonshire, was my closest friend. Poor Gee was trapped in an unhappy marriage with the duke—a very taciturn sort of fellow. Lady Jersey, a weasel in silk and rouge, made a cuckold of her husband with any man that would have her—"

"The scandal," Jack gasped in mockery. "And these are the matters of the elite across our vast ocean."

"Yes. And before my memory returned to me, my origins

were dubious at best, so Georgiana held a masquerade to introduce me to Society as Miss Cavendish..."

Jack stiffened at the name. *Benjamin Cavendish. I should ask her about the gentleman...*He shook himself of the thought. *Perhaps at a later date, I can inquire her of the gentleman.*

"...London's *ton* is comprised of licentious, two-faced gossipers," she continued. "Everyone takes a lover, or three, so long as they've birthed an heir. One day you're the listener to a most delicious, scandalous tale, the next, your own detailed gossips fly from the mouth of your previous day's confidante."

His mind whirled with Benjamin Cavendish, and the child he fathered with Jane. *I'm no better than London's lustful profligates.*

"A few gentlemen were kind," Annalisa said. "Mr. Fox, Mr. Beauregard, and Mr. Fitzherbert. But others were scoundrels."

"*Monsieur* Claude Beauregard?" Jack asked, his interested piqued.

"Yes. Know you him?"

"Zounds!" He laughed. "I met the gentleman years ago when Oliver and I visited Versailles. Beauregard was my contact in France..." He wondered how Mr. Deane fared in Paris. *How long ago Congress's summons seems...*

"He was the doctor directing my care when I was in Paris. A kind man, from what I recall." She smiled. "How strange I met someone across the Atlantic with whom you were acquainted. Even Mr. Fitzherbert reminded me of you...at first—though I knew not who you were."

Jack frowned. "How close you came to forgetting me forever."

"I know." Annalisa shivered, and he pulled her close. "I wish it could be like this forever."

Jack kissed the top of her head. "So could I, love."

"Then let's hope the sun never rises again."

"If only I could contain the sun and give you the moon. Then for us, it would always be like this. We could forget the war...and everything else unfavorable."

Her head perked up from his shoulder. "You mean to say our army does not do well?"

"Our victory at Trenton was uplifting, but who's to say at winter's end we'll have enough men left to continue the fight. The conditions are deplorable at Morristown."

"Are my brothers well?"

"George is captain of his militia. He meets with General Washington on occasion. I daresay, he's the bravest man there. I've not seen William. He remains at Ticonderoga."

"Will George marry Abigail?"

"If she can divorce Essex. It pains me to know she was as much prisoner in her own house as you were to your mind, as I was aboard HMS *Lively*. She may petition with desertion, or adultery if he's been unfaithful."

Annalisa was quiet for some time. "Could you petition something similar?"

He considered what Jane had threatened, and his breath quickened. *If I had but one sip of laudanum...no, 'tis gone from my life. I must quell it on my own. Annalisa can never know what befell me.*

"What is it?" Annalisa asked.

"Nothing, dear heart. We can discuss more of these things tomorrow. 'Tis getting late and I must return—"

"Nonsense. I'll burn as many candles as I must until the sun rises, and you've explained to me enough why we can't be together when I know we can."

"Peace, Annalisa. 'Tis not so simple."

She rose, the chair squealing across the wooden floor.

"Then my worst fear has come to pass. All the torment of the past year has been nothing compared to this—"

"What fear do you speak of?"

"You love me no longer."

She looked as though her very soul had flown from her, leaving behind a ghostly pall of a person. The sight of her anguished face crushed him. He loved her more than he valued anything in this world, and to hear her speak such folly with such conviction was unbearable. His breath tightened, and he stood with her. Unable to endure his own suffering, he drew her into his arms and blended his mouth with hers.

She melted into his embrace, and between kisses, Jack said, "Dearest love, that is simply not so."

"Then let me have you. Just tonight."

Forsaking Jane's threat and Thomas Paine's credos on conscience and conduct, he deepened his kisses. The assuredness of her love overtook, and warmth spread through his body as Annalisa clung to him, awakening desire and longing. *No amount of opium could supplant this feeling. I feel.*

"Annalisa," he sighed pleasurably. "I'll spend every second of this night proving my love for you. I swear it."

◈◈◈

JACK REACHED FOR ANNALISA, BUT THE SPACE WAS EMPTY. His heart raced. *Was it a cruel dream? Had she never been there at all?* Several mornings he'd awakened similarly, the laudanum having confused him into believing her ghost had laid with him the night prior. He sat up.

Annalisa stood before the mirror, brushing her hair. She faced him and beamed. "You're awake."

He sighed and flopped against the pillows. "I reached for you and you were gone—I thought it all a dream."

Annalisa set the brush on the bedside table and approached their bed. "Last night was no dream." She took his hand and placed it over her heart. While he couldn't feel it beat, her chest warmed his hand. "I'm as alive and real as you."

"And you must remain so until I'm no longer living." Jane's threat, though idle as it was, haunted him. *How can I live with myself if Jane poisons my son? Or Annie?* His eyes misted and he averted his gaze from her.

"Jack, what is it?"

"I'm fearful of losing you again—"

"Losing me again?" She cocked her head. "You mean to death?"

"Jane made some unfounded intimidations when I went to see her and the child."

"You said nothing. What did she threaten?"

He hesitated. "She would poison you."

To his surprise, Annalisa laughed. "I'm hardly fearful of her physick. She knows nothing, Jack. Of the two of us, I'm the one who could poison her. But I would never stoop so low." A heaviness settled between them, and with more solemnity, she added, "What else did she say? Would she injure you as well?"

Jack rubbed his neck, then pulled the tie from his hair. "She said she would harm herself and the child if I divorced her."

Annalisa's face fell. "That is grave, indeed. Would that she attempted to kill me instead." She reached for the *wampum* necklace at her throat. "She sounds irrational. Pray, was she of right mind when she spoke to you? Were you quite convinced of her candor? If you were, she shouldn't be left alone to her own devices. Our nephew's life is innocent."

His heart skipped at her mention of his son—the child he

could not acknowledge. Jack held his face in his hands. "I know not what to do. If Jane commits the sins she's threatened, I have her blood, and the boy's, on my hands. If she harms you, I could never live with myself. Never."

"I needn't anyone to shield me, especially from Jane. But from all you say, it sounds like she needs protecting from herself." Annalisa sat on the edge of the bed and smoothed the creases of her linen chemise. "Thank you for obliging me last night. I know you're in an impossible position. I just...I... c-can't believe what's come to pass. I grieve it more than I grieved your d-death when I was at D-Devonshire House." She paused, drew in several breathes, and slowly, she spoke, "At least...then...I believed you...gone."

Jack lifted her hand and kissed it. "Don't I know it well. Had I known you lived, I never would have agreed to marry Jane. Would that I never took us on that ship."

"What's d-done is...done." Annalisa crumpled the edge of her chemise. "I apologize. M-my stutter sometimes returns when I'm...disconcerted."

He quaked at her words, and the injury that left his darling girl afflicted, one year later. Jack pulled her into his arms, and she rested her head upon his chest. *How many months have I pined for her, yearned to hold her?* And now she acquiesced, most readily, to the most ridiculous of arrangements. After all she'd braved upon that distant shore, her kindness and compassion prevailed. But he prickled at the image of Jane last night, fatigued and pale. Though she'd spoken with bitterness and cruelty, she'd just given birth. *Can I blame Jane for such irrational words?* Perhaps it would only be a matter of days, or weeks at most, for her to return to her usual state of health; then he could speak to her with reason, and plant the seed for divorce. Yet, last night, he committed adultery, leaving him no better than Jane the night she came to him, still married to Oliver.

Perhaps I truly am a lecher...a licentious profligate.

He focused on Annalisa's steady breath. She belonged in his arms. After all their time apart, he owed it to her, and himself, to be with her one final time. For last night, he'd never regret their adultery.

❦ 37 ❦
JACK
TOPSFIELD, MAY 1777

THE SNOW OF MARCH had long since melted, leaving the grass verdant and smelling sweet. Colorful flowers decorated his mother's garden, but none bloomed as vibrantly as those within Annalisa's. Jack pleasantly recalled her beloved flowers planted beside the kitchen garden, adjacent to the barn at the Howlett farm. *How those vibrant blooms fade when she's among them.* He wondered if she sat amongst the new garden she'd started with Addy at their old house. The thought sat bitterly within him. *The house we shared...*

"Jack? Are you even listening to me?"

Jane's soprano cut his thoughts, catapulting him back to his mother's garden and their argument about the Continentals. George had written of their departure from Morristown, and where Jack was to meet them upon his arrival to New York.

"You know I have a responsibility to the militia. I've signed myself on for one year with Washington's army. 'Tis a contract. To desert would be akin to treason."

"Treason?" Jane's cheeks bloomed pink. "Your fighting the

British is treason. 'Tis well known militia abandon and desert. Why should you hold yourself to grander expectations?"

"What's the manner of man you wish me to be? An absconder? A man lacking integrity? A man who steals away under cover of night fearful of defeat?" Jack lifted Robby from her and cradled him to his chest. Each time he gazed upon the child that should have been his namesake, the old pains returned to his heart. *He should be my heir.*

He continued, "That sort of man holds no honor, no respect. Is that the sort of man you wish for me to be with the boys? Teach them to lack integrity when it suits them most?" Jack gazed into his son's small face, this new life he must love, and impart on him the ways of their budding new world. "Whether we're victorious or no, I'll keep to the course of my actions, madam. And please you, Jane, hold your temper. 'Tis most disagreeable on you."

"Forgive me, sir, but you've let your foolish dreams of rebellion and war carry you away from your duties at home. You can't shirk all you're responsible for in the name of justice. You must get me with child so I can give you a true heir. Robby can't inherit your titles in the way he was conceived—and you've kept from my bed since I gave birth."

Jack chilled with the spring air. "And I shall continue to do so until you're healed from childbirth. But this war affects you and your future well-being—including those freedoms of the children. So please you, don't pretend I fight of my own accord, or presume to know the tedious and burdensome nature of my scruples."

"Please, Jack. Don't leave us like this. I don't wish to quarrel with you." Jane reached for Robby.

Jack started at the way the sunlight caught his son's face as he handed him to her. For a brief moment, he reconsidered leaving, but the thought was fleeting. "You're entitled to your opinions of me, but you must know by now I do nothing that doesn't serve a purpose. I consider your well-being as much as I do the children's."

"And Annalisa," Jane spat. She turned from him with Robby at her shoulder, and the boy's eyes fluttered open; a deep azure, far different from Jane's arctic blue. *Annalisa will notice they're not brown as Tommy's, or as Oliver's had been.* He cringed at the lie he must withhold from her.

"Yes. And Annalisa's." Jack went to the lilac bush—Annalisa's favorite flower—and inhaled the perfume. He would leave her a bouquet later today. "I ride at dawn."

Jane's lovely face drooped. "I know Tommy is not yours, but Robby is. Please, stay for him. Keep our family whole, Jack." She moved toward him and cupped his face. "For the sake of the children."

Robby's round little cheeks tugged at his heartstrings. But it was no matter—the child would still be his whether he remained in town or not. Jack leaned over and kissed Robby's tiny forehead. "My sweet boy, be good for your mother, yes?" In four strides, he quit the garden for the stable, and tacked up his horse. He needed to say his good-byes.

Jack rode down the narrow lane, now green in springtime, until he reached the gristmill. There stood the brown saltbox he shared with Annalisa when they were married. Smoke piped into the May breeze from the wide, central chimney. A great purple lilac bush decorated the front of the house. *How did I miss this bit of shrubbery before now?* Enthralled, he dismounted and tied Morgaine to the wood fence, then made his way toward the bush. Using his knife, he cut several blooms and placed one upon the iron scraper embedded within the stone front-door steps.

From within the house, a rich contralto sang. He peered through the window. Annalisa, wearing just her stays and petticoat, whirled about, her long curling hair unbound. Sarah's voice harmonized with hers as the two danced about.

Smiling, and struck with a design, Jack placed another bloom upon the path, followed by another, and another, until he reached the stable.

"Good day, Quinn."

Quinnapin looked up from brushing his horse. "Jack! *Wuneekeesuq.*" He threw down the brush and grabbed Jack's hand. "How good to see you, Friend. You're looking well."

"Thank you, Friend. Likewise."

Quinnapin lowered his voice, "Pray, you've been free of laudanum, yes?"

Jack nodded. "Yes, I've been quite rid of it since you helped me. I swore never to take it again."

"I've not told Miss Anna of your struggles. 'Tis not my information to tell. But if you wish to build more harmony between you, 'tis something you might wish to unveil."

"I'm shamed by how I coped, Quinn. She'd look upon me as a coward."

Quinnapin's hand rested on Jack's shoulder. "Think on it. Trust is built through honesty, and time."

Jack smiled. "You're quite right."

"Come, have you called for Miss Anna?"

"Aye, I heard her and Miss Sarah singing inside the house. Would you mind asking her to come out the front door—I've a surprise for her."

Quinnapin grinned. "Of course."

Jack sat atop a wooden barrel with the rest of the lilacs and waited for Annalisa to find him. With each passing minute, his nerves tingled at the anticipation. He closed his eyes and imagined her in her stays, as she just was, singing and dancing about the house.

"Jack?"

He opened his eyes.

Annalisa poked her head into the stable, a small bouquet of purple lilacs in hand. He stood from the barrel and held out the rest of the flowers to her.

"You found me."

She rushed into his arms. "Finally, you've come. 'Tis been days...nay, since Sunday, at the meetinghouse."

The floral scent of her hair dizzied him. "I know. I've received word from George."

"Then you're leaving." Annalisa pulled from him and sat on a wooden crate. She adjusted the yellow-dotted neck hand-kerchief tucked into the bodice of her blue linen day dress. "I suppose I knew this day would come."

"Aye, and it pains me to leave you."

"You can't speak like this to me anymore, Jack."

He knelt beside her and lifted her hand to his lips. "How can I not? I pray every night I might make things right by us, but I know not how I can. I've been poring over my law books for weeks—"

"You've forsaken God. To whom do you pray?"

He glowered. "To whatever Deity will listen."

"Then mayhap your prayers have been answered by this unknown god." Her lips curled, then spread into a beautiful grin.

"How so, dear heart? Tell me."

"I've not told anyone, 'tis but a scandal...I've been absent of the morbid flux since we coupled that night."

"You mean it?" Giddy from the news, Jack covered her face in kisses. "I've gotten you with child?"

"My courses were absent in March and April, and I've missed them again for May. Forgive me for not telling you sooner, but I wished to have failed at least three before revealing such news."

"Of course." He kissed her again, this time sweetly and tenderly. Jack wound his arms about her and placed a hand over her stomach. Though her torso remained conical and flat within her binding stays, their growing child would round her belly, and come December, she'd be mother to their babe. He warmed each time he glimpsed her holding and playing with her niece and nephews. *Annie deserves to love a child of her own, a son or daughter who may bear her green eyes and golden skin.*

"Now you may petition for divorce," Annalisa said. "In a few months' time, there'll be no way for me conceal the infidelity."

His body tensed. By summer's end, her slender frame was sure to show, and would be an obvious indication of his marriage betrayal. He pictured Robby and heard Jane's threat.

"Would that you could come with me to New York," he said.

Annalisa's face alighted. "You need only ask it of me."

"'Twill be the only way to conceal what we've done."

Her brows knitted. "Jack, this is our chance to be married again. To start our family. Whyever would I wish to hide this?"

"Because Jane will end herself, and Robby, or she'll poison you. She's threatened as much each time I discuss divorce. 'Tis madness."

"She'd never do something so heinous. She speaks only to coerce you into staying with her, and you comply, perhaps out of fear. But once she sees she can hardly keep you from me, she'll realize her empty threats are made only in vain." Annalisa clasped his hands and kissed them. "I swear it. The children will be safe, and so will Jane. You needn't worry. There'll be no blood on your hands, or mine. I swear it."

Quelled by her fine words, he leaned in and kissed her. "I never meant to put us in this position, Annalisa."

"I'm as guilty as you. We both lay together that night believing it our last. But we must look upon this as a sign from God...or whomever." She winked. "We're meant to be together, else this child would never have taken hold within my womb."

He stiffened at her words. That singular night with Jane had also caused her to get in the family way. Was he then, too, meant to be with Jane? His stomach churned at the thought. Perhaps everything was chaos, with no meaning behind anything at all; just mere events come to fruition at the behest of poor decisions. At least this child was conceived with his beloved, and without laudanum.

⚜

THAT NIGHT, JACK'S PARENTS HOSTED A FORMAL DINNER. Abigail sat to his right, Annalisa to his left. Across the table, in her rightful place as his wife, Jane looked on Annalisa with triumph.

Over the clank of silver, Abigail said, "Annie, have you had the madeira?"

"Yes, 'tis wonderful." She sipped from her glass, then added, "Louisa is growing into such a pretty little girl."

"She is, but God knows as she's strong as a Bixby," Abigail replied.

Andrew chuckled. "But she's also part Perkins, which makes her quite stubborn and prone to poor decisions."

They all laughed.

"I concur, Brother," Jack said. "Just last week, I caught Louisa in Father's study with Tommy. Tommy watched her pull out Father's maps and books from the bookcase—quite large, in fact. I was astounded by her strength. When I lifted her, she ripped a page from the book and knocked a burning candle to the floor. She is very much George's daughter."

Jane sipped her wine. "Tommy's a good boy. He always listens to what he's told. Ollie would be proud."

"I'm certain Robby will be just as well-behaved with such a good older brother to admire," Mother replied.

"I'm not so certain." Jane studied Jack, and he thought she might reveal the nature of Robby's conception. "He might have a bit of a rebellious streak in him."

"How can you tell a child's personality at two months?" Annalisa asked, setting down her fork.

"When you have a child one day," Jane quirked an eyebrow, "That is, if you can...you'll know."

Annalisa held her sister's stare. "I beg your pardon?"

"Jane," Abigail scowled. "That is hardly appropriate."

A simper lifted Jane's face. "I meant no harm, only that once she bears a child, if she's able to detect their personality, she will. It also helps to know the father's character when determining the disposition of one's children."

Jack's neck heated as Annalisa's gaze met his. She grinned but withheld her news from the table. Such information could hardly be offered when he remained married to Jane. It would be months before he could petition the divorce, and several more before the magistrates at Salem, and potentially Boston, would deliver a verdict. Until then, they three must linger in nuptial standstill, his conscience divided between love and duty.

❧ 38 ❧
ANNALISA
TOPSFIELD, JUNE 1777

A S ABRUPTLY AS JACK returned to her, he departed for New York. With Addy and Sarah for company, and occasionally Quinnapin, Annalisa frequented her family's farm to visit Mary and Henry, and to sit by the ancient oak.

That afternoon, Annalisa sprawled in the shade with Mary. The tree's wide limbs hovered over the earth and reached toward her family's farm. Two years prior, she and Jack had perched upon the lowest hanging branch the night of the Strawberry Festival, the night he'd confessed his love for her.

An annual event, the festival was that night, and though she yearned to taste Addy's strawberry desserts and dance to fiddles and fifes, Annalisa wondered if she could withstand the display of cheer knowing Jack and her brothers remained at war. *I should be with them.*

Mary's head upon her lap, Annalisa read aloud a letter from George. He was back in New York with Washington's army, and hopeful of meeting with Jack. *Will they try to retake the city, then?*

She imagined George at the encampment, barking orders at his militia, as he used to snap at their brothers on the farm. She grinned at the memory. It was George she was closest to than any of her other full-blooded siblings. Save for Mary, perhaps.

Her sister peered up at her. Mary would be fifteen come August, and already her face had lost its childhood roundness. Mamma would surely have her come out to Society next spring. *I wonder if she's yet gotten the morbid flux.*

"Think you George will come home soon?" Mary asked.

Annalisa shook her head. "No, I think not."

"'Tis no matter. He'll survive the battles he sees. I know of no other man taller or stronger."

"I think you're right."

Mary sat upright, then stood, wiping leaves from her petticoat. "I'm going to ready for the festival. Come with me?"

"In a bit. I'm quite enjoying our tree."

"Fair enough. I've missed sitting with you beneath it." Mary blew her a kiss. "'Tis been a dream having you home, Annie."

"'Tis been a dream being back." Annalisa returned her sister's kiss. "Go ready for tonight's festivities. I'll be along presently."

The oak's leaves cast lacelike shadows upon her skirts and bodice. Annalisa rested her hand upon her stomach. For the first time, she had to loosely bind her stays to accommodate her belly beneath. *This is the furthest along I've been with child.* She thrummed at the realization, thankful Mary had not noticed.

"You're glowing, Miss Anna." Quinnapin stood with his firelock slung over his shoulder, his bronzed skin peeking out from his linen shirt.

"Thank you, old friend." Annalisa patted the space beside her. "Come, sit."

He knelt and removed his effects, then sat, his buckskin breeches barely touching her skirts.

"I'm sorry about Weetamoo," she said. "She was a lovely girl. I liked her very much."

Quinnapin's lips pursed. "We cannot speak her name, Miss Anna. We don't wish to disturb her in rest."

"Forgive me, I knew not. Addy said the Iroquois had taken her..."

"A Mohawk took her life. On our way through New York."

"How'd it happen?"

His face hardened. "We were not far into the lands you call New York. We were traveling with a Mohican friend of mine, when we encountered Mohawks. It was determined they were in allegiance with the British and ordered to kill any who were not of the Iroquois nation. I fought but could not save her."

"I'm so sorry, Quinn."

"No apologies. How could you know?" He ran his hand over the bits of grass, dirt, and dried leaves beneath them. "We buried her with everything she could need in the afterlife."

Annalisa wondered if they buried Weetamoo with plenty of cooking tools. Though Annalisa knew little of the Natives to whom her grandmother belonged, Weetamoo, a Wampanoag, had generously taught Annalisa receipts her grandmother may have cooked. For that modest, but monumental, gesture into her grandmother's past, she was grateful.

Quinnapin closed his eyes. After several moments, he said, "Death is a reminder of the cycle of life, Miss Anna. As it is destructive, it is also a renewal...like planting seeds in winter for them to grow come spring. We buried her facing southwest. The southwest wind is the warmest, most pleasing, and is the house of the Great Spirit, Keihtánit. There, she will only ever enjoy pleasant weather, bountiful harvest, and plenty of game."

Annalisa smiled. "That sounds like a wondrous afterlife... like Heaven. Think you the Agawam go there as well?"

Quinnapin's brow creased. "Miss Anna, Agawam is a place, not a people. The Natives who occupied that village were Pawtucket, of the Abenaki nation. It is likely your grandmother was Pawtucket. She may also have been Pennacook."

"Zounds. My papa always told me she was Agawam. I'm mortified—"

"Peace." Quinnapin smiled gently. "A mistake made by your English people, though I'm saddened your grandmother never corrected the error. Perhaps she never spoke of her people to your father."

Annalisa frowned. "She died when my Papa was a child. He remembers little of her. 'Tis all I know."

"My grandfather knew the Abenaki language from traveling north, and he taught me some. I know enough to understand, but cannot speak it. Their rites and sacred ceremonies are something I know nothing of, but I implore you to speak to your ancestors and listen when the grandmother spirit speaks, *nokummusanit auntau*."

"I should pray to her?"

When he did not offer more information, Annalisa thanked for him sharing.

"There is much I cannot say, Miss Anna. They belong to our *Wôpanâak* sacred ceremonies—my father is Medicine Man, and when he dies, my sister will become Medicine Woman—but one day, I welcome you to observe the rites, though you cannot partake."

She brushed his shoulder. "I would be honored, Friend."

Quinnapin gestured to her bodice and smiled. "*Wuttau-niyeu*. It means 'she bears a daughter.' "

Annalisa gasped. "A daughter? Can you be sure?"

"Jack planted the seed of life within you. May you long prosper beneath this sacred *nootimus*—oak tree—may you forever take refuge in its shade, and may your children—*kuneehanak*—one day climb its branches."

"Thank you," she whispered, unable to find her voice, and she blinked away her tears.

"Miss Anna, you are kind, and deserving of a good life."

"As are you, Quinn."

He gripped her hand. "These are not days to lament. Jack, George, and William may be at war, but Spirit will decide when we meet them again." Quinnapin lifted her from the ground with him. He stood tall, like her, and lean. "Miss Addy and Miss Sarah have come with Abigail and Jane. They planned a feast for dinner to celebrate the festival tonight."

There was no reason for her to feel despondent. Quinnapin was right—despite the war—good still persevered, and she would see her brothers and Jack soon enough. *The worst is behind me.* She lifted his firelock and slung it over her shoulder, then linked her arm with his.

"I've missed carrying one of these," she said with a laugh. Her menswear from London was laundered and tucked deep within her clothing chest at the foot of hers and Jack's bed. *I'll need it one day. I'm sure of that much.*

Quinnapin joined her. "You've got your musket, Miss Anna. 'Tis ready for you when the spirit decides the time is right."

Savory roast chicken with root vegetables basted in butter and chives, buttery fish and cheese pudding, fresh spring salad, and sweet strawberry tarts lined her parents' dining table. Bottled madeira and ale flowed freely, and about the table sat Mamma and Papa, Henry and Mary, Jane, Abigail and Andrew, Quinnapin, Sarah, Addy, and Liza. It was rare for Liza and Addy to sit and eat with her family, but on the evening of the Strawberry Festival—as well as the corn husking in October, and Twelfth Night in January—Papa made exception. Lord and Lady Perkins had been invited but were promised to Mr. Hooper at his summer house in Danvers.

Jane, having regarded Annalisa little in the months she'd been home, spoke kindly, and even refilled Annalisa's glass of madeira. Jane, with cheeks rosy and her mouth upturned, proved to be in high spirits, and Annalisa couldn't help but share in her sister's good humor.

"Come, Annie, you mean to tell me you danced a minuet at Devonshire House in London?" Jane asked. "And you didn't stumble?"

"No," Annalisa laughed. "I danced several minuets—each one as beautifully danced as though it were you."

Jane lifted her glass. "Then I salute you. You finally learned the dance."

They toasted and drank. *I wish our kinship could always be this easy.*

"And at a masquerade," Mamma said. "A clever way for the duchess to introduce you, my dear."

"Georgiana was so kind to Annie," Abigail chimed, her freckled cheeks rouged with wine. "No better person to have rescued her, am I right, Miss Devonshire?"

Sarah nodded. "Quite, Lady Essex. I loved Her Grace as though she were my own kin." She eyed Addy and Liza. "I imagine you feel similarly, Miss Addy, Miss Liza, regarding your lovely Howletts here?"

Addy smiled. "Oh, yes. I've known these children since they were babes. Mr. and Mrs. Howlett have always been good and gracious."

"Liza's indenture is nearly up," Papa said. "Two more years and she can return home if she so desires."

"Will you travel to Ireland?" Mary asked.

"Aye, I miss Ireland. I grieve t' leave Topsfield, but me mam 'n da will be wantin' me home," Liza replied. "I miss me brothers, as ye miss yers, now."

"What of you, Quinnapin?" Henry asked. "Will you join my brothers in the war?"

"I made one attempt." Quinnapin eyed Annalisa as he replied, "And I think I will try again, but I'm awaiting the correct time."

"And when is that?" Abigail asked. "If you go, will you take me with you so I may see George?"

Quinnapin chuckled. "When the spirit decides, Miss Abigail."

"But Abbie, what of Louisa?" Andrew asked. "Will you take her with you?"

"I assure you, an encampment is no place for a child," Jane said, setting down her fork. "I would know, having been aboard HMS *Lively* with Tommy."

Abigail tilted her head as though she hadn't considered this. "But George must meet his daughter, no?"

"George will be busy, my dear. He's captain of his militia," Papa said.

"He'd make time for you, I know he would." Annalisa reached for Abigail. "Louisa's his daughter."

Mamma studied Annalisa. "Annie, you haven't touched the

fish and cheese pudding. 'Tis your favorite. Are you feeling poorly?"

Annalisa scraped the soft, cheesy casserole across her plate to make it appear she'd eaten some. "I have. I've just taken my time. I don't wish to rush through it."

Abigail leaned in and whispered, "It tastes metallic. Like the poultry." She speared a piece of chicken and ate it with a smirk.

Annalisa's hairs bristled. "How did you know?"

"It happens when you're with child," Abigail murmured, her glance darting briefly at Annalisa's stomach. She sipped her madeira, then whispered, "Jane's bound to find out. Your waist never looks this wide in your stays."

❦

TOPSFIELD'S LUSH COMMON TEEMED WITH MUSICIANS AND lanterns to be lit. The people of town who'd baked portions of their strawberry crop into shortcakes, pies, and tarts, gathered about wooden tables with their delectable treats. Captain Gould of the militia organized his kegs from the Whispering Willow Tavern, along with an array of tin tankards and cups.

"I'm well on my way to becoming disguised," Abigail said. "Far too much madeira at dinner."

Annalisa laughed. "You sound like George."

"George would guffaw and say, *'rogues, let's have you wrapped in warm flannel!'*" Jane's delicate soprano mimicked their half-brother's bass vocals.

They giggled.

"Well done, Janey," Annalisa said. "You sound just like him."

"Thank you, but I think your voice is more attuned to such pitches than mine," Jane replied with a small grin.

"I should like to meet your brother, Calais," Sarah said. "He sounds like he would get along well with the rowdiest bunch in London."

"George hates Society," Annalisa replied. "I don't doubt he'd enjoy a tavern in the lower parts of London."

Fanny Shepard, Lizzie Balch, and Hannah French paraded toward them like an ostentation of peacocks. Annalisa hid her scowl for Hannah French. *If they three were in London, the* ton *would consume them alive.* The thought lifted her lips in time for her to greet Martha Perley, William's paramour, who followed behind.

"How wonderful to see you again, Mrs. Per...Miss Annalisa." Fanny Shepard's plump face flushed the color of the strawberry dessert she carried. "I apologize, I know not how to address you."

"'Tis a complicated matter, Miss Shepard," Annalisa replied tartly.

"It has been nice seeing you again at the meetinghouse on Sundays, Annie," Martha said. "I pray William is faring well at Ticonderoga. I miss him terribly."

Annalisa smiled. "Has he written you?"

Martha offered a shy grin. "Yes, but 'twas only two letters. I imagine he must be quite busy."

"He'll write more," Abigail said. "And if he does not, then you must write him."

"Pray, I hear you've left your husband, Lady Essex," Hannah said. "May we still address you as such, *my lady,* or shall we soon be calling you Mrs. George Howlett?"

Abigail's nostrils flared, and she stepped forward, baring her teeth. "I've friends in higher places than you, Miss

French. Speak to me again in such a manner and I shall ruin you."

Hannah huffed and stomped from their grouping.

"My apologies, ladies," Abigail said. "My time in London, with all I endured was...significant. As was Annie's. You needn't call me Lady Essex, though I'm not officially divorced from Charles. And no, I don't presume to one day be George's—"

"But you've birthed his child," Lizzie Balch interrupted. "Surely, he means to marry you."

Jane's face reddened. "My brother has yet to meet the child. Not that it would change his disposition. I'm certain he'll marry Abigail as soon as her divorce petition is validated by the courts. But I don't believe you've filed one yet, have you, Abbie?"

"I've not..." Abigail replied softly.

Mary bounded toward them, and clasped Annalisa's hand. "Good evening, ladies." She appraised Annalisa. "La! You've eaten quite a bit of strawberry treats, Annie. Did Abigail have to loosen your stays?"

"Mary, 'tis quite rude to make conjecture on such things. Annie barely ate any of her supper..." Jane's gaze fell on Annalisa's waist and her eyes grew wide. "How could you?" She turned from the group of ladies and hurried into the crowd.

"Jane, wait." Annalisa weaved through the townspeople until she reached the Common Rock, a large boulder at the far end of the common. There, Jane stood with her back to the festival.

"You're with child, aren't you? Did Jack lay with you?"

"Jane, not here," Annalisa replied.

Her sister turned, her face blank and eyes hollow. "Tell me once, and I'll believe you if you say it. Are you with child?"

Annalisa crumpled her skirts and averted her gaze. *Fie, Mary! I should've known she'd notice my waist.* "Aye. We lay together once. I never thought it would be enough to get me in the family way..."

"Once is enough." Jane's face contorted with what Annalisa perceived to be anguish. "You were supposed to be dead." Her delicate whisper cracked.

Annalisa reached for Jane. "We lay together once. But I was his wife before ever you were."

"We were betrothed before ever you wed," Jane cried. "And then you died!"

Annalisa stepped back. "But I didn't. I'm alive. What will you have me do? Return to London and live out my life at Devonshire House? Forget myself, my name, and everyone I love? Because I d-did that, Jane. I remembered n-none of my life or myself. N-nothing!" Her heart skipped at the stutter, and she composed herself, reciting Mad Madge under her breath. "There's nothing you can say that will change how I feel about Jack. We eloped, yes, but if he petitions for divorce by means of adultery, he may marry me again. I'm sorry if that means you must lose him, but he was never yours to lose." Annalisa looked down, unable to hold Jane's icy glare. "It seems you would rather me dead."

"I don't wish it, Annalisa," Jane snapped. "Only that you would leave us be. This was the original arrangement, lest you forget. Jack was meant to marry me." She stared at the Common Rock. "Do away with the child. Could you do that for me? For your nephews?"

Annalisa's skin crawled. "How could you ask that of me? You know how long I've wished to be a mother. I'm sorry you were widowed with Oliver's children. I'd not wish that fate upon anyone. But Jack is this babe's father, and we will build a family together. Jane, I'm his wife."

"Were." Jane wandered toward the festival, then turned. "You *were* his wife. And until he petitions for divorce—which I know he won't—you'll simply be his mistress. His concubine. No better than the harlots at Mount Whoredom and Damnation Alley."

G EORGE SCRAMBLED FOR HIS quill and dipped it in ink. He'd written to Abigail a dozen times since Jack left for, and returned from, Topsfield. But he'd not received one letter. *It must be that dandy plum, Essex, is with her. Perhaps 'tis he who withholds her mail, as he did in London.* Aggrieved, he gritted his teeth. *I must know my daughter. I must learn more of her.*

How strange to be a father, yet never know one's child. If it had been any other girl, he might have contested the birth. But it was Abigail, and he lay with her several times before enlisting with the army, before she wed Lord Essex. How foolish he'd been to not take better precaution. She'd been reckless as well. Surely, she could've prevented the child from taking hold with one of Addy's magick teas.

But it was no matter. What was done was done. He fathered Abigail's daughter, and he would meet her and hope-fully be her father. *Can I be a father?* The thought irked him. Pa was the only father he'd known, having reared George since infancy. Yet, Captain Bixby remained ever prevalent. *An image.*

My aunt and Mother tell me I'm an image of my father...a man who is just a name to me. A ghostly emptiness settled over him for the man he so resembled, but never knew. Had he any other traits of his father? Was he also stubborn and defiant? Had Captain Bixby not died at sea, would George, too, have become captain of a ship...

I'm a captain. Of my militia. The hair on his arms lifted. *Is captain in my blood?* He could hardly bemoan his birthright if it were so, though he'd done it independently of Captain Bixby. With resolve George placed the pen to paper and started to write. *I will not just be a name to Louisa, a man she conjures each time she peers into a looking glass and ponders her face...*

"Captain Howlett—" Bartlett burst into his tent.

"Zounds." George peered up from his page. "What is it?"

"You've a letter, sir." Bartlett, now pockmarked from their winter at Morristown, held out the sealed envelope.

George took the letter and broke open the unfamiliar seal.

7th July, 1777
Ticonderoga

Dear Brother,

It is with great Lamentation I Wryte to you. The British have overtaken Forrt Ticonderroga. We saw Burgoyne's men, their bonfyres upon Sugar Loaff Hill, and we knew we were Sarrownded. General Schuyler ordered us to Evacuayte at once. I shall Wryte againe when I can. May we meete soon.

Yours &c,
Will

George's face tingled as he glanced up at his friend. "'Tis from William. Ticonderoga's fallen."

Bartlett's beady eyes widened. "Fallen?"

"Aye. They've succumbed to Burgoyne." George rose from his chair. "I must to my superior."

Jack hurried into George's tent, his face careworn. "Cousin, Ticonderoga's been overtaken."

George held up the letter. "So I've just learned."

His cousin cocked his head. "Who's written?"

"William." George tossed the page onto his small desk. "They fled like cowards. No doubt they'll continue to march south."

Jack's lips pursed. "No, not cowards."

"Whatever's to be done?" Bartlett asked.

George ran a hand over his stubbled chin. "'Tis clear from his advancement upon Ticonderoga, Burgoyne means to isolate New-England from the rest of the colonies. To separate us would mean to squelch the rebellion."

"To truly decapitate the snake's head, Howe and his men must march north from York Island," Jack replied.

George offered a grim chuckle for Jack's analogy. "Aye. I'm sure Washington expects this. Mayhap, we can give them a fight to remember."

"But...how we can do that?" Bartlett asked. "We're wildly outnumbered."

"We split up," George said. "Find more men to join the militia—local men from the area who know the land. The more militias we incorporate, the better. Then, we meet upon the battlefield."

"What of William?" Jack asked. "Is he unharmed? Or has he been taken prisoner?"

George stiffened. He hadn't considered this. A rush of guilt flooded him for the way he'd referred to his brother as a coward. He'd presumed, since he received a letter, William had escaped. Perhaps the note was written in haste, and clandestinely given to a courier.

"I'll learn the names of those taken at Ticonderoga," George said. "If William's is among them, we're headed north, rogues."

ANNALISA

TOPSFIELD, EARLY AUGUST 1777

A S ANNALISA PASSED TWENTY weeks of pregnancy, she sat in her small house with the doors and windows ajar to allow for a breeze. Careful to avoid Jane at the meetinghouse on Sundays, Annalisa hadn't spoken to her since the festival in June. But this afternoon, Abigail, flushed and rather anxious, called, insisting she visit the Perkins estate.

"No. I will not see Jane, and I'll not apologize, Abbie. I did nothing wrong." Annalisa fanned herself, but only wafted hot air across her perspiring face.

"Please, I wish for you to come over to see the children." Abigail paced before the unlit kitchen hearth. "Little Robby is growing fast. You wouldn't believe it. And Louisa and Tommy are the best of friends."

Burdensome guilt settled over her, and Annalisa replied, "Only if we sit outside. I can hardly stand this heat."

Abigail clapped her hands. "Of course! Oh Annie, Louisa will be so happy to see you."

Abigail led Annalisa around the back of the house to sit in the garden. In the shade of an old willow, they sprawled a blanket to sit upon, while Louisa and Tommy wobbled about the yard. Jane, beneath her straw hat and umbrella, sat in a chair with little Robby. It was no wonder Jane remained porcelain even in the height of summer, a feat that had earned her the title of the *town gem.*

Annalisa, happy to be quite bronzed, tossed her hat aside and stretched upon the blanket with Tommy and Louisa. The children crawled over her, and she laughed.

"Oh, you're so heavy, both of you," she cried. "Come here, let me give you a kiss."

Annalisa scooped up Louisa and planted kisses about the girl's face. Though her dark brows and hair rendered her serious, Louisa laughed often—the essence of George. Annalisa turned her attention to Tommy, who nestled into her lap and rested his flaxen head against her. *The boy is solemn, but sweet. Would that he remains so.* Each child appeared quite like their respective fathers. Except Robby.

Annalisa appraised the babe at Jane's bosom. His marine blue eyes and soft brown hair rendered him different than Tommy, and hence, Oliver. *Robby looks like Jane. Perhaps the second child is more like the mother.* She ran a hand over her belly. Would it look more like her, or Jack, or a perfect amalgamation of them both?

"Annalisa."

Jane's soprano commanded attention, and Annalisa looked up. Her sister glowered, but still looked lovey.

"I want to apologize for how I behaved at the festival. 'Tis been hard for me, knowing I may lose a second husband."

Jane blinked several times, then shifted under Robby's weight. "It makes me wonder what is wrong with me."

Annalisa knelt at Jane's feet. "There's nothing wrong with you. You're the town gem, and every gentleman's dream. You've only a spur of bad luck. Perhaps 'twill now be broken."

Jane nodded. "I pray you're right."

Annalisa gave a small smile, and eyed Robby. "May I hold him?"

"Of course." A smirk lifted Jane's full lips, and she handed the babe to Annalisa. "How ready you are to be a mother. I'm sure you've dreamt of the day you might hold Jack's son or daughter."

"I have." Annalisa kissed Robby's forehead. "You've no idea how long I've wished and dreamt it."

Abigail glanced up from her needlepoint. "And you'll finally come to know it. December, yes?"

Annalisa nodded. "Yes. I can hardly wait."

Jane reached for the pitcher of tea with lemons, and refilled Annalisa's glass. "Here. 'Tis too hot not to drink. Especially if you're with child."

"Thank you." Annalisa gulped the cool tea. "This is lovely. Did Mercy make it?" She held out her glass for another, and Jane refilled her cup.

Abigail shrugged, then held out her glass for a pour. "I know not, but 'tis refreshing, is it not?"

Annalisa finished her third glass. "Somewhat minty, with a hint of sweetness, like chamomile, but not quite." She'd familiarized herself with Addy's receipts for physick, and now, Sarah's. But this tasted unlike any of their teas. Although, there was one Sarah had described to her, but not made; one with a mint-like taste...a sweetness like chamomile. *What was she describing?*

Jane replied, "I'm glad you enjoyed it."

When they'd drunk the rest of the tea, and the sun had ascended beyond the trees, Annalisa slid a hand over her brow. It slipped over the perspiration with ease. "'Tis too hot. I think I must retire."

"I thought you'd never ask." Abigail threw down her needlepoint and lifted a sleeping Louisa from the blanket.

Jane took Tommy's hand and asked Annalisa, "Mind you carrying Robby?"

Dizzy with the heat, Annalisa shook her head. "Of course, not. He's such a darling boy." She held the baby to her bosom and nuzzled his round face. "How perfect you are, little Robby."

They returned indoors, where it was only moderately cooler. Annalisa groaned, and with her free arm, clutched her stomach. "I've terrible cramps."

"Do you need the necessary?" Abigail asked. "My stomach is feeling a bit off, too. Perhaps 'tis the heat."

Her gut wrenched and strained her insides, and Annalisa dropped to her knees on the parlor floor. "My God, I've never felt cramps this terrible." Clutching Robby, she writhed over herself to stop the sensation.

"Annie, are you all right?" Abigail asked. "You look pale. Jane, take Robby so she can lie down."

Annalisa gritted her teeth. "'Tis agony."

Robby squealed over her wail.

"Zounds! You're bleeding." Abigail tried lifting her from the ground. "Jane, take Robby."

On her knees and using one hand, Annalisa pushed onto her feet but slipped on the blood soaking her skirts. She collapsed backward into Abigail. Her friend steadied her and cradled her against her lap.

Annalisa asked, "Am I giving birth?"

Jane knelt and snatched Robby from Annalisa, murmuring, "The only child of Jack's you'll ever hold."

"What was that?" Abigail's flustered cry resonated through the parlor.

Jane's honeyed soprano crooned, "It must've been too much tea. You really should've been more careful. Hopefully, you'll pass the babe in no time at all."

Icy dread coursed through Annalisa as Jane took her children and quit the room.

"Jane, come back here at once," Abigail shrieked. "Get help, please!"

The room grew blurry as Andrew, Mercy, and Lady Perkins dashed into the parlor. Heavy tears dripped onto Annalisa's face as Abigail held her head to her bosom.

"The tea?" Annalisa asked. "It tasted so lovely...quite refreshing..." Her eyes closed, though it felt as though her insides would tear her apart.

❧ 41 ❧

ANNALISA

TOPSFIELD, AUGUST 1777

BIRDS CHIRPED AND CHATTERED beyond the casement, and a cascade of yellow sunlight bathed the room in hot, summery glow. Annalisa slid her hand across her forehead and sat upright. Slowly, the room came into focus; her room, or, rather, the bedchamber she'd shared with Jack.

From a chair in the corner, Sarah rose. "Calais, you're awake." She hastened toward the bed and felt Annalisa's face with her rough hand. "You bled much. Here, drink this." She handed Annalisa a cupful of liquid.

"Am I back in Paris?" Annalisa asked, then sipped from the cup. The bitter fluid burned, and she coughed. "This is terrible."

"Buckwheat. It helps to stop the bleeding."

Annalisa gulped the remaining liquid, grimacing as she swallowed. She lay back into the pillows and threw an arm over her face. "Tell me 'twas a nightmare."

"I wish I could. Lady Essex and her brother brought you home...'tis been two days, Calais. We feared we would lose you, but Mr. Quinn was quick to help, with Miss Addy."

Annalisa removed her arm from her face. "Was I delivered of the child?"

Sarah nodded.

Her lip trembled. "A boy, or a girl?"

Sarah reached for her hand and squeezed. "A girl. A tiny baby girl."

Forcing back tears, Annalisa asked, "Can I see her?"

Sarah shook her head. "I'm sorry...she did not survive."

A silent scream left Annalisa's mouth, followed by a blood curdling wail as she bent over herself. "God, why! What have I done to deserve this? How did this happen?"

"Hush..." Sarah's hand smoothed her hair. "We think it was the tea. Someone brewing the tea used pennyroyal... perhaps by accident. Lady Essex has not been able to determine how it happened."

"'Twas Jane," Annalisa sobbed. "She did this to me."

"She denied it. Your sister would never intentionally hurt you or your unborn child."

Yes, she and Jane had been ill at ease in one another's company, but to accuse her of such evil was too much, even for Jane and all her jealousy. *But Mercy would know better than to accidentally brew tea with pennyroyal.*

"Be still, dear friend. Miss Addy wrapped your girl in muslin. Would you like to see her?"

Annalisa wept, "How can I gaze upon her without dying myself?"

"She looks as though she sleeps."

Sarah's hand smoothed her hair once more, and Annalisa reached for her. She heaved into Sarah's shoulder, inhaling her scent of chamomile and cinnamon, until she could sob no more. *I must see her. I must hold my daughter.*

"I must give her a name. If he'll help me, I'd like to speak with Quinnapin."

Sarah nodded. "Of course. Let me fetch them. Addy's made a strong venison soup, and chamomile tea."

Not five minutes in agonizing solitude, and Addy entered the bedchamber behind Sarah, with a bowl of soup and cup of tea. Though she had little appetite, Annalisa ate several spoonfuls of the savory broth, rich with iron from the deer, and finished the mug of chamomile.

Quinnapin stepped inside the room with a small box in hand. He set the vessel upon the bed and stood by her. His mere presence exuded a gentleness, cloaked in calm strength. Annalisa drew in a shaky breath and opened the box.

A tiny girl child, no larger than two pounds, rested peacefully within. Annalisa lifted the baby, still snug in her muslin cloth, and cupped her in her hands. She sniffled and blinked away the tears.

Annalisa trailed one delicate finger across the girl's gaunt, dimpled cheek, and whispered, "My Eliza. Eliza Perkins. *Kuwamônush.*" She looked to Quinnapin. "I will no longer speak her name...today I renounce my god, for he has forsaken me." Silence settled over the room, but when she spoke again, she steadied her wavering voice, "Quinn, will you help me bury her? I would like her to face southwest, toward Keihtánit's house."

He knelt and squeezed her hand. "Of course, Miss Anna."

꧁❀꧂

AT SUNSET, ANNALISA SAT BEHIND QUINNAPIN UPON HIS stallion as they rode to her family's farm. In silence, they trudged into the fields toward the ancient oak. Beneath its ample shade, at the base of the trunk, Quinnapin dug a small, deep hole.

"When a child is buried, the father often will cut a piece of his hair to leave with them."

He offered her his knife, and Annalisa readily cut a lock of her hair. She placed the curling tresses upon the baby's tiny torso, then leaned down and gently kissed the infant's forehead.

"Good-bye, my love."

"*Wachônuq ahkee,* the land keeps her."

Before she could further contemplate the matter, Annalisa closed the box and planted her into the earth, facing south-west. She and Quinnapin poured dirt into the hole, while he chanted something in his native Wampanoag—a mystery rite she was not privy to know but was grateful he now shared.

As the sun set below the horizon, they settled in stillness beneath the sheltering oak. Quinnapin had once warned her to beware the *Puk-wudjies* after dark, but this evening, they remained unaltered and unbothered by the dwindling light, protected by the oak's vast canopy. The tree's spirit vibrated and buzzed, shielding them from all manner of unpleas-antries, but one creature passed within the sage abode. Yellow flashes of light sparkled, illuminating the space beneath the trunk. Lightning bugs congregated over the tiny gravesite, as though they meant to carry Eliza's soul to Keihtánit's house.

At the thought, a strange tranquility settled over Annalisa. Her daughter would go to a place of pleasant weather, boun-tiful harvest, and plenty of game to keep her from ever hungering. She imagined her underdeveloped baby growing into a little girl with glowing bronzed skin, ocean-blue eyes, a dimpled smile, and curling honey-brown hair. *I'm safe, Mamma. I'm happy, Mamma. I'm at peace, Mamma. Kuwamônush,* the girl said.

The lightning bugs dispersed, the noble tree's vibration

eased to stillness, and Annalisa knew her daughter had made it to Keihtánit's house.

She was at peace.

✣ 42 ✣

ANNALISA

TOPSFIELD, AUGUST 1777

WHEN SHE HAD REGAINED her strength from
the miscarriage, Annalisa rode to the Perkins estate
to call on Jane.

Mercy opened the door.

"Miss Annalisa, Mrs. Perkins is in the drawing room, shall
I take you to her—"

Annalisa pushed past the housekeeper and down the hall
—she knew the house as well as her own—until she reached
the drawing room, and threw open the door.

Jane sat by the window with a book in one hand, and little
Robby, now five months, curled at her bosom. Tommy, at
eighteen months, waddled about the room. Annalisa's grief
returned as she yearned for the daughter that had been taken
from her.

Jane peered up from reading. "You're looking better."

Annalisa clenched her fist. "Did you kill my daughter?"

"I beg your pardon?" Jane closed the book and placed it on
the round table beside her.

"You heard me. Did you put the pennyroyal into the tea?"

"Annie, that is absurd. I cannot—"

"The miscarriage nearly killed me, and you've remarked more than once how you thought I was dead. Why not poison me and my unborn child?"

"How could you propose such a charade? I'm your sister!"

"Yet, you wear many masks, Janey, and the face I see now bears one of contempt. I've learned well enough a mask may reveal a person's nature. How can I trust it wasn't you? How can I be certain that in your envy and desperation to keep your family intact, you didn't harm mine?"

"I'm still Jack's wife, Annie. You and he have no family. Now."

Her blood curdled and turned cold. "You did do it, didn't you?"

Jane returned to her book as though Annalisa no longer remained in the room. "The well-being of my children is of utmost importance. And one day, when you have children of your own, you'll understand."

"How dare you."

"Does reputation mean nothing to you, Annalisa?" Jane spoke with exasperation, but her countenance remained poised, unaffected. "Besides, adultery is sure to persuade the magistrates, but without a child as evidence, who's to believe it? 'Tis what Hannah French says, anyway."

"Since when have you befriended Hannah French? Damn Hannah French! Think you I care what she says? Reputation be damned, Jane."

Jane set down her book once more. "Look at me, Annie. Have you two children who need a father? What other man of good breeding may have married me in my state? I require Jack more than you, and you'll not take him from me." Her face softened. "I'm grief-stricken for what you've endured. No mother deserves to lose her child. But we all make mistakes.

Perhaps 'twas by divine Providence that God punished you for your sins."

"My what?" Annalisa fisted her hand, wishing to strike her sister.

"Your adultery."

"By murdering my daughter? My *innocent* daughter?" She glared at Jane. "I curse God as I curse you, Jane Catherine *Howlett*. May your future children turn to ash within your womb. May your health leave you when you need it most. Should you ever look upon me again, may your eyes fail you with blindness."

Jane clutched Robby to her breast. "Annie, please, stop it—"

"And may your children learn to love me more than they'll ever love you—their bitter, soulless, harpy of a mother. No better than the harlots at Mount Whoredom, or Damnation Alley." Annalisa spit at Jane's feet and made sure to utilize her sister's full name once more. "You're dead to me, Jane Catherine Howlett." She fled the drawing room, charging past Mercy and outside, to her horse.

❧

THAT EVENING, ANNALISA SAT AT HER KITCHEN TABLE WITH Quinnapin, Sarah, and Mary, who called on her for supper. Outside, crickets chirruped and an owl hooted. Annalisa wondered from where the owl made his presence known to them. *The stable? Or perhaps a tree?* She set down her salad fork, ready to take a walk outside.

"You must eat, Miss Anna," Quinnapin said. "Regain your full strength."

Annalisa studied the trencher before her. The greens

wilted in the humidity. "I know Jane did this. She won't admit it, but I know 'twas her."

"And you cursed her as you should," Sarah replied. "Now, let's focus on healing."

Annalisa eyed her musket hanging over the hearth. She always supposed womanhood would be too much, and here she was, a young woman, husbandless and childless, having survived miscarriage most certainly at the hands of her own sister. As a man, she would never have endured such hardships in the militia. *Only different ones, I suppose.* She would write to Jack this evening of the miscarriage. He needed to learn the fate of his unborn daughter. Yet, the thought of writing such words crippled her.

"I can't believe Janey would do something so terrible," Mary said. "But I know she's jealous. She always has been. I've seen it for years."

"What else have you seen?" Annalisa asked.

"I don't see nearly as much as I did when she lived with Mamma and Papa. Since she's been at the Perkins's, I see her very little. Only when she calls on Sundays with Tommy and Robby." Mary hesitated. "I wonder if Jane still thinks of Oliver, if she wishes he were alive."

"What makes you speak so?" Annalisa asked.

Addy came forward with a tankard of cider, set it upon the table, and sat with them. "You think far too much on the subject, Miss Mary," she said gently.

"Just a thought, really," Mary replied. "Because sometimes I wonder how he died. What happened to him...if he'll come back like you and Jack did."

"Oh, Mary." Annalisa reached for her sister. "'Tis unlikely. General Burgoyne signed and sent the letter to Lord and Lady Perkins. I'm certain Jane thinks of him. She has reminders in her two children. As for how he died, he probably took a ball to his chest." She sat back in her chair with her tin cup. Though she loathed her brother-in-law, she hoped he died with the honor befitting a soldier; he was, after all, the father of her innocent nephews.

A cooling breeze blew in from the open windows, a refreshing reprieve from the stuffy, summer heat. Annalisa shivered.

"Shall I shut the window, Miss Annie?" Addy asked, lifting from her seat.

"No, no. 'Tis quite nice," she replied. "I rather enjoy summer nights."

Sarah chuckled. "Then you would despise Barbados, Calais. It was hot and humid all the time, from what I remember."

"Yes, it were." Addy grinned. "Sunshine beating down, palm trees swaying lazily in the breezes. It were magick, really."

Mary rested her elbows on the table and set her chin in her hands. "Tell me more. It sounds like a dream."

Addy looked to Sarah. "Shall I? Or will you?"

Sarah pursed her lips. "I don't remember much, Miss Addy. I was taken young."

"Very well." Addy sipped her drink. "The water were real blue...turquoise, and so very clear you could see all the way to the bottom, because the sand was pure white and soft...like Miss Jane's skin." She laughed, and they chuckled with her.

"What happened, Addy?" Mary asked. "How'd you come to leave it?"

Annalisa straightened in her chair. "Mary—"

"No, 'tis all right, Miss Annie. I never told you girls how I come to America. Never wanted to give you girls nightmares. But you're both grown now and have seen your share of horror." She drank again from her mug. "I lived five-and-forty years on that island. Five-and-forty years. Until they came and took me, my daughter, and granddaughter."

"Was it the British?" Mary asked.

"The Spanish, Miss Mary. In their big sailing ships. They packed us all in. We were to be sold. Sold like cattle, or horses." She peered into her empty cup, then set it down. Annalisa poured her more cider. "I thank God we weren't sailing to Spain, because they packed us in real tight. But the journey was long enough. When we arrived in St. Augustine, we were kept in chains, and dragged into the streets to an open market. My daughter were real sick from the journey. I think she got sold off to some plantation in Charleston. I was surprised my granddaughter kept her health. She had these big, round eyes, bright with wonder and curiosity...well, she never opened them, not once, to see where we was at. She got sold off to some British gentleman..." Addy paused, looking to Sarah, who held her head in her hands. "What is it, Miss Sarah?"

Fat, heavy tears coursed between Sarah's fingers. When she lifted her face from her hands, her cheeks glistened. "I remember it all...just as you say it, Adjubah."

Addy gasped and stood. "Phibbah?"

"Phibbah, yes. That was what my mother called me." Sarah wiped her cheeks, but the rivers continued to flow. "I'm that little girl who never opened her eyes."

Addy clutched Sarah tightly. They swayed as they sobbed —joyful tears, Annalisa hoped, though suspected they were forlorn for the years they'd been torn apart by that unforgivable abomination, the slave trade. *A disgrace of humanity.* Annalisa looked to Quinnapin, who'd been silent the past half-hour. He hung his head, and Annalisa reached for his hand and held it.

Every moment of distress she'd experienced while in

Europe paled in comparison to the torment and suffering Addy and Sarah had endured at the expense of trade— including Quinnapin and his Wampanoag nation; Natives like her grandmother and the Pawtucket, who no longer occupied the very land on which her family's house stood.

It mattered little that Addy had been free for decades, working for Mamma and Papa as long as Annalisa could remember; or that Sarah had been free, and well-educated while in the service of the Duchess of Devonshire. At one point, they weren't free, and knowing that was the cruelest truth of all.

Annalisa recalled the night she and Jack spent beneath the oak after the Strawberry Festival. They'd spoken of the abolition of slavery, something she'd only ever contemplated, but never expressed. Jack had hoped their new country could be a free land where everyone was created equal, and to her surprise, the sentiment had been stated in Congress's declaration of independence. She could only hope such ideals would be upheld should they win the war. For Addy and Sarah. For Quinnapin and the Wampanoag, and every other Native nation the English, Spanish, and French had wrongfully displaced. Natives like the Pawtucket, and her grandmother.

For the first time in months, her spirit vibrated with renewed hope for their cause, for the war Jack and her brothers fought. *The war I should be fighting with them. Freedom is worth fighting for—it is the only thing worth fighting for. And I've truly nothing left for me here...*

She looked at each face about her kitchen table: her sister Mary's, pale, and so full of youthful candor; Quinnapin's, tawny and wizened beyond his twenty-some-odd years; Addy's shining and umber, etched with the lines and wrinkles of a storied life; and Sarah's, smooth, with sparkling, round eyes teeming with hopeful conviction.

How honored, how grateful she was to be among such strong people, who against all odds, rose above the fates dealt them. *I must rise above mine, too. I must again become Benjamin Cavendish.*

Quinnapin met Annalisa's gaze, and it flickered toward her musket hanging over the hearth. "*Manut-oo auntau,* the Creator speaks. It is time, Miss Anna."

❧

ABIGAIL PACED BEFORE THE KITCHEN HEARTH. "YOU MEAN it? You're going to New York?"

"There's nothing for me here, Abbie."

"That is far from true," Abigail cried. "You have a niece and two nephews who adore you."

The thought of leaving her family constricted Annalisa's breast. She'd never see them again should she fall in battle.

"I know, and it grieves me. But I'm far more lamented by my own losses. My daughter was my final hope. She would've been the reason Jack petitioned for divorce...we could've finally been a family. But now, there's little reason a magistrate would grant him such a decree. There's no evidence of his adultery, and he'll hardly abandon Jane and her children." She was silent for a moment. "I could never ask him to do it. As much as I'm loath to admit it, Jane's right. Her children require a father more than I need a husband...and I can't bring myself to be in her presence again."

Abigail looked on as Annalisa, dressed in her breeches and waistcoat from London, removed her musket from the hearth and set it on the floor beside her haversack and cartridge box.

"Then take me with you," Abigail said.

"Quinn and I ride at dawn for Bemis Heights. He heard

from a gentleman at Gould's tavern that General Gates is encamped there."

"Louisa must meet George."

"I would if I could, but I know not whether George is at Bemis Heights. And you heard Jane...as much as I hate to admit she's right...again...the army is no place for a child, especially a little girl." Annalisa drew up Abigail's hands. "You must stay in town so I have someone besides Mary to write to. Sarah and Addy have plans to sail to Charleston in a fortnight to find Sarah's mother. That is where you'll tell everyone I've gone."

"That you've gone to Charleston?" Abigail frowned but pulled Annalisa into her arms. "I'm going to miss you so much."

Her friend's rose and bergamot perfume surrounded her, and Annalisa kissed her cheek. "I'll write as often as I can, and when I find George, I'll send for you and Louisa. It may not be until we go into winter's quarters. There'll be no fighting, then. But for now, we must travel light, and quickly."

"Of course." Abigail bit her quivering lip. "You're too brave for your own good, Annalisa Howlett."

GEORGE

FORT TICONDEROGA, NEW YORK,
SEPTEMBER 1777

U NDER COMMAND OF GENERAL Lincoln, who had been charged with coordinating the New-England militias, George led his men, with Bartlett and Jack, north to Fort Ticonderoga. It was as good a mission as any; he suspected William had been taken prisoner. He meant to free his brother if it was the last thing he did.

They'd been traveling since Bennington, where they left behind General Stark and the First New Hampshire Regiment—who held victory over the British and were now encamped at Pawlet—and continued north.

Buzzing cicadas stifled the humid air. George wiped sweat from beneath his cocked hat and loosened his neckpiece. Fort Ticonderoga was located at the southern end of Lake Champlain, not terribly far from Lake George. At least there'd be plenty of water for him in which to cool off—a stark contrast to the last time he'd been there, in the dead of winter. These late-summer New York breezes felt far thicker than the air at home this time of year, though the nights grew quite cool. The daytime heat might crush him before they ever reached their destination. That, or the Natives. News had run rampant about a beautiful girl called Jane, who'd been brutally murdered by the British-allied Iroquois while traveling to see her Loyalist husband. George bristled. If it weren't for news of Oliver's death, he would've believed the story about his half-sister.

But Oliver was dead, and Jane was married to Jack, and Annalisa had returned from the dead. The irony shifted his mouth into a grimace. Truly, God was cruel. *But at least Annie lives.* He'd written her before the militias departed on this expedition, but only divine Providence knew if he'd hear from her before the harvest. The mail was wildly unreliable, and with his constant movement about New York, receiving letters proved problematic.

George glanced beside him at Jack. His cousin had returned to New York after having reunited with Annalisa. A tinge of jealousy surged through him. *I wish I'd been able to join him. Abbie must be cross with me for not meeting her and the child.* But they would meet again. He was determined to be father to his daughter, and husband to Abigail, no matter Lord Essex. *The plum.*

They came to the heights south of Sugar Loaf Hill, and their marching stalled.

"Cogswell's regiment, we set up camp here," George ordered.

Jack set down his things. "This wilderness is nigh impregnable. There's no way the British may send out patrols for any distance in these woods."

"Aye." George dropped his effects and turned to his prisoner, Captain Fleming, whom he'd marched all this way tied with rope. The captain's auburn hair matted to his face in dirty tresses, his filth-coated chin and cheeks patchy with an unshaven beard. "And you're going to help us, reptile."

"And what if I don't?" Captain Fleming's cracked, dry lips split, and a trickle of blood seeped from the fissure.

"Then you'll be left here to die," George snarled. "The Mohawks are known to scalp their enemies before burying a tomahawk into the skull."

❦

IN THE CHILLED HOURS BEFORE DAWN, GEORGE AND HIS party set out for Sugar Loaf Hill. A dense mist had settled in, and George grinned wryly to himself. *Blessed fog! You aided our evacuation to York Island, and you'll serve us today.* With firelocks primed and loaded, they carefully ascended Sugar Loaf Hill.

Atop the mount, a battery of British artillery overlooked Fort Ticonderoga, now wreathed in thick fog. Only a dozen Redcoats, and one sergeant, manned Sugar Loaf.

"Fire!" George ordered.

Snap-crack!

A symphony of musket-fire splintered the morning calm, and the British scurried about in disorganized formations.

"Fall in, gentlemen. Prime and load."

George advanced with his militia, and the other militias followed suit.

"Make ready...fire!"

"Zounds!" A ball whizzed past Bartlett, who reloaded his fowler and fired upon the assailant.

As more rounds fired, the few Bloodybacks remaining fled their post, and George and his militia, with the other provincial militias, overtook the battery.

"Men, carry on to the bridge," George shouted.

"Think you they'll allow us to cross?" Jack breathed heavily as he tried keeping pace with George.

"Aye. 'Tis what Fleming is for." George turned to their

prisoner, who marched beside them, now unbound and clean shaven. "Where are we from, Fleming?"

"Halifax," Captain Fleming replied with a grunt.

They reached the wood bridge, and as George had planned, Captain Fleming approached the guard. Believing them Canadian, the guard allowed their party to cross.

When they'd traversed the La Chute River, Captain Fleming faced George. "I've done your will. You've no other use of me. Release me, you fiend."

"Never," George growled. "You spied for the Bloodybacks and nearly ruined the lives of my sister and cousin. You belong to me now, squeeze crab." He gestured to Bartlett and Jack, who re-bound Fleming's raw wrists in rope.

"I've atoned for my mistakes, I swear it." Captain Fleming lunged after George, who'd already strode several yards ahead. "If you release me, I'll return to Rhode Island, neither Loyalist nor Patriot."

George turned. "You'll return Patriot, or not at all."

"I was responsible for the Gaspee," Fleming blurted.

Jack, George, and Bartlett formed a circle about Captain Fleming.

"You were responsible for the Gaspee?" Jack asked, quirking an eyebrow.

"Aye." Fleming cleared his throat. "My brother was captain of the packet ship, *Hannah*, they'd been pursuing. 'Twas I who sent notice to my friend ashore, Abraham, who then boarded and torched HMS *Gaspee* when it ran aground in shallow waters."

"Can we believe him, Captain?" Bartlett asked. "Seems too plausible for a Rhode Islander to know of such an affair and claim status."

"Seize him," George ordered.

Jack and Bartlett restrained Fleming as George stepped

closer. He towered over Captain Fleming by at least six inches —as he did with most men—and glared hard. "What made you a turncoat? Why betray yourself to the British when they ran your packing ship aground?"

Captain Fleming held George's stare. "They promised me land. And five hundred pounds per annum." He hesitated, licking his dry lips. "After the Gaspee affair, I was ruined. I had nothing, save my barque, *Liberté*."

George studied the captain. The falls at the mill this side of the bridge thundered like storm clouds. No musket-fire, or intercourse between them, could be heard over the roaring waters. "Then will you turncoat again?"

Captain Fleming shifted his weight. "If it means I may march with you unbound."

"You will pledge yourself to the Continental Army," Jack said. "This is your only chance, Fleming—"

"You will pledge yourself to *me*," George sneered. "'Twas my family you nearly killed. My family you betrayed."

Captain Fleming nodded. "I swear to you, Captain Howlett, I'll fight in your militia under your orders."

"And when this war is ended and we return to the province, you will be indentured to my sister as stablemaster and coachman, for no less than five years," George added.

"Ten years," Jack said.

"Ten years?" Bartlett asked. "'Tis a bit much—"

"Ten years," George agreed.

Captain Fleming collapsed to his knees. "I'll do it. I swear upon my deceased mother, I'll do it. Please, release me. I'll serve you, Captain Howlett, Mr. Perkins. I swear it."

"Lieutenant Perkins," George corrected.

"Lieutenant Perkins." Captain Fleming was near tears, though his jaw stiffened.

George eyed Jack, and together they unbound Fleming's

wrists, which were bloodied with eruptions of sores from months of imprisonment.

Captain Fleming stretched his wrists. "If you're searching for your brother, Captain Howlett, my bet is he's yonder." He gestured to a wooden barn, situated beside a small, decrepit house, not far from the mill at the falls.

George advanced toward the structures, keeping Captain Fleming close. As they neared the wooden buildings, several men emerged, their eyes round with wonder.

A thin boy with patchy, dark beard stared at George. He jogged toward the boy, and when he neared, realized it was no boy. The young man's pale eyes pierced through him, as his mother's often had.

"*Wilhelmina.*" George threw his arms about his younger half-brother, the first of his family to embrace in over two years. He wrinkled his nose against the fetid stench clinging to William and stepped back to appraise his brother's condition. William was quite emaciated, and caked in grime, his clothes torn, and fingernails embedded with dirt. His hollow cheeks and bony chin boasted a light beard peppered with dirt and flecks of bread crumbs.

"My God, look what the Redcoats did to you. Pray, Hessians, too?"

"You've c-come...for me," William sputtered.

"Aye." George draped an arm about him. "We're taking you back with us. From now on, you don't leave my militia." To his regiment, he ordered, "Cogswell's, gather the other imprisoned."

Jack, Bartlett, and Captain Fleming, along with several others who'd arrived on the scene, scattered toward the dazed prisoners.

William hugged himself, a pathetic, sad creature from the

soft boy he'd been on the farm. No, he certainly wasn't George, but he never was.

"Are you...are you disappointed we lost Ticonderoga?" William asked.

George shook his head. "No. I'm only glad we found you alive."

William grinned. His bottom first molar was rotting. "One more Howlett to withstand the British and Hessians."

"Aye." George chuckled. "And Annie's alive, if you can believe it."

William started to sob. "Annie's alive? Praise God...praise God."

George held William close. "There's much news to share, Brother."

✿ 44 ✿

ANNALISA

BEMIS HEIGHTS, NEW YORK,
SEPTEMBER 1777

B Y THE TIME QUINNAPIN and Annalisa arrived at
Bemis Heights, the site had been fortified, and housed
thousands of tents. The area, a densely wooded plateau with
scattered acres of farmland below, nestled beside the Hudson
River to the east, and stood just outside Saratoga. It was clear
to Annalisa the vantage was well-chosen by the Continentals;
its elevation provided a clear view of the land and
commanded the only road to Albany along the river.

"*Seep-oo.* It means 'river'."

"*Seep-oo,*" Annalisa repeated.

"Look." Quinnapin pointed west, toward a vast expanse of
woods. "That wilderness will offer much resistance to any
marching army, particularly one trying to move guns." He sat
by their campfire and stretched his legs. "I'm glad we finally
made it. I was beginning to tire."

She lowered herself beside him and pulled a loose thread
upon her stocking. "'Twas a long journey, but I'm hopeful for
victory." Annalisa peered about the encampment at the rows
of canvas tents and crackling fires, the soldiers in blue

uniforms, and militias in old coats of brown, green, and grey. The mix of militia returned her thoughts to Jack and her brothers. "Pray, think you we'll find George among these men?"

"I know not." Quinnapin raked the embers of their small fire, and she handed him a cast iron pan. They'd camped many nights now, and she was used to their ritual. "There are thousands of men. I suppose 'tis possible he's here with Jack, but it will prove difficult finding them."

She leaned in close and whispered, "And concealing my identity."

Quinnapin stiffened as he leaned over the fire. "Aye. That, too."

THE SUN ROSE INTO REDDENED SKY, WREATHED IN CLOUDS. Beneath a misty blanket, the flaxen fields below shimmered and glittered with dewdrops. Annalisa memorized the ethereal scene as she warmed herself by the smoky fire. Something about the howl of wind last night crept beneath her skin, lodging itself with an unsettling sense of purpose. She shielded her eyes from the harsh rays now spilling over the horizon, and her sensibility heightened. The camp had grown quiet, and a trepidation seeped from within.

Around ten o'clock, the crisp air gave way to cannon fire. Her skin prickled at the cacophony, tugging her back to Bunker Hill. Beside Quinnapin, she shivered and rubbed her arms.

A militiaman eyed her. "Never heard guns before?"

"Quite the opposite, I fear," she replied, deepening her contralto voice. "I was at Bunker Hill. 'Tis a sound that haunts me at night."

The men around her nodded. "For Bunker Hill," a few said, clapping her on the back.

"Sir!" A scout, perched high in a tree shouted, "I see the glint of bayonets."

Annalisa glanced up at the boy who could be no older than sixteen, then returned her gaze to the men about her. She anticipated a reaction, but they continued to eat and talk amongst themselves.

"Should we not act?" she whispered to Quinnapin.

"I've not fought in battles like these before...Ben." He was careful to use her alias. "I know not how the men should or shouldn't respond to information."

"No, you wouldn't," barked a militiaman behind them. "Your tribes fight for the British. How can we suppose where your allegiances lie, savage?"

"You dare call him *savage?*" Annalisa said, her lip curled.

Quinnapin snapped his head toward the militiaman, his dark eyes narrowed. "The Mohawks fight with the British. I'm Wampanoag, and I fight with the Continentals. Unless you wish for me to step over your dismembered body when your skull's been scalped by Iroquois, I suggest you shut your potato trap and give your tongue a holiday. *Savage.*"

The militiaman's face fell, and he scampered away from their campfire.

A lanky soldier replaced him. "Fall in, rogues, we're moving out. General Arnold's orders."

A mile from their encampment sprawled Freeman's farm —much like her family's she left behind in Topsfield. The expanse of grassy fields gave way to a small wooden farmhouse at the outskirts of the plain. A small tuft of smoke swirled from its chimney. *The owners are still inside.* Her stomach lurched.

What would my family do, where would they go, if the Redcoats and Hessians marched upon them? Such had been the fate of Tabitha Nelson's farm in Lexington. Since the battles at Lexington and Concord, Annalisa often worried of the sound of muskets and cannon-fire upon her home, the dead littering the narrow lane, and her family tending to the wounded only to be charged with treason, no matter the uniform from which blood spilled...

At the bottom of a hill stood the British center lines. With each advancing step, she gripped her Brown Bess, knuckles white. At Bunker Hill, it had taken fortitude to hone the skill of rapidly loading her musket. Now, her aim and speed were required more than ever. This time, she knew what to expect of battle. *I wonder how Nathaniel is...* Her friend from the Danvers militia with whom she'd fought that day at Bunker Hill...the friend she'd saved after the British maimed him.

"We march into the clearing," Major General Arnold hollered over the chest-rattling musket-fire.

Annalisa looked to Quinnapin. His hardened face showed neither fear nor anxiety. She swallowed the dryness within her mouth and adopted his energy.

"Charge!"

The order came as though from nowhere, and Annalisa, clutching her musket with bayonet affixed, ran down the hill toward the British lines. "For Bunker Hill!" she cried.

"For Bunker Hill!" Quinnapin echoed.

Their onslaught pushed the Redcoats back, but the British charged on them, forcing her militia back into the clearing. Musket rounds sped through the air as Annalisa loaded her Brown Bess, aimed, and fired. A Lobsterback dropped to the ground, splattering hot blood onto her face. The redolent scent of iron flooded her, overwhelming her with the ambience of Bunker Hill. She forced away the memories and quickened the pace at which she loaded.

"Use your bayonet, Cav," Quinnapin shouted, as he swung his tomahawk and caught a Redcoat's arm. Quinnapin finished the soldier as he collapsed in a bloodied, red heap.

Annalisa fired at an advancing Redcoat, then hoisted her bayonet, stabbing another in his neck. The soldier gasped and fell as blood spurted from his puncture. Fueled by an electrifying energy, she jumped over his body, and swung her bayonet into an oncoming Mohawk. He crumpled to the earth, gargling his final breath.

Annalisa advanced and retreated with her militia several more times, while bodies of the dead and wounded piled both within the clearing and at the outskirts of the woods. Like Quinnapin, she cavorted through the field, sidestepping and hopping over the deceased, a lethal dancer of the revolution. For only a moment, she thought, never had she been this light of foot at a ball. *This is the strangest masquerade yet!* If only Sarah or Gee could see her now.

At twilight, the British still held the field, though neither side claimed victory. Weary of when she would again have to fight, Annalisa returned to her tent and scrubbed the dried blood from her face and arms. She opened her physick diary and located Addy's receipt for a skin wound poultice. She'd left the field mostly unscathed, save for a laceration to her forearm, which wasn't at all deep, though it burned. Annalisa reached into her haversack and retrieved a box of dried herbs, plants, and roots that Addy and Sarah had given her prior to leaving Topsfield. She crushed what she needed into a poultice and mixed it with Addy's oil, packed it into her wound, and bound her arm in clean linen.

"May I enter?"

It was Quinnapin.

"Of course."

Quinnapin stepped into her tent. "You fought bravely today. I see you've Miss Addy's physick. Perhaps we should take our aid to others who are wounded."

Annalisa appraised his arm. He'd been bayoneted in the shoulder and had already dressed the injury.

"Aye." She gathered her poultice supplies and fled the tent with him.

"Let's separate," Quinnapin said. "I'll go down this way, and you take Addy's physick down that queue of tents."

Annalisa made her way through the line, asking, "Any wounded in need of physick?"

"I do," a man called from within his shelter.

She dipped inside the tent to find a portly fellow, bearing a hole in his calf from a round. Annalisa examined the wound. The lead wasn't trapped inside. She crushed the herbs and mixed them with Addy's oil, packed the shallow cavity with the poultice, then wrapped his leg.

"Thank you kindly, sir. What's your name, lad?"

"Cavendish. Ben Cavendish," she said, and hurried into the night.

Annalisa found her way into several tents where she remedied bayonet lacerations and musket wounds. At the edge of the encampment, she lingered a moment before entering another tent from which she heard shouts and groans.

Inside, a militiaman squirmed upon his cot, his face crimson as he chewed upon a piece of wood. Two other men seized him. Annalisa gaped at the surgeon cutting his leg, four fingers below a tourniquet, until he reached bone. Using crooked needles, the surgeon tracked aside arteries and placed a leather retractor upon the bone. He pulled it back to get a clear view. The militiaman bucked against the men holding him down and screamed despite the wood between his teeth.

The surgeon grabbed his bone saw and, in no longer than fifty seconds, drove it through the man's femur, severing the leg above the knee. With a thud, the limb fell to the ground. The surgeon then buried arteries into the tissue and sutured a skin flap over the stump. When he finished, he stood and glimpsed Annalisa.

"He's all yours."

Nauseated, she started. "Sir, where are you going?"

"There are others who need amputations, sir." The surgeon ducked from the tent with his instruments, and the other two men who'd held the militiaman upon the cot.

Alone with the man, she swallowed through the roiling nausea, and ran a hand over the man's sweltering brow. He'd fallen unconscious, no doubt from shock. But it was no matter. Annalisa inhaled a slow breath and focused upon the task. She rummaged through her physick diary and decided upon a receipt. When she'd concocted the poultice, she covered the fresh stump in a green-brown paste, then wrapped it in fresh white linen.

Annalisa stepped from the tent, a foreboding dread settling in. Few men survived amputations, and that man would be no different. A fate she wouldn't wish upon anyone, not even her greatest foe. Silently, she prayed to whatever god would listen, *may Addy's physick heal him. Please.*

Quinnapin jogged toward her. "Pray, how did your services go, Cav?"

"Well, I suppose." She walked with him back to their tents. "Quinn, to whom can I pray?"

"The Great Spirit." He rested a hand upon her shoulder. "Keihtánit always listens and will guide you if you ask."

When she reached her tent, she said good night to Quinnapin, and rested on her cot. Staring into the blackness above her, she whispered, "Great Spirit, please heal that man and the others we've touched. Please, let us be victorious, that their injuries were not in vain."

৩৮৩

ON THE FIFTH DAY FOLLOWING THE BATTLE, QUINNAPIN met Annalisa by the campfire. He sat beside her and stretched his long legs before the flames. The air had grown cool, rustling leaves in the trees. Already, they started to turn, and would soon be engulfed in vibrant yellows, reds, and oranges. Back home, Papa would be preparing for the annual corn husking.

Quinnapin rubbed his hands over the fire. "I overheard one of the militia captains saying our losses were great. Apparently, General Gates has written to Congress for reinforcements."

"Reinforcements?"

"Aye. 'Tis not over, Cav. We've a chance, yet."

Hopeful for victory, she smiled. *I'll have to write to Abigail and Mary.* Annalisa wondered how Louisa grew, and if she looked more like George. She imagined her black-haired niece playing with Tommy and Robby. *Eliza would've played with them, too, had she survived.*

Quinnapin's hand met her arm. "Keihtánit's house is pleasant this time of year, as always."

Annalisa stiffened, and she nodded, taking solace in his words. But she knew not how to tell Jack when next they'd meet, particularly if it were here, at camp. She could hardly greet him as Benjamin Cavendish. *He must never know my secret.*

❧ 45 ❧

ANNALISA

BEMIS HEIGHTS, OCTOBER 1777

SNAP-CRACK! BOOM!

Annalisa awoke and sat upright in her cot. Her breath puffed in little clouds. She shivered. Autumn was truly upon them.

Crack-boom!

The stink of sulfur wafted into her tent. *Another round of musket-fire. A skirmish, perhaps.* There'd been several the past few weeks since the Battle at Freeman's Farm. She swung her legs over the edge of her cot and stood. Promptly, she bound her breasts in linen, pulled on her shirt, threw on her waistcoat and jacket, and re-plaited her hair into a queue. She sucked down the bitter liquid in her tin cup she'd prepared the night before. The magick behind her guise had been tempered only by the mixture of herbs she drank each morning—a concoction Sarah had detailed to her that would keep the morbid flux at bay. As long as her monthly courses remained absent, she could masquerade as Benjamin for months. So far, she need not stuff her breeches with a bulky period apron, as she had that day at Bunker Hill.

Annalisa quit her tent with her Brown Bess and cartridge box and hastened to Quinnapin's. The crisp autumn air nipped her cheeks and nose. Soon, the first frost would encase the grass in glistening chill. Come harvest, it wouldn't be long until their encampment retreated to winter's quarters. *Will I follow them? Should I summon Abigail and Louisa? Or return to Topsfield?*

Quinnapin emerged from his tent and stood with his effects. "Another skirmish this morning."

"Aye. Let's join."

They hustled toward the commotion of musket-fire, along with several others from their militia. At the outskirts of the encampment, in the clearing below, a band of Natives marked with red and black face paint, charged with tomahawks. Dawning sunlight highlighted the baldness surrounding hair and feathers sprouting from the middle of their heads. Alongside the Natives, a few white-skinned British, adorned in similar warpaint, wielded muskets.

Quinnapin brandished his tomahawk. "Those are Mohawk. Affix your bayonet, Cav."

Annalisa slid her bayonet onto the muzzle of her Brown Bess and followed Quinnapin toward the chaos.

Her musket loaded, she fired on a British soldier. He gripped his chest and toppled into the dewy grass. An oncoming Mohawk swung his tomahawk, and she caught the blow with her bayonet; Quinnapin buried his tomahawk in the Mohawk's neck. The Native's knees buckled, and he collapsed. Quinnapin sliced the Mohawk's hair from his head.

Annalisa thrust her bayonet into another Mohawk's abdomen. She twirled the weapon around and whacked his jaw using the butt of the musket. Quinnapin finished him with the tomahawk. Shouts and cries echoed throughout the clearing, and several more militia entered the skirmish.

Annalisa glimpsed the fighting. *This small band of Mohawks and British won't survive the onslaught of our militia without the support of the full British army.* Her skin raised. That day was certainly coming.

"Cav, look out!"

A white British soldier with face painted red, and garbed in buckskin breeches, charged toward her. His dark, menacing eyes startled her as she lunged with her bayonet. The Redcoat crumpled to the ground, gasping. She'd only managed to pierce his side. Quinnapin ran toward her and reached down. His tomahawk raised in one hand, he gripped the soldier's blond hair with the other.

"Wait, stop," Annalisa cried. The face, though painted, she recognized. Her heart racing, she lowered her voice. "Oliver?"

Quinnapin released the lock of hair and knelt. "Oliver Perkins?"

The soldier's face distorted with a grimace as he held his bleeding side. "Aye, 'tis me," he said with a cough. "Know I you?"

Annalisa eyed Quinnapin. "We must get him to our camp at once."

"Wipe off the warpaint and we might have a chance," Quinnapin replied.

INSIDE QUINNAPIN'S TENT, ANNALISA STRIPPED OLIVER from his bloodied shirt and tossed it to the ground. Quinnapin shuffled through his haversack.

"Who are you?" Oliver slurred his words, his eyelids drooping. "Why've you brought...me...here—"

"He's unconscious." Frantic, Annalisa looked to Quinnapin. "Are you certain no one saw us take him?"

"Without the warpaint, he passes for wounded militia." Quinnapin removed bandages and a bundle of herbs from the haversack and set them where Oliver lay upon the cot.

"Should we keep our identity from him?" Annalisa asked.

"For now, let's get him bandaged. When he awakens, we'll tell him—"

"He cannot not know I'm here, Quinn."

Quinnapin mumbled something in Wampanoag, and worked quickly, his fingers packing the wound with dark green paste. With Annalisa's help, they rolled Oliver side-to-side as they wrapped the linen about his torso, over the healed wound of a musket round to his abdomen. When they finished, Quinnapin cleaned his bloodied hands on another piece of cloth.

"Aye, he can't know you, but he will remember me. Thankfully, the wound is not deep. He will live. If it had been further..."

"He already died," Annalisa replied. "Lord and Lady Perkins received a letter from the British stating he expired in battle." She shook her head, bewildered. "Now we've three who've survived our alleged deaths."

Quinnapin chuckled, then his countenance resumed candor. "There is a reason you've been spared life."

Annalisa rose from the chair. "I must write to Abigail. She needs to know her brother lives—" Her throat tightened. "Jane must learn he lives. Her husband lives, Quinn!"

She studied Oliver, who slept upon Quinnapin's cot. His warpaint removed, his face appeared angular, his complexion tanned from too much sun. Her fists clenched. *And he'd had the audacity to comment upon my own bronzed skin when first we met. Now, he is but a shade lighter than I. Yet, he'd dared put his hands upon me.* The thought behind her, she released her fists. This man was her brother-in-law, her sister's rightful husband, and the father of her nephews. The courts should now have no objection to any divorce petition from Jack. A sense of relief washed over her. *Jane's deceased husband lives! Oliver is alive. Much may return to as it was.*

⚜

THREE DAYS AFTER THEY DISCOVERED OLIVER PERKINS, A New Hampshire militia led by Enoch Poor arrived at Bemis Heights. Anxious, Annalisa paced outside Quinnapin's tent. Within, Oliver slept, having received bandages and physick from Quinnapin that morning. She lifted the flap as though to enter, then abruptly closed it. She hurried from the row of tents and found her friend by the fire.

"He'll return to the British at first chance," Annalisa said. "Especially now we've seen reinforcements arrive. He has no loyalty to the Patriot cause. I was a fool to have saved him."

Quinnapin flipped a johnny cake in his iron skillet. A bit of uncooked batter spilled over the edge and landed in the flames with a sizzle. "We did right by him, Cav. I think his allegiance may shift knowing we rescued him."

"I think you give the scoundrel too much credit," she replied.

"He remembers me and has thanked me for saving his life. I think 'tis you who give him too little credit."

His words gave her pause. "I can't go to him. He'll recognize me, Quinn."

"I think you're unrecognizable in those clothes," he replied.

She shook her head and muttered, "I pass for a man amongst the others only because they know me not. Oliver does. I fear he'll uncover my identity, then take me to the British. I'll be hanged, Quinn." Annalisa shuddered at George's warning: *You will be charged with impersonation—and jailed. At worst, hanged, if you're found by the enemy. And I along with you, for knowing.*

"You'll be hanged, too, Quinn."

Quinnapin shook his head. "You're unrecognizable. Talk to Oliver. You need to let him know about Jane and his sons. 'Tis not my information to tell."

Slowly, she lifted from the campfire log. "Is there a magick to further cloak my identity?"

Quinnapin laughed. "Go. Now."

Annalisa removed herself from the fire. In the distance, trees swayed in October's breeze, their orange, ochre, and crimson leaves swirling from their branches. She stopped outside Quinnapin's tent. There was no turning back from this. Quinnapin was right—Oliver needed to know his second son was born, and that Jack had wedded Jane. She sucked in a breath and ducked inside the tent.

Oliver sat up in the cot, his muscled chest bare, save for the linen wrapped about his torso.

His brown eyes turned to slits. "'Tis you. You bayoneted me, then chose to save me. Why did you change your mind? Do I know you from somewhere? You knew my name—"

"I do know you but you don't know me. I'm Benjamin Cavendish, a relation to the Howletts of Topsfield."

"Benjamin Cavendish?" Oliver adjusted his position on the cot and swung his legs over the side. "I know not the name, but I'm cousin to George Bixby Howlett, Mr. Howlett's adopted son."

"Yes, I know George," she said, deepening her voice. "I'm a relation to Mr. Howlett, not his wife, so George is no cousin of mine."

Oliver rubbed his temples, as though trying to recall how George was related to him. "Ah, I see. Why did you spare me?"

"I could hardly return to town with your blood on my hands." She paced the length of the small tent. "You're thought to be dead at home, but you've much to live for."

He chuckled. "Aye. So I was. Nearly. Then the Iroquois found me. Know you my wife, Jane?"

"Aye, sir. I do. That is why I saved you."

"Pray tell, is she well? I've not been able to find my way home, nor send a letter. Though it seems the British had little trouble in notifying my family of my death. Had they even checked my body, they'd have found I was alive."

"Then why continue fighting for them?"

"'Tis what I know, Mr. Cavendish." Oliver hesitated. "May I call you Ben?"

"Cav. 'Tis what Quinn calls me."

"Very well, Cav. I can't well be a turncoat. My brother and I—surely you know Jack—are at odds. When last we met, he was prisoner aboard HMS *Lively*, and my wife aided his escape with our son...tell me, have you seen young Thomas?" His face softened at the mention of his son, and Annalisa's heart trembled.

"Aye, the boy is well, and growing fast—"

"Then I can rest tonight." Oliver grinned. His teeth had yellowed from the last time she'd seen him.

"Jane's remarried," she blurted. "She needed a husband for her children—"

"Remarried?" Oliver's face fell. "To whom? Know you the man?"

Annalisa quaked. "Jack. She wed your brother...at the behest of your father."

Oliver's hands fisted, and he slammed the cot. "Damn him! Damn them both!"

"No, please. There's hope yet, now you're alive. Jack may petition for divorce...his wife, Annalisa, is alive, too—"

"What?" Oliver's head jerked up, and he studied her carefully.

"Y-yes...Annalisa lives, too. And n-now, so d-do you."

Oliver rose from the cot and stood to his full height, only two inches taller than she. He made his way toward her, grazing the chair for balance as he passed by. "Annalisa Howlett lives."

"Annalisa Perkins," she corrected him. "She was Jack's wife..."

He cupped her shoulders and slid his hands down her wool-encased arms. Her hands tingled, and a trickle of perspiration dripped between her bound breasts.

Oliver stepped back and held her stare. "Is. Annalisa *is* Jack's wife. And she indeed lives...right here before me."

❧ 46 ❧

ANNALISA

BEMIS HEIGHTS, OCTOBER 1777

ANNALISA BACKED AWAY FROM Oliver. "You know not what you're talking about—"

"Your disguise is well done. I'll give you that. You had me fooled, even with the scar beneath your right eye. How could I have missed it?" Oliver returned to the cot, smirking. "But at the mention of Jack, something in your face turned. You're unmistakably you, Annalisa Howlett."

She grimaced at her name upon his lips. It was true, she was Annalisa Howlett, and no longer Annalisa Perkins. If it were any other time, she would have chided him for his cruelty in reminding her of it, but he knew not Jack had been wedded to Jane and suffered similarly.

Oliver sucked in a breath and winced. "Thank you for saving me."

"I beg your pardon?"

"You saved me. After you bayoneted me." He winked. "But you saved me, nonetheless. I've no doubt it has to do with your loyalty to my son, your nephew."

"Well, that was part of it. I could hardly let you die.

Twice." She returned his wink. "And besides, you've two sons. Jane was with child—"

"Two sons?" Oliver had started to lie down but bolted upright to the edge of the cot. His face glowed crimson from the pain, then greyed. "She lay with Jack?"

"No—she...apparently you got her with child when last you were together. Is that not possible?" Annalisa's face numbed. *Did Jack sire Robby? Did he lie to me?*

Oliver massaged his temples. "I think we did strum upon HMS *Lively*, but I can hardly remember much before Quebec and *Trois-Rivières*."

Her fingers prickled as the blood returned to her hands. "Then you've two sons. Tommy and Robert."

Oliver grinned. "Two boys."

"And you've a niece from Abigail. Louisa, after your—"

"Grandmother. I remember her well." His smile widened. "Then our family is growing. Pray, how fares Abigail? Has she yet returned with Lord Essex?"

"That is another tale for another day," Annalisa replied.

"Quite." Oliver bit his lip, then returned to a recumbent position upon the cot. "We've a bit in common now, you and I. Both of us taken for dead, both of us victims of marriage charades made in haste."

"Aye."

"Does Jack know you're alive?"

"He does."

"Yet he remains married to Jane."

"He...it is quite complicated," she replied, neglecting to tell him about her pregnancy and miscarriage. "But I imagine Jack could petition for divorce now that we're both alive."

"Annalisa, we were presumed dead. Unless Jack deserts Jane, or commits adultery, I see no reason for the courts to grant him a decree."

She pulled up Quinnapin's chair and sat, elbows upon her thighs. "If the magistrates deny it, then what?"

Oliver cleared his throat, eyeing her from his periphery. "We fight, Annie."

Her skin raised. Oliver had never called her 'Annie', and he looked upon her now with solidarity. *Can his candor be believed?*

"We return home and fight to get our spouses back." A mischievous smile pointed the corners of his mouth. "I'm sure we'd have no trouble at all causing them to commit adultery on one another."

This is true, as Jack and I have already performed the sin. "Aye, wherever Jack may be."

"Ah. Then he's not in Topsfield with his wife?"

"No, he left for the army. I've not heard of his whereabouts. Or my brothers'."

"Sounds like Jack," Oliver huffed.

"You left Jane, too, for the British," Annalisa spat.

"Fair enough. She's been an obliging wife, allowing both her husbands to leave for war. Is she, too, a turncoat now that she's married a Patriot?"

"I know not. We haven't spoken since before I left with Quinn, and I shan't speak with her again."

"Very well. Then should I expect to venture home myself?"

"No. I'll join you. At least Jack will know where to find me when he returns." She stood and held out her hand. "Shall we shake upon it?"

He laughed, then winced, clutching his side. "A gentleman's agreement?"

"Aye. A gentlemen's agreement. We return home before we go into winter's quarters, so you may be with your wife and children—and you will keep my secret."

"And what secret is that?"

"My guise. Benjamin Cavendish."

He hesitated for an uncomfortable moment before saying, "Agreed." Oliver lifted his arm, and she shook his hand.

Annalisa turned to leave the tent, but he stopped her by reaching for her. "Cav, you're rather impressive with that musket of yours."

"I only have my brother to thank for it." She was about to dip from the tent when Quinnapin blocked her and stepped inside.

"Reinforcements have arrived." He whispered, "And I think your brothers are among them."

"George and William?" Annalisa gasped, her heart skipping a beat. "Are you certain?"

Quinnapin did not reply but stiffened as he glanced at Oliver.

Sensing his disquiet, she placed a hand on his arm. "He knows, Quinn. But we made a gentleman's agreement—he will keep my secret."

Quinnapin's shoulders relaxed. "I see."

"What of my cousin, George?" Oliver asked, a sneer upon his lips.

Annalisa cried, "Oliver Perkins, you are now a turncoat. You will befriend my brother once more—"

"Yes, yes." He rolled his eyes. "But truly, George is here?"

"Aye." Quinnapin replied. "I overheard someone talking about a Captain Howlett. Unless there is another militia captain called thus, I daresay it is he."

Annalisa quaked with anticipation. She longed to see her beloved George, but she'd promised him she would never resurrect Ben Cavendish after her stunt at Bunker Hill. He'd never forgive her if he discovered her here. Neither would William.

"They can't know—"

"I gave you my word, I'll not divulge it," Oliver replied. "Besides, I'll hang if you're uncovered."

She faced him, eyes wide. "Then George spoke true—we will all hang—"

"If the British find you. I doubt the Continentals would hang you. You'll merely be charged with impersonation—"

"And jailed," she said, finishing Oliver's sentence.

"Aye."

"But you knew it was me. How can I be certain they won't recognize me?"

Quinnapin reached into his haversack and retrieved a bundle of dried herbs and bark. "I'll make something for you to drink." He ducked from the tent.

When he returned, he presented a steaming cup of tea, and a smoking bundle of bark.

The smokiness enticed her toward him. "What is it?"

"Drink it. I think your eyes give you away."

"Yes," Oliver agreed, sitting forward on the cot. "Green eyes are less common than brown or blue."

"This will dilate the pupils, giving your eyes a darker appearance."

She drank the liquid and grimaced. "What is it?"

"I'd never poison you," Quinnapin replied. "You can trust me. Drink."

As she drank, he swirled the bundle of bark about her. Its earthy aroma clung to her clothes and hair.

Oliver sat upright on the cot, his almond eyes growing round. "Well, I'll be damned," he quoted George.

Annalisa chuckled. "Yes?"

Oliver stood and approached her. "'Tis uncanny, Quinn. I would believe her more now than ever I did earlier. Your eyes, Annalisa. They're nearly black."

Quinnapin set down the bundle of bark, which had ceased to smoke. "Now, come. Let's find your brothers."

"Have you a looking glass?" Annalisa asked. "Will I see myself, or another?"

"You will see your face," Quinnapin replied. "'Tis a mask, of sorts, for others not to recognize you."

They left Oliver within the tent.

The sun had already begun to set below the trees, typical for autumn days when daylight was scarce and night reigned true. At home on the farm, Annalisa recalled the height of the darkest months—which fast approached—when they saw only eight hours of daylight. A stark and dismal contrast to her favorite season of spring, which offered sixteen glorious hours of sun.

Amidst the descending twilight, Annalisa followed Quinnapin through the encampment. Men she'd known since arriving at Bemis Heights gathered with unfamiliar men of the newly arrived militias and built campfires. Quinnapin turned toward her, and pointed. There, upon a log, sat her younger brother, William. He appeared shockingly thin and rather pale.

"Come with me." Quinnapin led her toward the infant fire that had just been lit. William leaned over the flames, fanning them. He looked up.

"Quinn?" William rose to his full height and embraced Quinnapin. "My God, finally! Are you with anyone else from town? Josiah Averill and Isaac Perley are over there...have you seen my brother? George is about here somewhere...and Jack."

Annalisa startled. *Jack is here?* She lingered behind Quinnapin until he introduced her.

"Will, this is my friend Ben Cavendish. We call him Cav. He's been helping me heal and bandage wounds."

Annalisa nodded to William. "Pleased to make your acquaintance, sir," she said, lowering her voice.

William grinned, exposing a blackened molar. "Likewise."

She relaxed and studied his familiar face, now with fewer red spots of late boyhood. At nineteen, he was a young man, and handsome despite the gauntness. When last she'd seen her younger brother, he'd just turned seventeen. That was two years ago. She repressed a shudder for the time lost. *I wish I could embrace him. Martha Perley will be glad to hear he looks well enough...and that Isaac, too, is alive.*

"Come, sit with me by the fire." William gestured to a few chairs scattered about the flames that now danced in the darkening twilight.

Quinnapin and Annalisa settled about the campfire with William.

"Tell me, Will, last I heard you were at Fort Ticonderoga," Quinnapin said.

William hugged himself. "I was. And 'twas overtaken by the British. I was imprisoned, along with Averill and Perley. I thank God George and his militia were appointed the mission to retake the fort. They failed, but were at least able to release us."

Annalisa held her breath. "I'm sorry to hear this."

"I'm quite well, now, but 'twas a grueling ordeal," William replied, then appraised Quinnapin. "How did you come to Bemis Heights?"

"I traveled with Cav, here. He was a member of the Danvers militia and offered to journey with me."

William grinned, and Annalisa warmed. His two front teeth overlapped slightly, an endearing trait she loved about his smile, but his lower molar had turned dark with rot.

"I'm glad you could accompany my friend, Cav. We've been trying to get Quinn to join the cause for months."

William jumped from his seat. "'Tis George." He shouted, "George, we're here. Look, I found Quinnapin."

Annalisa followed William's gaze. Her hulking older brother turned to face their campfire. He looked much as she remembered him—clean-shaven and well over six feet in height, broad shouldered, and with long hair as inky as night, plaited into a queue. He neared the fire and Annalisa appreciated his green eyes beneath thick brows, and his strong, square jaw. When George caught sight of Quinnapin, his lips upturned, and he guffawed a deep, boisterous laugh.

Embracing Quinnapin, he said, "You look well, old friend."

"As do you." Quinnapin released George and gestured to Annalisa. "Captain Howlett, this is my friend, Cav."

Annalisa quickly tipped her hat. "Captain Howlett."

"Pleasure's mine, Cav." He studied her a moment, and his bass voice boomed, "Pray, what is your full name, Private?"

She stiffened. He knew the name; she'd told him after Bunker Hill. *I pray he doesn't remember.* "Benjamin. Benjamin Cavendish."

George's jaw hardened. "Indeed."

A rotund, portly fellow joined. "May I sit with you, Will?"

"Of course, Bartlett." William gestured to a chair beside him and introduced the young man. Bartlett then placed an iron skillet over the flames and plopped several sausages into the pan.

"Pray, were you at the battle on September the nineteenth?" William asked.

"Yes, and what a battle it was," Quinnapin replied.

"We heard neither side claimed victory, but that the British held the field," William said.

"'Tis true." Annalisa kept her voice deep, and her cocked hat low upon her brow.

"I hear Howe sent reinforcements to Burgoyne," Bartlett added. "I'm certain battle will ensue any day now. Or so Captain Howlett suspects."

At the way Bartlett referred to her brother, Annalisa hid her grin. As she tilted her hat, George's gaze met hers from across the fire, and his brows creased. She bit her lip and shook her head slowly. *He knows.* Ignoring the butterflies whirling about her stomach, she kept her face steady.

Her voice low, she added, "We suffered heavy losses that day, but I daresay, I heard we have over ten thousand men, now."

"Cav fought fiercely," Quinnapin said. "And in the several skirmishes since. Even killed some Mohawks and took a British soldier prisoner."

George held her stare. "Well done, *Cav.*"

❦ 47 ❦

GEORGE

BEMIS HEIGHTS, OCTOBER 1777

G EORGE QUIETLY FOLLOWED BENJAMIN back
to his tent, and let him disappear inside. The following
morning, before dawn, he returned with a lantern in hand,
and sneaked inside. All was dark, save for Benjamin
Cavendish upon his narrow cot.

"A word with you, Private."

Benjamin stirred from beneath his blankets and sat
upright, rubbing his eyes. "Sir?"

"A *private* word, Private."

No doubt sensing his irritation, Benjamin stood at once.
"Aye, sir."

"Dress yourself and meet me outside."

George stormed from the tent, leaving his lantern for
Benjamin to use while he dressed. As he waited in the early
morning darkness, George's face heated, and he opened and
closed his fists several times, cracking the knuckles.

When Benjamin emerged with the lantern, George
marched the young man from the fortification down to the
shore of the river flowing east of the encampment. When

they were beyond earshot of anyone, he swallowed through the tightness building in his throat. His beloved sister, whom he thought dead the better part of a year, now stood beside him. But this was not how he wished to reunite. *She must know I'm not pleased.* Yet, he wavered, unsure of how angry he should be.

George faced Benjamin, or rather, Annalisa. She was taller than he remembered, and slender, without her petticoats to hide her form. Standing before him without her linen cap to cover her curling hair, now plaited beneath a cocked hat, she adorned breeches and a coat that had been tailored to fit her frame. She appeared every part the young militiaman. If not for the name, she would have been unrecognizable to him last night.

"Goddammit, Annalisa. Or should I say, *Cav?*" Her downcast gaze and silence lit a flame within him, and he growled, "Have you nothing to say for yourself?"

She met his stare. "George, please. I've s-so longed for this. I simply w-wished to join the cause which w-we so firmly b-believe."

What is this stutter? He relaxed his shoulders, unclenched his fists and, after a moment's pause, wrapped his arms about her. "Peace, Little One."

"I'm s-so sorry George. I...I tried to w-write." Her voice muffled against his shoulder. "I n-never meant for you to discover me here...l-like this."

"Peace, Annie. I'm not angry. Only disappointed we're reunited here, and not at home." He held her at arm's length and examined her. "I'll say, you're convincing. I applaud you that."

She smirked. "Not convincing enough to fool *you* though."

He chuckled and sat on the sloping shore of the river bank. *How much time has passed since last we met? Two years? And how much have we endured? Surely, she's not the same sister I left behind that brisk August morning before dawn.* It struck him, and he shivered. The sun had not yet risen, and twinkling stars still dotted the sky, just as it had that morning he'd left her.

"No, not enough to deceive me. Though, I barely recognized you last night. And you've certainly convinced poor *Wilhelmina.* 'Twas the name. I remembered it from Bunker Hill. Old Ben and his tomfoolery."

"I feared you would." Annalisa settled beside him, drew her legs to her chest, and encircled her arms about her knees. "William will discover me soon. Quinnapin's tea only keeps my eyes appearing dark for so long." With one hand, she picked a blade of grass. "Is Jack here?"

"Aye. Will you keep this from him as well?"

"I must. No one can know I'm here, especially him." Her voice cracked. "I remember what you told me...about women dressing as men in the militia. He cannot hang, George. I can't let him know 'tis me...if I'm discovered, he'll hang. You'll all hang!"

"Peace, Little One. I won't tell." He wrapped an arm about her. "How did you leave Topsfield? Does no one know your whereabouts?"

She hovered her gaze on the swelling river. "I told no one, save Abigail and Mary. Everyone believes me to be in Charleston with Addy."

"And Jane?" From his periphery, he noticed her jaw set.

"Jane is dead to me."

Her icy tone sent a chill up his back. "What passed between you?"

Annalisa did not move or speak for nearly a minute, as she perhaps tried to gain composure, or withhold tears from spilling from her eyes.

George reached for her. "You can trust me, Little One—"

"Jane murdered my child."

He stiffened. "She what?"

"You gave Jack leave to return to town not long after Abigail and I returned from England—"

"Aye, I meant to go with him, but I couldn't obtain leave."

"As you can imagine, our reunion was one of love and desperation. Our time apart was hideous on both accounts. What followed was a blessing—it was only one night, but he got me in the family way." Her cheeks colored in the lantern light. "You must remember we were trying to have a family after we eloped, but all my pregnancies ended in miscarriages. Naturally, I guarded my joy, but the babe survived five months."

She sucked in a breath, and when she collected herself, continued, "One hot afternoon, I was sat with Abigail and Jane in the Perkins's garden. Jane offered me some tea we'd been drinking. 'Twas refreshing, so I drank several cups. Later that day, I miscarried. I nearly died, George. And when I'd recovered, Addy and Sarah told me the tea had been brewed with pennyroyal."

His neck and face heated. "Fie. For what purpose has Jane to poison your unborn child?"

"Her niece. I miscarried a daughter." Annalisa paused. "'Tis true. I swear it, though I can't prove it." She faced him, and he appreciated a glisten upon her cheek. "She has every-thing to lose now she's married to Jack, and my daughter would've interfered. With my daughter gone, she can refute Jack's adultery...I assume 'tis what he would've issued had he filed a petition for divorce. No magistrate will grant divorce without reasonable cause. There's little reason for him to file one, now. Though he knows nothing of the miscarriage..."

As angry as he was, a deep sorrow nestled at the sight of his precious sister, so vulnerable after having endured such hardship. George kissed her temple, and she rested her head on his shoulder. "I'm sorry, Little One."

She trembled beneath his arm. "I'm loath to give Jack such awful news after all we've endured. But he can't learn I'm here, George. He can never know I'm Benjamin Cavendish. Can you tell him about the miscarriage? Tell him a letter got through to you from me."

George rubbed his side whiskers. "I can, though I grieve to relay such news. He'll certainly mourn as he mourned you... I know not if he has the strength to endure much more, Annie." He hesitated, unsure of whether he should divulge to her the nature of Jack's torture and how he'd coped by using laudanum. "He's been quite...tormented. I'm not sure what he told you when you met in springtime, but he's...much altered since being imprisoned."

"But he must learn the fate of his stillborn daughter."

"Did you name her?" *What if I received such news from Abigail about Louisa?* George's chest tightened.

"Eliza," she whispered. "But I cannot say her name. Quinn buried her with me. She's at rest at Keihtánit's house."

George tingled. *Then she has forsaken our god as I have.* A lump formed in his throat. "She would have been a great playmate to Louisa, I'm sure."

Annalisa smiled sadly. "Louisa is the joy of my life. She's so like you. I can't wait for you to meet her."

A surge of energy burst through him, and he turned to face her. "Tell me more."

"She looks like you. Hair, eyes...she's bold, and impatient, and so clever. She always has us laughing."

"Zounds," George guffawed. "Pray, Abigail is well?"

"When last I saw her, she was in good health. She's such a good mamma to Louisa. You would be proud to see them."

His heart ached. "Would that I could be father to the child, and husband to Abigail."

"We escaped Lord Essex. He remains in England. Surely, Abigail may petition for divorce and marry you."

George started. "He didn't travel with you?"

She looked down. "No. He was not the man we believed him to be when they married. He withheld her mail, George. I daresay, we never would have made it home if not for the Duchess of Devonshire, and my plan to masquerade as Benjamin. I returned us safely...which is why you can't make me leave this place. I belong here. And I will continue to fight, because 'tis what I believe. We have people in our lives who need the freedoms we're fighting for. The declaration inspired me, George. I fight here with Quinn, for Addy, and Sarah...Addy's granddaughter."

He considered all she spoke. They were bold words, confident words. And in their time apart, she'd endured and survived much. *She is strong. Relentless.*

"I can hardly protect you from life, Little One, though I've tried. 'Tis clear you'll partake in this war of your own volition, with or without me." He stood, lifting her with him. "You're now under my command, Private Cavendish. I know how much it means for you to fight. I'm keen for you to join for the sole purpose that by some mysterious consequence, you survived Bunker Hill *and* Freeman's Farm."

"I fought in the center lines on Freeman's Farm. I killed and wounded many Redcoats. In the past fortnight, I even killed Mohawks in skirmishes."

"Aye. And the agreement is that when next we battle, which may be soon, I'll see with my own eyes your capability. I'll near myself to you at all times." George hesitated before offering his final thoughts. "I couldn't live with myself if I allowed you to run recklessly into the field and meet a bayonet, or musket-fire." He shuddered, recalling the wound that nearly killed her at Bunker Hill. She'd been more than fortunate that day.

To his surprise, Annalisa smiled, and kissed his cheek. "I'll oblige. You have my word, sir." She held out her hand. "An agreement between gentlemen—Captain Howlett."

"An agreement between gentlemen." He laughed and shook her hand, then pulled her into an embrace. "How I've missed you, Little One...Private Cavendish."

❧ 48 ❦
ANNALISA
BEMIS HEIGHTS, OCTOBER 7TH, 1777

ANNALISA WIPED THE SWEAT and grime from her face and, clutching her musket, hurried after George and Quinnapin. Her brother sought General Benedict Arnold, who rode wildly up and down the lines atop his brown gelding. Annalisa thought the general might fall from his horse with the force of his vigor.

"Rally, men, rally! To Breymann's Redoubt!" General Arnold galloped into the fray toward British and Hessian lines.

Annalisa regarded George and Quinnapin. They'd all been fighting most of the afternoon, and the British had retreated back to Freeman's Farm, all their advancements from the first battle gone. Breymann's Redoubt, to the British far right, appeared weaker than Balcarre's Redoubt, heavily defended by both British and Hessians forces, and situated mid-field.

"He's daft," George said, "but if we can overtake that fortification, we'll be behind British lines. This will be a decisive victory, Little One."

With lips pursed, Annalisa nodded. Her musket loaded

and bayonet affixed, she sprinted into the fray with Quin-napin; George fell behind.

"By my side, Cav," George shouted over the deafening boom of cannon and musket-fire. He wielded his firelock on a charging Hessian, but the soldier sliced Annalisa's right arm.

"Fie!" She hollered.

Her brother discharged his fowler on the assailant, and with a sputter, the German fell. George turned to her. "Quick, your neckpiece."

Blood spilled from the gash as she untied the linen cravat from her neck, and with George's help, wound it tightly about her arm.

"I'll be fine," Annalisa said, though it burned.

She loaded her musket then fired, striking a Redcoat in the chest, then thrust her bayonet into an oncoming Hessian. Beside her, George reloaded his fowler with expert quickness, firing three volleys a minute at the onslaught.

"Quinn!" Annalisa fired her Brown Bess on advancing British. Quinnapin swung his tomahawk into their opponent, an echo of their coordinated efforts at Freeman's Farm.

The battlefield ebbed with smoky, sulfuric discharge of gunpowder, the scent mingling with coppery blood. Such sights and smells often returned Annalisa to Bunker Hill, but she peered ahead. At the foreground of their ambuscade, General Arnold rode recklessly about the field. *If only we had someone like him at Bunker Hill. Then we may have proved victorious that day.*

Cloistered amidst her charging militia, Annalisa lost sight of General Arnold, and fired upon a Hessian foolish enough to advance, despite his retreating army. The soldier toppled to his knees and landed upon his face. He gurgled and gasped into the earth. Pitying him, Annalisa bayonetted him, and his gurgle ceased. *Would that this unknown German have done simi-*

larly for me had I fallen. With a shiver, she cradled her wounded arm, stepped over his body, and hastened after George.

Quinnapin, who just maimed a Lobsterback, cleared his blade on the soldier's red coat. Beside him, George nodded to her arm, now soaked with blood.

"Would that I'd killed that Hessian before he got to you," he said.

"Worry not, 'tis but a scratch," she replied, recalling his gruesome injury from Lexington and Concord, of which he'd said the same. Her right bicep throbbed viciously beneath the tied cravat, but she was confident she could treat it once they returned to camp.

"They retreat!" a militiaman shouted above the roar of explosive gunpowder.

As the sun made a lazy departure toward the horizon, the Redcoats and Hessians hurried from the field, leaving behind the dead and wounded. Freeman's Farm, empty of Burgoyne's army, left the Continentals and militia behind Breymann's Redoubt. Her body beginning to ache, Annalisa wound her good arm about George and together, they hobbled through the body-littered field. *This must be how Oliver was presumed dead.*

Quinnapin sidled up beside them. "That looks to be a nasty wound, Cav. Have you enough within your supplies to remedy it?"

"I do." With nothing to distract her, the searing burn of the gash amplified, but she withheld a grimace. *The cut is deep, but not long.*

"Cav!" A familiar voice rang through the evening smog, and William, encrusted in blood and dirt, bounded toward them with Bartlett at his heels.

"What is it, *Wilhelmina?*" George asked.

"'Tis General Arnold," he replied, his face pink beneath a layer of grime. "He's been badly wounded."

Annalisa stared at Quinnapin, whose healing capability far eclipsed her own.

"How bad is his injury?" Quinnapin asked, catching her glance.

"We know not, only that he was shot in the leg, and had fallen from his horse," Bartlett answered for William.

"Where's Jack?" George asked.

"I know not," William replied. "I've not seen him since this morning."

Bile rose into Annalisa's throat. *What if he's wounded, or dead? I must search this field for him...*

"Josiah and Isaac are with Captain Fleming and the rest of the Massachusetts regiment burning British tents," William added. "Arnold is with the Connecticut regiment. You must go, quickly."

Annalisa hesitantly followed Quinnapin as he weaved through the confusion of men and tents.

"He has surgeons and doctors enough, I'm sure," Annalisa said. "How could they know to ask for us?"

"We've a reputation, Cav," Quinnapin replied, looking back. "We healed many after Freeman's Farm."

The sky quickly darkened, as autumn is wont to do, but the mask of night hardly obscured the vestige of battle. Campfires and lanterns lit the smoky landscape in eerie glow, and Annalisa choked on the sulfur still clogging the air. She quivered, unsure if it was her untreated wound, or the otherworldly nature surrounding her.

I'd rather be any place but here, tonight. And we must find Jack...

After much questioning as to General Arnold's whereabouts, Quinnapin and Annalisa discovered his large tent, crowded with various ranking officers of the Continental

Army, and a couple of alleged healing women who had traveled with the Connecticut regiment.

One man recognized them and dragged them through the throng to General Arnold's side. The general clutched an open bottle of rum as he writhed upon a cot. Sweat trickled down his temples.

"Who...are...who are...these people?" His voice sounded tight as he spoke through clenched teeth.

"Sir, I'm Private Benjamin Cavendish, and this is Quinnapin, his father is Medicine Man of the Wampanoag. We've been summoned to treat your leg, sir." *Hard to believe this is the very man who gallantly rode upon a gelding this afternoon.*

One of the women stepped forward. "Are you a doctor?"

Careful to avoid her gaze, Annalisa replied, "No, madam. Just a young man learned in the art of healing."

The woman squinted as Annalisa opened her sack of supplies.

A man, clearly the surgeon, set down his saw. "He's refusing amputation."

An amputation will lead to a lengthy, painful death. A flash of the first amputation she'd seen pushed into her mind, and the man who perished days later. Annalisa tamped away the memory and regarded the general.

"General Arnold, you wish to keep your leg, sir?"

Though he bit a piece of leather, his words were quite clear: "I...will not...have it...amputated."

"This is folly." The surgeon threw up his hands. "He must lose this limb. There's no other way to save it."

"If I may, sir, I believe we can salvage his leg, though he may suffer from deformity after 'tis healed," Quinnapin said.

The surgeon's brow creased. "And who are you?"

"Quinnapin, sir. My father is Medicine Man of our Wampanoag nation."

"I would trust Quinnapin with my life, sir," Annalisa added. "I'm no trained surgeon either, but Quinn and I have healed many in this war. If Mr. Arnold would like to keep his leg, I suggest you allow us the space to treat him."

The surgeon, flanked by each of the women, stepped back, and Annalisa and Quinnapin moved in to assess the injury. The wound was extensive, and would require splinting, their strongest poultice, and a potent tea regimen. Quinnapin prepared the poultice and packed the wound. After wrapping the leg in clean linen, he swirled about a smoking bundle of dried herbs and bark.

Annalisa prepared a tea from the bark of a provision tree —the bark, according to Addy, was incredibly rare, and to be used sparingly for persons of dire need—to aid with blood loss.

When they finished, General Arnold slept, and she and Quinnapin quit the tent. The commotion of alleged victory buzzed about the encampment, but Annalisa leaned on Quinnapin as they walked.

They returned to her tent and removed the bloodied bandage about her right arm.

"'Tis deep, as you suspected, but we can heal it," he said. He mixed a poultice, and with skilled fingers, packed the wound. "You won't fall ill like Bunker Hill."

Annalisa bit her lip from the pain. "Thank you, Friend."

Long after Quinnapin left her tent, Annalisa lay in darkness, her fingers grasping her Bunker Hill musket round. She'd still not seen Jack. For all she knew, he writhed within his own tent as some surgeon amputated his leg, or arm. The thought chilled her, and she curled beneath the blanket. *He must learn of Eliza.*

She'd endured much these two and a half years; witnessed scathing brutality at Bunker Hill, death and miscarriages, deceit, and now, more bloodshed. *I'm far from the girl I was when this war began. But how many more years must we endure? Surely, we can't all withstand the length of this war. And what did George mean with regards to Jack? What befell him aboard that ship, and after?*

She kicked off the blankets and breathed into her throbbing arm.

They'd won this battle, or so it seemed, but could they win the war? Such was not for her to know, and by the end of it all, how many of them would still be alive to tell the tale?

49

ANNALISA

BEMIS HEIGHTS, OCTOBER 1777

ANNALISA SPENT THE NEXT three days nursing her wound within her tent. George brought her food, and Quinnapin changed the bandage. But on the fourth day after the battle, Annalisa left her tent for Quinnapin's, to see how Oliver fared from his bayonet wound.

She lifted the flap. Quinnapin squatted, mixing a cup of tea.

Oliver, perched upon a chair, smirked. "Cav, good to see you. I heard you were wounded but somehow managed to rescue Benedict Arnold's leg?"

She grinned. "Aye, with Quinnapin's help, of course."

"Pray, how long do you think you can keep up this masquerade? Surely, your brothers and Jack must suspect."

"As long as we're here," Annalisa replied. "And I've not yet seen Jack, only George and William. George knows, but Will doesn't. Soon, you and I can return to Topsfield, like we agreed. I've written Abigail twice these past three days."

Oliver nodded, his lips taut. "And you won't keep me prisoner like George and Jack's pet, Captain Fleming?"

"You're no prisoner of ours, Ollie," Quinnapin said.

"Are you feeling better?" Annalisa asked. "Would that you left this tent and made your presence known to them. I'm sure they'd be glad to see you're alive."

"No. You and I will leave here in the dark of night. No one will know I'm alive until we reach Topsfield and I'm reunited with Jane." Oliver twisted in the chair to check his wound and scowled. "The injury still pains me, but I daresay I could ride home with ease. I'm feeling much better than I was a fortnight ago."

As dusk blanketed the encampment, Quinnapin offered Annalisa the tea to darken her eyes. She drank it with haste, then left the tent with him, leaving Oliver to rest. Quinnapin guided their way through the fort, toward several fires that had been lit. In the distance, drums sounded, and Annalisa wondered if it was Natives at Burgoyne's fortification yonder.

"*Nun-oo-tam puhpeeq*, I hear music," Quinnapin said, turning to her. "Mohicans who fought with us."

"Where are they?"

Quinnapin hesitated, pausing his step. "There."

The sound of a fiddle joined the drumming, and Annalisa's chest constricted. "I know that fiddle…I'd know it anywhere."

Quinnapin smiled. "Then go to it, Cav."

She reached for his hand, and her bicep twinged with the stretch. "Will you come with me?"

"I will, but first, I promised Ollie some food."

They parted ways and Annalisa followed the music. The song was unfamiliar, but the sound drew her nearer the camp-fire. *Music, it is always music that binds us.*

Jack stood beside a drumming Mohican, his fingers upon the fiddle's neck, the bow gliding swiftly, as any accomplished musician's would. *He's proficient no matter what he plays, be it*

Bach or Handel, or the Gobby-O. When the song ended, she stepped closer, relieved he appeared unharmed from battle.

She clapped and deepened her voice, saying, "Well done, sirs."

Jack glanced up, and his cheeks dimpled. "Thank you, sir. Come, join us."

Josiah Averill and Isaac Perley sat about the fire with two other Mohicans, and a freckled-skinned man with auburn hair. She settled beside one of the Mohicans and warmed her hands over the flames. The air had turned quite cool, and her breath puffed into delicate clouds.

Jack handed the fiddle to Josiah, who'd often played with his father at the Whispering Willow Tavern in town, and soon, *Dribbles of Brandy* erupted from the instrument. Jack sat on the other side of Annalisa.

He tipped his hat to her. "I'm Lieutenant Perkins. I don't believe we've met. Were you at the battle?"

How friendly he is to others. She grinned, hoping to return his friendliness. "Aye, sir, I was. I'm Ben, but the rogues call me Cav."

"Pleased to make your acquaintance, Cav." Jack gestured to the others seated about the campfire, two of whom she knew from Topsfield. "Josiah Averill and Isaac Perley come from my hometown, and Moskim and Muxkweeno are from the Mohican turtle clan." He hesitated before acknowledging the red-haired man. "And this is Captain Fleming...a turncoat."

Captain Fleming scowled. "I wish you wouldn't introduce me as such, Perkins—"

"'Tis Lieutenant Perkins, to you," Jack snapped.

"A turncoat?" Annalisa asked, keeping her voice low.

"Aye, Fleming here was a Patriot in Rhode Island—or so he claims—who sailed his ship for the British to the price of five hundred pounds...the ship that destroyed my life and the life of my late wife, Annalisa..." Jack shook his head. "'Tis a long, convoluted tale I shan't bore you with. But Fleming is once again Patriot. He fought with us the other day."

Her breath tightened and Annalisa no longer noticed her throbbing wound. *Jack still refers to me as his late wife? And that Captain Fleming...captained our ship,* Liberté? Her neck and face burned, and she dug her nails into her fist. "Then you're a man of little honor, Captain Fleming," she sneered. "How can we trust you won't turn again?"

Captain Fleming, with torn clothes, un-mended shoes with holes, and matted, coppery hair tied with twine, looked on her with weariness. "I fought with you three days ago, did you not hear the lieutenant? Besides, I care little for what you think, *Cav.*"

"Battle or no, I'm sure Lieutenant Perkins would share a different sentiment were his lady still alive," she continued.

"Peace, Cav. Fleming has atoned for his sins," Jack said.

"Has he? Has he made amends with your deceased wife, then?"

"You speak as though you knew the lady yourself," Captain Fleming replied. "Pray, what is your full name?"

"Benjamin Cavendish, and I—"

"Benjamin Cavendish, say you?" Jack's face fell and a dark shadow crossed his pleasant face. "Then you know Miss Annalisa Howlett of Topsfield."

"Know? Is she living, then?" Annalisa asked, hoping to deflect his cold entreaty.

"Aye, against all odds, she lives," Jack replied. "Come, lad. I know you know the lass."

"Why do you ask?"

Captain Fleming laughed. "You're an odd fellow, Cav. Dare

I say I'm rather adept at reading people? You, sir, most readily know Lieutenant Perkins's former wife."

Jack gripped her coat. "Speak true, Cav—how do you know Miss Annalisa Howlett?"

Her heart raced. *How does he know to associate me with Benjamin? Has he read my poetry book, then?* She grew light-headed. "I...I did know the lass—Miss Annalisa...she's m-my—"

"She fondly regards you. Do you feel the same for her?" Jack barked.

Confused, Annalisa replied, "Aye, I've always thought well of her, sir..."

"Villain!" Jack cried. He leapt to his feet, dragging her with him. "How do you know her?"

Trembling, she said, "I met her...I have...she has...she regards you highly, sir. She loves you—"

"Ah, but she does not feel for me as she does for you, sir?" Jack's breath smelled strongly of rum. Perhaps he was disguised, and not thinking clearly. *Is this the altered state George referred to?*

"Sir, she loves you, I swear it—"

"Then why did she write about you upon the pages of her book? Know you we were married? Know you how much I still love and cherish her? That I would give my life for her? Would you, sir? Would you die for Miss Annalisa Howlett this very night?"

Captain Fleming chuckled darkly. "Say yes, boy. Or no. Either way, you're a dead man."

Jack's eyes glimmered in the firelight, and Annalisa thought he might weep, but the anger in his voice prevailed. "Speak, villain!"

"I...I know not, sir," she cried.

"Then I challenge you," Jack growled. "I challenge you here, at daybreak."

Josiah Averill's music had vanished, as he and Isaac looked on in horror.

"Peace!" George sprinted toward the campfire with Quinnapin. "Jack, unhand this lad. There is no challenge."

"George, know you this young man?" Jack asked.

He released the edges of her coat, and Annalisa sank back and bumped into Quinnapin, who stood with William.

"Peace, Cousin, I know Cav," George said, his eye wild. "We met before the battle."

"Has he mentioned he knows your beloved sister? That reptile is written upon the pages of Annie's poetry book... words of affection..." Jack choked on the last word and turned from the campfire. "I've wondered for months who the man is written upon the pages of her book, the man she regards so highly...and now he's here. I challenge you, Benjamin Cavendish—"

"No." George held Jack from her. "No, I knew no such things, but Annalisa loves you well, more than she loves this rogue here, if ever she loved him at all. You'll not challenge this young lad. 'Tis not worth it, Brother."

"I think 'tis a fair challenge," Captain Fleming said.

"Shut it, Fleming, you worthless fartleberry," George roared.

"Captain Howlett speaks true," Annalisa said, lowering her voice. "Annalisa—"

"Miss Annalisa," Jack corrected with ire.

"Miss Annalisa never loved me. You can rest assured of that, sir. I would never lie to you."

Jack broke free of George's grip, and advanced. "You must tell me how you know her, else I'll meet you at dawn with pistol loaded."

She wished to cower from him, but it was Jack. While he was imposing in his enraged, irrational state, Annalisa stood tall and stepped forward, her own anger bubbling over the sharp throb within her bandaged arm. *Enough is enough. He is now married to Jane. He will not divorce her. And Benjamin is innocent.*

Exasperated, she replied, "I knew Miss Annalisa, and I did love her. But last I heard, you married her sister, Jane. I'd never have done that to her. What have you to say of that, reptile?"

"Fie, Cav," George shouted. "Leave it be, rogue."

"No, let him speak," William cried. "Pray, how *do* you know my sister, Cav?"

Quinnapin grabbed Annalisa's wrist and tugged her to him, whispering, "Do not provoke Jack, he is serious in challenging you. Are you mad?"

"I'm quite incensed, Quinn. He's married my sister, and referred to me as his late wife," she hissed. When she returned her glare to Jack, his face had fallen.

"I never wished to marry her sister. I loathe the very occurrence. For you to propose it was by my own submission, then you are the villain, boy, not I. During my time at home, I spent one night with Annalisa, and now she carries my child. What say you to that?"

William gasped, "Is it true?"

"Aye," Jack replied. "Annie is with child, and I will petition for divorce from Jane for my sins. Is that what you wished to hear from me, Cavendish? Would you be a better husband than I? I've no doubt about it. I've become a lecher, it seems. But 'tis I who shall rise to the occasion for my sins...if loving someone can be considered thus. 'Twas I who faltered and lapsed in judgment, but 'tis I who shall make amends with Miss Annalisa for the sake of our unborn child."

Annalisa clenched her jaw until her head pounded. *George hasn't told Jack of the miscarriage. He still believes me pregnant.* A roil of queasiness rocked her.

Jack continued, "So I challenge you, Cav. Tomorrow at dawn. We may have both survived the last battle, but now God may decide our fate. George, I name you my second." He turned and left the campfire with Captain Fleming.

Annalisa looked to George and Quinnapin, who circled about her. William convened with Josiah, Isaac, and Bartlett, who'd overheard the commotion and joined the grouping.

"What do I do?" she asked in a hushed tone.

"I'm his second." George bared his teeth. "You couldn't leave it be, could you? You had to aggravate him."

"And you didn't tell him I miscarried?" she hissed. "You've had three days since the battle to tell him."

"I couldn't. Not last night. He was curled up in his tent writing you a letter. All he could do was talk of you and the unborn child. He told me he wished to name it after you it if was a girl..."

Her heart plummeted into the pit of her stomach. "What can I do now? I can hardly duel him. I love him," she whispered. "And he's clearly tormented..."

"Whatever did you write upon the pages of that book?" George asked.

"Shh, William and his friends." Annalisa tugged George and Quinnapin from the campfire and into the darkened perimeter. "It matters little what I wrote, only that he believes me capable of loving someone else."

"I agree with Cav," Quinnapin replied. "But I don't think Jack is in his right mind. We all know him well, and this is not him. Your friendship has endured more than most, and I believe such stress may have taken its toll."

George glowered. "I also may have offered him more rum tonight than I should have..."

"But what shall I do come dawn?" Annalisa asked. "Should I meet him with a pistol? I haven't even a pistol of my own, and my arm still heals—"

"Then that's what you'll do," Quinnapin said. "Meet him at dawn—I'll be your second—and show him you've come without a weapon, that you have no intention of dueling him."

"But what if—"

"Quinnapin speaks with reason," George said.

"Perhaps we can alter his decision come morning," Quinnapin added. "He hardly has a reason to duel you. You've done nothing to him. The fault lies with him."

Annalisa considered this. Jack's jealousy led him to challenge Benjamin Cavendish and not his own shame, though, she supposed, it played some role in his madness. She'd all but begged him to lie with her the night he returned to Topsfield, but they were both to blame for the act. Now, they must bear the consequences. *But I've suffered enough. I'm the one who buried our daughter...*

That night, Annalisa lay awake beneath the blankets on her cot. Her arm pulsated with a crude sharpness, and her mind whirled. *How can I sleep knowing I may have to duel Jack come morning?* And yet, she fumed. The more she perseverated upon their intercourse, the more she questioned his sense. *When did he become so irrational?* Certainly, the time he was imprisoned aboard HMS *Lively* had taken its toll, and now, his time in the militia. Morristown had sounded as tortuous as HMS *Lively*, then to discover she was in fact very much alive after he'd wedded Jane, well, perhaps it was more than any person's sanity could handle. Now, Benjamin Cavendish was to endure and suffer his illogical mind.

50

JACK

BEMIS HEIGHTS, OCTOBER 1777

J ACK BARELY SLEPT, HIS spirit vibrating with an anxiety he'd not known since his days aboard HMS *Lively*. *Why did I challenge the boy? I thought I was rid of those irrational feelings. What's become of me?* He tossed about his cot, and finally, sleep evading him, threw off the blankets, and dressed himself for the duel. *Perhaps he will not wish to engage. Perhaps we can part as mere acquaintances.* It mattered little to him they'd won the battle against Burgoyne, who now—he'd heard—contemplated surrender. Jack had nowhere to go. Should he return to Topsfield at the end of his contract, he would be forced into a life with Jane while Annalisa grew ever rounder with his child. Only after the birth could he suppose filing a divorce petition. No magistrate would grant it without reasonable cause, and adultery was one in their favor. *No child as evidence, no divorce.* He shuddered at the thought of his darling girl, home in the house they'd shared, spending her pregnancy in seclusion, save for Abigail's calls. His sister, no doubt, would visit often with Louisa.

But would the Howletts understand? Certainly not, no

matter Annalisa's survival of the shipwreck. *How could I have done this to her?* The guilt and shame bubbling up, part of him hoped Cavendish would win the duel.

Jack stepped from his tent and into the dark October morning. The east brightened from indigo to periwinkle, and the trees upon the horizon etched black against the sky. He drew up his pistol to examine it. *Where's George? The sky quickly lightens...*

From the shadows, his cousin approached, looking grim. "Perkins, you've made a grave error."

"Thank God you've come. I fear I've lost my mind."

"You have. Pray, you're not taking the laudanum—"

"No, never." Jack shuddered against the October chill. "I swore never to take it after Quinnapin helped me recover."

"Then I'm grateful you've at least partly come to your senses. Though, I see you carry your pistol. Mean you to duel the lad?"

"I must, mustn't I? 'Twas I who challenged him..."

George's great hands rested upon his shoulders. "No, Brother. You needn't go through with it. This has been a misunderstanding...if only you knew the truth—"

"The truth?"

George sucked in a breath through his teeth and said, "Annalisa's—"

"Where shall we duel, then?" Benjamin asked. The rogue appeared with Quinnapin. "Quinn's my second, Lieutenant Perkins. I hope you mind not."

Jack's chest heated with indignance. He'd considered not dueling Cav, but seeing him now, with his own friend named his second, Jack could hardly stand it. He urged George and Quinnapin to decide on a location, which they begrudgingly chose by the river.

As the orange sun peaked over the trees, the black river

waters faded to blue, and rippled reflections of gold and crimson leaves. Jack handed his pistol to George, and his heart thudded as he eyed Benjamin, who carried no weapon.

"Mean you to forfeit?" Jack asked.

"I mean not to participate, Lieutenant," Benjamin replied.

Jack curled his fist and released it. "Find the man a pistol so we may fight as men." He looked to Quinnapin and George, who said nothing.

"I think it would behoove you to cease this challenge, Jack," Quinnapin replied. "No good can come of it, I swear to you, old friend."

"If you are indeed a friend of mine, you'll find your man a pistol so he may duel me with honor, Quinn."

Shaking his head, Quinnapin fled the river bank. In ten minutes, he returned with a pistol that appeared to be British. Quinnapin checked the weapon, then handed it to Benjamin, whispering something Jack could not hear.

Jack held out his hand for his pistol, and George planted it in his palm.

"You will regret this," he murmured.

George's ill-omen trilled down Jack's back, standing his hairs on end beneath his coat. *Shall I ask him why he believes thus? Is he so friendly with Cavendish he fears I may accidentally kill the boy?* Jack resolved not to murder Benjamin, but only further wound the boy's dominant arm.

They moved several paces apart and Jack settled into the earth, staring hard at his opponent.

"Lieutenant Perkins, I have no intention of dueling you. I was wrong to have spoken to you in such a manner of your beloved Miss Annalisa. I would never dare to slander her name, or yours, sir—"

"If you should duel anybody, Brother, it should be me."

Jack recognized the voice as one from beyond the grave,

and he faced the ghostly sound. "Ollie. You're alive." He gasped, not knowing if it was elation, relief, or fear, that he looked upon his brother's form. Jack lowered his pistol.

Oliver made his way toward Benjamin and snatched the weapon. "I stand here for Cav. 'Tis me you should challenge, not the boy."

"No, Ollie, please," Benjamin pleaded.

"I must, Cav." Oliver stared hard at Jack. "My brother and I have unfinished business to attend to...and I heard you've wed my wife."

Jack grimaced. "I did so to appease Father. You must believe it. We all thought you dead—same with Annalisa. Jane was left with Tommy, and pregnant...I did what we all thought to be the honorable thing."

"There's no decency in what you did, now we're both alive. This marriage is the greatest offense to my integrity, and Annalisa's. I challenge you for the both of us."

"Peace, Ollie." George stepped between them. "Zounds! I'm stunned by what I see before me. Your family learned of your death through Burgoyne's army. We all had little reason to believe the message false."

Oliver said bitterly, "Had they checked me after battle and not left me for dead, they'd have known I lived. I owe my survival to the Iroquois." He peered at Benjamin and scowled. "I loathe this, Jack. But I must stand between you and Cav. Either you accept the lad's apology, and you apologize to me for wedding my wife, or you duel me."

Jack's head spun. He didn't wish to duel Oliver over marrying Jane, but he did wish to injure his brother for refusing to rescue him from imprisonment.

"I know not what I can say to placate the matter. You were a villain on board HMS *Lively*, having left me to rot inside that cell while Lieutenant Dickens tortured me day and night. To this very moment, I'm tormented by my time in that cell. Know you what you did to me, in your own blinded need for justice? You left your brother to be brutalized, like some rabid cur. I swore I could never forgive your betrayal, and yet, I chose to honor you in death...I married your wife so your children would not be fatherless...or worse, stepchildren to a lesser man. Now, you stand here before me a changed gentleman? I doubt your scruples have altered much these eighteen months." Jack lifted his pistol and pointed it at Oliver. "No, you'll get no apology from me, Brother. 'Tis I who require one from you."

Oliver raised his weapon. "So be it, Brother."

"Stop, this is madness," George bellowed.

"Step aside, George. I'll not stand for injuring you if you do not," Jack said.

"Aye, your hulking form is blocking my view," Oliver added, one eye squinted.

George hesitated before moving to join Benjamin and Quinnapin, who stood, clearly in trepidation, by a tree.

Jack's heart bounded as he pulled back the cock, and honed aim upon Oliver's thigh. He would not seriously injure his brother, only wound him. He prayed Oliver would do the same. Jack inhaled a shaky breath, and when he exhaled, pulled the trigger.

Crack-boom!

"Cav, no!" Quinnapin cried.

It all happened so fleetingly, Jack hadn't noticed Oliver pointed his pistol to the sky and fired his round. And Benjamin Cavendish writhed on the ground, gripping his leg.

51

ANNALISA

BEMIS HEIGHTS, OCTOBER 1777

GEORGE, QUINNAPIN, AND OLIVER crowded about Annalisa as she lay upon the cot. She squirmed, biting hard upon the piece of wood Quinnapin placed between her teeth.

George unbuttoned her breeches and she kicked him with her right leg. "No!" She spat the wood to the ground. "No, please, I can care for this injury myself."

Quinnapin knelt beside her. "Peace, Friend. We're all here, and we know 'tis you. We're going to care for this wound. The round is stuck within and must come out. We have to remove your breeches."

Oliver loomed over Quinnapin. "I can't believe you. Why did you do something so foolish? I wasn't going to shoot him, Annalisa, and I could've sustained any injury incurred from his foul pistol—"

"Enough," George growled. "What's done is done. I knew this would happen. I warned Jack when he made the challenge, and I warned him again this morning. He'll learn soon enough."

"No," Annalisa shouted. "He can never know what he's done to me...that it was me."

The men surrounding her said nothing, and somehow, she knew they would keep her secret.

Quinnapin's gentle hand found hers. "Please, we must remove your breeches. Will you let us?"

Annalisa swallowed hard. The round had embedded itself, rather shallowly she suspected, within her outer thigh—too high for them to roll the breeches up from the knee. She nodded, and George unbuttoned the garment, and slid it from her hips. She squeezed her eyes shut and threw her arm over her face, mortified to be fully bare before them. Jack was the only man to have seen her body, and he'd worshipped every inch of her. *He would be devastated to know he'd inflicted this wound.*

"'Tis not deep at all," Quinnapin said. "Here, bite this."

The piece of wood reentered her mouth, and she clenched it between her teeth. Pressure upon her left thigh, followed by a sharp, ripping sensation, consumed her leg.

"'Tis not bleeding much, Little One." George's deep voice surrounded her, and she felt his hand upon her head. "You're lucky it missed your vital artery."

Annalisa quaked, though it wasn't from the chill of that autumn day, or her exposed legs; she'd scarcely escaped losing her leg, and hence, her life. The memory of that man's amputation after the Battle at Freeman's Farm forced its way into her mind, and she heaved. Unable to contain the lurch of her stomach, Annalisa sat upright and retched, covering Oliver in last night's rations.

A scuffle of men sounded from beyond her tent, and a man barged inside.

"How is he?" Jack asked.

Quinnapin and Oliver shielded her from Jack, and George lunged forward, shoving Jack from the tent.

"He's fine. He'll be riding to winter's quarters in no time," George replied. "Now, go."

The commotion from beyond the tent dwindled to a lull of murmurs, and Quinnapin and Oliver removed themselves from her cot. Oliver wiped the vomitus from his coat, and Quinnapin wrapped a piece of linen about her slender, sinewy thigh. She warmed with each wrap, his hand growing near to the space between her legs. Yet, his gaze never once strayed from the task, and for that, she was thankful.

"That was close," George said, sitting beside her. He hung his head and shook it. "Another scar to match the others. Though, I'm certain neither of us considered you'd incur such an injury this way."

"I had to," she said. "I thought maybe I'd do it in time to stop either of them from shooting, but I was too late."

Quinnapin finished wrapping her leg, and Annalisa pulled up her breeches, buttoning them about her waist. The bandage left her thigh quite bulky beneath the fitted garment. Unlike petticoats, which hid legs and bulky period aprons, she learned years ago little could be concealed beneath fitted breeches.

"Thank you, Quinn." She reached for his blood-smeared hand and squeezed.

He nodded. "Of course, Miss Anna."

It was the first time he called her thus since they'd left home. Though she often felt more herself as Benjamin, part of her missed Annalisa, though Jack had made that quite impossible.

Quinnapin stared hard at her, as though reading her thoughts. "Jack is unwell. That much is clear." He stood, and washed his hands in the basin. "I'm going to him. If you'll excuse me."

He dipped from the tent, leaving her with George and Oliver; two old foes, though they were cousins. Now, they stood before her, united in what befell them that morning. Her thigh seared with pain, but she sat upright on the cot, holding Oliver's stare.

"I never thanked you for what you did today," she said.

"I could hardly let him duel you," he replied flatly, but she knew he was sincere. "In the time you've known me, I've not been the greatest of gentlemen. 'Twas the least I could do to atone for my behaviors of years past."

George said nothing, though he nodded with satisfaction.

Oliver turned to leave. "I should go. If you need anything, I'll be in Quinn's tent." He ducked into the grey day beyond, leaving her with her brother.

Relieved to be alone with George, with the reality of the morning's duel, Annalisa wailed. Her brother held her and let her heave against him. His strong, muscular hand brushed the matted hair from her face that had been plaited into a queue these last few months. She was barely a woman anymore.

"There, there, Little One." His thumb swiped the droplets from her cheek and grazed the scar beneath her right eye.

"I'm so very sorry I did this, George."

"Shh. I'm not angry. Not like Bunker Hill." He paused. "I still think you a fool, but 'tis no matter."

She wiped her face. "I am a fool. I never should've come here with Quinn—"

"You did what you must. I'll never chastise you for that. Not anymore. You can hold your own on a battlefield, and in a camp. The men like you, respect you, even." George inhaled sharply. "I'm proud of you, Annie. I wish I could tell each man here that you're my sister. But I'll settle for only being your relative through marriage, in this masquerade." He chuckled. "Did I get that correct? You're a cousin to our family?"

She smiled, though tears still blurred her vision. "Aye, you're no relation of mine, Captain Howlett."

They both laughed.

"How you ever fooled the Danvers militia is beyond me. But you're convincing, and your story is believable. I only pray that when Jack finds out, he's as understanding."

She stiffened. "Think you he knows?"

"He has no idea. But when he does, Annie—and he will—you must be prepared for the consequences."

"Should I return home before he finds out?"

George shook his head. "You're in no condition to ride. But when you are, I'll send you home with Oliver. Jane needs to know her first husband's alive."

"I wrote to Abigail. Hopefully everyone already knows."

"I won't be surprised if they don't. The mail's been unreliable since the war began. But when you see Abbie, can you tell her I've written her several times as well? I wish to know Louisa. Fie! I wish to marry Abigail."

"Would that you could return with me, then bring Abbie and Louisa to camp. The Hessians have their families with them. I know Abigail wishes to join. She asked to leave with Quinn and me, but I told her *no*."

George grimaced. "Had she come, I wouldn't have been surprised, but I'm relieved she didn't. A camp is no place for a little girl. Louisa is still a baby."

"She'll be two next May," Annalisa replied.

"Even still. She's a child. If she became ill with the pox, I'd never forgive myself."

Thoughts of Eliza flooded her, and she hardly noticed the dull ache in her right arm, or the burst of acute sharpness in her left thigh. Annalisa studied her brother as he looked upon her, and she knew he thought of Eliza as well.

"I'll tell Jack. When I'm able," she said.

"How?"

"I know not. But I'll tell him. You needn't burden yourself with such news when 'tis mine to give."

52

ANNALISA

TOPSFIELD, LATE DECEMBER 1777

ANNALISA AND OLIVER RODE down the narrow lane. It was only wide enough to allow two horses to pass, and that was how they traveled. A light snow had fallen, dusting the stone wall that lined the edges of road. The Perkins estate sprawled only two miles from her family's farm, and a quarter-mile from the house she and Jack had rented from his father's cousin, David. But it made little difference now. When she and Ollie had arrived at the small saltbox, they discovered David had let the house to other relatives now that she and Jack were no longer married.

Dejected, she trotted the lane with Oliver, though she knew she'd been lucky to have lived there that spring and summer. Now, she must return to her family's homestead and reside with her parents, and Mary and Henry. *Things could be worse. I could have to live with Jane still sharing a bed with Mary and me.*

Before venturing to her family's farm, she decided to see Oliver home. As much as she detested Jane, she yearned to witness their reunion. Oliver had been kind to her these several months, and quite transformed in his sensibility from youth. If she was being honest with herself, it was Oliver she cared to see reunite with his wife and children. Not Jane. *George was right. Life is rarely what we think it should be.* If she spoke to herself as that young girl Oliver had assaulted seven years ago in Boston, she'd have never believed she'd one day seek to share in his joy. *I suppose we all can change.*

The Perkins's yellow house, situated on a small hill, came into view from the road.

Oliver peered at her. "I feel my nerves beginning to shake my hands. Look at the reins." He lifted the leather strap, and it wavered.

"Your family will be nothing but overjoyed to see you. I swear it."

Oliver chuckled. "Think you we can celebrate Twelfth Night this year? 'Tis only next week."

"It seems strange to celebrate anything while we're at war," she replied. "But I'd be remiss not to. We've plenty of little ones now to spoil with molasses candy and trinkets."

Oliver removed a small satchel from his coat pocket and tossed it to her. She opened the bag and peered inside.

"Lead soldiers, for my boys," he said. "I bought them from a minuteman at camp whose son had died of the pox."

"I remember William had similar toys when he was a boy." Annalisa laughed, recalling her younger brother stretched across the wooden floor of the drawing room as he posed the lead soldiers beneath tables and chairs. Sometimes, if she wasn't careful, she'd step on one and flatten the arms. George had been especially guilty of such charades, though sometimes he did it purposefully to provoke poor William.

They ascended the drive, then descended the hill toward the barn, where the groomsman stabled their horses. Annalisa hastened after Oliver as he strode up the pathway to the front door. He knocked, and they both awaited Mercy to answer.

"Mr...Oliver," Mercy gasped, opening the door.

Poor Mercy, how many more times must she answer that door and discover our deceased selves on the other side? Annalisa followed Oliver indoors, where Mercy took their hats and riding cloaks, and showed them into the parlor. There, by the roaring fire, Lady Perkins, Jane, and Abigail sat with the children, and Susan and Charlotte.

The color drained from Lady Perkins's face as she rose from her chair. "My God. My God." Her shaking hands covered her mouth, and she wailed. "Oliver, my God!"

Oliver embraced her. "I'm here, Mother."

Abigail was already before Annalisa with her arms about her. "Oh, Annie, I'm so very glad you've come home."

As Abigail held her, Annalisa eyed Jane, whose delicately rouged cheeks had grown wan.

Oliver focused his attention on the little boy who toddled at his feet. Lifting Tommy into his arms, he kissed his cheek. "You've grown into quite the young lad." Then, he went to Jane, who remained poised upon the sofa with little Robby, now nine months, in her lap.

He knelt beside the sofa and lifted the babe. "Hello, Robby, I'm your papa." Oliver planted a kiss on the child's forehead. Robby's little face dimpled with a gummy smile, and in that moment, Annalisa thought the child far more resembled Jack than Oliver or Jane. Her insides coiled. *Can it be that Robby belongs to Jack, and not Oliver? No...* The baby had been conceived in springtime, when Jack was prisoner aboard HMS *Lively*, and Oliver not yet presumed dead. *No...'tis unlikely. The timing is quite off.*

"Aunt." Louisa tugged at Annalisa's frock coat, and she knelt before the girl.

"How's my favorite niece?"

At almost twenty months, Louisa looked more like George than she did before Annalisa left town. The girl's eyes had deepened to a dark forest green, and her black hair had grown to her shoulders.

"She's missed you almost as much as I have." Abigail kissed her daughter's round face, then tugged Annalisa into a corner of the room.

When they were beyond earshot from the others, Annalisa whispered, "I can hardly wait for George to meet her. He asked me all manner of questions about her...I know he'll make a wonderful father."

Abigail pouted. "You never sent for us. Why?"

"'Twas not safe, and I was injured badly in the middle of October. It took the remainder of that month, and into November, before I could ride any significant distance. By then, the troops were preparing to march to winter's quarters at Valley Forge. Had I made it there, I would've sent for you—"

"I would've gone with Louisa. 'Tis been agony, Annie, living each day not knowing whether you, or George, or Jack lives—and having to keep your whereabouts secret from our families. 'Twas madness. And now, Ollie comes home to us..." Abigail stepped aside and went to her brother, who'd joined Andrew and their young sisters.

Annalisa stood with Louisa at her hip, watching the Perkins family unify as nearly whole. Jack, now at Valley Forge, would be the only one missing once Lord Perkins arrived from Congress.

"Let me call for Mercy to get you settled in, and some hot water for washing," Lady Perkins said. "Miss Annalisa, will you be staying with us for dinner? I'm certain you're weary from your travels from Charleston. Pray, how does Addy and Sarah?"

"I left them quite well, Lady Perkins," Annalisa replied. "I'll be headed to my parents', presently. I only wished to see Oliver home, and the joy upon your faces."

"But you must tell us how you came to meet and travel with Ollie," Andrew said.

"Divine Providence took us to the Wayside Inn, along the road to Boston," Annalisa blurted.

"What coincidence," Lady Perkins cried. "And to think, you, a lady, traveled all the way from Charleston—"

"Oh, please stay, Annie," Abigail said. "Louisa's only just seen you. Surely, you can spend the night and venture home on the morrow. I've plenty of dresses for you to borrow..."

Annalisa eyed Jane, who remained seated upon the sofa with Robby. Her sister hadn't looked at her but once since she stepped into the parlor. But it wasn't Jane she came to see. Annalisa strode across the room and plucked Robby from her lap.

"How's my sweet nephew?" Annalisa kissed the boy's dimpled cheek, then set him back in his mother's lap. He reached for Annalisa and howled.

"Look what you've done," Jane hissed. "He was perfectly content until you took him from me."

"'Tis not true," Oliver replied. "He missed his auntie."

"Yes, he missed me," Annalisa said, then to Lady Perkins, "I shall stay the night, my lady, thank you."

ANNALISA LAY BESIDE ABIGAIL WITH LOUISA BETWEEN them. The girl had long since fallen asleep, but Annalisa stared at the dark canopy above them. It had been months since she'd slept in a bed, or in the company of women. Now, she knew not what to say.

"Have you heard at all from Sarah and Addy?" Annalisa asked finally.

"Last I heard, they made it to Charleston, but have yet to find Sarah's mother." She fell silent a moment. "I pray they do, but I'm fearful they won't."

"What makes you say so?"

"If Sarah's mother was sold as a slave, and was ill at the time, she may no longer be living, Annie."

Annalisa hated to think Sarah's journey had been for naught, but she needed to hope, for Sarah's sake, that against all odds her mother lived.

"And poor Addy," Abigail continued. "To live all these years never knowing whether her daughter or granddaughter lived."

"I'm ashamed to be a part of such a society that allows for it to happen."

"You mean the slave trade?" Abigail asked.

"Aye."

Silence passed between them, and Annalisa wondered if Abigail, too, considered the heinous nature by which their society thrived; how families were made wealthy and boasted extravagant lives. Though her own family never owned slaves, they were hardly removed from civilization, one made prosperous by the capture and captivity of others. Sickened, Annalisa turned to face Abigail. In the candlelight, her friend's cheeks glistened with tears.

"'Tis why I fought, Abigail. For Sarah and Addy. If we win this war, I pray our new country recognizes and acknowledges everyone as free and equal."

"We've a long way to go, Annalisa."

"Aye, but we must begin somewhere. We know 'tis wrong

to enslave people, we know 'tis wrong what we did to Quin-napin and the Native nations. And many more realize it now, too. There's a chance we can change our world. Why wouldn't we fight for that?"

A small grin lifted Abigail's lips. "You sound much like Jack. Pray, did you see him at New York while you were away?"

Annalisa bit her tongue, unsure of whether she should reveal the nature of their duel, and his brief insanity over Benjamin Cavendish. "I did. He didn't know me, so I was glad for Quinnapin's magick tea."

"Did you bring Addy's physick to camp as well?"

"I did. Quinn and I healed many. We even saved General Benedict Arnold's leg from being amputated. Quite a feat, I must say. The same leg had been wounded twice. I'd never wish amputation on anyone...not even Jane."

Abigail shuddered. "I fear thinking of all you saw. The blood, the brutality. How can you withstand it?"

"I'm not without it affecting me. Nightmares from Bunker Hill still plague my sleep, though they diminished quite a bit when Jack slept beside me. I'm loath to admit they've returned with a vengeance."

"'Tis also why you went away, was it not? To escape the pain of losing the baby?"

Annalisa swallowed thickly. "I've fought hard to forget but can't."

"Would that Jack could marry you again. Now Oliver's returned, I daresay it should be far easier for him to petition divorce."

"Quite. But we won't know until Jack returns from Valley Forge," Annalisa replied. "What of your own marriage? Have you heard from Lord Essex? Does he remain in England?"

Abigail scowled. "I've not, and I pray it remains so. The

longer he's absent from my life, the better. Then I may ask Jack to help me fashion a divorce petition on grounds of abandonment."

"Aye, Jack will be busy with divorce petitions," Annalisa chuckled. "Mayhap he will build his law practice around it."

They giggled.

Abigail shifted onto her side and grasped Annalisa's hand. "Let it be so, sweet friend. Then we may finally be married to the men we're supposed to. I'm through with appeasing Society."

🐝 53 🐝
ANNALISA
TOPSFIELD, JANUARY 1778

A S THOUGH THE COLONIES weren't at war with Britain, Annalisa and Mary helped Liza decorate the house for Twelfth Night. Garlands of cedar and evergreen dotted with holly berries, hung from each fireplace mantel and doorway, and bundles of mistletoe dangled from the entryway. Warm scents of clove and cinnamon mingled with the woody cedar.

From his chair by the fire, Papa pulled from his pipe. A tendril of sweet tobacco smoke swirled over his head. "The house is looking wondrous, ladies."

"Are you yet finished?" Mamma's hands settled on her hips. "The Perkinses will be here shortly. Liza, have you finished the pie?"

Liza nervously bobbed a curtsey. "No, marm." She scurried to the kitchen.

"I think we've about finished, Mamma," Mary said. "I don't mind helping Liza—"

"Absolutely not." Mamma stared at Annalisa. "You may help Liza. Go to."

Annalisa slinked into the kitchen, leaving behind Mary's aggravated protestation, "Mamma, if you will send Annalisa, then I should follow!"

Henry sat at the wide kitchen table before the hearth, and Annalisa joined him. "Is it always like this?"

He shrugged. "Aye. Since everyone left, Mother's done everything to ensure Mary is accepted into higher society. Every Saturday, Jane's been teaching her the minuet." Henry chuckled. "She's coming out this spring."

Annalisa shook her head. "I still see her as that young girl watching me learn those horrid dances."

"Mother will do anything to ensure Mary is more like Jane than you," Henry said.

Annalisa leaned close and murmured, "And look how Jane is—surrounded in scandal. Like me."

They laughed.

Mamma hurried into the kitchen, her face flushed. "They're here. Come, quickly." She fled the room as cursorily as she entered, leaving a gust of rose perfume in her wake.

Henry stood, shaking his head. "I know not why Mother is always so harried when entertaining the Perkinses. They're practically family."

"They *are* family," Annalisa said. "But no matter how we marry their issue or bear children to their sons, their station is still higher than ours, and for that, Mamma will never let us forget."

They quit the kitchen and commenced down the hall, into the parlor, where they greeted the ever-growing Perkinses: Lord and Lady Perkins, Jane and Oliver, who stood awkwardly at a distance and each with a child in their arms, Abigail and Louisa, Andrew, Charlotte, and Susan.

Mary, fifteen and looking quite grown in her crimson dress, took Susan Perkins, eleven come springtime, and her sister Charlotte, soon to be four, into the drawing room. Annalisa marveled at Charlotte, only two years older than their niece, Louisa. *Charlotte and Louisa will grow up to be very close.*

Oliver stepped forward and kissed Annalisa's hand. "It does me well to see you again, Annie."

Ignoring Jane, Annalisa pecked her nephews' cheeks, and replied, "Likewise, Ollie."

Lord Perkins's creased eyelids drooped from his long drive from Pennsylvania. No doubt his stresses were great within Congress—they had been displaced to some undisclosed location in Pennsylvania after Philadelphia fell to the British in September. Despite this, he smiled, and reached for her.

"Miss Annalisa, you're looking well. It always does me good to see you, my dear. Pray, was your journey from Charleston a good one?"

She nodded. "Likewise, sir. I'm glad to see you've arrived home safely. And yes, my travels were filled with wondrous chance, as I'm sure Ollie told you."

Lord Perkins chuckled. "Yes, he did. Our families have been through quite the tumultuous couple of years, but I daresay we've been equally blessed."

"Hear, hear, Perkins," Papa said with a nod.

⚜

AFTER DINNER, ANNALISA SAT AT THE SPINET WHILE BOTH families squeezed into the modest drawing room. Her fingers at the keys, she imagined Jack behind her with his violin, and started *The Gloucestershire Wassail.* As she played, she pictured George and William bellowing the tune as they walked about with Addy's potent bowl of spiced wine. Her throat tightened at their magnified absences. How incomplete her family was this Twelfth Night, yet they were as whole as could be, when other families celebrated with loved ones forever lost. This Twelfth Night, neither her family, nor the Perkinses, believed any of them dead, and for that, she was grateful.

"Annie, this time last year we were at a masquerade in London." Abigail sat beside her upon the bench.

Annalisa tittered, remembering Lord Essex in his gown, though that night had ended dreadfully. "How has it been a year? It feels as though much more time has passed."

"Would that this year is an improvement on the last two," Abigail said with a raise of her glass.

Annalisa stopped playing and reached for her madeira. She clanked her glass to Abigail's. "Hear, hear, dearest friend."

"You mean, *sister*," Abigail replied. "You were married to Jack and will be again."

"And you'll marry George. Then we'll be sisters twice," Annalisa laughed.

"Let us toast to it happening this year. This will be our best year yet!" Abigail cried.

Annalisa resumed playing, and Andrew and Oliver approached the spinet.

"What are all these toasts we're missing?" Andrew asked, a grin dimpling his cheek.

Annalisa appraised the eighteen-year-old. *How alike to Jack he is.*

"We've decided to make this year our greatest yet," Abigail replied. Her cheeks flushed, and Annalisa knew her friend was disguised on madeira.

Andrew raised his glass. "Hear, hear, ladies."

The room filled with Annalisa's playing, and she looked out on the sea of familial faces. Not even Jane scowled, but rather laughed with her sons, their faces sticky with molasses candy. Mamma and Papa played cards with Lord and Lady

Perkins, and Liza, with Charlotte and Louisa upon her lap, serenaded the girls with Susan.

To Annalisa's right, Abigail chatted and drank heartily with Oliver and Andrew; to her left, Mary and Henry studied her playing with awe. Such joy was the very physick her soul needed after so much time away, and in that moment, Annalisa forgot the war, that George and William, and Jack and Quinnapin remained at Valley Forge.

From the front door, there came a banging.

Annalisa stopped playing and looked about the room to see if the others had heard it. Liza went to stand, but Papa rose from the card table. "Allow me, Liza. Perhaps 'tis Mr. Averill come to join, or some insolent mummers come to obtrude."

Annalisa chuckled, recalling the old traditions of holiday mummery. *Would that I was a mummer this year, masked and frolicking house to house.* She resumed *The Gloucestershire Wassail,* her glances steady upon the drawing room door for their dancing intruders.

❧ 54 ❧

GEORGE

TOPSFIELD, JANUARY 1778

G EORGE HOPPED INTO THE drawing room with
William, bellowing:

"Our bowl it is made of the white maple tree,
With the wassailing bowl we'll drink to thee!
Drink to thee, drink to thee!"

"George, William!" Annalisa cried.

Annalisa, Mary, and Abigail jumped from the spinet
bench, and crowded them in the doorway. George wrapped
his arms about Annalisa and Mary.

"'Tis been too long, Little One," he said with a wink.

Annalisa returned his gesture with a mischievous smirk,
then moved into William's embrace. After George kissed
Mary, he faced Abigail and drew her into his arms. Her head
to his chest, he held her as she sobbed. Engulfed by her
pleasant rose perfume, George closed his eyes. He'd been long
consumed by the vile stench of war and illness.

"Shh, 'tis all right," he crooned into her hair. "I'm here.
I'm quite well, and unharmed."

"Where's Jack?" Jane asked from the sofa.

"He's taken ill and was unable to ride, else he would've come," William replied. "But worry not, he's under Quinn's capable care. I've no doubt he'll be recovered by the time George returns to Valley Forge."

"Then you intend to go back?" Mother asked.

"Aye, my contract ends in June." George held Abigail at arm's length, and his heart skipped. "Let me see the child."

Her face bloomed with a joyous beam, filling him with a warmth not even Gould's flip could conjure. And when Abigail lifted Louisa from Liza's lap, his chest swelled. George pursed his lips and cleared his throat.

"Zounds. Well, I'll be damned." He pressed his face against Louisa's cheek and breathed in her scent. He'd never imagined children had their own smell, but Louisa did, and he'd never forget it. "I'm your Papa. Can you say that? Can you say 'Papa'?"

"Pa!" Louisa bellowed.

The room erupted in laughter.

"Abigail, this girl is quite my daughter," he guffawed. "Pray, has she given you much trouble?"

"She's always giving me trouble, George Howlett," Abigail laughed. "But you'll be glad to know she's as strong-willed as her Pa."

George drew Abigail to the sofa where Jane sat with Tommy and Robby, and placed Louisa in his lap. She crawled about him, and ran her hands along his face, slapping him.

"Zounds," he said, his cheeks squished between Louisa's sticky hands, "Did you teach her do this? Am I being punished for being away?"

Annalisa returned to the spinet, and the room erupted with William, Oliver, and Andrew bellowing the 'fa la la las' of *Deck the Hall*.

"Pray, you mean it Jack will heal?" Jane asked.

"Aye. He's merely suffering from some body aches and a sore throat. Quinn's been most diligent in giving him teas. I doubt not he'll be recovered by the time we return." George hesitated, studying the nephews he'd never met. How alike to Oliver the elder one was, and how alike to Jane the younger. "Your boys are handsome. Think you now that Ollie lives, you'll try to rebuild your family with him?"

Jane averted her stare and focused upon the younger one in her lap. "I know not what Jack will do. Oliver's said nothing of the matter to me, only that Jack's learned of his survival. How complicated things have become. Would that they were not—"

"Then you would rather both Annie and Oliver were gone?" Abigail asked.

"No, of course not...only that, when they were presumed dead, things were much simpler," Jane replied as she studied Oliver by the spinet.

George stiffened at her words. "Annie wrote to me of her pregnancy. Knew you about that?"

Jane straightened in her seat. "I did, though she wished it not be known to me, even though I'm Jack's wife."

"Then you must see how convoluted this is truly become, since Annie no longer carries his child," George replied bitterly. "Know you anything of her miscarriage?"

Jane's head snapped toward him. "How do you know she miscarried?"

Abigail said, "She's clearly not pregnant, and would've borne the child by now."

"She wrote me," George added.

Jane shifted Robby to her other thigh and smoothed her skirts. "I know nothing of the miscarriage, only that it occurred before she left for Charleston."

"I see." He had to navigate these intercourses carefully,

lest Jane come to know Annalisa had spent her time in the army with him. *Thank the devil Abigail is quick to reply!*

"George, Louisa has your snuff box," William shouted from the spinet.

George peered down and saw the little tin square in his daughter's hand. He pried her fingers from the box, and she shrieked. "Easy, love. This is mine."

Louisa screeched until Abigail removed her from his lap. "She's persistent, to say the least."

"I can tell," he replied.

"Children are only persistent if you lack disciplining them," Jane said, smoothing the chestnut brown hair from Robby's forehead.

George watched Tommy, who played quietly upon the floor with a set of lead toy soldiers. As though he knew his uncle watched, Tommy drew a soldier to his mouth.

"Tommy, no," Jane scolded. "You'll choke." She reached down, pulled the soldier from his mouth, and smacked his hand. "Naughty boy, we don't put toys in our mouth."

Tommy erupted with a shrill cry, and Annalisa stood from the spinet, the music ending abruptly. "What's happened?"

Oliver hurried to his son and lifted him from the floor. "You needn't scold him for playing with toys I gave him."

"He put it into his mouth. He could've choked," Jane snapped.

Oliver cradled the screaming boy. "But he didn't, did he?"

"Had you been here to help raise him, you'd have known not to give a toddler toys small enough for them to swallow," Jane replied.

"Enough of these ill tempers," Lord Perkins said, raising his head from his hand of cards. "'Tis an evening of festivity, lest we forget. Small children can be a nuisance, and you've both done well given the circumstances. Now, their fathers have returned and shall father until duty calls them away again. That is how it is until this conflict is ended."

The room fell silent as the full gravity of the war descended upon them, as those who were absent, amplified. George looked to Annalisa, who sat upon the spinet bench, surrounded by Mary, Henry, and William. *Every Howlett is present, but Jack is missing from the Perkins brood.* Andrew remained beside Oliver, and Liza sat quietly with Susan and Charlotte. Jack's absence left the crowded room feeling empty, and he knew Annalisa felt it, too.

As though to fill the void, Annalisa started to play, and George rested his head back. He reached for Abigail's hand and clasped it, wishing this night would never end. For some reason or another, a grave feeling settled over him that this would be the last time they'd all be together in the same room.

55

ANNALISA

TOPSFIELD, FEBRUARY 1778

WITH CANDLEMAS UPON THEM, Twelfth Night felt to be years ago, not mere weeks. Annalisa and Mary sat in the parlor. Her sister worked on her needlepoint, and Annalisa reread Thomas Paine's *Common Sense*. The pamphlet was now two years old, but the radical words still rang true. She harkened back to the night at the Black Water Inn when Jack, William, and Quinnapin gathered about to read the pamphlet for the first time; before any of them, save George, had left for the army.

George was returning from the Black Water today, and would be home within the hour, she supposed. Three years had passed since he last stepped inside his own establishment, and two years since Annalisa had seen Elisha Porter.

She glanced at Mary and smiled. Her darling younger sister would have her debut come spring. Annalisa pondered the kind of gentleman who would ask Mary to dance, and perhaps, court her. *My little sister, my dearest Mary. She can't be courted by just anyone. But who remains to attend these local balls? What young, eligible gentleman hasn't joined the war?*

Mary seemed unaffected. Her little needle pointed up, then down, her fingers fast at work embroidering a rose. Mary was far better than she or Jane ever purported to be at needle-point. Annalisa bit her lip to hide her smirk. Her own stitching was base at the best of times, and Jane had always been the accomplished one among them. Now, Mary seemed to surpass even Jane.

"You're quite good," Annalisa said.

Mary looked up. "I suppose with you and Jane gone I've had much time to master these old, hackneyed patterns."

Annalisa set aside her pamphlet. "I'm sorry I left you alone here."

"Don't be. You were married, and then terrible things befell you. I could never blame you for any of it. I've only missed you, 'tis all. Would that I could've joined you."

"Mary, you know 'tis too dangerous."

Mary set down her canvas. "What makes you think I don't wish to partake in this war? What makes you think I couldn't learn to fire a musket as you have?"

"I wouldn't wish what I've seen upon anyone, especially you. Battle is full of horrors. If you wish to partake, then weave your own textiles, as other ladies are wont to do—"

"How can you rebuke me so? You of all would scoff at such trite displays of rebellion."

Annalisa frowned. Mary was right. She could hardly sit by and spin her own fabric while the men left for battle. "Well, if you don't fight, and you'll not weave or spin, what will you do?"

"I go with Henry every other week to George's tavern. I've taken to listening."

"Listening?"

"Aye. I've come away with quite a bit of information," Mary replied.

"And to whom have you relayed such knowledge?" Though Annalisa chuckled, she remembered the few times she'd been at George's tavern and overheard Loyalists speaking of British generals and such. A tavern was an easy way to garner intelligence, but it was a matter of ensuring the news ended safely, and in the right hands.

"I've told Henry, of course," Mary replied.

"Ah, then he takes it to his contact?" Annalisa asked.

"I suppose. I know not where he takes my information." Mary picked up her canvas and continued with her perfect rose.

Espionage. 'Tis what Mary does. She spies. Perhaps she could be employed by someone within the Continental Army. No one would suspect her... The thought covered her in goosebumps. Spies, if uncovered, always received capital punishment. *No, I can never involve her. The dangers are too great.*

She suddenly understood the fear George felt all these years about her masquerading as a man. He cared too much for her to see her languishing in a prison, or potentially hanged.

The front door swung open, and George strode into the parlor. "My two favorite sisters," he bellowed. "I come bearing gifts from Elisha." He handed them each a parcel wrapped in paper.

Annalisa tore it open and sniffed the beef mince pie. Her mouth watered at the buttery crust. "How I've missed these."

Mary carefully put away her canvas then ripped open the paper, and bit into the pie without moving to the kitchen.

Annalisa and George laughed.

"These pies are so delicious, George," Mary said, her mouth full and her eyes rolling back into her head.

"Careful, with such vulgar manners, Mother won't let you have your debut this spring," George howled. He sat beside

Annalisa and drew up the pamphlet she'd been reading. "I've read this thing nearly a hundred times."

"I've but read it twice." She leaned against him and closed her eyes.

A knock sounded at the door, and Annalisa lifted her head.

Abigail hurried inside the parlor with Louisa clutched to her breast, her eyes wild, and frantic.

"What is it, Abbie?" Annalisa asked. "You look a fright."

Shaking, Abigail handed her a letter. "Read it, I don't mind."

Annalisa unfolded the page, and George leaned in to read alongside her. When they finished, they peered at one another, then to Abigail, who bit her lip.

"He's here. He's coming for me," she whispered.

"Who?" Mary asked.

"Lord Essex," Annalisa and George said in unison with Abigail.

"What should I do? Where should I go?" Abigail cried. Louisa shrieked in her arms, and George reached for the girl. How much smaller she looked tucked against his strapping chest, snuggled within his bulging arms.

"We can go to the Black Water," Annalisa said. "He won't know to look for you there."

"No." George rose from the sofa with Louisa. He paced for several moments, then turned to face them, huddled together with Mary. "Come with me to Valley Forge. You, too, Annie. Essex will never know you're there. 'Tis a secluded place, a day's ride from Philadelphia—"

"But the British hold Philadelphia," Mary said. "What if he travels yonder?"

"A sound thought, Mary, but unlikely," George replied.

"Let me come, too," Mary said.

"No," Annalisa said with George. They looked at one another, then Annalisa added, "You're more valuable here. When Essex comes for Abigail, listen to everything he says, but play the unwitting coquette, then write to us. Can you do that?"

Mary nodded.

"No, don't involve her," George barked.

"She wishes to help. Whyever can she not?" Annalisa asked.

Abigail added, "'Tis true, George, no one will suspect her."

The way George looked upon Mary with devastation, made Annalisa's blood run cold.

"She and Henry are the last of us to be removed from this war. I wish to keep it so," he replied.

Mary crossed her arms. "I'm hardly removed from it, George."

George towered over her. "Is that so, young miss?"

"I can keep to myself, I swear it," Mary said. "We don't even know for certain Lord Essex poses any threat to us. Should he call here, Mamma and Papa, and Henry and I shall host him as fondly as we ever hosted gentry."

Annalisa asked, "Is William leaving with you, too? Or can he remain here?"

George shook his head. "*Wilhelmina* has been honorably discharged. After the year he's had, I doubt he wishes to sign on for another."

"What is this?" William asked, stepping into the parlor.

"Lord Essex has written," George replied. "He's landed in Boston and means to come for Abigail. I've insisted she, Louisa, and Annalisa return to Valley Forge with me. Mary has offered to garner intelligence on Lord Essex should he come to the house seeking Abigail."

"Why should Annalisa go with you and leave me behind?"

William said with a scowl. "Surely I'm of greater assistance at Valley Forge than here—"

"No, you've been honorably discharged," George said. "You'll be better help here. You and Henry can guard the house should anything suspicious arise because of Lord Essex's presence within the province. I doubt it not he has allies within the colony and means to use them."

"But why would he call here? Should we not warn the Perkinses?" William asked.

"My papa already knows, and Ollie is aware," Abigail said. "They'll ensure he does nothing to compromise my family."

"Only until Congress reconvenes," Annalisa added. "Then your father will be away. Think you Ollie and Andrew will be sufficient?"

"Of course, which is why William and Henry must remain here," George said.

At this, William nodded. "Aye, but when will you, Quinn, and Jack return?"

"Jack's been ill since Twelfth Night, else he'd be here now, perhaps to remain. Quinn won't return until Jack's beyond his convalescence."

William sighed. "Aye, sir."

"Mary, you'll be in charge of writing to us with any information. I'll put you in contact with an individual I met while stationed at York Island. He'll instruct you on learning to write in cypher and will supply you with sympathetic stain."

Mary nodded. "Aye, sir."

George kissed Louisa's forehead, then regarded Annalisa and Abigail. "Ladies, we ride at dawn."

56

ANNALISA

VALLEY FORGE, LATE FEBRUARY 1778

THE DAY BEFORE a blustery storm, Annalisa arrived at Valley Forge with George, Abigail, and Louisa. Snow blanketed the lone road winding through the winter encampment, imprisoning them all. Wind whistled down the chimney of their small cabin. The stale air suffocated, but it was too cold to crack a window. In the modest bunk she shared with Abigail and Louisa, Annalisa tossed about, unable to warm.

"Miss Anna."

Annalisa stuck her head out from the wooden bunk. "Quinn?"

Quinnapin hastened toward her. His tawny complexion appeared quite ashen, his silhouette thin, and cheeks hollow. He knelt beside where she lay.

"What is it, old friend? Where's George? He left us an hour ago."

Quinnapin reached for her. "Jack's unwell, worse than he's been. He's so bewildered with fever he doesn't remember being honorably discharged from the army."

Annalisa slid from the bunk. "Mayhap there's a tea in Addy's physick book that will aid him."

"You can certainly try," Quinnapin replied. "Perhaps your mere presence may help."

Determined to battle fate, Annalisa wound her cloak about her, and with Quinnapin, stepped into an icy gale. Sleet and heavy, wet snow pummeled her as she followed Quinnapin down the row of log cabins until he paused outside one.

"He's in here," he said, gesturing to the doorway.

Annalisa stepped inside.

The fetid odor of illness stung her nostrils, a noxious reminder of the death gripping Valley Forge. At one end stood a small stone fireplace, flanked on either side by wooden bunks stacked three beds high. Three poorly soldiers lay upon their narrow beds, each turning restlessly in cold sweat. Jack lay upon the bottom bunk.

She hurried toward him and knelt, placing her hand upon his brow. It burned. Though he huddled beneath a blanket, beads of perspiration congregated at his forehead and temples.

"Your wife is here, Perkins," Quinnapin said.

"Quinn, no—" Jack held up a hand to her. Clouded by fever, his gaze migrated toward Quinnapin. "My...what?"

Quinnapin replied, "Your wife."

Jack reached for him. "Quinn, they said my w-wife is here, but I don't see Jane," he croaked.

Annalisa's insides churned as though they curled about a capstan. *Even in his fever delirium, he wishes for Jane.*

"Your *real* wife is here," Quinnapin replied.

"Annie?" Jack's bloodshot, watery eyes opened.

"Jack." She gripped his stiff, icy hands. "You're freezing and burning."

"Is it...r-really...y-you?"

Using the ends of her cloak, she dabbed away the perspiration from his temples and forehead. "Hush, my love. 'Tis really me." *He must believe me a visage, or a ghost.*

"They said my wife is here," he perseverated for a moment.

Annalisa forced a chuckle. "No, just an old friend."

Releasing her cloak, she scraped the damp hair from his face. His chestnut brown locks hung freely, framing the perfect sculpt of his jaw and chin. Jack reached for her, and his dry, cracked lips parted into a dimpled grin.

"My dear, dear...heart..." he huffed, tugging her close.

Feeling the bony ridges of his spine through his clothes, Annalisa's eyes welled. "My God, you're but bones and flesh." She pulled from him and wiped the tears.

Jack reached to cup her face. "All is r-right...n-now you're here." His voice sounded stiff but sincere, as he pressed his lips to her forehead.

"What shall I gather from your bag?" Quinnapin asked.

Annalisa told him the herbs she required for the tea, and he retrieved them as she knelt by Jack. When Quinnapin returned with the tin of steaming liquid, Annalisa placed it to Jack's lips. He drank thirstily until he finished the cup, then rested his head back. His eyes closed as he clasped her hand, and she wondered if he could now rest.

Quinnapin crouched beside Annalisa. "I've not seen him sleep in days. He takes great comfort knowing you're here."

"Then I'll not leave him," she said.

Quinnapin squeezed her shoulder and kissed her temple. "I'll return come morning. But please you, allow yourself rest, too, Miss Anna."

THE FIRST WEEK OF MARCH HAD COME AND GONE, AND George stood over Annalisa with a hard, bland biscuit. "Some firecake, Little One."

"Still no rations?" Weary, she raised a cup of tea to Jack's lips.

George shook his head. "We're still waiting. But you must eat, or you'll grow poorly yourself."

Annalisa set down the cup and took the firecake. She nibbled its tough, crusted edges from baking in the fire's ashes. Though bland, she appreciated its smoky aftertaste.

George settled beside her and peered at Jack. "Has he improved at all?"

"'Tis been a fortnight, George. I'm afraid I've done all I can." She sopped her tears with the edge of her cloak, realizing Jack's birthday was upon them. He would be six-and-twenty, far too young to perish. "Quinn and I healed countless men at Bemis Heights, but now, I can't even save Jack."

George wrapped an arm about her though she noticed his jaw stiffen. "Don't speak it. I've already lost Samuel, I won't lose Jack, too. He's suffered much, but he's strong. Remember that, Little One. Try and get some rest until morning."

When he'd left the cabin, into the March storm, Annalisa returned her gaze to Jack, who slept with slow, steady breaths. His cough had improved, but the fevers still left him delirious. If Jack was to die, he needed to know about his daughter.

Her heart heavy, Annalisa smoothed the hair from his forehead. "Jack, darling, the baby died," she choked. "I miscarried again. But you needn't worry. If you wish to see her, and you soon may, you need only go to Keihtánit's house." Biting her lip, she smiled through her tears. "You lost your faith, and so did I. But I found hope through Quinnapin." She trembled as she spoke the words aloud and covered her face with her hands.

"A d-daughter?" Jack muttered.

"Jack, you can hear me..."

"Aye, love." He reached for her. "W-what did you c-call her?"

She whispered, "Eliza."

A blustery gale wheezed down the small chimney, threatening to extinguish the fire and creaking the walls of the cabin. Annalisa quavered from the arctic chill, and Jack pulled her into his bunk. They lay in a silent embrace on the solid planks, the tips of their noses touching. As she wept, she wound her arms about him, as she had the night of the shipwreck. This time, the storm raged on beyond the walls of their small cabin, and there were no ocean waves to part them, only disease and war. Clutching him close, Annalisa did the last thing she could do; she prayed to the Great Spirit Jack would make it through the night.

☙❧

ANNALISA STIRRED TO SUNLIGHT STREAMING THROUGH cracks in the walls. Beside her, Jack breathed easily. Relieved he'd not yet perished, she placed a hand upon his brow. He felt cool. Her body flooded with calm and she sighed. Leaning back against him, she closed her eyes.

"Annie? When did you come? Do I dream?"

She turned to face him. "Aye, you dreamt in fevers. I've been here a week."

Jack rubbed his dreary eyes. "You said something to me last night...about a daughter?"

"Aye. I miscarried back in August."

His lower lip quivered, and she thought he might weep. "Pray, did you name her?"

"I did. But I cannot say her name—"

"Whyever not?"

"I spoke it last night to you." She shivered. "I think..."

The force of last night's storm felt to be more than the work of divine Providence; at the mere mention of her daughter's name, the air had changed, perhaps provoking something in the ethers she did not understand. Something in her prayer to the Great Spirit had been heard. Perhaps it had been their daughter who listened.

"I believe she may have cured your fever." Annalisa ran her hand over Jack's forehead and down his cheek. His hand reached up to cover hers. "She's at rest at Keihtánit's house. I shan't disturb her again."

Jack's brow knit in a way she suspected he wished to understand, to know more. "Where is Keihtánit's house? May I go there to see her?"

"No—well...not yet, I pray. But when you return to Topsfield, on a day when Jane doesn't expect you, I'll take you to where she's buried. 'Tis a place you're fond of, as am I."

"The oak." He closed his eyes and ran the heels of his hands over them. "Annie, how have I done this to you? To us?"

"You did what you believed was right. I blame you not." She leaned over and kissed his forehead. "I must return home, but Abigail and Louisa are here with George. I daresay they may leap the sword."

Jack tried to smile, but his face fell. "I pray I'm well enough to witness it."

Though something in her spirit told her he would recover fully from his illness, her heart remained in the trenches of her body. Annalisa slid from the bunk and gathered her things, for, if she lingered a moment longer, she'd never leave his side.

Jack gripped her hand. "Dearest love, wait—"

"Jack, you can't call me thus anymore." She withdrew her hand from his, then added, "I'm comforted your fever broke, but I must return home. I entrust you to Quinnapin's capable care. I'll let Jane know you've made it through the worst."

She fled the cabin, leaving Jack to reach after her.

❧ 57 ❧
JACK
VALLEY FORGE, APRIL 1778

I T WAS NO DREAM at all; Annalisa had been there to care for him and restore him to health. At least that was what Jack remembered while in the throes of his fever dreams. News of their daughter, and her untimely end, forged an everlasting space within him, though he couldn't recall the girl's name. *Annie bore a daughter. We created life. Now, she's a tiny angel.* A small girl with Annalisa's warm complexion and curling hair stood by a pleasant stream. The girl beamed up at him with blue eyes to match his own, and her cheek dimpled with a smile. *I'm happy here, Papa. Now, go. Go find Mamma.*

A surge of air filled his lungs, and Jack started awake. He ran a hand over his chest, his shirt damp beneath his palm. *A dream, and no more.* Catching his breath, he slid from the wooden bunk, pulled on his waistcoat and coat, and hobbled from the cabin into the early spring day.

"You look better today," Quinnapin said, meeting him by the entry. He carried a cup of tea and offered it to Jack.

"Thank you, old friend. I feel my health returning." Jack drank the warm liquid. "Pray, how long have I slept?"

"'Tis just after noon," Quinnapin replied. "George and Abigail are ready. Shall we?"

Jack followed his friend down the muddy path through the barracks, to a grove of oaks. There, amidst the grey, barren trees, ripe with chartreuse spring buds, George stood with Abigail. His sister clutched Louisa's hand. Abigail had come to him after Annalisa left, but it had been months since he last saw Louisa. She stood much taller than he recalled. *How she looks like George. I wonder how Robby is. Does he look at all like me? He should be one now...*

Jack's own birthday, also in March, had passed. He was now six-and-twenty, far too old to be as disestablished as he was. *Father must be ashamed. And Uncle.* As his father's and Lord Brunswick's heir, Jack's station within Society required far more of his reputation than what he conjured.

"You're looking well, Perkins," George said with a laugh. "Come. Stand beside me. I've good news from General Washington."

"Pray, tell."

"France has finally signed an alliance treaty with us."

Jack's shoulders relaxed. "'Tis about time. I suspect 'tis because of Burgoyne's surrender in October."

"I assumed the same." George grinned at Abigail. "And today I finally get to marry this young lady."

"Then you mean to leap the sword," Jack laughed, shaking his cousin's hand.

"'Tis the only way," Abigail said. "Mary wrote that Lord Essex has called now twice since arriving in Boston, and means to take up residence at his Cambridge home until I arrive. We can't return to town, Jack. He'll find me and bring me back to England."

Jack gripped his sister's hand and kissed it. Lord Essex would have to overcome both he and George before ever attempting to bring Abigail back to England. "Peace, Abbie. We'll never let him do that, I swear it."

"When we leave this place, you and Louisa will be safe at the Black Water," George said.

Warmed by the sentiment, Jack added, "I'd like to journey home with you, if I may." *Now, go. Go find Mamma.* The girl's voice in his dream rattled his chest, and the blood drained from his face.

George slapped his back. "Of course, so long as you're able to ride. Are you feeling well enough, Brother? 'Tis been weeks since Annie left you, and your health has only improved."

Abigail's smile faded. "What is it, Jack? You look pale."

He shook his head. "'Tis nothing. I only mean to see Annalisa as quickly as possible."

"Then you do plan on petitioning for divorce?" Abigail asked.

"Aye. Ollie lives, and I'm certain he wishes to remarry his wife," Jack chuckled, but his countenance readily eased to soberness. "I love Annie. And I know she bore our daughter."

"Eliza," George said.

Abigail gasped. "I knew not her name. She never spoke thus. What a lovely name for our little baby angel."

"Eliza." Jack's heart fluttered at the sound, and his skin puckered with goosebumps as he spoke her name aloud. "My daughter." An image of the girl from his dream returned. *I'm happy here, Papa. Now, go. Go find Mamma.*

"We can no longer say her name," Quinnapin said. "She's at Keihtánit's house, at rest. I helped Miss Anna bury her."

Jack's hand found Quinnapin's shoulder. "I've no words to convey the depth of my gratitude...and sorrow...that you were with Annie at that most horrific time..." He choked on the final word and blinked away the sting of tears. "And I was not."

Quinnapin clutched Jack's arm. "No gratitude is necessary. We are brothers, and Anna, *numusees,* my sister. We laid your daughter to rest, planted her as a seed beneath the treasured oak. The southwest wind guided her to Keihtánit's house, where she will remain in pleasant days, will never hunger, nor grow cold."

His throat tight, Jack could not speak. He merely nodded, then in an overwhelming rush of emotion, reached for Quinnapin and held him close. Within his friend's embrace, Jack sobbed. Losing his daughter and his unyielding love for Annalisa, the trauma of HMS *Lively*, his abuses of liquor and laudanum which led to an unwitting adultery with Jane who bore him the son he could never claim as his own, and the unmitigated loathing for Oliver and Benjamin Cavendish— two men who neither deserved nor warranted his hatred—all poured from him in an outflow of tears he swore he'd never shed.

"'Tis all right, my brother," Quinnapin said. "You have everything you require."

"Perkins, all will be well." George's cavernous voice surrounded him, and Jack felt his cousin's hand upon his back. "You've much to live for, and the past is behind you. There's no use perseverating on things that can't be undone."

Jack knew George spoke with Samuel in mind. His cousin rarely mentioned their old friend, claimed by a battle wound he incurred at Kip's Bay. But Jack suspected George suffered that loss greatly, even if he never spoke the words aloud.

"Come, today is for celebrating," George added. "We've an alliance with France that can only help our cause, and Abigail and I will marry...we've certainly waited long enough for this day. Soon, perhaps when this war's won, you'll have your day again with Annie."

Jack released Quinnapin. "Thank you, Brother." He looked to George. "How right you are, Cousin."

"You may call me 'brother' as well, you know," George replied with a smirk. "You were married to Annie, and you're still married to Jane."

Jack chuckled through his tears and wiped them from his face. "You both have been more brothers to me than my own."

"I think when you return home, you'll find Oliver a changed man," Quinnapin replied.

Captain Fleming and Bartlett joined them in the oak grove. A chilly April wind rustled the branches in the oak trees, and Captain Fleming pulled his navy woold cloak about him.

"Shall we get on with it, then?" Captain Fleming asked.

"Aye, we're awaiting my superior," George replied.

As he spoke, a tall, portly gentleman sporting a blue coat with buff facings, and epaulets on both shoulders, strode into the grove. Jack recognized the familiar face from his days in Boston.

"Knox," George bellowed.

"Captain Howlett." Henry Knox tipped his hat to George, then bowed to Abigail. "My lady. Shall we begin?"

❧❦❧

JACK'S FINGERS TRILLED UPON THE NECK OF HIS FIDDLE, emanating the familiar tune, *Dribbles of Brandy*. George held Louisa in one arm and spun Abigail with the other as they danced about the campfire. Jack followed the song with *The Gobby-O*, then in memory of Samuel, *The Parting Glass*.

"Sluice your gob, rogues," George hollered. His face flushed with the glow of far too much rum as he sang:

"And all I've done for want of wit
To memory now I can't recall
So fill to me the parting glass
Good night and joy be to you all!"

Captain Fleming and Bartlett clanked mugs. "Huzzah!"

The scene, reminiscent of Jack's elopement with Annalisa, lifted his lips into a joyous grin. Now, it was Abigail's turn. Only God knew the life she'd suffered with Lord Essex before this night, but she was deserving of their cousin, George. Now, she could be happy. *My sister, the daughter of a lord, married to a lord, now dances as wildly and happily as any should. Would that her marriage to George be long and fruitful.*

Jack played until his fingers ached, and the calloused tips bled. Many months had passed since he last held a fiddle, but he persisted, envisioning Annalisa at her beloved spinet. In his mind, she performed Mozart, the music he bought for her in Vienna.

There was much he didn't know of her time in London, and more he wished to ask her, particularly about Benjamin Cavendish. The poor lad had seemingly fled camp, perhaps having deserted, like many others, after he recovered from his wound. *How cruel, how lost my mind was that day. I'll never forgive myself for harming that boy. And Ollie.*

Oliver's survival had come as more surprise than relief, though now, Jack flooded with joy. His brother would wish to return to Jane, which would aid in his quest for a divorce proposal...except Oliver didn't know that Robby belonged to Jack. No one could know. The information would come about someday, he supposed. Someone, either of their family or the town, would suspect and make a conjecture, then it would be all over. The truth would be there for everyone to know, and Jack could finally live as the boy's father. *I owe it to*

Oliver, myself, and Annalisa. I must convince Jane to confirm what's true.

Yet, a darker thought entered his mind...

What if Oliver insists on raising Robby as his own? What if Annalisa rebukes me forever?

He'd never know until he returned to Topsfield, and he was nearly well enough to ride the distance. Perhaps by the first week of May, he could pack his things and travel north. *I must see her, I must go to Annalisa, whether she will have me, or not.* His daughter decreed it so, and he would listen.

❧ 58 ❧

ANNALISA

TOPSFIELD, APRIL 1778

SOMEONE HAD SPOKEN HER daughter's name, for Eliza came to Annalisa in a dream. The girl laughed with that dimpled smile, so alike to her father's, and her curls bounced as she frolicked about the garden. *Mamma, Papa is coming home, by the sea.*

Annalisa sat upright in the canopied bed she shared with Mary. Beside her, her sister slept. Beyond the wavering, imperfect windowpane, the sky grew light, but the sun had not yet risen. *Is Jack returning to Topsfield? But by the sea? Will he sail to Boston, rather than ride?* It was unlikely. Washington's army remained at Valley Forge, perhaps through spring. And Jack, undoubtedly, persisted in convalescence.

She gently shifted from the bed, and laced her front-lacing stays, tied on her petticoats, and pinned on her day dress. The mornings still proved quite cool, so she slipped on a pair of wool mitts, and pulled her neck handkerchief over her bosom, tucking it beneath the strings of her linen apron. Quietly, Annalisa opened the bedchamber door, and sneaked down the stairs. In the kitchen, she grabbed an egg basket and made her way outdoors to the chicken coop.

There, amidst the brisk spring morning, damp with sparkling dew, she knelt and gathered eggs. In the distance, Henry and William tilled the fields with Papa, Dane, and Zeke. *George used to be among them.* Her brother's absence magnified in the rising sun, but she was glad at least William remained home.

Annalisa ducked behind the barn and made her way beyond the fields to the ancient oak. Beneath the tree's heavy boughs, she set down her egg basket and sat on the lowest branch, now worn smooth from years of sitting. The space where she and Quinnapin had buried her daughter was only a patch of dirt covered with brown leaves. *Dearest girl, whatever do you mean? Your papa comes to me by sea?* Annalisa closed her eyes, awaiting the answer. High above the branches, a mourning dove cooed, but no words came from her daughter. Tempted to speak her name, Annalisa bit her tongue. *No. I'll not disturb her.*

She rubbed her thigh, over the healed wound from the duel with Jack, and shivered. How close he'd come to knowing he'd challenged her, and not Benjamin. *He can never know.* Yet, she couldn't understand why he was made so irascible by her muse. Jack didn't know Benjamin, only that Benjamin supposedly knew her. *'Twas a victimless crime, to be sure. So why challenge Cav, and not Captain Fleming? He is the villain. Not Cav.*

Troubled, Annalisa rose from the branch. She'd only been in town a few weeks, and had spoken to Jane but once, on that first Sunday she was home, at the meetinghouse. She'd relayed the course of Jack's illness, and that he'd markedly improved by the time she left Valley Forge, but said no more. Her sister had gone on to sit awkwardly between Andrew and

Susan Perkins, as far from Oliver as possible, which left Annalisa wondering if Jack had to be the one to petition for divorce, or if Oliver could file it. The situation was far too convoluted for her to understand the workings of the courts. That was for Jack to interpret. He was the lawyer. But he wasn't there.

Annalisa lifted her basket of eggs and wandered from the tree. Tomorrow would be the third anniversary of the Battles at Lexington and Concord. *How has it been three years since that fateful day?* From what she recalled, it had been a similar morning, her father and brothers tilling the fields when George left his plow mid-furrow to respond to the call. How she'd wished to join him.

Since that day, I've seen my share of battles. Burgoyne had surrendered after Bemis Heights—the victory was theirs—and now, there was an alliance between the colonies and France. *With France's aid, this war may now end.*

As she neared her house, the front door opened and closed, and Mary stepped outside holding a letter. Catching sight of Annalisa Mary gripped her petticoats and jogged toward her.

"What is it?" Annalisa asked. "You look flushed."

"You just missed Andrew Perkins. He delivered this note —Lord Essex is calling on them tomorrow, and our family has been invited to dinner."

Annalisa's heart skittered. "Does William know? I can't go to that dinner. Lord Essex will ask me where Abigail is—he knows 'twas I who stole her away—"

"Essex knows not you and Abigail have been home. When last he called while you were at Valley Forge, I told him you'd written but had neglected to mention your whereabouts. You could be anywhere."

"Did he believe such a tale?"

"He couldn't refute it," Mary replied. "You need to go to George's tavern in Portsmouth. He knows not about the Black Water, nor where it is, or that it belongs to George. You'll be safe there while he's in town. I'll write to you when 'tis safe for you to return." Mary quickly added, "And be not alarmed by the patronage who now visit there. 'Tis by no mistake, I assure you."

"I can't live like this, Mary. Essex may call on us one day without the warning of a letter—"

"'Tis unlikely," Mary replied. "Cambridge is not so close as Ipswich, which may lend itself to an unannounced visitor from time to time. No, he will need to spend the night at the Perkins estate, as he did the last time he called." She hesitated. "He is their son-in-law, and by all means has every right to call on them."

Annalisa sighed. "You're right. Must I leave at once?"

"As quickly as you may pack your things. Shall I ask Henry or William to take you?"

"No. I can ride myself, as much as Mamma abhors it," Annalisa muttered. "Pray, think you Essex has the intention to send paid men searching for us? Not that his accounts can afford it..."

Mary tilted her head. "I think not."

Annalisa gasped. "What of Jane? Could she...would she reveal our whereabouts to Lord Essex? She has no allegiance to me, or Abigail—"

"She's married to Jack, and Abigail is her sister-in-law. Jane has little reason to divulge such information. And until Lord Essex's cruelty toward Abigail is filed in a divorce decree, Lord and Lady Perkins may host him within their house as they see fit."

Annalisa neglected to mention Abigail's desperate intention of wedding George while at Valley Forge by leaping the sword. *That marriage will hardly be legal...she's not even divorced from Essex!* A beat of silence passed between them, and Annalisa reached for Mary.

"I'm in awe of you. How you've grown. I'm remiss to have missed the moment you turned from girl to young lady."

Mary gave a small smile. "You never missed it, Annie. You were always with me, even when you were away."

She tugged Mary into an embrace. "Dear sister, come to Portsmouth the first chance you get. Otherwise, write to me. I'll remain at the Black Water until you alert me 'tis safe to return home. And please you, keep a close watch on Jane. I've a feeling she might betray Abigail and me."

"I'll be your eyes and ears, Annie. I swear it."

Annalisa released Mary but clung to her hands. "And above all, please be safe."

Mary replied with candor, "I always am. I promise. Mr. Culpepper sent me the sympathetic stain."

Annalisa cocked her head with curiosity, and Mary grinned, adding, "Invisible ink."

⚜

THE ROAD TO GEORGE'S BLACK WATER INN WAS LONG, BUT Annalisa had traveled it much over the years, and in spring, it proved a fine journey. Trees and shrubbery, popping with chartreuse buds, waved and rustled in the spring wind, and birds chattered and sang. Strawbery Banke in Portsmouth was situated on the Piscataqua River, which opened into the sea. Near the port city lay the island of New Castle, on which she'd hoped to one day build a summer home with Jack. That dream had dissolved as transiently as their marriage.

The stable-hand at the Black Water Inn took her horse, and Annalisa carried her belongings inside the three-story establishment. From the bar, Elisha Porter beamed as he caught sight of her.

"Miss Annalisa, you've returned." He left the bar and retrieved her trunk. "Shall I put you in your usual room?"

"Just the small chamber on the third floor, please. I'll be here alone for some time, I'm afraid."

"Pray, have you seen Mr. George?"

"At Valley Forge, weeks ago. He was in good health. I pray he'll return soon."

Elisha nodded, satisfied. "Henry and Mary have diligently maintained the bookkeeping. William, I'm afraid, has been relegated to your farm."

"Yes, that is by George's design," Annalisa replied.

Elisha glanced about, then whispered, "We've seen an uptick in Loyalists. Know you anything of it?"

Annalisa bit her lip, confused. "You mean to say the Black Water has become a Loyalist inn?"

Elisha's brow puckered. "Aye, 'tis by no design of Mr. George, I'm sure."

At first, Annalisa pondered how this could happen, then she held her breath, remembering what Mary had said about the tavern's patronage. *Henry and Mary. They can listen for intelligence if it comes from Loyalist tongues. How cunning! If only George had had the foresight to establish this place as a Loyalist dwelling long before he opened its doors.*

"I think Mary mentioned the sort—perhaps these travelers have nowhere else to go in Portsmouth...everyone is welcome here, I suppose." Annalisa smirked, then leaned in close to murmur, "But we're still Patriots."

Elisha grinned. "I thought as much, Miss Annalisa."

❧ 59 ❧

JACK

VALLEY FORGE, MAY 1778

A LETTER FROM MARY reached Valley Forge the day before George, Abigail, and Jack meant to ride for Topsfield. Sat about a small campfire in early evening, Jack anxiously watched over George's shoulder as he opened the letter.

"The reagent." George removed a bottle from his coat pocket and brushed the contents over Mary's letter. In a matter of minutes, hidden messages appeared between the lines of an otherwise mundane letter about the farm.

George handed the letter to Jack, and he read the note. "Lord Essex called again...he plans on staying a fortnight with my parents."

"The squeeze crab," George rumbled, then snatched the letter from Jack and crumpled the page into their campfire. "I'll challenge him should we meet again."

"La! Speak no such folly." Abigail slapped his shoulder, then frowned. "Now we must delay our journey home."

George eyed Abigail, his thick brows raised. "You think I would lose a duel to that fart catcher, Mrs. Howlett?"

"Faht...catch-hurr." Louisa giggled in George's lap, and he placed a hand over her mouth.

Jack laughed. "Peace, Brother. You would end Essex in a duel, but your wife makes a standard point—as it was foolish of me to have challenged Benjamin Cavendish, it would be equally imprudent for you to challenge the viscount."

Abigail's face fell. "Jack, you did what?"

He shook his head. "Some young lad at camp. I challenged him."

She gasped. "Whyever would you wish to harm that young man? What offense could he have made upon you?"

Jack's head tilted. "Know you the man?"

Flustered, she replied, "No...but I can't imagine any man insulting you enough for you to challenge him. 'Tis most unlike you."

He hung his head. "'Tis true, I had no right to challenge him. His insult was borne of my jealousy. The boy knew Annalisa, and I feared she may have loved him in return—"

"Annalisa has loved no one but you the entire time I've known her," Abigail snapped, her cheeks rouged. "How dare you presume she's loved anyone else. You know nothing of the torment she's endured from loving you."

His sister's words struck him, and he bit his lip. "I'm shamed for how I behaved. Believe me when I say I've not been myself since the shipwreck." Jack's gaze settled on Louisa, who climbed over George's lap. "When I learned of... my daughter...something in me healed. My God, I cherish her, and yet, I'll never know her. It devastates me that Annalisa and I created something, someone, powerful enough to heal my heart from the spirit world. I look at you, George, and I see a father. I see Ollie, and also see a father. But when I look at myself, I have no children—" his throat tightened at the thought of little Robby, "—no issue to take my name, and I cling to the image of this little girl. She's come to me in my dreams, but I know 'tis no dream. I know 'tis her. I'm her Papa, and I feel...complete."

"Then you must ride home without us, Perkins," George said. "You're recovered enough to withstand the journey on your own."

It was true. With Lord Essex in Topsfield, George and Abigail must now delay. "I know I can, but I'm fearful of being pursued by the British. They still search for me, I swear it, since I escaped HMS *Lively*."

"You've never mentioned such," Abigail replied, her hand to her breast.

"I never wished to trouble you. But as an escaped prisoner, if I'm discovered on the road, I may have an appointment with the gallows."

George squeezed Jack's shoulder. "You made it through Loyalist New York when you found Fleming and managed to facilitate the officers' escape from Fort Washington. I think you can return safely." He hesitated. "Why don't you bring Fleming with you? He's committed to you and Annie for ten years of indenture."

"Not until the war's ended. 'Twas the agreement," Jack replied.

George shook his head and skewered a sausage from the spider over the fire. "Bring Fleming, and ride north with haste. Annalisa awaits you. I've already written to her."

Jack eyed the barracks for Captain Fleming, who was never too far from George and him. "I suppose." He stood and lifted his haversack. "I'll write as soon as Essex departs Topsfield."

George shook his head. "We'll not return to Topsfield while that squeeze crab is in the province. We'll to the Black Water. Annie may be there as well while Essex is in town.

We'll leave with Quinnapin when Washington orders us from winter's quarters. Should give Essex plenty of time to return to his haystack in Cambridge."

Jack nodded, kissed his sister and niece, and pulled George into an embrace.

"Give our love to Annie," George said.

Abigail added, "Tell her we'll be attending the Strawberry Festival next month, if we can manage it."

⚜

JACK SPENT TWO DAYS ON THE ROAD WITH CAPTAIN Fleming since leaving Valley Forge, and the latter part of the previous day getting through New York. He'd traveled to Pennsylvania on more than one occasion, but such journeys never felt as tedious as this; at the end of this venture was his beloved Annalisa. As they rode through Connecticut, Jack adjusted his bauta mask, the bridge of his nose growing sore beneath the plaster. *If we keep this pace, we'll reach the Wayside Inn by nightfall.*

"I think there's hardly a Redcoat upon this highway," Captain Fleming said. "We've made it through the worst of Loyalist territory when we passed through New York yesterday. Why don't you just remove that hideous mask?"

"Any tavern we stop at could be Loyalist, housing British regulars. Don't be a fool," Jack snapped.

"No one knows your face, Perkins. Put the mask away."

Hesitantly, Jack slid the bauta from his face, and slipped it into his haversack. He sighed, relieved of the pressure upon his nose and to feel cool air upon his cheeks.

They'd already ridden eight hours, and the sun hung low in the sky.

"I think the horses need rest," Captain Fleming said.

"Can't we continue until we reach the Wayside?" Jack asked.

"No, the horses need water. We needn't linger at the inn, just to water and feed the beasts—and ourselves—and we'll be off before dawn. If we maintain this pace tomorrow, we'll be at your house in another day or so."

In Sturbridge, a small town just over the border of Massachusetts, Jack and Captain Fleming located the Publick House, a newer establishment, where they watered and stabled their horses, and purchased a room for the night. Seated across from Fleming in the dimly lit tavern, Jack appraised his indentured servant. The captain drank heartily from his tankard and dried his mouth on his sleeve. He'd been loyal to them since they'd captured and taken him prisoner, but would he remain so?

'Tis the best kind of mercy I can provide the man who nearly destroyed my life and Annalisa's. Jack peered about the finely furnished room, complete with shiny tables and chairs. "This Publick House is quite a difference from the first tavern we met at in New York. Just built in '71, I believe."

Fleming belched, then chuckled. "Aye. And not a Redcoat to be found."

Jack bristled at the mention of Regulars. "Speak not so loudly. We know not whether this is a Patriot establishment—"

The door to the tavern opened, and in stepped several officers donning crimson. Jack's heart sank.

"We require rooms, by decree of His Majesty's Royal Army."

At the voice, Jack's hair stood on end, and he stiffened in his seat. His bauta mask still hidden within his haversack, he glanced through his periphery to visualize the speaker.

Lieutenant Dickens, from HMS *Lively.*

Jack lowered his head and stared into his tankard.

"Poor timing on my part," Fleming chuckled darkly.

"You planned this, didn't you?" Jack hissed. "You knew this was a Loyalist inn, and you led us here...you spineless cur—"

"Fie," Captain Fleming whispered. "*You* led *me* here. I knew nothing of the sort. Think you so little of me, still?"

"How can I trust a turncoat? I was foolish to believe you—"

"You can trust me. I swear it upon my life." Fleming glanced at the officers who sat about a table near the window. "Unless you recognize them, 'tis unlikely they'll know you."

"Lieutenant Dickens," Jack muttered. "My torturer aboard HMS *Lively*. He's the tallest one...thin, with a sour-looking face."

Captain Fleming's face deflated. "Zounds. All right, here's what we do. We keep our heads low, and when I say to move, I block you when we stand, and make our way to the room for the night. We ride before dawn. Can you do that?"

Chewing his lip, Jack nodded. Beneath the table, he noticed Captain Fleming readying his pistol. *Will they hear the click when he cocks it?* Jack held his breath.

Click.

His head low, Jack peered at the officers' table. None seemed to notice over the gentle chatter of two gentlemen at one other occupied table. A pot boy scurried over to the officers' table and set down four tankards.

"Ready, Perkins," Captain Fleming uttered. "Now."

They stood, and Captain Fleming blocked Jack from view of the Redcoats. At a deliberate pace, they navigated the room in three strides, but at the door, one of the officers stood.

"You there, about face."

"Upstairs, Perkins," Fleming murmured.

Click.

Another pistol cocked, and Jack glanced before him. Lieutenant Dickens pointed his weapon at them. "I said, about face."

"What's the meaning of this, officer?" one of the men seated at the other table asked, rising from his chair.

"Be seated, sir. I assure you, 'tis necessary I take action," the lieutenant replied.

No, I will not run. I will confront the fiend. Jack stepped around Captain Fleming and faced the room.

"Lieutenant."

The lieutenant's lips twisted into the yellowed sneer from Jack's nightmares. "Upon my word, freedom looks well on you, Mr. Perkins. I thought it was you."

"Know you this man, sir?" Captain Fleming asked, his pistol aimed at the lieutenant.

The two men at the other table watched in horrified silence. *Are they Patriots? Or Loyalists?* Jack wondered if the innkeeper would soon materialize to assess the scene.

"I'd know that pretty face anywhere," Lieutenant Dickens scoffed. "We've been searching for you, whelp. How fortunate you chose this safe establishment for the night."

"You've found me, Lieutenant. But I won't be returning to your dreadful ship," Jack replied.

"That is unlikely, Mr. Perkins," Lieutenant Dickens said. "You're an escaped prisoner. Come now. Let's not cause a fuss...or what is it I've heard you heathens say? A *jerrycummumble*? You've a date with the gallows."

Captain Fleming fired his pistol on the lieutenant and missed. The round lodged into the green painted wall behind the officers' table. To Jack's dismay, the men seated at the other table continued to watch. *Unhelpful. They must be Loyalists.*

A second discharge rang out and struck Captain Fleming's chest. He gripped his chest and collapsed to the floor. "Lobsterback bastard," Fleming choked.

Now, the gentlemen seated at the other table rose and hurried from the tavern room, most likely to seek help, or a doctor, Jack hoped. He dropped to the floor and pressed firmly upon Fleming's wound, his hands slipping with the outflow of blood.

"Hang on. Keep with me," Jack croaked.

Captain Fleming's face grew pale. "I see it now...Perkins... the light, and the...darkness." His eyes slowly closed.

"I struck a vital artery, Mr. Perkins. Not a very challenging task at this range, unfortunately for him. If he'd been a better shot, perhaps it would be me upon this floor in a pool of my own blood—"

Heated with anger and fueled by remorse for Captain Fleming's final year on Earth, Jack reloaded the pistol, his bloody hands slipping over the metal, and stood. "I challenge you, Lieutenant Dickens, for the death of my friend."

Lieutenant Dickens smirked. "Challenge accepted, whelp." He loaded his pistol.

"Sir, would you like me to be your second?" one of the officers asked.

"And must we provide a second for the Rebel?" another added.

"Silence," Lieutenant Dickens barked. "I will not entertain the rules of a duel with a Rebel. There will be no seconds, and we shall duel here—"

Jack fired, marking the lieutenant precisely in the leg—the same leg Jack had injured in the wreck. At such close proximity, the round had certainly shattered the bone.

"You vile wretch!" Lieutenant Dickens cried.

"Why should I behave as a gentleman when you yourself

wished to forgo the rules of engagement with a Rebel?" Jack asked. Hastily—and to his guilt-ridden dismay—he removed Captain Fleming's effects from his person and fled the room.

"You cannot escape, Perkins," Lieutenant Dickens shouted from the tavern, where he clutched his devastated leg.

As Jack reached the inn door, the innkeeper barreled after him, shouting. Not waiting to hear what was being said, Jack pushed through the inn door and ran toward the stable. His hands trembling, now sticky with congealed blood, he tacked up a horse and rode into the night, his bauta mask fixed over his face.

JACK

THE PROVINCE OF MASSACHUSETTS BAY, MAY 1778

JACK GALLOPED THROUGH MASSACHUSETTS wearing his mask, never once removing it. He could take little chance of being discovered again, even as he closed in on rebel-held Boston. As he neared Topsfield, he almost felt Annalisa's energy, and was tempted to ride with his face exposed once more. His town was safe...*No, I will not be a fool. My fears were confirmed, and poor Fleming, though I accused him unfairly, paid for it with his life. Another regret I may add to the others.* But he'd narrowly escaped the gallows.

The road at the outskirts of Topsfield rose into a great hill, then sloped downward. This it did two more times. *Home.* He turned down the narrow lane and paused near Mile Brook Bridge, which passed over the Ipswich River. Safe within the boundary of his treasured town, he tied his horse to the bridge and washed and scrubbed his hands of Fleming's blood in the river. The water wavered with crimson tendrils, but the rust-colored remnants clung to Jack's cuticles and beneath his trimmed nails. Unable to rid himself of the blood, he wept. *I'm so sorry, Fleming. I've caused you nothing but agony in your final years of life.*

He could have lingered beneath that bridge for hours, wallowing in Fleming's untimely death, but George's reminder came to him: *there's no use perseverating on things that can't be undone.*

Composed, Jack returned to his horse and galloped away from the peaceful bridge, down the lane which led to his family's estate, and also, the Howlett farm.

The familiarity of the Howlett's verdant acreage stretched beneath the clouds overhead. It mattered little the day was less than fair—he was within reach of his beloved Annalisa. His horse slowed to a trot down the drive, where he hopped from the beast and tied it to the fence. He removed his mask and hastened up the path to the front door.

Liza answered before he knocked. "Mr. Perkins."

"Pray, is Annalisa home? I must speak with her most urgently."

Liza shook her head, and Mary stepped up to the front door. "She's away, Mr. Perkins, but please come inside—"

"I'll ride to her at once. Where is she?"

"Jack!" William bounded to the door, and settled beside Mary. She stepped from the house and closed the door on Liza and William.

"Annie's at the Black Water—"

"I should've known. How long has she been in Portsmouth? Shall I go to her now? Or will she be returning soon?"

Mary shook her head. "Lord Essex seems to have over-stayed his welcome at your parents' estate, and there remains. You may go to her, but I suggest you first visit your parents and your wife, and your...nephews."

Jack grimaced, the exhaustion of the overnight ride

consuming him. "Aye. Will you write to Annie and let her know I'll be coming?"

"I trust the couriers even less. I can give a letter to Henry. He's traveling thither on the morrow."

"Thank you." His conscience heavy for what he would encounter at his family's estate, Jack returned to his horse. *The way Mary studied me...Robby must resemble me already. 'Tis only a matter of time before the truth is revealed.*

Two miles down the lane proved more tedious than his midnight ride through Massachusetts, but it wasn't long before his family's yellow house, perched on the hill, came into view. He rode his horse toward the stable, and noticed Lord Essex's coach within the carriage house, and his father's parked in the drive.

"Mr. Perkins, how good to see you sir," the groomsman said, taking Jack's horse.

"Likewise, sir." Jack nodded to the man and hurried up the path to the front door.

"Mr. Perkins." Mercy opened the door. "How good to see you, sir." She took his travel coat and led him into the parlor.

Oliver sat in a chair reading, one leg over the other, while Lord Essex sat beside Jane on the sofa with her two children. Mother perched in her chair by the unlit fireplace stitching her needlepoint with Susan, and Andrew peered out the window, smoking a pipe with Father.

His youngest brother turned from the window. "Jack!" Andrew, as tall as he, crossed the room and embraced him. "Look at you, you do look well. At Twelfth Night, George said you were quite ill when he left Valley Forge."

"I had proper healing," Jack replied.

Oliver grinned, rose from his chair, and placed the book on a table. "It does me good to see you, Brother." They did not embrace, but rather, bowed politely.

"Likewise, Ollie." Jack then kissed his mother and Susan, and shook Father's hand, before turning his attention on Jane and Lord Essex upon the sofa.

The viscount had risen and extended a polite bow. "Mr. Perkins, good to see you again, sir," he said, his smirk deepening his chin divot.

"My lord," Jack replied, unable to conjure more than that. His attention on Jane, Jack kissed her hand.

"Tommy, Robby, give your Papa a kiss," she said flatly.

At the address, Jack's breath caught, and he looked at Oliver, who bit his lip and crossed his arms.

"'Tis all right, Jack," Oliver replied.

Jack shook his head. "No. 'Tis not all right. This child—these children—are your sons, and should know you as their father, whether or not I'm married to Jane."

"Jack, please," Jane hissed. "We've much to discuss. Give Tommy and Robby a kiss, and we'll into the study."

Tommy, at two, ran into Jack's arms. "Papa Jack!"

Behind him, little Robby took four unsteady steps, then toppled over. Jack scooped up the boy and kissed his round, dimpled cheek. "You boys have grown much since last I saw you."

"Pa," Robby said with a giggle. Jack's heart swelled at the life he'd created, and held him snugly in the crook of his arm. When he turned to face the room, his family fell silent.

"Shall we into the study, then?" Oliver asked.

"Aye." Jack set down the child and followed his brother across the parlor. "Jane?"

She stood, smoothed her skirts, and glided toward them, then out the door, leaving a wake of lavender for them to follow. Jack's stomach wrenched at the scent.

Oliver closed the study door behind them and made his way to Father's mahogany desk. He sat and removed a ledger.

"I've drafted everything as per Father's instructions, but I leave it to you, Jack, to review for correctness."

He joined Oliver at the desk and read the page: a divorce petition. His shoulders loosened as he continued reading the document Oliver had written with their father. Jack suddenly stiffened. Robby was listed as one of Oliver's two sons, and there was no mention of their adultery to end the marriage, only 'abandonment'.

"Does he not know?" Jack asked, staring hard at Jane.

Her cheeks colored.

"That you strummed Jane and produced Robby? Aye, I'm aware. And I'm certain our family now knows it as well. The child is an image of you, Jack."

"Then, it would behoove us to list adultery."

"Then list it," Oliver replied.

His quill upon the page, Jack hesitated, studying his brother a moment. "May we discuss the matter, first?"

"There's nothing to discuss. You both believed yourselves widowed and took comfort in one another." Oliver sighed. "I blame you not."

Jack exhaled the breath he hadn't realized he'd held. Oliver was forgiving their betrayal only because he knew not they lay together before they received word of his death. *I should tell him the truth.*

"And I'm grateful, Ollie, you've been so kind and understanding," Jane said. "And that you love both boys as your own."

"Whyever should I not? My blood runs through their veins regardless, no?" He gave Jack a small grin that caught him off guard.

"You mean to name Robby as your son?" Jack asked.

"Yes. We must keep our family together," Jane replied.

"But...he's my son. I'm happy to name him my heir—"

"'Tis too late for that," Jane said. "He knows he's Robby, not John Jackson Perkins IV."

Oliver shrugged. "I suppose if you're willing to tell Annalisa, and if she'll accept him, I can't see the harm—"

"No!" Jane cried.

Jack and Oliver up righted themselves in their seats.

Jane smoothed her skirts again and composed herself. "No, I think such an act would defile my name and yours, Ollie. We must keep our family intact, as well as our reputations."

Oliver scowled. "It frightens me how little you consider my raising Jack's son as my own. Have you considered his feelings in this at all, madam?"

Jane regarded Jack with a softened gaze. "Please. We made a mistake. Let me atone for it by accepting this burden from you. It will be best Annalisa never knows."

A sourness seeped into Jack's stomach. "She will uncover the truth. 'Tis only a matter of time. And when she does, she'll forgive none of us."

"So be it. I can accept the blame for it," Jane replied.

Oliver asked, "What if I don't wish to be part of such a charade?"

"Since when do you care for Annalisa?" Jane snapped.

"Since I realized she..." Oliver trailed off. "Since she forgave me. We rode back to Topsfield after meeting at the Wayside, and I've much changed my opinion of her. She deserves not to be hurt, not by us, and especially not by Jack."

Jane pursed her lips. "Very well. We shall reveal the nature of Robby's birth to our families, and Jack, you may name him your heir."

"At last, some sense is spoken," Oliver sighed.

"And I shall tell Lord Essex where Abigail is hiding," Jane continued. "'Tis only fair he reunites with his lawful wife."

"You wicked harpy," Oliver muttered, and left the desk. He glanced down at the family signet ring upon his littlest finger. In one swift motion, he slipped off the ring and placed it upon their father's desk. "Jack, I believe this is yours," and left the room.

"Require you anything else from me, sir?" Jane treated him to a coy smile as she lifted from her chair.

"Sit down," Jack ordered, nearly forgetting he was no longer in the militia. "I wish to look at you as I redraft this petition."

Her brows lifted at his terse address, and she settled in one of the Windsor chairs opposite the desk.

Jack drew up the quill. With each dip of his pen into the inkwell, he lifted his gaze to Jane and wrote the reasons they should be parted, and their marriage dissolved. When he completed the document, he signed, then asked for her signature.

Reaching for the gold signet ring from where Oliver had left it, Jack studied their family's seal etched into the top. He folded the page and dripped crimson wax over the fold. As though he'd never lost the ring, he stamped the document, sealing it, and replaced the ring upon his little finger.

Coldly, Jack said, "I'm quite finished with you, Miss Howlett. You may go."

Her face as stone, Jane rose from the chair and bobbed a formal curtsey. "My lord." Soundlessly, she drifted from the study.

Closing his eyes, Jack leaned back in his chair and released a long-held breath. He did it. He was rid of her. For now.

🙟 61 🙟

ANNALISA

PORTSMOUTH, THE STATE OF NEW
HAMPSHIRE, MAY 1778

A T DAWN, ANNALISA WANDERED the rocky shoreline perched above swelling waters. The Atlantic, looking quite blue, offered her little reprieve from the anxiety coursing through her. She hadn't heard from George since he'd written for her to expect Jack sometime in the coming weeks. But worse, she hadn't heard from Mary. *Does Lord Essex still remain in Topsfield at the Perkins estate? Whyever does he persist there? Why won't he return to Cambridge?*

She paused in her walk and sat upon a rock overlooking the sea. East, across that vast expanse, lay England. How far she was from Gee, the Duchess of Devonshire, and all her kindness; London, and all its antics; France, and *Monsieur* Beauregard. Those days seemed far removed from her, now. To the south, she wondered how Addy and Sarah fared in Charleston. She'd received their last letter shortly after returning from Valley Forge; they still hadn't found Sarah's mother, but they were well, enjoying the warmer weather.

In the rising sunlight, Annalisa lifted her face to the sky

and closed her eyes. The warmth flooded her skin, and she sucked in the salty air. *Eliza, my love, you are missed.*

"Great Spirit, please keep my daughter well, and guide me in this life without her and her father."

"I beg your pardon, Miss."

Startled, Annalisa turned at the gravelly voice. A man wearing a Venetian bauta mask stood beyond the rock.

"Sir?"

"Charming creature, whyever do you cry?" the masked man asked.

"I'm waiting for a faithless young man," she replied. "I was told he'd meet me here, but I'm beginning to think my brother was mistaken."

"Pray, what's the man's name? Perhaps I've seen him on my travels."

Unnerved, Annalisa cocked her head. "Why do you wear that mask? I've not seen one since I left London."

"A man hunts for me," he replied. "But I'll remove it if it frightens you—"

Annalisa held up her hand. "No need, sir. I'll not be the reason you're discovered."

The man nodded with gratitude and adjusted his black riding cloak. "Pray, the name of the man you seek?"

"Jack. He was away with the army at Valley Forge—"

"Fie. I wouldn't depend on Jack. 'Tis not likely he'll meet you here if he's traveling from Valley Forge. Washington's men are still encamped. But you may tarry with me in yon fishing town. New Castle is quite nice. You needn't fear a thing."

Annalisa said nothing, her senses heightened. *I should run from this strange man before he captures me.*

Taller than she, the man stepped closer, casting a shadow across the stony ground on which they stood. "Your Jack was traveling north with a captain. Last I heard they were at a tavern in Sturbridge, where Redcoats assaulted them. He took a ball to his chest."

She gasped. "No, 'tis not true. You lie, sir." Tears gathered and dripped down her cheeks. "I thought I lost him once. If I'm to lose him again, I swear I'll take no other man. For his sake, I'd rather wander this earth alone."

The man fell silent, then reached for her. "Peace, dear heart." His voice had softened to a musical baritone, and her skin prickled at the sound. He tugged her close and lifted the mask. "'Tis me, Annie. I'm the man you're seeking, the cause of all your agony."

Through her tears, Jack's handsome face came into focus. "Your cur, you tricked me." She slapped his chest, but flew into his arms.

"Annie, I'll never be parted from you again, I swear it. Not ever in this lifetime will I leave your side."

She pulled from him. "What of Jane?"

"We signed a divorce petition...Jane, Ollie, and I...and I filed it with the magistrate at Salem two days ago. Annalisa, you're my heart, and I can't bear the thought of being parted from you."

She gasped. "By the sea. I dreamt this from Eliz—" She stopped herself.

"From Eliza?" Jack pressed his forehead to hers.

"Yes, our daughter."

"I've dreamt of her as well."

Annalisa's eyes clouded again. She blinked and her cheeks cooled with tears. "Pray, what does she look like when she comes to you?"

Jack wiped the tears from her face. "Like you, my darling girl, but with my eyes, and smile."

"Aye, she does." Annalisa heaved against him until she

summoned enough composure to step back. "But you did not see her in life as I did. Jack, she was a tiny thing—fit into the palm of my hand."

His eyes closed, and a few droplets clung to his dark eyelashes. "And she is our little one. We will create more life between the two of us, Annie."

She looped her arms beneath his and held him close. "Promise me she won't be the only one."

He kissed the crown of her head and murmured, "I promise."

Annalisa pulled from him. "Pray, did you speak true? Does a man truly hunt for you?"

His jaw tightened. "Aye. The British are searching for me." With a shiver, a shadow passed over his face. "Lieutenant Dickens...I wounded him at the tavern after he murdered Captain Fleming, but he'll not stop hunting me."

She started. *Captain Fleming! That turncoat.* She could hardly ask about him, since she'd only met the man when she was masquerading as Benjamin. "How do you know this lieutenant?" she asked instead.

"He was my torturer aboard HMS *Lively*."

Annalisa shuddered. "Then 'tis not safe here, either, Jack. The Black Water has become a haven for Loyalists. If we're to remain here, we must adopt an alias."

Jack pursed his pleasantly shaped lips. "A clever thought. Pray, what name shall we be called, then?"

She considered several, but only one surname stood out to her as worthy of their masquerade. "Bixby, after George's natural father."

Jack chuckled. "That was the name I adopted when I met Captain Fleming—God rest his soul—and he believed me Loyalist, for a brief time, anyhow. Well, Mrs. Bixby, what shall I call you in private?"

"Anna is fine," she replied. "I think we may keep our Christian names."

They returned to George's tavern, and Jack followed her to her private quarters on the third floor. She hadn't expected Jack would stay with her, but he helped move her things into the larger guest room on the second floor they'd shared over two years ago.

She sat on the bed and chuckled. "It feels as though no time has passed between us, and yet we've suffered so much."

He sat beside her on the bed. "When the time is right, when my divorce is granted, you have my word as a gentleman, I'll ask you to marry me."

"Then shall we not spend the night together?"

"No, no. Oliver and Jane have resumed their life together at my parents'." He shook his head. "'Tis all so strange."

"Aye, it is." She grinned. "Pray, how are our nephews? I've not seen them in weeks."

"They're in good health. They're very kind boys."

Annalisa chuckled. "'Tis surprising, given who their parents are. But I must say, Oliver's surprised me. He's much changed."

"Yes, he is." Jack drew up her hands. "Would that Robby... and Tommy, and Louisa were here. I know how much you cherish them."

"Yes, and one day we'll have own to love."

He kissed her, then rested his forehead against hers, their noses touching. "Would that I could give you a child."

She brushed her lips against his and lifted his hand to her breast, where he plucked the neck handkerchief from her dress and tossed it to the wooden floor. "If you're able," she breathed against his mouth, "I'll have you this moment."

Jack gave an impish smirked and muttered, "Oh, lass, I'm able."

Spellbound from his kisses, she pulled him onto her and hiked up her skirts—careful to conceal her petticoat over her healed leg wound—as he positioned himself atop her. He unbuttoned the flap of his breeches, and she accepted him into her. Annalisa savored the closeness, the most they'd been in over a year—and this time, she enjoyed him knowing it wouldn't be their last, that he would one day again be hers.

❧

ANNALISA SAT IN THE SMALL GARDEN BEHIND GEORGE'S tavern. There, sweet and savory herbs would soon be in full bloom, ready for their uses in either the kitchen or Addy's physick. Annalisa flipped through her physick diary, searching for a tea. The morbid flux had been erratic and irregular since stopping the tea she drank while masquerading as Benjamin Cavendish—it had been of utmost importance it never came upon her while wearing breeches. And with her menses now upon her, Addy's physick had returned her courses as expected.

"What do you study today, dear heart?" Jack kissed her forehead and sat beside her.

"The morbid flux is upon me with a vengeance. I must find something to quell the cramps."

Jack's cheeks rouged. "Ah. Ladies' troubles. Something I can hardly relate to, but I do sympathize. Before long, you'll be with child, I'm certain of it." He smiled and withdrew a letter from his pocket. "My uncle's written. He plans to visit."

"Lord Brunswick?"

"Aye."

Her brows lifted. "Your uncle, Lord Brunswick, is visiting us *here*, at the Black Water?"

Jack laughed. "Aye, love. He and Aunt Catherine. Is this not a fitting establishment to accommodate his lordship?"

She shook her head. "Jack, I—"

"Peace, dear heart. He won't be sleeping at the inn. He's staying with the governor but means to pay us a visit."

"More news from Congress?" Annalisa asked, leery.

"I doubt it. Though, my father is returning to Pennsylvania soon. I shan't be joining him."

"I give thanks to the Great Spirit."

Jack cocked his head. "What, you don't wish to be parted from me?"

"You cur," she laughed, gently shoving him. "You know where I stand on that."

"I know. I'll not leave you again, and I'm in no hurry to travel."

The gravity of Jack's circumstances settled between them, and she replied softly, "No, I can't imagine you are."

Jack kissed her hand. "I swear, we'll be safe here. No one will suspect 'tis me so long as we keep to our alias as Bixbys —" He stopped, then added, "Save for Captain Duncan, my rescuer from HMS *Lively*. Pray, you've not seen a man by that name since staying at the Black Water, have you?"

Annalisa shook her head. "No, I've not. Mostly Loyalists pass through, thanks to Henry and Mary. They've taken to listening, though I'm not sure where Henry takes his intelligence."

Jack stiffened, and she noticed a relative unease wash over him. "They're spying? The twins?"

"Aye. Henry and Mary have always been clever and observant, and Mary's persistent in wishing to partake in the war. I've been strict with her, she cannot join as—" Annalisa stopped. *Jack can never know I've been in the war, that I'm*

Benjamin Cavendish. "She cannot join like George and William."

He studied her for a moment. "Knew you a young rogue called Benjamin Cavendish?"

Her chest constricted. "I...d-did." She sucked in a breath, soothing herself. "Why do you ask?"

Jack frowned. "I'm ashamed to admit, I dueled the boy... while we were at New York."

"You didn't. He was always such a kind fellow," she replied, frowning.

"I'm afraid I did...I was driven mad. I foolishly believed you loved him." He hesitated. "Did you ever?"

"N-no, of course not. I've only ever loved you."

Her answer seemed to placate him, but in the way he studied her, she wondered whether or not he believed her.

Jack's thumb glided over the scar beneath her right eye. "I pray over the course of our lives, you may learn to trust me with the secrets of your heart, Annalisa."

Her heart pattered. "M-my secrets?" *I should tell him, perhaps he won't mind. No, I can't. He'll be hanged if I'm discovered. But if he's discovered, we'll both hang. Perhaps there is no way out...*

"Aye. 'Tis true every woman keeps them, yes?"

"I have n-none that I k-keep from you." She bit her tongue, irritated. "Damn this stutter!"

Jack's gaze softened. "My darling girl. Where was the injury that plagued you so?"

She placed his hand upon her head. "Here, there was a great bruise which caused me m-many headaches, and d-dizziness." Annalisa closed her eyes. *"Beauty, you cannot long devotion keep: The mind grows weary; senses fall asleep..."* When she finished the poem, she opened her eyes. "Reciting Mad Madge always sets it right."

He frowned. "I've caused you pain. I remember you said it

returns when you're upset." Jack kissed where the bruise had once been, then with his hands in hers, lifted them both to standing. "Come, let's inside. My victualing office is rumbling."

Annalisa smiled. "Aye, 'tis almost time for nooning."

Jack cocked his head and laughed. "Since when have you called it thus? We did so at Washington's camp."

"'Tis something I learned from William since he's been home," she lied, and followed him back into the tavern. *Hiding my time from him as Cav is going to prove much harder than I imagined it would...*

JACK

PORTSMOUTH, THE STATE OF NEW HAMPSHIRE, JUNE 1778

LORD BRUNSWICK ARRIVED AT the Black Water Inn with Aunt Catherine at precisely the hour he meant to. The main tavern room still bustled with patrons, but Jack had instructed Elisha to keep the back two rooms closed. At the front foyer, Jack greeted his aunt and uncle with Annalisa.

"Jack, my boy." Lord Brunswick kissed his cheek. "It does me good to see my heir apparent after all this time."

Hesitant, Jack forced a smile. His uncle, always quite thin, appeared far more so. "Likewise, my lord." He gestured to Annalisa. "You remember Annalisa, sir."

Aunt Catherine, her chestnut brown hair now streaked with grey beneath her hat, stepped forward. "Of course." She clasped Annalisa's hands. "How good to see you, my dear." Smiling, she faced Jack and cupped his cheek. "You look well, Nephew. As handsome as ever."

"Come, let's sit in the garden." Jack led their party through the empty rear tavern rooms, and outside through the back door.

"Pray, you've help here, yes?" Lord Brunswick asked.

"Elisha Porter is George's tavern-keep in his stead," Jack replied. "But Annalisa and I have been taking up residence here while...while George is away."

Beneath a sturdy oak, Lord Brunswick and Aunt Catherine sat on a bench, and Annalisa and Jack sat opposite them on another.

"'Tis agreeable here. Pray, how was your time in Washington's army? You look to have avoided most soldiers' ailments," Lord Brunswick said with a chuckle.

Jack eyed Annalisa. "I was honorably discharged in January, my lord. I was inoculated at Morristown two winters ago, but this past winter at Valley Forge I fell ill for several months. Thankfully, I've made a full recovery." He paused. "George should be arriving home soon, ending a three-year contract."

Lord Brunswick adjusted himself on the bench, looking quite uncomfortable. "Yes, your cousin." He cleared his throat. "You're probably aware that our visit is not without cause—"

"We wished to see you, Jack—both of you," Aunt Catherine chimed. "We were devastated by all that's passed these two years for your families."

"Yes, yes, of course," Lord Brunswick said. "But there are pressing matters of which I must speak with you."

Jack sat forward. "Go on, sir."

"I've heard some distressing news from my friend Lord Essex. Most distressing, indeed. He visited us at our home on Tory Row, without his wife...your sister. He told us she fled England last January and cannot be located."

"Perhaps he's not searched enough for her," Annalisa replied.

Lord Brunswick studied her. "A husband who's lost his wife grieves for her, I assure you, Miss Howlett."

"Mrs. Perkins," Jack corrected him, and quickly added, "My lord."

"Not according to your father," his uncle quipped. "I'm not sure what charades you've been involved in, but these convoluted marriages must be cleaned up at once. I must return Abigail to Lord Essex in all haste, and this disgraceful living arrangement between you two must end. Our family has a reputation to uphold. Have I made myself perfectly clear?"

"My lord, Abigail will not return to Lord Essex. He's not the man we all believed of him, and she will no longer endure his abuses," Annalisa said.

"My word, you give your opinion rather decidedly for a woman, young miss," Lord Brunswick replied.

Jack's jaw tightened. "I'll not remain married to Jane, sir. She belongs to Oliver, as she once did. I've signed a petition to divorce her, Uncle, so I may again marry Annalisa. Until then, we'll continue to live as though we are. I'll not have you sit here and speak to her as though she were some petulant child. At two-and-twenty, she's a woman grown, and has much experience to recommend her."

"He's right, my darling," Aunt Catherine said. "Jack, we only wish for what's best for you and our family. As your uncle's heir, you recall you must be married to a woman of upstanding character—"

"Of which I was, before our ship was wrecked and we were both presumed dead," Jack replied. "Forgive me, Aunt. I grow weary of defending my actions. Oliver is no longer deceased, and neither is Annalisa. We each hope to return to our rightful spouses to whom we married in 1775."

"Therein lies the issue, Jack." Lord Brunswick shook his

head. "I've come from your father's house and Oliver will not remarry Jane. He's refused."

Jack looked to Annalisa, then back to his aunt and uncle. "He won't? Whyever not?"

"Jane has left with Lord Essex," Lord Brunswick replied. "'Tis most unseemly she should travel thither to Cambridge with Essex. I daresay their friendship is rather uncouth..."

Jack's heart sank. "Has she taken the children with her as well?" *I'll be damned if she absconds with Robby.*

"I believe she has," Aunt Catherine replied. "But Oliver made no mention of their intentions to remove themselves from Cambridge."

"She will insist they go to London," Annalisa replied. "I know my sister, and she cares only for herself. Her reputation is ruined here, but in London, with Lord Essex, she may flourish as the wife of a viscount."

Lord Brunswick studied her a moment. "You're quite astute, Miss."

"If Essex has gone away with Jane, why did you insist I send Abigail to him?" Jack asked.

"Because if his rightful wife is returned to him, he will be required to leave your brother's wife alone," his uncle replied.

Silence settled between them, when the backdoor of the tavern flew open, and George stomped into the garden with Abigail and Louisa.

"We're home, Perkins!" George bellowed. He set Louisa on the ground and she ran toward their party. "We've guests?"

Jack stood with his aunt and uncle. "Cousin, you've met my uncle, Lord Brunswick, and my Aunt Catherine—my father's sister."

George, looking rather uncomfortable, bowed clumsily. "Aye, my lord, my lady." He looked to Abigail, whose cheery face had withered as an autumn leaf after peak season.

"Aunt Catherine, Uncle." She went to them and offered each a kiss on the cheek.

"Is this the little one?" Aunt Catherine beamed and lifted Louisa from the ground.

Louisa threw a rock at her. "Fie!"

Startled, Aunt Catherine replaced the girl on the ground, and George scooped her into his strong arms.

"Aunt," Louisa shrieked, reaching for Annalisa.

George handed Annalisa the girl, and said, "My apologies, Lady Brunswick."

Aunt Catherine rubbed her nose where the rock had struck her, then sat. "'Tis all right."

"Young lady, you've much to explain." Lord Brunswick regarded Abigail and gestured for her to sit beside his wife. "I've heard much from Lord Essex, and this behavior is most unseemly. You were bred far better than to behave thus."

Abigail's lip quivered, but she forced her shoulders back, refusing to sit. "Essex was a monster, Uncle. I'll not return to him. He withheld mail from me that indicated Jack was alive after the wreck, and I could never understand why he kept it from me." She hesitated. "He was also cruel."

Lord Brunswick's stern face softened. "I knew this not about him."

"Oh, you poor dear." Aunt Catherine reached for Abigail's hand.

"Pray, was he unfaithful to you?" Lord Brunswick asked.

"I can't prove he was, my lord, but most men in London take a lover," Abigail replied. "It would surprise me little if he had."

Jack looked to George, then back at Abigail. "Uncle has told us Lord Essex returned to Cambridge...with Jane."

Abigail gasped. "What of Ollie?"

"The wicked doxie," George growled.

"Doxie!" Louisa shouted.

"Shh." Annalisa placed a hand over her niece's mouth.

"Oliver has refused to remarry her," Jack replied. "I filed the divorce petition, and according to Uncle, Oliver would not have her back."

"Whyever not?" Abigail asked. "They have children."

Jack bit his lip, heart pounding. *This is not how Annalisa should discover this information. But our families must know. They should've known the moment he was born.* He sucked in a breath, then exhaled. "Robby is mine."

"La!" Abigail gasped, clutching her bosom. "You didn't! You couldn't have," she shrieked.

Annalisa handed Louisa to George. "I won't remain here and listen to this."

Jack chased after her. "Annie, wait!" But George stopped him.

"You've much to explain. Stay. I'll go to her." George left with Louisa and returned to the tavern.

Lord Brunswick shook his head, sitting again beside his wife. "What else has passed between you? How might I expect things to grow even more complicated, Jack? Does your father know?"

"No...no one knows, save for Oliver." Jack licked his lips. "Sir, Jane and I...we were...it happened during my darkest hour, when I believed myself widowed of Annalisa."

"At least you were honest with poor Ollie," Aunt Catherine replied, her face grim.

Jack spun his signet ring, eyeing the tavern yonder. "I wished to relay the truth the day Robby was born. But Jane made several unfounded threats...an extortion of sorts, which made me hold my tongue against my better judgment. I'm not proud of my actions."

"Oh, Jack," Abigail sobbed. "How could you? How could you do this to Annie?"

"I regret it, Abbie. Think not I enjoyed myself!" Flustered, he stood and paced the garden. "Imagine my utter chagrin when Jane announced herself in the family way...and then Annalisa came home with you."

Aunt Catherine rose from the bench and met Jack by a lilac bush. Her gentle hand upon his shoulder, she said, "Jack, we all make mistakes in youth, and when we're suffering." Her gaze returned to the tavern behind them. "If she truly loves you, she will forgive you, and understand."

Jack shook his head. "Annalisa needn't forgive me. 'Twas my mistake, and I accept the consequences of those actions. I neglected to tell her when we reunited a fortnight ago out of a misplaced sense of fear." He regarded his sister. "Abbie, Jane had threatened she would disclose your location to Lord Essex if I revealed the truth about Robby. Perhaps that was the moment Oliver decided he no longer wished to have her as his wife."

"This is grave, indeed." Lord Brunswick joined them by the lilac bush. "Even more so if Jane leaves for London with her children."

Abigail scurried toward them. "Jack, you must go to Annie. Tell her everything you've told us. I know she'll forgive you. She loves you. I know she'd wish for you to keep Robby if you could." She faced their aunt and uncle. "Now, if I may share my bit of gossip with you about Louisa..."

His sister was right, of course. Determined, Jack left their party and commenced toward the tavern.

❧ 63 ❧

ANNALISA

PORTSMOUTH, JUNE, 1778

LOUISA SQUIRMED OVER GEORGE as he sat at one of the empty tables. She tugged his hair from its queue.

"Zounds, that's painful. Be still, child." He gripped the girl's hands and tucked her into his lap. "Annie, I swear I knew not this news. I'm as shocked as you. Had he told me, I would've divulged it to you."

Annalisa paced the small room that had been blocked off for their guests. From the window, Jack still congregated with his sister, aunt, and uncle in the garden. *Jack fancied Jane before ever he noticed me. He must've fallen in love with her in my absence.* At the thought, her wounds from Bemis Heights and the duel started to ache, and she gritted her teeth against the anger of betrayal.

She turned to face her brother, who sat with his own love child in his lap. He'd lain with Abigail before she married Lord Essex. *In their moments of intimacy, had George any consideration of marrying Abigail? Are all men scoundrels, then?*

"I don't believe you," she hissed.

"Fie." George's cheeks colored. "You've little reason not to trust me. I've not spilled a morsel of your gossip to Jack about your muse Cav, and his antics at Bemis Heights—that he dueled you instead of some poor young lad."

"This is different," she cried, her rage bubbling over. "He lay with Jane. They produced a child, and he chose to keep this from me. He either loves her, or he's a scoundrel. Oliver truly is the better man, and I *never* thought I'd speak such words."

George rose from the table and met her by the window. "Peace. Oliver is much changed, yes, but Jack is no scoundrel, nor does he love Jane. He's honorable. What he did, not so much, but I'm certain there's reason behind it. He does nothing that serves no purpose, Annie. You know this. And he would never wish to intentionally cause you pain."

"Yet he has." A churn of nausea coiled her insides, and she wished to leave the tavern forthwith. "I know not whether I can ever marry such a man."

"Enough." George peered out the window. "Here he comes. You needn't accept a marriage proposal from him today, but at the very least, please listen to all he has to say."

The back door opened, and Jack stepped into the room. "George, may I speak with Annie alone?"

"'Tis Miss Annalisa to you, Mr. Perkins," she snapped.

"Annie, enough," George barked. Louisa giggled and grabbed his ear. He set her down and stood beside Annalisa. "If you don't mind, I wish to hear how this came about, since I, too, was not privy to such intelligence. After all the time we've spent together fighting, you not once told me you lay with Jane, and that Robby was yours."

Jack's face sagged. "George, I..." He looked to Annalisa. "Annie—Miss Annalisa, I should've told you the day he was born, but we were just reunited after a long year of believing the other dead. When I went to Jane, I asked to name him after my father, as is tradition, you know, and insisted we tell our families who fathered him. She refused, citing her reputation, and proceeded to threaten to poison herself, the child, or you, if I petitioned for divorce."

First, Annalisa's neck heated, then her face. She ground her teeth to prevent the outburst, but it fired from her as violently as a round ignited from her musket. "She did p-poison me, Jack! Jane m-murdered our child, yet you still k-kept her secret!"

Annalisa fled the room, hurried through the main tavern room, and out the front door. Portsmouth's houses and rowhouses sped past in a blur as she sprinted down several side streets until she reached the wooden bridge leading to Peirce Island, or as it was known in town since the construction of Fort Washington in 1775, the Isle of Washington. Annalisa hastened up a small hill overlooking the mouth of Piscataqua River, which opened into the ocean. Across, lay Seavey's Island and the shores of Maine. Below, salty waters lapped the shoreline. Her face throbbing and hot, Annalisa contemplated briefly whether or not to fling herself into the swelling tide.

No, Mamma. You can't come to me yet. Papa loves you.

"Eliza," she cried. "N-no, he d-does not!" Gasping, she clawed at her neck handkerchief and flung it. The fabric floated on the breeze before dwindling to the waters below, where the tide swallowed it whole. Annalisa crumpled to the ground. Between sobs, she massaged the arm that had been wounded at Bemis Heights, whispering a verse of Mad Madge's poetry, *"I conquer all, am master of the field; and make fair Beauty in love's wars to yield—"*

"Please, cry not."

Annalisa lifted her head. Blurred through her tears, she made out a girl child, no older than five. She stared hard at Annalisa with eyes to match the waters before them. Had she come from the barracks at Fort Washington yonder?

"Run along, child..." Annalisa wiped her tears, and her throat tightened. "Eliza?"

"Mamma. I promise I'll protect you."

Nothing about the visage caused alarm, but rather, a haze settled over Annalisa with an overwhelming sense of love and calm. "Can you protect me from your Papa?" she asked.

Eliza's small, bronzed hand touched Annalisa's arm, and she chilled at the sensation.

"No, Mamma. Papa loves you, as I do." Her hand faded through Annalisa's forearm, and the girl grinned, her cheeks dimpling. "He comes this way, by the sea. Be not angered by him."

Her daughter faded, and Annalisa reached for her. "No, please, don't leave me, my love."

Jack advanced up the hill, and held out his hand. "I have no right to ask your forgiveness, but I do wish to explain."

Annalisa glanced about, the otherworldly haze leaving her. Eliza was nowhere to be seen. *No...what child would be this near to a fort?* "Did you happen upon a small girl on your way to the island?"

Jack's brow lifted. "A girl? No."

Her face fell. "'Tis no matter." She adjusted the pins in her dress, then met his harried stare. "Continue, sir."

Jack fiddled with his signet ring as he stood before her. "Not a day has passed I haven't regretted what occurred between Jane and I that night." He drew in a shaky breath. "I was a coward, a man incapable of facing the agony of losing you, and the torture I experienced aboard that ship...I'm ashamed to admit..." Jack pinched the space between his eyes. "I'm shamed, Annalisa. I became a man you would never wish to call 'husband'. I drank heavily, and deeply depended upon laudanum to dull the pain and despair. I was numb, and felt nothing... because I wished to feel nothing. And 'twas in my altered state Jane came to me wearing your perfume, and I did the task."

Annalisa twirled the musket round within her pocket. "She seduced you."

"So it seems. I can't remember much of the event...only that we woke together the following morning and I loathed myself more than I ever have before, or since." He drew up her hands. "I must be honest with you. I was not myself. I was overcome by opium and liquor, Annalisa. Poisons to my mind and self...I depended upon both."

"How did you quit the stuff?" She bristled as a gust of air blew off the briny waters, cooling her face. "Have you?"

"Yes, I have. Quinn, by the grace of God, took me in and cared for me as the opium left my body. I was sick for days, Annie. Nearly a week."

Quinn knew about his ailments, aided him in this time of need. It made sense to her now why Quinnapin had told her Jack was quite ill.

"I learned of Jane's pregnancy," Jack continued, "and after she gave birth...well, you heard what I relayed."

Somewhat softened, Annalisa asked, "But why did you not tell me when we met a fortnight ago?"

"Jane threatened she would reveal Abigail's location to Lord Essex if Oliver and I divulged the truth to our families... I was wrong, Annalisa. I should never have kept it from you, no matter her threats. And now it matters little. She's gone with Lord Essex and—"

"She took the children with her." Her anger melted,

quickly turning to pity. "Well, we must find Robby and take him back."

Jack's sagging face lifted. "You mean that? You know I would never ask it, or even expect it of you..."

"Yes. He's your son—" The last word felt thick with tears. She composed herself and repeated, "He's your son." Her throat closed again and she fought the tears. "This is too hard."

Mamma, I'm here.

A tenderness returned to Jack's face, and he caressed her hand. "You know I would never ask you to raise him as your own—"

"He's my nephew, I already love him. 'Tis no great task to love him."

"Annalisa..."

"I'm pained to think you could not call him your own— and that Jane has attempted to sever your manhood by declaring the child hers and not yours by means of threats!" Her blood boiled at the image of her perfect sister, always so coy and charming with Society, but a wicked, soulless witch beneath her prim and fabricated exterior.

"Robby has a birthright as your son." Annalisa thought of the daughter who now looked over her as a guardian and imagined the anger and torment she'd feel if Eliza had lived, but if she could not call her 'daughter'. *What heartache...to watch one's child live and grow up as someone else's.* Annalisa shook herself of the thought and rested her forehead against his. She hadn't realized they'd drawn quite close as their conversation progressed.

She whispered, "She was here. Before you came to me."

"Eliza?"

Her fingers flew to his lips. "Shh. Speak not her name."

"I'm here, Mamma, Papa."

The small voice carried on the breeze, and they turned. Jack's hand, clasped in Annalisa's, tightened.

"Do you see what I see?" he asked.

"'Tis her."

Laughing, Eliza skipped up the hill toward them, her honey-brown curls bouncing. "I'm returning to Keihtánit's house. You should find my brother."

As she faded away, Jack faced Annalisa, his eyes round with wonder. "I'm lost for words."

"I never believed in ghost stories as a child, but she was here. Or have we both gone mad?"

Jack shook his head. "No, dear heart. She was here." He kissed her hand. "No more secrets between us, I swear it."

A lump formed in her throat. She yearned to speak about Benjamin Cavendish, but no good could come of it—a hanging, at worst, if she was discovered by the British. At least Robby was a small child. She could learn to love him as her own if it came to it. As his aunt, she already did love him. *No, Benjamin Cavendish must remain my secret to bear.*

"Of course...but..." she drew in a breath, "Jack, I'm no longer the girl who hurried to marry you at nineteen. We've endured much, and breached one another's confidences, deeply. When you've given me reason to restore my trust in you, I'll consider marrying you again. Until then, we part here as lovers and friends, and no more."

He sighed. "Quite. Of course, I understand. I'll spend the rest of my life proving you can trust me. I've nothing to hide from you. I know I can be the gentleman you deserve—"

She placed her hand to his lips once more. "In time, love. Shall we return to the inn? We've a dinner to start with your aunt and uncle."

Jack lowered his gaze, and she could tell he was bruised by her reluctance, but he remained steadfast in his composure. "Aye. I pray Abbie revealed to them her news of Louisa."

Annalisa chuckled, eager to lighten the air between them. "Your poor uncle. He's going to leave here more distraught than when he arrived."

❦ 64 ❦
JACK
PORTSMOUTH, JUNE 1778

AFTER DINNER, LORD BRUNSWICK took Jack aside and handed him a note. "To begin your new journey."

Jack broke open the seal and read, *"A sum of five thousand pounds.* Sir, I cannot accept this." He fought the urge to frown, wondering if he would ever get to spoil Annalisa, shower her with all that was deserving of being his wife. *If she chooses to be my wife...* Her hesitancy had startled him, but did not surprise him. She had every right to feel as she did, and he would now do everything in his power to show her he was worthy of her.

Lord Brunswick laughed. "Of course, you can. You're to inherit everything when I'm gone."

"I'm grateful you still wish it of me after the news you received today," Jack replied.

"I'm dying, Jack," his uncle said.

Jack started, though he suspected as such from his uncle's frail appearance. "Sir, I'm devastated to hear so."

"I don't believe I'll live through this winter. I certainly won't be returning to England. Your aunt and I will carry out the rest of my days in Cambridge. This should get you by until I pass—" He added with a dark chuckle, "Since your father seems to be in good health."

"I shall put it to good use, sir. I assure you—"

"Build that summer home by the sea, if you will," Lord Brunswick said. "Start a second law practice up here. When this war's ended, you'll need something with which to bide your time." He eyed Annalisa on the other side of the room, who sat with Aunt Catherine and Abigail. "Or bequeath some of it to your cousin and sister. They may renovate this tavern into something truly special...perhaps something fit to host General Washington himself."

Jack smiled, and gripped his uncle's bony shoulder. "Thank you, Uncle. I'd say I know not how I can repay you, but that seems of little consequence. Would that you enjoy your days in Cambridge with Aunt."

"I shall. I'm truly not deserving of her. I fear I've spent the majority of our marriage split between two mistresses— England and America. She was patient with me that I could not give her children to distract her when I was gone. But she loves me well, and for that I'm the luckiest man in the world. I see something similar in your Annalisa. I hope you know I was wrong to have judged her those years ago."

"You did mention it, but I'm glad to hear it again, sir."

"As for your little love child with Jane...we've all one of those, don't we?" His uncle laughed and clapped his shoulder, reminding him of Captain Fleming. Jack wanted to chuckle, but only one thought came to mind. *Are we men all scoundrels then? Truly, we deserve not the women in our lives.*

When his aunt and uncle left, Jack and Annalisa gathered with George and Abigail in the main tavern room. Men congregated about the wooden tables, drinking ale and consuming mince pies. Elisha brought them a large pitcher of flip and a plate of freshly baked pies.

"Enjoy. 'Tis a relief to have you all here," Elisha said.

George looked up at his faithful tavern-keep. "It does me good to be back. Come, sit with us and enjoy the fruits of your work. This tavern would never have become what is it today were it not for you, rogue."

Elisha grinned. "Thank you, Mr. George, but you've another of your party I'm waiting for."

"Quinnapin?" Annalisa asked.

"Aye, Mr. Quinn," Elisha replied. "And these arrived for you today, Mrs. Bixby." He handed Annalisa two letters.

"Mrs. Bixby?" George asked, his thick brows raised.

Jack and Annalisa laughed.

"We'll explain later when there are fewer patrons in the room," Jack said.

"I thought I missed something as well," Abigail giggled, then looked to Annalisa. "Are either of those notes from Sarah?"

Annalisa turned one over and read the script. "Aye, this one." She broke open the seal. "They're in Charleston still... nothing yet on finding her mother, but they've moved into a small house of their own, courtesy of a captain." She looked up. "I'm so thrilled for them."

"I bet you miss them well," Jack replied.

"I do. I pray we shall meet again, soon."

"Who's written the other letter?" Jack asked.

"Mary." Annalisa broke the seal and unfolded the page. "I need the reagent, George."

George handed Annalisa the bottle and she brushed the contents over her Mary's letter. Her hand rested upon her bosom when she finished reading and looked to Jack. He swallowed thickly, fear rising.

"Mary's in Cambridge with Lord Essex and Jane. The children are there. And Mary's uncovered a note." Annalisa eyed each of them. "'Twas Lord Essex who paid off Captain Fleming...at the behest of Lord North."

Jack's innards twisted at the mention of the late captain. "Zounds."

"That dilberry," George roared.

"What!" Abigail shrieked.

"'Tis true." Annalisa lowered her voice, "He spied for the British the entire time we've known him, Abbie. Of course, it makes sense he wished to marry you—the daughter of a proclaimed Patriot. 'Twas so he could gather intelligence."

"This is unbelievable," Abigail cried. "How could I have been so foolish?"

"Hush, there are Loyalists about," Jack said, peering about the room.

George's hand rested on Abigail's shoulder. "Peace. You knew not, bid as your father would have you do. Pray, Annie, does my uncle know this information?"

Annalisa shook her head. "Mary's not written such. But I imagine Lord Perkins is ignorant of the fact, else he would not have hosted the gentleman for nearly a month."

"The cock robin, the plum," George muttered into is tankard, then gulped the remainder of his flip. "Would that I travel to Cambridge on the morrow to challenge Essex—"

"No, George," Abigail said. "Mary's there now. She'll be our eyes and ears." She looked to Annalisa. "Yes, Annie?"

Annalisa nodded. "Aye. So she told me before I left home."

A stillness settled over their table, and Jack wondered how his son fared, now he was in Lord Essex's domain. *How could Jane do this? What has Oliver to say of the matter? His son is gone, too. At least Mary is there to watch them.* Jack drank his flip, then pushed the tankard from him. "I must get word to Ollie."

George refilled his tankard from the pitcher. "There's not much either of you can do at this time, Brother. Essex is a powerful man, and if he seizes Jane and the boys, there's not much can be done about it."

"'Tis not as if Charles can name either of them his heirs," Abigail replied. "And he has none. He truly has no use for them."

"Think you Jane will try to convince him to name Tommy his heir presumptive?" Jack asked.

"They aren't even married," Annalisa said with a chuckle. "Jane is merely visiting Cambridge with Mary, and they're staying with Lord Essex. 'Tis a bit unseemly, but not unheard of. At least that's what I've garnered from Mary's letter. Of course, there's an inherent risk, as we all know Jane's proclivities toward finer things, but I think we shouldn't rush to a conclusion when there's little harm done. Yet."

As much as Jack wished to ride for Cambridge with Oliver, Annalisa was right. They must wait and abide their time. Mary would continue to write, and they would have time to conjure a plan should something arise. "Quite. Jane may return to Topsfield within a fortnight with Mary. Only time will tell."

Annalisa gazed at him and placed her hand over his, a tender, monumental gesture that warmed him, given their intercourse earlier that day.

"If Mary writes otherwise, and Jane and Lord Essex set sail for England with those boys, you have my word, we'll buy passage on the first ship to set sail." She smiled at Abigail. "I have acquaintances in high places in London, and the Duchess of Devonshire is a dear friend. I know she'd help if I asked."

❧ 65 ❧

ANNALISA

NEW CASTLE ISLAND, THE STATE OF
NEW HAMPSHIRE, JUNE 1778

ANNALISA GRIPPED JACK'S HAND as he led her over what she imagined to be rocks and sand, and adjusted the cravat he'd tied over her eyes. Despite his intoxicating amber perfume that lingered upon the fine linen, she asked, "How much longer must I wear this?"

"We're nearly there, I promise." He steadied her as she stumbled. "Careful."

She laughed. "Perhaps if I weren't blindfolded."

"Where's the pleasure in that?" Jack stopped walking, and she felt his lips upon her hand. "'Tis but a masquerade."

"I've been to masquerades. Everyone can at least see, though you can't appreciate their face."

He walked her for several more minutes, and the roar of the ocean grew louder. Engulfed by sea air, Annalisa surrendered to her blindness, and stepped lightly, caring little where he took her. To her dismay, tonight was the Strawberry Festival in Topsfield, and they remained in New Hampshire. In the light of his journey to Portsmouth last month, Jack was leery of travel. Though he seldomly spoke of Captain Fleming, she suspected his death affected him greatly.

We will attend next year. And we will have Robby. Will Jack wish to call him John Jackson IV?

Jack stopped and pulled her beside him. "We've made it. Wish you to see where we are?"

She giggled. "Of course."

He tugged the cravat from her head, and bright sunlight flooded her eyes. Annalisa blinked to adjust her sight, and slowly, her surroundings came into focus.

Sprawled across a stretch of green grass, George and Abigail played with Louisa upon a blanket. Quinnapin knelt before a large basket, removing mince pies, cured meats, cheese, and bread. He handed them all to Oliver, who placed them on wooden trenchers. William, with Martha Perley, stood facing the ocean. The Atlantic stretched for miles, perhaps to England from this vantage. The view left her breathless, and she eyed Jack beside her. He beamed, and she knew he did this for her.

"They've made it," George bellowed. "Come, the ale is ready for you, Perkins."

William turned. "Annie! I hope you don't mind I've brought Martha."

"Of course, not." Annalisa smiled, then turned to Jack. "What is this place?"

"Do you like it?" His cheeks dimpled with a crooked smile.

"I'm in awe. 'Tis magnificent."

"Good. I made a payment for it yesterday."

She gasped. "You don't mean it."

"Aye." He smiled and lifted her hand. "'Tis the site of our summer house—should you wish to marry me, of course."

Annalisa beamed, then winked. "You've done well to convince me, Mr. Perkins."

"You deserve nothing less," he replied, rather soberly. "I've not yet heard back from the magistrates, but I'm hopeful by autumn my divorce will be granted. I wish to do everything right this time, Annalisa."

Appreciating his sincerity, she slipped her hand into his and kissed it. "Thank you, sir."

They approached the picnic. William and Martha had joined the others on the blanket, and Oliver handed Jack a tin cup of ale. It was strange seeing Oliver amongst them, getting along so well with everyone, but she could hardly complain. He'd been an unlikely ally this past year, and she was forever grateful for his turn of heart, and coat.

"Good to see you, Brothers," Jack said.

Quinnapin smiled. "*Wuneekeesuq*, Miss Anna, Jack."

A good day it was, she thought. "*Wuneekeesuq*, Quinn."

Annalisa sat next to her old friend and drew Jack down beside her. Louisa crawled to him and sat in his lap. Jack cuddled the girl and kissed her cheek. *He will make a wonderful father.* The thought pained her for only a moment. Jack already was a father, and he would care for Robby as his own, she was certain of it. *And one day, we might share in a child of our own.*

"Jack, I think this is the perfect place for your new house." Abigail raised her mug. "May we celebrate much at this very place in the years to come."

"Hear, hear!" They all saluted.

"Huzzah!" The gentlemen clanked mugs.

"Dare we presume you a turncoat, Cousin?" George asked Oliver.

Oliver's cheeks pinked, and he regarded Annalisa. "Much has happened these two years. I'd be a hypocrite to deny it—

Jack, we suffered equally under the hands of the British. I'd be an even worse brother, cousin, and brother-in-law, to forsake you all now." He raised his cup again. "To the rebel cause, and those who were parted from us because of this war—Samuel, and Captain Fleming."

"To the rebel cause, Samuel, and Captain Fleming," they all saluted.

Annalisa ate and drank until she thought her stays could contain her stomach no longer. The others had gone to explore the plot of land, leaving only Jack seated beside her upon the blanket. They faced the sea, their fingers entwined.

Despite the overwhelming vastness of the ocean before them, and the war still raging in the southern colonies, Annalisa breathed through her sense of trepidation. In this moment, Jack was here, and they were surrounded by family; the only thing that mattered. Her heart belonged to him—she knew that much—no matter what passed between them. As Quinnapin had taught her, and she now accepted, only Spirit knew when their time would come—to marry, raise a family, be free of the constraints brought on them by war. Yet, she yearned to sit with Jack beneath the oak, the site of their daughter's tiny grave, and mourn with him.

Until then, she needed to be content with the unknown, as endless and trying as the ocean before them, as unpredictable as the storm that parted them two years ago. These recent developments with Jane and Lord Essex left her burning with unease; she could only imagine how Jack felt. Yet, with Jack and her family by her side, she knew they could withstand the storm and overcome anything this world, or war, set against them. Including Jane. Thankfully, Annalisa had many on her side to help. Suspecting their journey was far from over, her grip on Jack's hand tightened.

"I see our children chasing one another along this stretch

of yard." Jack's gentle baritone settled over her, tugging her back into the moment. "When this war's ended, our dream is within reach, Annie."

She smiled at him. By this time next year, she could be sitting in her summer kitchen, entranced by this view, perhaps the war having been ended now that France had allied themselves. *He's right. Our dream is within reach.* "Pray, if I agree to marry you, make sure the builders foster a place that holds both our muskets, yes?"

Jack laughed, then cupped her cheek. Softly, he placed his lips to hers. "My darling girl, our grandchildren will never believe our stories."

His kiss covered her in goosebumps, and she returned it with as much love as she felt for him. When she pulled away, leaving him wanting more, she swiped her thumb over his lips and smiled.

"*Kuwamônush,* John Jackson. The more remarkable our stories, the better."

THANK YOU

Thank you for reading *Muskets & Masquerades*.
Please consider leaving a review. Reviews not only help other readers find new books, they help readers find which books may end up being their new favorite!

18TH CENTURY & NEW-ENGLAND VOCABULARY, PHRASES, AND SLANG

ABRAMS: men/gentlemen
APPLE DUMPLING SHOP: a woman's bosom
BAGPIPE: fellatio
BANNS: (marriage banns) an announcement of impending marriage
BAWDY BASKET(S): a lady or group of ladies
BEAR-GARDEN JAW: rude or vulgar language
BENEFIT OF CLERGY: avoiding the death penalty as a Christian by pleading benefit of clergy; one would be branded on the thumb with the letter of their crime: F for felon, M for murder, T for theft; this was so the benefit could not be claimed more than once.
BLOODYBACK: redcoat in His Majesty's Army
BUNDLEBAG/BUNDLING: an old New England tradition in which parents would arrange courting couples to spend the night together. The gentleman would be sewn into a canvas sack to prevent copulation prior to marriage. Other times, a long wooden board was placed between the couple.
CHRISTMASTIDE: the twelve days of Christmas, beginning

on December 25th and ending on Twelfth Night, Epiphany, January 6th. (Sometimes the dates observed are Dec. 24th – Jan. 5th) Christmas itself was rarely celebrated in New England.

COCK ROBIN: a soft, easy fellow

CURTAIN LECTURE: an instance of a woman reprimanding her husband in private

DANDY PRAT: an insignificant or trifling fellow

DILBERRIES: excrement stuck to the hairs of one's arse (dingleberries in modern terms)

DISGUISED: drunk

DOXIE(S): lady/ladies

DRESSED TO THE NINES: dressed to perfection

FARTCATCHER: a servant who follows closely behind their master

FIE: used to express outrage or disgust.

FLIP: tavern drink made of rum, ale, molasses, and eggs, then beaten with a hot fire poker to create a nice froth, topped off with grated nutmeg. Each tavern had their own version of flip.

FOWLING PIECE/FOWLER/FIRELOCK: Smooth bore flintlock, muzzle-loading gun, used primarily to hunt fowl. Was a typical household weapon in New England.

GAOL: old spelling of *jail*

GO OFF: to orgasm

HOOPS (see *panniers*): undergarments worn beneath ladies' petticoats to give wide skirt appearances classic to the 18th century

INTERCOURSE: conversation

GREEN GOWN (to give someone): to have sex with a woman in the grass

GOLLUMPUS: a large, clumsy fellow

JERRYCUMMUMBLE: to shake or tumble about

KEIHTÁNIT (*Cautantowwit, Kautantowwit, Keihtán*): The Great Spirit. Spelling varies among the Algonquin nations. Keihtánit is the Wampanoag spelling.

LA: expression of surprise

LEAPING OVER THE SWORD: a military marriage

LET-GO: to orgasm

LOBSTER/LOBSTERBACK: redcoat in the His Majesty's Army

LOOKING GLASS: mirror

MARM: ma'am

MORT(S): lady/ladies

MUMMER(s): masked dancers who cavorted through the streets on Twelfth Night and visited homes unannounced to beg for holiday drinks and treats.

MUSKET: smoothbore barrel, muzzle-loading gun. Less accurate but was usually used within the military because of quicker loading and the ability to attach bayonet.

NECESSARY: bathroom/loo/privy/outhouse

NOOZED: married, hanged

OWL IN AN IVY BUSH: said of a person who wears a large, frizzed wig

SPATTERDASHES: made of wool, leather, or linen, they covered a man's leg from mid-shin to top of the foot. Worn by military, sporting, or working men for warmth.

SPILL: a piece of rolled wood or paper used to light a fire

PANNIERS (see *hoops*): these were worn beneath a lady's petticoats to give the wide, 18th century skirt silhouette.

PEGO: a man's penis

PHYSICK: medicine

PLUM: a fortune of £100,000 or someone with such fortune.

POMADE: hair grease used with powder to create desired hairstyles

PUK-WUDJIE (various spelling): translating literally to

'Person of the wilderness'. Little people of the forest in Wampanoag folklore who are mischievous in nature.

RECEIPT: recipe, old spelling

ROGUE: men/gentlemen

REMEDY CRITCH: a bowl/chamber pot, usually porcelain, in which to urinate

RUN GOODS (to take): virginity, or, to take one's virginity

SHENEWEMEDY: some historians believe it is Topsfield's name, according to the Pawtucket, meaning "the pleasant place by the flowing waters." Some believe it was how the Pawtucket pronounced Topsfield's first colonial name of New Meadows. It was changed to Topsfield in 1648, and the town incorporated in 1650.

SHITTING THROUGH THE TEETH: vomiting

SHUT YOUR POTATO TRAP AND GIVE YOUR TONGUE A HOLIDAY: to shut up

SLUICE YOUR GOB: to take a hearty drink

STAYS (pair of): whale-boned corset that gives conical shape to torso that is classic to the 18th century woman's silhouette

STRUM: to have sexual intercourse

SUIT IN DITTO: a man's suit where all pieces (breeches, coat, and waistcoat) are of the same color and fabric

SQUEEZE CRAB: a sour looking, shriveled, diminutive fellow

SYMPATHETIC STAIN: invisible ink used during by spies during the Revolutionary War

TIP THE VELVET: to put one's tongue in a woman's mouth, or cunnilingus

VICTUALING OFFICE/VICTUALS: stomach

WHIP JACKETS: men

WHOLE NINE YARDS: clothing took nine yards to make; to be the whole nine yards meant your outfit was of cut of the same nine yards of dyed fabric, which meant everything matched perfectly; sometimes dyes differed.

WIBBLE: cheap or bad liquor

WRAPPED UP IN WARM FLANNEL: drunk with spiritous liquors

ZOUNDS: an exclamation of surprise or indignation

ABOUT THE AUTHOR

LINDSEY S. FERA is a born and bred New Englander, hailing from the North Shore of Boston. As a member of the Topsfield Historical Society and the Historical Novel Society, she forged her love for writing with her intrigue for colonial America by writing her debut novel, *Muskets & Minuets*, a planned trilogy. When she's not attending historical reenactments or spouting off facts about Boston, she's nursing patients back to health. *Muskets & Masquerades* is her sophomore novel.

Ingram Content Group UK Ltd.
Milton Keynes UK
UKHW012054190423
420461UK00015B/293/J